CIVIL LIABILITY
in criminal justice
fourth edition

Darrell L. Ross
Western Illinois University

 LexisNexis®

 anderson publishing
A member of the LexisNexis Group

Civil Liability in Criminal Justice, Fourth Edition

Copyright © 1987, 1994, 2003, 2006
      Matthew Bender & Company, Inc., a member of the LexisNexis Group

   Phone 877-374-2919
  Web Site www.lexisnexis.com/anderson/criminaljustice

Library of Congress Cataloging-in-Publication Data

Ross, Darrell L. (Darrell Lee), 1951-
    Civil liability in criminal justice / Darrell L. Ross--4th ed.
       p. cm.
    Includes bibliographical references and index
    ISBN 1-59345-328-0 (softbound)
    1. Tort liability of police--United States. 2. Tort liability of criminal justice personnel--United States.
I. Title.

   KF1307.B37 2006
   344.7305'22   2006029692

Cover design by Tin Box Studio, Inc.

EDITOR Elisabeth Roszmann Ebben
ACQUISITIONS EDITOR Michael C. Braswell

Acknowledgments

While a book may be the work and dream of the author, many individuals assist in the final product. First I would like to thank Michael (Mickey) Braswell, Ph.D., of Anderson Publishing for giving me the opportunity to revise this edition of the text. His friendship, insights, patience, and suggestions greatly assisted me throughout the course of updating the book.

The substance of the text would not have been fully completed without the influence of three individuals. Thanks to Robert L. Parsons, Ph.D., who has been my mentor. He first introduced me to several attorneys who have over the years used me as an expert witness in a variety of civil cases with police and correctional agencies. Dr. Parsons encouraged me to pursue a Ph.D. years ago, and his continued guidance, advice, and strategies for working on civil cases have been immeasurable. A debt of gratitude is owed him for sharing his knowledge in policing, use of force, and civil litigation.

Many thanks to Joe Seward and Chris Johnson, civil litigators, who successfully defend criminal justice officers and agencies in civil litigation matters. Working with them on civil cases has greatly increased my knowledge of the civil process. Their legal skills and talents illustrated during discovery, motion preparation, and in the courtroom are unmatched and have enhanced my ability to write about defenses.

Many thanks go to Elisabeth Roszmann Ebben for her tireless efforts in editing this revision. She provided numerous editing suggestions and recommendations.

Much appreciation goes to three civil liability scholars who may not be aware that their work and research in civil liability has greatly influenced my interest in the subject for the last 14 years. Thanks to professors Rolando del Carmen, Victor Kappeler, and Michael Vaughn for their pioneering and continued research and publication efforts in this area. These three individuals are without question leaders in criminal justice regarding civil liability issues. Their work has been an inspiration to me to further research, write, and publish on civil liability topics. Thanks for your work.

Many thanks go to the professors, students, and practitioners that have used the text in order to increase their knowledge in this continuing changing area of the law.

And last, but certainly not least, I would also like to thank my wife Judy and my daughter Gretchen for understanding my commitment for endeavoring to update this work.

Preface

Civil litigation filed against criminal justice agencies is an increasing phenomenon. Due to the proliferation of civil litigation against criminal justice agencies, professors and trainers can no longer just concentrate on the criminal law. As a response, college courses and training have been developed to expose students and practitioners to the civil liability process at the university, community college, and agency levels. This book has been written in an attempt to provide information that will aid in better understanding the civil process.

Due to the nature of civil litigation today, students and practitioners must not only have a working knowledge of the criminal law, but also possess a firm grasp of the civil law process. The two systems have distinct differences and implications. In contemporary society, a criminal justice practitioner must know how to function in both systems. Students must be aware that their actions as a practitioner will more than likely be probed by a citizen or a prisoner plaintiff claiming that their actions or inactions deprived them of their constitutional rights. Likewise, practitioners must be continually updated on judicial decisions that affect their job performance. This edition of *Civil Liability in Criminal Justice* has been updated with 100 new cases, including several United States Supreme Court decisions, which have in some cases changed prior practices in a certain topic area. The text is written with the needs of college students, academy recruits, veteran practitioners, administrators, and agency trainers in mind. Acquiring a complete understanding of the distinctions of both systems will greatly benefit the reader.

The book can be a stand-alone text for a legal course or a supplement to an administrative course. The text has not been written as legal advice, because only attorneys may provide such advice. Rather, the text provides general information relative to the civil liability process that affects police and correctional situations. Therefore, the text has been structured to integrate United States Supreme Court decisions and to provide lower court decisions in order to illustrate how different cases have been applied to police and correctional situations. The text also integrates research on civil liability that underscores pertinent legal issues, liability trends and patterns, policy and procedure issues, training issues, and individual officer and administrative responsibilities. Combining these features not only provides useful information in understanding the court's decision-making process, but also provides the reader with realistic examples and research on how cases are applied at the criminal justice agency level.

About the Author

Darrell L. Ross is professor and chair in the Department of Law Enforcement and Justice Administration at Western Illinois University.

Contents

Chapter 1

Overview of Civil Liability

Overview

The intrusive nature of the duties that criminal justice personnel perform exposes them to higher degrees of liability than other occupations. This is not to suggest that physicians, psychologists, social workers, therapists, teachers, or administrators are unlikely to be the subject of a civil lawsuit. It is because criminal justice practitioners restrict citizens' and prisoners' liberties and rights, and therefore are more likely to become involved in litigation than members of other professions.

Among the many job functions that criminal justice personnel perform, responding appropriately to street- and institution-level situations is paramount. Criminal justice personnel must also exercise a high degree of skill in using their authority and discretion when implementing department policy and enforcing the law. Legal actions against law enforcement officers frequently arise out of situations in which they have restricted the rights of citizens or prisoners. Other litigation may result from allegations of failing to perform legally assigned duties, performing duties in a negligent manner, misusing authority, using excessive force, or intentionally depriving a prisoner or other person of his or her constitutional rights.

Filing a civil lawsuit in the United States has become all too common since the 1970s. American society has become highly litigious, resorting to filing civil lawsuits without hesitation. Litras and DeFrances (1999) conducted a study for the Department of Justice on the overall trends of 500,000 tort cases filed in the United States during fiscal years 1996-1997. Civil cases arising out of the 75 largest counties were studied. Types of claims ranged from personal injury actions, such as airplane accidents, assaults, libel and slander, and medical malpractice, to motor vehicle accidents, and product liability. Motor vehicle accident claims accounted for 20 percent of the cases, while product liability cases accounted for 15 percent and medical malpractice cases accounted for eight percent. Plaintiffs won 45 percent of all cases filed. Plaintiffs were awarded damages in 86 percent of these cases, and punitive damages in 18 percent. The median award was $141,000. In 10 percent of the cases, the plaintiff was awarded more than $1 million, and in eight percent of the cases, awards exceeded $10 million. Approximately $2.7 billion was awarded in combined compensatory and punitive damages.

Cohen (2005) performed an updated study on the trends of federal trials and verdicts decided during 2002-2003, representing 512,000 cases filed. He reported that since the 1970s there have been highs and lows in the number of civil tort filings. Tort cases actually tried in court have been declining since 1985 by 79 percent, from 3,600 to 800. Cohen noted that the growing use of alternative dispute resolution is cited as the primary reason for the decline in the number of tort trials.

Cohen also reported that 20 percent (98,786) of the claims filed by plaintiffs involved an injury, a loss, or damages. Of these claims, 71 percent were decided by a jury trial in U.S. District Courts and the remainder were adjudicated by a judge. Personal injury claims accounted for 90 percent of the total claims while property damage accounted for the remaining 11 percent. Overall, plaintiffs prevailed in 48 percent of the cases and won less frequently in medical malpractice (37%) and product liability lawsuits (34%). Plaintiffs are more likely to win in a bench trial, 54 percent versus 46 percent, but juries are more likely to grant monetary awards, $244,000 versus $150,000 granted by a judge. Among all torts filed, the median awarded amounted to $201,000. Median awards for personal injury claims amounted to $181,000 and property damage awards were $321,000. While claims of medical malpractice were less frequently won by plaintiffs, they accounted for the highest in median awards granted, $600,000. More than 90 percent of the claims filed took from one to four years to terminate.

In a separate study, Cohen (2005) studied the trends in punitive damage awards in civil trials in the 75 largest counties in the United States during 2001. He reported that slander (58%), intentional tort (36%), and false arrest/imprisonment (26%) represent three of the most common categories in which punitive damages are awarded. Of the 6,504 cases studied, the plaintiff was awarded punitive damages in six percent of the cases. This percentage has remained stable since 1992. Juries are more likely to grant punitive damages than judges. In one-half of the verdicts, the plaintiff was awarded $50,000 or more, in 12 percent $1 million was awarded, and in one percent, $10 million was awarded. Punitive damages exceeded compensatory damages in 43 percent of the cases. Medium and maximum ranges of punitive damages were reported on the three common categories: intentional torts ranged from $16,000 to $4.5 million; slander ranged from $77,000 to $700,000; and false arrest/imprisonment ranged from $8,000 to $100,000.

Criminal justice agencies and personnel are also vulnerable and easy targets for litigation. During the 1980s and 1990s, there were unfortunately a number of high-profile civil liability cases that brought to the forefront the problem of police and correctional officer misconduct nationally. The city of Philadelphia, Pennsylvania, paid out approximately $3.2 million in 1996 in two separate lawsuits related to a bombing incident that occurred in 1985. Police officers dropped C-4 explosives from a helicopter on a residence in order to drive out members of an antigovernment group. The bomb ignited and fire spread through numerous residences, destroying 61 structures and killing 11 people.

Other incidents have created controversy about police conduct and have resulted in civil litigation. The beating of Rodney King in 1991 led to three Los Angeles police officers being criminally indicted, convicted, and sent to federal prison. Later, the city of Los Angeles, California, paid out $3.8 million in a civil judgment to King. In 1993, two Detroit, Michigan, police officers were prosecuted, convicted, and sentenced to prison for the beating death of Malice Green. In 2000, several New York City police officers were convicted and sentenced to prison for beating Abner Louima and forcing a toilet plunger handle into his rectum.

Moreover, there have been successful outcomes in high-profile cases alleging officer misconduct. In the spring of 2000, four New York City police officers were acquitted of criminal charges in the shooting death of Amadou Diallo. In that case, the officers fired their weapons 41 times. Officers approached Diallo and he made a sudden reaching movement for his wallet. Because of poor lighting in the doorway of the apartment complex, visibility was poor and officers mistakenly took his movements as threatening and the appearance of the wallet for a weapon.

In the summer of 2000, the Federal Bureau of Investigation prevailed in a civil lawsuit brought by survivors and families of the Branch Davidian group in Waco, Texas (Garcia, 2000). Agents of the Bureau of Alcohol, Tobacco, and Firearms (ATF) were executing a warrant for the arrest of David Koresh for firearms violations, when they encountered lethal resistance from him and members of his cult in February 1993. Several agents were injured and six were killed. For more than 50 days, Koresh and his followers refused to exit their compound and submit to arrest. The siege ended with the main housing structure being burned as FBI agents attempted to enter the building.

Four million dollars in damages was paid out for a deadly force incident in 1995. The Ruby Ridge standoff incident in Montana left one U.S. Marshal and the wife and two children of Randall Weaver dead. An FBI sniper shot and killed Vicki Weaver and her infant child, and a U.S. Marshal shot and killed the Weavers' 14-year-old son, Samuel. Federal agents were attempting to arrest Weaver on suspected charges of possessing and selling illegal firearms.

While individual civil lawsuits filed against police officers have gained momentum since the 1980s, the federal government, through the Department of Justice, has brought civil lawsuits against several police departments. These lawsuits have been brought under § 210401 of the Violent Crime Control and

Law Enforcement Act of 1994 (Title 42 U.S.C. § 14141). The Pittsburgh, Pennsylvania, and Steubenville, Ohio, police departments were the first police agencies to complete federal oversight through a consent decree for five years through this law (DOJ, 1997; 2005). Since this law began to be used by the Department of Justice in 1997, 22 police agencies have been investigated and are in various stages of a five-year consent decree or a Memorandum of Agreement (MOA) (DOJ, 2005). Further, eight agencies are currently under DOJ investigation for allegations of police misconduct under § 14141 (*see* Chapter 8 for a full review of § 14141).

Jails and prison systems in the United States are also subject to prisoner civil litigation and many have sustained consent decrees. Koren (1994) reported that the number of correctional systems under court order/consent decree increased from 11 in 1988 to 39 in 1994, largely due to prisoner litigation. Correctional entities have also been targets of prisoner litigation. In 2000, the Michigan Department of Corrections settled several civil lawsuits involving sexual abuse of female prisoners by male officers. In Texas, a privately operated jail incurred litigation stemming from a shakedown in which officers were alleged to have used excessive force and physically abused prisoners, violating their constitutional rights. The actions of the "shakedown" were videotaped and later broadcast on *Dateline NBC* in 1997. The videotape showed officers and command personnel requiring prisoners to crawl across the floor nude, while officers kicked, pepper-sprayed, and prodded them with stun guns, then used a dog to move them out of their cells. On several occasions, the video showed the dog biting various compliant prisoners. This incident resulted in a civil litigation claim against the sheriff, the chief deputy, and a county official in charge of the detention center's emergency response team (*Kesler v. King*, 1998). The claim alleged the use of excessive force, failure to train, failure to supervise, and a failure to screen prospective officer candidates prior to employment. The court ruled against the county, holding that it was not objectively reasonable to use force or the canine in this situation, in which prisoners were compliant.

The purpose of this chapter is to examine the prevalence of civil liability in police and correctional work. Since the 1960s, citizens and prisoners in the United States have, with increasing frequency, filed civil lawsuits against police and correctional officers. Trends and the subject matter of these lawsuits are still emerging, and accurate data that fully tracks this area of the law is sparse. Recognizing this, emerging trends and patterns of citizen and prisoner litigation are presented.

Trends in Police Civil Lawsuits

Much of the previous scholarly research on police civil liability has focused on precedent-setting cases decided by the United States Supreme Court (Barrineau, 1987, 1994; del Carmen, 1993; del Carmen & Smith, 1997;

Franklin, 1993; Kappeler, 1997; Klotter, 1999; Smith, 1995; Wardell, 1983). Specific police civil liability research has addressed issues of police actions "under color of law" (Vaughn & Coomes, 1995; Zargans, 1985); deaths in detention due to suicide (Kappeler et al., 1991): police misconduct (Littlejohn, 1981; Meadows & Trostle, 1988; Schmidt, 1976; Silver, 2005); negligent operation of police vehicles and failure to arrest drunk drivers (Kappeler & del Carmen, 1990a, 1990b); officers' attitudes toward police liability (Garrison, 1995; McCoy, 1987); liability for abandonment in high-crime areas and moonlighting (Vaughn, 1994; Vaughn & Coomes, 1995); trends in settling civil cases (Bureau of Justice Statistics, 1995, 1999, 2005); liability in sudden, wrongful custodial deaths (Ross, 1998, 2005); and liability trends in the police use of force (Ross, 2002).

While a great deal of research exists relative to civil suit analysis, a dearth of accurate statistical information exists regarding the trends and types of lawsuits filed against police. It is difficult to precisely assess the true nature of lawsuits filed against the police, partly because the courts publish only a portion of the cases they decide, and judges are selective in documenting those cases. There is no systematic method for collecting information specific to police civil litigation. The Administrative Office of the U.S. Courts (AOC) tracks federal civil actions annually, but does not specifically report cases filed against the police. Current literature reveals that civil lawsuits against police are widespread (Worrall, 1998), frequent (Kappeler, 1997), increasing (Kappeler et al., 1993), and a major concern to law enforcement officers (Garrison, 1995; Scogin & Brodsky, 1991), police chiefs (Vaughn et al., 2001), and government leaders (MacManus, 1997).

In the absence of this information, researchers are forced to speculate about the trends and patterns of police civil litigation. A limited number of researchers in the past have used surveys or content analysis methods to examine trends in police civil litigation and they suggest that the number of cases filed against police officers is growing (Americans for Effective Law Enforcement, 1974, 1980, 1982; Barrineau & Dillingham, 1983; International Association of Chiefs of Police, 1976; Kappeler, Kappeler & del Carmen, 1993). Surveys administered by Americans for Effective Law Enforcement (AELE) report civil lawsuits filed against the police rose from 1,741 cases in 1967 to 3,894 in 1971, a 124 percent increase. They also report that by 1976 more than 13,400 cases were filed against the police (1982), making a 500 percent increase from 1967. More than 40 percent of all suits during this period alleged false arrest, false imprisonment, or malicious prosecution. Claims of excessive force by officers amounted to 27 percent of the allegations, and six percent of the claims alleged the misuse of firearms. The International Association Chiefs of Police (IACP, 1976) indicated during this same period that one in 34 police officers was sued. In the early 1980s, AELE estimated that more than 26,000 cases were filed annually (1982), and one legal scholar has estimated that since the 1990s, police have faced approximately 30,000 lawsuits annually (Silver, 2005).

Prior studies have revealed a variety of monetary awards for plaintiffs. A survey conducted by the National Institute of Municipal Law Enforcement Officers revealed that the 215 municipalities surveyed faced costs of more than $4.3 billion in pending liability lawsuits (Barrineau, 1987). The average cost of a jury award against a municipality is reported to be about $2 million (del Carmen, 1987). In the mid-1980s, there were more than 250 cases in which juries awarded at least $1 million (National League of Cities, 1985). A study of § 1983 police lawsuits from 1983 to 1997 in two federal district courts in New York revealed that monetary damages were awarded in 30 percent of the cases (Chiabi, 1996). Damages awards ranged from $400 to $950,000, averaging $50,408. During this 14-year period, the total monetary awards amounted to $4,536,702. Damages were more likely when a case was settled (47%) as opposed to when a jury or court awarded monetary relief (22%).

In studying liability trends of § 1983 litigation in U.S. District Courts between 1978 and 1995, Kappeler (1997) found that the average award (and attorneys' fees) against police departments was $118,698, ranging from $1 to $1.6 million. Scarborough and Hemmens (1999) examined U.S. Courts of Appeals decisions from 1989 to 1993. They reported monetary damages in only 27 cases, ranging from $1 to $7,559,000. Attorneys' fees ranged from $12,500 to $325,000, with a mean of $65,898.

These figures obviously do not reflect cases that are settled out of court, which represent a majority of police litigation. Moreover, these awards do not reflect the personnel time, resources, and legal and expert witness fees spent in defending the case. Chiabi (1996) reported that 32 percent of all police litigation in two federal district courts in New York was resolved through settlement. Worrall and Gutierrez's (1999) survey of 50 attorneys representing cities with police departments with more than 100 officers found that 41 percent of cases were settled.

A study of the New York Police Department conducted between 1987 and 1991 showed that the city paid out $44 million in claims to settle police misconduct litigation. During this five-year period, the average settlement or judgment awarded to the plaintiff more than doubled, from $23,000 to $52,000. In 1996, the New York Police Department settled 503 police misconduct cases for $27.3 million and complaints made to the civilian review board increased sharply (Sontag & Barry, 1997). In 1991, the Los Angeles Police Department paid $13 million in damage awards for police misconduct (Christopher Commission, 1991). A Justice Department study of Los Angeles County found that county officials settled 61 police misconduct cases, paying plaintiffs between $20,000 and $1.7 million per case. In 1999, the LAPD paid $2 million in monetary awards and settlements (McGreevy, 2000). In 1991, the city of Detroit paid $20 million in damage awards (del Carmen, 1991). One officer cost the city of Detroit $2.4 million over several years as he incurred 13 lawsuits, primarily due to excessive force claims (Ashenfelter & Ball, 1990). All of the civil lawsuits were settled.

Other studies have documented trends in police civil litigation. Swickard (2005) reported that the city of Detroit has paid out more in police civil litigation than any other large city in the country. Swickard reported that a city council study showed that Detroit paid out more than $118 million from 1987 to 2005 and nearly $45 million from 2001 to 2004 to settle police misconduct lawsuits. This rate accounts for about $4,000 per officer, or about $17.00 per person living in Detroit. Of the 4,100 officers, 261 were named in more than one suit, and 107 of these officers were sued in three or more cases. Suits naming these officers cost more than $32 million from 1997 to 1999. By comparison, the city of Los Angeles, California, paid about $3,000 per officer to settle police civil lawsuits, while New York paid about $1,300 and Chicago paid just under $1,000 per officer to settle such lawsuits.

While comparisons of the trends of civil litigation among cities are problematic, general patterns are worth noting. The city of Chicago paid slightly more than $17 million in settlements for police lawsuits from 1997 to 1999 (Swickard & Hackney, 2001). In Cicero, Illinois, the city paid out $1.1 million to settle two sexual harassment lawsuits and one excessive force lawsuit from 2000 to 2003 (McNeil, 2005). From 1991 to 2001, the city of Cincinnati, Ohio, paid about $2.4 million to settle 56 cases (McLaughlin, 2001). The settlements are but a portion of the $685 million that it takes to operate the city annually. In their largest payout in the history of the department, the city of Oakland, California, settled a class action lawsuit claiming that a few "rogue" officers victimized more than 100 citizens, amounting to $11 million (DeFao, 2003). A court awarded $1 million against the city of San Jose, California, in the wrongful death of a mentally impaired man (Associated Press, 2005).

From 1994 to 2001, the West Virginia State Police paid out $7.8 million due to wrongful arrests; $700,000 in 2001 for the same charge; $88,000 in 2002 and $44,000 in 2003 for claims of failing to train and supervise officers (U.S. Commission on Civil Rights, 2004). From 2001 to 2004, the city of Los Angeles, California, paid out more than $4 million in police civil lawsuits ranging from sexual discrimination against gay police officers, and two cases involving the use of lethal force (*Los Angeles Times*, 2004).

These examples show the importance of the subject matter, show some indication of the sheer volume of the claims filed, the staggering settlement amounts, and the ongoing attention that officers and administrators need to pay to the issue. Concern about being sued has been examined by several researchers. Del Carmen (1991) commented that the fear of being sued is an occupational hazard. Breslin, Taylor, and Brodsky (1986) suggest that job performance may be hindered by a preoccupation with litigation. Scogin and Brodsky (1991) surveyed police cadets in an Alabama training academy and reported that 84 percent believed their fear of being sued was rational and nonexcessive. Only nine percent reported that their fear of litigation was irrational and excessive. A study of Kentucky police cadets (Kappeler, 1997) found that 50 percent were worried about civil liability and 31 percent thought they worried to excess.

Perhaps the most comprehensive research regarding longitudinal trends in police civil liability was reported in a content analysis by Kappeler, Kappeler, and del Carmen (1993). They reported on 1,359 § 1983 cases filed against the police that were published from 1978 to 1994 and found that police prevailed in 52 percent of the cases (706). The analysis examined 20 major topics of civil liability. Major findings revealed that plaintiffs are more likely to prevail in claims of illegal strip searches (76.4%), inadequate policy (68%), coercion (63.6%), excessive force (59.6%), infliction of emotional distress (56.7%), inadequate training (53.5%), inadequate supervision (55.4%), assault and battery (55.4%), and failure to protect (51.2%). Three of the major topics of frequent litigation pertain to managerial functions: policy, training, and supervision. The average award and attorney's fees assessed against police departments were determined to be $118,698. Vehicle pursuits and excessive force claims averaged the highest awards granted to plaintiffs, $1.2 million and $178,878, respectively.

Ross and Bodapoti (2006) completed a longitudinal analysis of the claims, litigation, and losses of law enforcement agencies insured by the Michigan Municipal Risk Management Authority (MMRMA). The trends and patterns of these claims were examined from official MMRMA records from 1985 to 1999. The total number of claims studied was 11,273 and represented incidents from municipalities (n=94) and sheriff's departments (n=57), including claims from detention facilities. Municipalities accounted for 89 percent of the total claims filed. These agencies were dispersed throughout the state and included metropolitan, suburban, and rural departments.

The average annual total costs paid for all claims amounted to $10 million, but from 1996 to 1999 the total amount paid out declined by three percent. Approximately 20 percent of the claims closed without a loss (a payout). A claim may include a lawsuit filed by an arrestee, detainee, or employee. A claim may also include property damage, personal injury due to a worker's compensation claim, a loss from an accident, or an act of God. Overall, county agencies were more likely to incur a claim, a loss, as well as incurring the most costs of all claims filed. The larger-sized agencies (100+ sworn officers) incurred almost twice as much in losses paid than smaller agencies. From 1985 to 1992, the average time to close a case from date of file took 40 months. From 1993 to 1999, the average time from filing a claim to closure was 18 months.

The analysis revealed 25 common categories in which claims were filed. Of these, 15 claims specifically emerged from law enforcement agencies and the remaining emerged from detention facility incidents (see the section below for a discussion on detention claims). The most frequent claim filed was an auto accident with an injury (40%) and it was classified as moderate in monies paid out. Other common claims included: administrative liability (14%), excessive force (11%), police pursuits with or without injury

(10%), false arrest/imprisonment (8%), denial of medical care (4%), property claims (4%), and wrongful deaths (3%). Common claims filed against agency administrators included failure to train, supervise, and direct. An emerging trend of claims filed against administrators were submitted by agency personnel for allegations of sexual harassment and discrimination.

On average, the agencies closed a claim without a loss in 78 percent of the cases filed. On average, claims were resolved without paying a loss in 81 percent of the cases. The highest average payout for claims lost and percentage of claims lost by an agency occurred in the following categories: wrongful deaths ($295,000/35%), denial of medical care ($151,000/38%), auto accident with injury ($50,000/80%), police pursuits ($48,000/59%), administrative liability ($40,000/20%); excessive force ($33,000/37%), and false arrest/imprisonment ($15,000/32%). The average costs to defend a lawsuit with an attorney amounted to $40,000. When an attorney was used to defend a claim in court, the defendant agency prevailed in 75 percent of the cases.

This study represents the first to longitudinally examine multiple agencies from one state, using official records to perform the analysis. The total number of claims is not alarming for the study period, nor is the average amount of payout for claims lost. Specific claim categories are similar to those of the Kappeler et al. study (1993), but the average amount of losses paid and losing percentages were less than those in their study. These seven categories represent incidents that officers confront with regularity and pose risk-management strategies for agency administrators. Further, administrators need to work toward reducing the number of claims filed by their own personnel for allegations of sexual harassment and discrimination.

In a comprehensive study conducted by Vaughn, Cooper, and del Carmen (2001), 849 Texas police chiefs were surveyed about their experience with civil litigation. The chiefs reported that the fear of lawsuits made it more difficult for them or their officers to do their job (53%). During the three years prior to the survey, 36 percent of the chiefs revealed that they had been sued by a citizen and 78 percent indicated they had prevailed in the lawsuit. The most prevalent liability issues filed against the departments were for excessive force (22%), false arrest/imprisonment (19%), and unlawful searches and seizures (10%). The chiefs revealed that they had lost 22 percent of the cases filed by individual citizens and 41 percent of the cases brought by their own employees. Of the cases in which monetary damages were awarded against the department, 82 percent involved settlements and 18 percent resulted from a jury or court verdict. In all, the cases settled for $8,810,400 (159 cases), averaging $55,411 per settlement. Court or jury verdicts resulting in monetary awards totaled $3,335,409, and averaged $98,100.

Additional scholarly research has examined several emerging trends in police civil liability. Using LexisNexis and Westlaw searches of equal protection § 1983 claims, Blackwell and Vaughn (2003) reported on civil litigation by plaintiffs claiming that the police violated their Fourteenth

Amendment rights when they improperly responded to a domestic violence call. Case analysis revealed that when the police treat a domestic violence call or arrest less seriously than other violent assaults, delay in their response to such a call, or discriminate in arrests based on gender issues, the likelihood of liability increases. Courts are seemingly more inclined to find in favor of a plaintiff when they can illustrate that the police failed to provide adequate response in domestic violence calls. They advise that the police need further training and education on family abuse in order to become more responsive to victims of domestic violence.

Cuing on the concern that civil liability poses for police officers, several studies have been designed to survey police officers' perceptions regarding civil liability. Hughes (2001) randomly selected community and beat officers from the Cincinnati, Ohio, Police Department in order to compare their perceptions regarding the potential of incurring a civil lawsuit. A total of 147 officers (29 community officers and 118 beat officers) responded to the self-administered Likert-type survey, which included 11 items. Overall, respondents held negative attitudes regarding the use of effectiveness of civil sanctions against the police. While a majority of the respondent officers had never been sued in their capacity as a law enforcement officer, the officers reported that, as seniority increases, the more likely it is that they will be named in a lawsuit. Hughes reported that most officers believed that they should be exposed to civil accountability, and that as length of service increases, the perception that civil suits are a barrier to effective law enforcement decreases. A majority of officers believed that the threat of civil litigation does not prevent an officer from violating a citizen's constitutional rights during an arrest, that civil liability is unfortunate inevitability of the job, and that it is not a significant method for controlling officer behavior. Differences were not, however, based on gender, ethnicity, or educational background. Female and African-American officers tend to view civil or as less of barrier in performing their duties. Further, the more highly educated (college degree or more) and more experienced the officer, the more favorable the perception was toward civil litigation. A majority (68%) of officers agreed that good recruitment, selection practices, and training are viable methods for protecting the department from a lawsuit. Only a slight majority (50%) believed that a strong disciplinary system reduced the department's liability.

A second study focused on a comparison of police and correctional officer attitudes toward civil liability. Hall at al. (2003) distributed a 22-item survey to deputies and detention officers of a county in a southern state and all but one municipality within the same county. Of 975 distributed, 607 surveys were completed. Police officers accounted for 500 of the surveys and 107 were completed by detention officers.

Using logistic regression analyses, the researchers' findings were similar to that of previous studies (Hughes, 2001; Garrison, 1995; Scogin & Brodsky, 1991). Police respondents were more inclined to know a peer who had been sued. Police responded more frequently than detention officers that a supervisor's order placed them at risk of incurring a civil lawsuit. Both police and detention officers were more likely to agree (62%) that they should be subject to civil liability for violating the civil rights of a citizen or detainee. A majority of both groups (60%) reported that they had received adequate training pertaining to civil liability and 48 percent agreed that the threat of civil liability deters officer misconduct. The researchers found that the higher the level of education the officer had completed, and the longer he or she had been employed, significantly influenced their favorable response to survey items. The researchers concluded that only a minority of officers believed that civil litigation hindered their ability to perform their duties and that future research should be directed toward identifying the varying influences that affect their perception regarding civil liability.

Novak et al. (2003) examined whether police officers' perceptions, years of experience, and aggressive policing styles were associated with civil liability. An 88-item survey was administered to officers from the Cincinnati, Ohio, Police Department. Officers were also observed in the field as they responded to various calls for service over a 13-month period. The researchers measured three primary propositions: (1) officer beliefs about civil liability in deterring unlawful police behaviors; (2) officer beliefs about liability and a willingness to engage in lawful behaviors; and (3) liability concerns have no effect on officer behavior. As in previous studies, officers agreed that they should be subject to civil actions but that knowing that they may be sued would not, or has not, deterred their aggressive behaviors in making a lawful arrest. A majority of the officers also agreed that being sued is "just part of the job" and that it would not influence their behavior significantly. The researchers suggest that more research be conducted to compare attitudes of officers before and after a civil liability incident to measure what factors may influence officer behaviors.

Because national detailed data is nonexistent, it is difficult to identify definitively the trends in police civil litigation. The Ross and Bodapoti study, however, provides a more detailed analysis of the trends in common types of civil liability claims, costs paid out, and prevailing trends in one state than that provided in previous studies. Other studies discussed here illustrate the concern of police officers about civil litigation while performing their sworn duties. These studies are helpful in providing data regarding what shapes officer behavior in light of potential civil litigation. What appears to be clear is that police have been and continue to be targets of litigation. Based on the nature of police work, it is also evident that the trend will continue.

Trends in Correctional Litigation

The United States Supreme Court established in *Cooper v. Pate* (1964) that state prisoners could bring lawsuits against correctional officials under Title 42 United States Code § 1983. Since 1964, prisoner litigation has flooded state and federal courts. A limited number of studies have examined the prisoner litigation trends. Turner (1979) examined 664 cases litigated between 1960 and 1977 in the federal districts of Virginia, Vermont, and the Northern and Eastern Districts of California. He found that a high proportion of these cases were filed *in forma pauperis*, and that a significant percentage (68%) of prisoner cases were disposed of at the pleading stage. The most prevalent issues raised were those of medical care, property loss or damage, and access to the courts.

McCoy (1981) analyzed 527 court records of the U.S. District Court for the Southern District of Ohio from 1975 to 1980. She found that the change in the court's philosophy regarding the acceptance of prisoner lawsuits resulted in an increase of § 1983 suits filed by prisoners from 11 in 1975 to 87 in 1979. The data, however, also revealed a marked decrease in both § 1983 suits and habeas corpus petitions filed during 1979 and 1980. A high proportion of cases sought monetary damages and a significant number were dismissed. Thomas et al. (1985) compared the filings between habeas corpus petitions and § 1983 lawsuits in the Northern District of Illinois from 1977 to 1984. They reported that prisoners filing civil rights complaints were more likely to be "repeat filers," while habeas corpus suits tended to be filed by "one-shotters." In a second study, Thomas et al. (1986) compared state and federal prisoner civil lawsuits to the general population's filing of civil rights complaints. They showed a slow but steady increase in prisoner filings from 1960 to 1984. This finding, however, failed to show strong evidence to suggest that prisoners are more likely than civilians to take complaints to court. They reported that as the national prison population increased, prisoners actually filed proportionately fewer lawsuits. In 1964 one of every 100 prisoners filed two lawsuits. The ratio reached its peak in 1981, when seven suits per 100 prisoners were filed. By 1984 approximately one prisoner in 20 filed a lawsuit, the lowest ratio since 1969.

Champion (1988) performed a content analysis of state and federal prisoner litigation trends for six southern states to determine the number and nature of civil filings by prisoners. State records were reviewed for five periods: 1975, 1978, 1981, 1984, and 1987. The study revealed a decline in the filing of habeas corpus petitions and a decrease in the number of filings under the Federal Tort Claims Act, but an increase in § 1983 lawsuits filed by state prisoners. His findings were consistent with other studies on the topic (Thomas et al., 1986; Singer, 1980; Turner, 1979).

Hansen and Daley (1995) researched 2,700 § 1983 lawsuits that were filed in nine states during 1992. They found that the aggregate profile of § 1983 prisoner litigation most frequently involved issues of physical security, medical treatment, and due process violations. The largest number of § 1983 lawsuits named correctional officers (26%), followed by administrators (22%), medical personnel (9%), elected officials (7%), and arresting officers (6%) as defendants. The overwhelming majority (94%) of the prevailing prisoners won little or nothing in terms of actual dollars. Virtually all prisoners acted as their own attorney (96%).

Using a content analysis, Ross (1997a) conducted a 25-year assessment of 3,205 published local jail and state prison § 1983 litigation. In 1970 the national prisoner population was 176,391 and 2,030 lawsuits were filed (1.2% of the population filing). By 1994 the prisoner population was 992,000 and 36,318 lawsuits were filed (3.7% of the population filing). For the 25-year period, 3.6 percent of the prisoner population filed § 1983 lawsuits. During the study period, state correctional officials won 57 percent of the cases.

The Ross study also revealed several common types of cases filed by prisoners. The more prevalent issues included medical care, access to the courts, discipline, administrative liability, conditions of confinement, failure to protect, use of force, and classification. In 92 percent of the cases, the prisoner filed *in forma pauperis*, without legal counsel. When a prisoner prevailed (43%), equitable relief was awarded in 87 percent of the cases. Equitable relief is a nonmonetary judgment whereby the court, through declaratory relief, declares to the defendant that a regulation is unconstitutional. A court, through injunctive relief, may also prohibit practices of the defendant by requiring certain measures to be taken or practices to be instituted to avoid further violations of the Constitution. Monetary damages were awarded in 13 percent of the cases and averaged $43,488 per case, while punitive damages averaged $30,667 per case. The total compensatory award per litigated topic ranged from $4,500 to $5.2 million during the study period. Punitive damages ranged from $12,345 to $414,000 per litigated subject matter. Nominal damages of $1.00 were awarded to prisoners on an infrequent basis. Cases involving failure to protect, medical care, administrative liability, prisoner searches, conditions of confinement, and use of force all amounted to significant compensatory and punitive damages as well as attorney's fees when a prisoner prevailed.

Ross (1997b) also reported that prisoners in jails/detention facilities were less likely to prevail in a civil lawsuit than their prison counterparts. Jail officials lost 56 percent of the detainee litigation. Study results indicated that jail inmates were more likely to prevail in cases involving administrative liability (63%), such as hiring and training of personnel, supervision of officers, deficient or nonexistent policies and procedures, conditions of confinement (62%), deficient facility (60%, i.e., overcrowding and defective buildings), medical care (60%), mental health (58%), use of force (55%), and access to the courts (52%).

As part of the MMRMA study discussed previously, Ross and Page (2003) examined claims stemming specifically from jail detainee cases in 57 jails/sheriff's departments in Michigan. These claims represented 11 percent of the total claims studied and covered 1992 to 1999. The claims filed named detention officers in 26 percent, administrators in 22 percent, medical personnel in nine percent, and elected officials in seven percent of the cases examined. The overall costs for the study period amounted to slightly over $7 million and average about 36 claims per year.

While the frequency of claims reported is small in number, there are several categories worth noting in which large payouts were common. The following claims were more frequent in occurrence than other claims and show the average payout when a loss was incurred, and the percentage of cases in which the plaintiff prevailed: attempted suicide ($271,000/65%); suicide ($175,000/60%); delay/denial of medical care ($158,000/44%); wrongful death ($125,000/88%), excessive force ($120,000/18%); conditions of the facility ($45,000/45%); administrative liability for claims of sexual assault, sexual harassment/discrimination ($24,000/25%), and failure to protect claims ($15,000/33%).

Like the findings in the police study, larger jails (number of detention officers more than 100) accounted more for claims, losses, and payouts. When an attorney was used to litigate the case in court, the agency was more likely to prevail—about 60 percent of the time overall.

As revealed in Figure 1.1, nine years' worth of prisoner litigation filing trends have been documented by the Administrative Office of the Courts (AOC, 2005). Since 1980, § 1983 civil actions have become the method most often used by state prisoners and jail detainees filing legal actions against correctional officials. These figures reveal that § 1983 claims filed by state prisoners and jail detainees reached an all-time high—41,952 cases filed. This figure is almost three times as high as the number of habeas corpus petitions filed by prisoners. Careful examination shows, however, that beginning in 1997, the number of § 1983 actions filed began to decline, with only negligible increases in 1999 and 2002. Habeas corpus petitions steadily increased during this period and since 2000 they closely match the number of § 1983 filings. Since 1996, § 1983 prisoner filings have decreased by approximately 51 percent, while habeas corpus filings have increased by about 60 percent.

Figure 1.1
Type of Legal Action Filed

Year	Section 1983	% change	Habeas Corpus	% Change
1996	41,952		14,591	
1997	28,635	–32	21,858	+50
1998	26,462	–8	21,159	–3
1999	26,993	+2	24,089	+14
2000	25,505	-6	25,219	+5
2001	24,118	-5	24,684	–2
2002	25,964	+8	23,863	–3
2003	23,964	–8	23,313	–2
2004	23,449	–2	23,569	+1

Source: U.S. District Courts (2005), *Prisoner Civil Cases by Nature of Suit*, Table C-2A.

These trends appear to be influenced by the Prison Litigation Reform Act (PLRA) passed by Congress in 1996. In part, the Act was legislated by Congress to curb frivolous lawsuits filed by prisoners. The Act established mandatory filing fees, restrictions on filing successive petitions, and requirements for exhausting administrative remedies before filing their legal action. It also increased the ability of the courts to immediately dismiss any lawsuit that is frivolous, malicious, fails to state a claim upon which relief can be granted, or seeks monetary relief from a defendant who is immune from such relief.

Summary

As the above discussion indicates, criminal justice personnel and agencies continue to be targets of civil liability. While the number of citizen and prisoner filings is high, officials often prevail in these actions. Research also reveals that a majority of lawsuits are settled out of court, and it appears that this trend is increasing. Civil litigation is costly, but many of the judgments have been instrumental in providing more resources with which to perform daily duties, and increased personnel training, and have assisted in developing more efficient policies and procedures with which to guide officer decisionmaking.

Research on liability issues shows the trends and impact that lawsuits have on criminal justice agencies in terms of money paid out and operational and policy changes. In response, scholarly research has documented the changes in the nature of civil litigation and the differing perceptions of civil liability between officers and supervisors. While education affects an officer's perception regarding civil liability, most officers report that such litigation is a barrier to effective law enforcement. Research on civil liability helps to pinpoint areas in which lawsuits are more likely to be filed. Officers and administrators should endeavor to work toward proactive measures to minimize lawsuits in these subject areas. Research suggests that quality efforts made in recruitment, training, workplace policies, and a strong disciplinary system can reduce departmental liability.

Civil lawsuits can be bothersome and stressful, and the outcome can be unpredictable. Administrators must remain committed to providing personnel with training, guidance, and legal updates to better understand how to perform their sworn duties. Officers must remain committed to performing their duties within the framework of the law. Maintaining this commitment can assist in defending the next legal action the officer or department faces.

References

Administrative Office of the United States Courts (2005). "Civil and Trial Statistics: Twelve-Month Periods (2005)." Table C-2A Annual Report to the Director (Statistics Division). Washington, DC: Administrative Office of the U.S. Courts.

Americans for Effective Law Enforcement (1980). *Lawsuits against Police Skyrocket*. San Francisco, CA: Americans for Effective Law Enforcement.

_____ (1982). *Impact*. San Francisco, CA: Americans for Effective Law Enforcement.

Ashenfelter, D. & Z. Ball (1990). "City, Not Cops, Pays for Brutality." *Detroit Free Press*, July 16:1A, 8A-9A.

Associated Press (2005). "$1 Million Awarded Against San Jose PD." (June 11): 2D.

Barrineau, H.E. (1987). *Civil Liability in Criminal Justice*. Cincinnati, OH: Pilgrimage Press.

_____ (1994). *Civil Liability in Criminal Justice*, Second Edition. Cincinnati, OH: Anderson Publishing Co.

_____ & S.D. Dillingham (1983). "Section 1983 Litigation: An Effective Remedy to Police Misconduct or an Insidious Federalism?" *Southern Journal of Criminal Justice* 8:126-145.

Blackwell, B.S. & M.S. Vaughn (2003). "Police Civil Liability for Inappropriate Response to Domestic Assault Victims." *Journal of Criminal Justice* 31:129-146.

Breslin, F.A., K.R. Taylor & S.L. Brodsky (1986). "Development of Litigaphobia Scale: Measurement of Excessive Fear of Litigation." *Psychological Reports* 58:547-550.

Bureau of Justice Statistics (1995). *Sourcebook of Criminal Justice Statistics—1995*. Washington, DC: U.S. Department of Justice.

_____ (1999). *Federal Tort Trials and Verdicts: 1996-97*. Washington, DC: U.S. Department of Justice.

Champion, D.J. (1988). "Some Recent Trends in Civil Liability by Federal and State Prison Inmates." *Federal Probation* 2:43-47.

Chiabi, D.K. (1996). "Police Civil Liability: An Analysis of Section 1983 Actions in the Eastern and Southern Districts of New York." *American Journal of Criminal Justice* 21:83-104.

Cohen, T.H. (2005). "Federal Tort Trials and Verdicts: 2002-2003." *Bureau of Justice Statistics Bulletin*. Washington, DC: U.S. Department of Justice.

_____ (2005). "Punitive Damage Awards in Large Counties: 2001." *Bureau of Justice Statistics Bulletin*. Washington, DC: U.S. Department of Justice.

The Columbus Dispatch (1999). "The Lawsuit." October 22:3A.

DeFao, J. (2003). "City of Oakland Settles Civil Rights Case." *San Francisco Chronicle* (February 19):1D.

del Carmen, R.V. (1987). *Criminal Procedure for Law Enforcement*. Monterey, CA: Brooks/Cole.

_____ (1991). *Civil Liabilities in American Policing: A Text for Law Enforcement Personnel*. Monterey, CA: Brady.

_____ (1993). "Civil Liabilities in Law Enforcement: Where Do We Go From Here?" *American Journal of Police* 12:87-99.

_____ & M.R. Smith (1997). "Police Civil Liability and the Law." In Dunham, R.G. & G.P. Alpert (eds.), *Critical Issues in Policing: Contemporary Readings*, Third Edition. Prospect Heights, IL: Waveland Press, Inc.

Department of Justice (1997). Consent Decree with the Pittsburgh, PA, Police Department, April 16. Available at: www.usdoj.gov/crt/split/documents/pittssa.htm.

_____ (1997). Consent Decree with the Steubenville, OH, Police Department, September 3. Available at: www.usdoj.gov/crt/split/documents/steubensa.htm.

Franklin, C.J. (1993). *The Police Officer's Guide to Civil Liability*. Springfield, IL: Charles C Thomas.

Garcia, G.X. (2000). "Davidian Decision is Not the End." *USA Today* (July 17):1A.

Garrison, A.H. (1995). "Law Enforcement Civil Liability Under Federal Law and Attitudes on Civil Liability: A Survey of University, Municipal and State Police Officers." *Police Studies* 18:19-37.

Hall, D.E., L.A. Ventura, Y.H. Lee & E. Lambert (2003). "Suing Cops and Corrections Officers: Officers' Attitudes and Experiences about Civil Liability." *Policing: An International Journal of Police Strategies & Management* 26:529-547.

Hansen, R.A. & H.K. Daley (1995). *Challenging the Conditions of Prisons and Jails: A Report on Section 1983 Litigation*. Washington, DC: Bureau of Justice Statistics.

Hughes, T. (2001). "Police Officers and Civil Liability: The Ties That Bind?" *Policing: An International Journal of Police Strategies & Management* 24:240-262.

Independent Commission on the Los Angeles Police Department (1991). *Christopher Commission Report*. Los Angeles, CA: Independent Commission on the Los Angeles Police Department.

International Association of Chiefs of Police (1976). *Survey of Police Misconduct Litigation: 1967-1976*. Washington, DC: IACP.

Josar, D. (1998). "Cops Cost Detroit Millions in Lawsuits." *Detroit News* (March 9):1A.

Kappeler, V.E. (1997). *Critical Issues in Police Civil Liability*, Second Edition. Prospect Heights, IL: Waveland Press, Inc.

_____ & R.V. del Carmen (1990a). "Police Civil Liability for Failure to Arrest Intoxicated Drivers." *Journal of Criminal Justice* 18:117-131.

_____ & R.V. del Carmen (1990b). "Legal Issues in Police Negligent Operation of Emergency Vehicles." *Journal of Police Science and Administration* 17:163-175.

_____, M.S. Vaughn & R.V. del Carmen (1991). "Death in Detention: An Analysis of Police Liability for Negligent Failure to Prevent Suicide." *Journal of Criminal Justice* 19:381-393.

_____, S.F. Kappeler & R.V. del Carmen (1993). "A Content Analysis of Police Civil Liability Cases: Decisions of the Federal District Courts, 1978-1990." *Journal of Criminal Justice* 21:325-337.

Klotter, J.C., J.T. Walker & C. Hemmens (2005). *Legal Guide for Police: Constitutional Issues*, Seventh Edition. Cincinnati, OH: Anderson Publishing Co.

Koren, E.I. (1994). "Status Report: State Prisons and the Courts—January 1, 1994." *The National Prison Project Journal* 9:9-12.

Los Angeles Times (2004). "LA to Pay $650,000 to Settle to Two Lawsuits." (December 26): 1D.

Litras, M.F. & C.J. DeFrances (1999). *Three Out of Four Tort Cases Settled Out of Court.* Washington, DC: Bureau of Justice Statistics.

Littlejohn, E.J. (1981). "Civil Liability and the Police Officer: The Need for New Deterrents to Police Misconduct." *University of Detroit Journal of Law* 58:365-370.

MacManus, S.A. (1997). "Litigation: A Real Budget Buster for Many U.S. Municipalities." *Government Finance Review* 10:27-31.

McCoy, C. (1981). "The Impact of Section 1983 Litigation on Policymaking in Corrections." *Federal Probation* 45:17-23.

_____.(1987). "Police Legal Liability Is Not a Crisis, 99 Chiefs Say." *Crime Control Digest* 21:1.

McGreevy, P. (2000). "Lawsuit Settlements by City of LA Increased 28% in '99." *Los Angeles Times* (January 11):2B.

McLaughlin, S. (2001). "City Pays for Police Lawsuits." *The Cincinnati Enquirer* (December 16):1C.

McNeil, B. (2005). "$1.1. Million to Settle 3 Lawsuits." *Chicago Tribune* (November 9):2C.

Meadows, R.J. & L.C. Trostle (1988). "A Study of Police Misconduct and Litigation: Findings and Implications." *Journal of Contemporary Criminal Justice* 4:77-92.

National League of Cities (1985). "Seeking Solutions on Liability Insurance." *Nation's Cities Weekly* (November) 25:3-5.

Novak, K.J., B.W. Smith & J. Frank (2003). "Strange Bedfellows: Civil Liability and Aggressive Policing." *Policing: An International Journal of Police Strategies & Management* 26:352-368.

Ross, D.L. (2005). "Civil Liability for Custodial Deaths Following Restraint Incidents." *Criminal Law Bulletin* 41:625-640.

_____ (2002). "An Assessment *of Graham v. Connor*, Ten Years Later." *Policing: An International Journal of Strategies & Management* 2:294-318.

Ross, D.L. & M. Bodapoti (2006). "An Analysis of the Claims, Losses, and Litigation of Law Enforcement Agencies in Michigan." *Policing: An International Journal of Police Strategies and Management* Vol. 29, No. 1:38-57.

_____ (1997a). "Emerging Trends in Correctional Civil Liability Cases: A Content Analysis of Federal Court Decisions of Title 42 United States Code Section 1983: 1970-1994." *Journal of Criminal Justice* 25:501-515.

_____ (1997b). "Section 1983 Jail Litigation: A Twenty-Five Year Content Analysis." *Corrections Compendium* 22:1-8.

_____ (1998). "Examining the Liability Factors of Sudden Wrongful Deaths in Police Custody." *Police Quarterly* 4:65-91.

Ross, D.L. & B. Page (2003). "Jail Liability: Reducing the Risk by Studying the Numbers." *American Jail Magazine* Vol. 2, No. 1:9-15 (January/February).

Scarborough, K.E. & C. Hemmens (1999). "Section 1983 Suits against Law Enforcement Officers in the Circuit Courts of Appeals." *Thomas Jefferson Law Review* 21:1-21.

Schmidt, W. (1974). *Survey of Police Misconduct Litigation: 1971.* San Francisco, CA: Americans for Effective Law Enforcement.

_____ (1976). "Recent Developments in Police Civil Liability." *Journal of Police Science and Administration* 4:197-202.

Scogin, F. & S.L. Brodsky (1991). "Fear of Litigation among Law Enforcement Officers." *American Journal of Police* 1:41-45.

Silver, I. (2005). *Police Civil Liability.* New York, NY: Matthew Bender & Co.

Singer, R.G. (1980). "Prisoner's Rights Litigation: A Look at the Past Decade and a Look at the Coming Decade." *Federal Probation* 44:3-11.

Smith, M.R. (1995). "Law Enforcement Liability Under Section 1983." *Criminal Law Bulletin* 13:128-150.

Sontag, D. & D. Barry (1997). "Using Settlements to Measure Police Abuse." *New York Times* (September 17):1A.

Swickard, J. (2005). "Police Lawsuits Drain Detroit's Pocketbook." *Detroit Free Press* (July 15): 1B.

_____ & S. Hackney (2001). "Detroit Police Lawsuits Costly." *Detroit Free Press* (August 3):3A.

Thomas, J.D., A. Aylward, M.L. Casey, D. Moton, M. Oldham & G. Wheeler (1985). "Rethinking Prisoner Litigation: Some Preliminary Distinctions between Habeas Corpus and Civil Rights." *Prison Journal* 65:83-106.

Thomas, J.D., D. Keeler & K. Harris (1986). "Issues and Misconceptions in Prisoner Litigation: A Critical View." *Criminology* 24:775-796.

Turner, W. (1979). "When Prisoners Sue: A Study of Prisoner Section 1983 Suits in the Federal Courts." *Harvard Law Review* 92:610-663.

United States Commission on Civil Rights (2004). *Police Practices in Civil Rights in America.* Washington, DC: U.S. Commission on Civil Rights (January).

Vaughn, M.S. (1994). "Police Civil Liability for Abandonment in High-Crime Areas and Other High Risk Situations." *Journal of Criminal Justice* 22:407-424.

_____ & L.F. Coomes (1995). "The Liability of Moonlighting: Are Police Officers Employed as Security Guards Acting Under Color of Law?" *Police Liability Review* 6:6-9.

_____, T.W. Cooper & R.V. del Carmen (2001). "Assessing Legal Liabilities in Law Enforcement: Police Chief's Views." *Crime and Delinquency* 47:3-27.

Wardell, M.J. (1983). "Section 1983: A Change in the Meaning of Under Color of Law: *Polk County v. Dodson*." *Arizona Law Review* 25:151-175.

Weinstein, H. (2000). "Judge OKs Use of Racketeering Law in Rampart Suits." *Los Angeles Times* (August 29):1A.

Worrall, J.L. (1998). "Administrative Determinants of Civil Liability Lawsuits against Municipal Police Departments: An Exploratory Analysis." *Crime and Delinquency* 44:295-313.

_____ & R.S. Gutierrez (1999). "Professional Notes—Potential Consequences of Community-Oriented Policing for Civil Liability: Is There a Dark Side to Employee Empowerment?" *Review of Public Personnel Administration* 19:61-70.

Zargans, E.H. (1985). "Under Color of What Law? A Reconstructed Model of Section 1983 Liability." *Virginia Law Review* 71:499-598.

Cases Cited

Cooper v. Pate, 382 F.2d 518 (7th Cir. 1964)

Kesler v. King, 29 F. Supp. 2d 356 (S.D. Tex. 1998)

Chapter 2

Foundations for Liability

Criminal justice personnel have increasingly become targets of civil lawsuits. Historically, it has been common to read about a police or correctional officer being charged with brutality. In contemporary times, issues of liability have expanded beyond limited allegations of police or correctional officer brutality to include virtually every task performed by criminal justice personnel. Liability principles apply to all public officers, not just police officers. Detention and correctional personnel, probation and parole officers, including supervisors and administrative personnel, are subject to civil liability today. It is important for all criminal justice personnel to have a fundamental working knowledge of the critical components of civil liability, regardless of their level of responsibility.

Liability under Tort Law

The most common area of liability in criminal justice today arises out of tort law. Torts allow recovery for personal injury. Personal injury claims include battery, negligence, and emotional distress. Most states have voluntarily passed laws known as tort claims acts in order to remove sovereign immunity obstacles. These laws have allowed numerous plaintiffs to file lawsuits seeking redress for violations of their rights.

From a broad perspective, all law is tort law, because the United States is a common law country (Silver, 2005). It is important to recognize that there is no clear definition of tort. While contract or property law is more clearly defined, tort law is loosely structured and often less clearly defined. A tort is a civil wrong. The term originates from the Latin word *tortus*, meaning *bent* or *twisted*. Initially, crimes and torts were treated the same, and an individual or a group would respond to the wrongdoing by personally taking action against the accused. Over time, as private vengeance gave way to criminal laws codified and prosecuted by the state in the name of the victim, torts and crimes evolved into separate legal concepts. Tort actions are civil legal actions arising out of situations between private parties. The injured party files a lawsuit seeking legal relief in the form of damages rather than criminal sanctions. Tort actions do not include breaches of contract.

Many criminal justice personnel are more familiar with criminal law than they are with aspects of civil law, because they enforce and apply criminal law on a daily basis. Because the liability of criminal justice personnel falls into the civil law arena, a brief comparison between criminal law and civil law is necessary (see Figure 2.1).

Figure 2.1
Criminal Law versus Tort Law

Components of Criminal Law	Components of Tort Law
A Public Offense	Private or Civil Wrong
State vs. Individual	Individual vs. Individual
Fines, Probation, Incarceration, Death	Monetary Sanctions
Guilt Beyond a Reasonable Doubt	Preponderance of the Evidence
Acquittal Normally not Appealable by the State	Both Parties May Appeal
The State Receives Fines and Restitution Goes to Victim	Plaintiff Receives Monetary Damages as Compensation
Both criminal law and tort law seek to control behavior and impose sanctions	

Criminal Law

Crimes are defined in terms of conduct that is forbidden or required and the mental state of the individual at the time of the prohibited act or omission (Gardner & Anderson, 2000). Crimes can also be defined in terms of harm done to a particular victim and against the state. Crimes are viewed as offenses punishable by the state in the name of the victim, through assessing fines, probation, community service, imprisonment, or death. In the American criminal justice system, the state—through the prosecutor—brings criminal charges against the accused. The state has the burden of proving its case "beyond a reasonable doubt," which is a high standard of proof. Should a jury or judge find the accused guilty, the judge will determine an appropriate sanction for the defendant, to be administered by the state. In a criminal case, the accused has numerous constitutionally protected rights and has the right to appeal a conviction. The state generally does not have the right to appeal an acquittal.

Torts

Torts are private injuries or wrongful acts that result in an injury or harm between individuals or their property. An individual who suffers a private injury may seek redress (damages) in a civil action, rather than through the criminal law process. The injured party (the plaintiff) seeks compensation from the injuring party (the defendant). The standard of proof needed to prevail in a civil action is that of "a preponderance of the evidence," which is a lower standard than "beyond a reasonable doubt." This means that a jury reviewing the case and evidence only needs to be convinced by a 50.1 percent margin to find in favor of either party. In a civil action, the state does not represent either party; rather, both parties may be represented by retained legal counsel, or an individual may bring the case to court without assistance of counsel (known as *pro se*). In civil cases the losing party may appeal the decision to the next higher court, including the United States Supreme Court. Should the plaintiff prevail in a civil suit, the defendant may have to pay monetary damages, including compensatory damages, punitive damages, court costs, and attorney's fees. The purpose of tort law is to compensate the plaintiff, provide justice, and deter others from similar behavior.

Some torts may also be crimes. Consider a police officer engaged in the high-speed pursuit of an alleged criminal. Should the officer operate the patrol car recklessly and hit and kill an innocent party, the officer could be prosecuted for manslaughter or murder, depending on the circumstances. If the officer is convicted of a crime, the state could impose a sanction such as a fine, probation, or incarceration. The victim's family could also file a civil lawsuit against the officer, claiming that the officer violated the constitutional rights of the deceased. Should the officer lose, the plaintiff could be awarded monetary damages.

Types of Torts

Dividing torts into categories can be problematic, because the dividing lines can be unclear. There are three general categories of torts: intentional, negligent, and strict liability. Criminal justice practitioners are most often sued for intentional and negligent torts. Strict liability torts are generally associated with activities that are so dangerous or hazardous that a person who engages in such activities can be substantially certain that the conduct will result in injury or damages (Silver, 2005); for example, workers performing duties that expose them to dangerous levels of hazardous chemicals and the potential for those chemicals to seep into the public water system. The company may be held liable for such conduct. Criminal justice functions normally do not fall under strict liability torts and will not be discussed here.

Intentional Torts

More than any other occupation, the work of criminal justice practitioners requires them to intrude into the affairs of many people. Stopping, arresting, detaining, frisking, searching, and performing other tasks have provided a steady flow of intentional tort litigation against criminal justice personnel (specific types of intentional torts will be discussed in Chapter 3).

Intentional torts may be committed against a person or property (del Carmen, 1991). This discussion will focus on torts against people, because it is more likely that an intentional tort claim would be assessed against an officer in criminal justice rather than against property. In order to prevail, the plaintiff must prove that an officer's behavior was intentional. Intentional torts are behaviors that are highly likely to cause injury to another. Intent is not easily defined, but in the context of tort it means to bring about some physical or mental harm, either through omission or commission by the actor. Further, because the intent is in the mind of the officer, the plaintiff may have difficulty proving an officer's intent in court. An example of an intentional tort is a classification officer at a prison reception center intentionally placing a prisoner in a housing unit next to known enemies, and a day later that prisoner is sexually assaulted by two other prisoners. Liability most certainly would attach, because the classification officer knew of the likelihood of harm to the prisoner and intentionally housed him in the unit knowing that harm could result.

Negligent Torts

Members of society owe a duty of reasonable care to one another (Silver, 2005). While intentional torts emerge from the purposeful conduct of an officer, negligent torts frequently arise from failing to perform a particular duty. Negligence is the breach of a common law or statutory duty to act reasonably toward those who may foreseeably be harmed. The distinction between intent and negligence is a matter of degree. The line has been drawn by the courts at the point where the known danger stops being only a foreseeable risk that a reasonable person would avoid, and becomes in the mind of the actor a substantial certainty (Prosser & Keeton, 1984). Negligence is the absence of care according to the circumstances, and requires a lesser degree of foreseeability than intentional torts.

The officer's state of mind is not in question when evaluating his or her conduct, because even inadvertent behavior that causes an injury may lead to liability. An important question to ask when assessing negligent conduct is: "Did the officer's conduct create an unreasonable risk for another?" For example, it is standard practice in policing to secure handcuffs on an individual by double-locking the single bars to prevent them from rotating so that they do not tighten around the wrist and cause injury. Liability may attach if an arresting officer fails to check the tightness of the handcuffs and double-lock them, and the arrestee sustains a wrist injury during arrest and transport. The criminal justice field is replete with situations in which negligence liability may arise. Some examples include use of equipment and vehicles, failure to protect, operating defective jails or prisons, and negligence in responding to calls for service.

Negligent torts are separated into two categories: Simple negligence means that an officer failed to exercise reasonable care in the performance of his or duties, which led to an injury. Gross negligence means that the officer performed his or her duties with reckless disregard of the consequences of the actions that caused harm to another person or property. The distinction between these two categories is important because liability depends on which type is alleged. Normally, gross negligence is required in order for a plaintiff to prevail.

Other Types of Liability

Tort law provides the foundation for potential liability of criminal justice personnel. There are, however, other areas of liability that affect public officers. State tort liability exists for every public officer. This area of liability will be discussed in Chapter 3. While each state has tort laws, they also have different areas of liability. State tort liability typically includes such torts as wrongful death, false arrest, failure to protect, assault and battery, and invasion of privacy.

State Civil Rights Laws

Some states have civil rights laws that are similar to various federal civil rights laws. These laws provide sanctions for violations and are implemented as federal rights laws at the state level. This provides for more effective enforcement of the law by state authorities. Normally, federal officials allow the states to implement federal law with minimal interference.

Criminal Liability

Public officers may incur criminal liability under state law. The penal codes of most states provide for criminal prosecution of public officials who commit acts that violate the civil rights of an individual. Criminal justice personnel acting within the scope of their employment may be charged with a crime if they intentionally commit unlawful acts against an arrestee or prisoner in confinement, mistreat an arrestee, intentionally subject a person in custody to bodily injury or death, or knowingly engage in sexual activities with arrestees or prisoners.

Criminal justice officers may also face criminal liability under federal law—Title 18 U.S. Code § 242 (Criminal Liability for Deprivation of Civil Rights) and § 241 (Conspiracy to Deprive a Person of Rights) which was enacted in 1886. Under § 242, the defendant officer must have acted under color of law, acted intentionally to deprive the person of a protected right, and the person must actually have been deprived of that right. The law provides for a criminal sanction and under § 241 punishes the violation for conspiracy to commit the act, which requires at least two participants. Title 18 § 242 states:

> Whoever, under color of any law, statute, ordinance, regulation, or custom wilfully subjects any person in any State, Territory, Commonwealth, Possession, or District, to the deprivation of any rights, privileges, or immunities secured or protected by the Constitution or laws of the United States, or to different punishments, pains, or penalties, on account of such person being alien, or by citizens, shall be fined under this title or imprisoned not more than one year, or both; and if bodily injury results from the acts committed in violation of this section or if such acts include the use, attempted use, or threatened use of a dangerous weapon, explosives, or fire, shall be fined under this title or imprisoned not more that ten years, or both; and if death results from the acts committed in violation of the section or if such acts include kidnapping or an attempt to kidnap, aggravated sexual abuse, or an attempt to commit aggravated sexual abuse, or an attempt to kill shall be fined under this title, or imprisoned for any term of years or for life, or both, or may be sentenced to death.

A former Detroit, Michigan, police officer was sentenced to 27 months in federal prison on one count of felony deprivation of rights under color of law under § 242 (*Detroit Free Press*, 1999). The officer stopped a motorist for driving with an expired license plate. The officer used a racial slur and the driver objected. The officer sprayed the driver with pepper spray and hit him in the head three times with a police radio. Two Detroit officers and one state police trooper witnessed the incident and testified against the officer. In addition to the prison time, the officer's sentence included two years of supervised release.

The Criminal Section of the Department of Justice Civil Rights Division is charged with enforcement of this title and investigating complaints made by citizens and prisoners. Between October 1, 1999, and January 1, 2005, 284 officers were convicted of violating this statute (U.S. Dept. of State, 2005). Below are some examples of this enforcement:

- Officer Justin Volpe was sentenced to 30 years in prison under § 242 for brutally sodomizing Abner Louima in New York, while acting under color of law (December 1999).

"Criminal" liability
Under Fed Law.

U.S. Code SEC 242
(Crim liability for
deprivation of civil
rights

SEC 1983 (for
deprivation of
Constitutionally
protected rights+)

icted of striking an arrestee
ton while the arrestee was
ar. He was sentenced to 13
vilful unreasonable seizure
).

ansas Department of Cor-
ced two naked and hand-
a cattle prod. During a
fendants shocked and beat
ately, five officers entered
victed at trial. The officers
ing from 24 to 78 months
under § 242 for imposing unusual punishment under color of
law (February 2001).

- A North Carolina police officer pleaded guilty to a felony civil
  rights charge for coercing women, whom he stopped or
  arrested, into having sex with him. He was sentenced to 10
  years in prison for wilful deprivation of liberty without due
  process under color of law (September 2003).

- An Oklahoma police officer was convicted and sentenced to
  prison for assault for fracturing the hip of a 67-year-old
  arrestee he stopped for a traffic violation. The officer was prosecuted under § 242 for the wilful deprivation of the victim's
  liberty without due process under color of law (July 2004).

- A Texas police officer was convicted on federal civil rights
  charges under § 242 for repeatedly assaulting a handcuffed
  man while the officer was acting under color of law. The
  officer first kicked and choked the man, then proceeded to
  stick the barrel of his gun into the victim's mouth, threatening to kill him. The officer attempted to cover up his actions
  by submitting a false report (September 2004).

Federal Civil Rights Laws

Criminal justice personnel may also incur liability for violating the
civil rights of another under federal law. Title 42 United States Code § 1983
provides remedies such as monetary damages or injunctive relief for violations of constitutional rights. The § 1983 lawsuit is filed in federal court,
and claims that the officer or official, acting under color of law, deprived the
plaintiff of a constitutionally protected right, either prior to or during arrest
or detention, during incarceration, or after release (parole).

Title 42 United States Code § 1985 (Conspiracy to Interfere with Civil
Rights) provides a civil remedy to plaintiffs who can show that two or more
officers conspired to deprive them of their civil rights. Under § 1985, the burden is on the plaintiff to prove that the officers actually agreed to participate

in the action. The plaintiff must also prove intent to deprive him or her of equal protection under the law. For example, two detention officers and the sheriff meet and agree to house a detainee in a cell with a known violent offender who would purposely beat the detainee on the sheriff's order. The three could be held civilly liable for violating the detainee's rights under § 1983, and under § 1985 for conspiracy.

Violent Crime Control and Law Enforcement Act

Police departments have a higher probability of incurring liability since the passage of § 210401 of the Violent Crime Control and Law Enforcement Act of 1994 (Title 42 U.S. Code §§ 14141 and 14142). Passed partly as a result of the Rodney King incident, it grants the Department of Justice (DOJ) extremely broad investigative powers and prosecutorial authority in cases of alleged use of excessive force. Sections 14141 and 14142 permit the Department of Justice to investigate patterns or practices of misconduct in local police departments and requires the collection of statistics on "police abuse." The Department of Justice has the authority to look beyond the acts of an individual officer and into the affairs of the entire police department. The statute also gives the Department of Justice authority to file civil actions on behalf of citizens to obtain declaratory or equitable relief. The Pittsburgh, Pennsylvania, and Steubenville, Ohio, police departments were the first two police departments in which the Department of Justice utilized the statute. Both departments were under five-year consent decrees with the federal government from 1997 until it was successfully completed in 2002. Since October 1999, the DOJ has conducted 22 investigations of law enforcement agencies. As abuses come to the attention of the DOJ, other agencies are investigated (*see* Chapter 8 for a detailed discussion on the trends of these consent decrees).

The Civil Rights of Institutionalized Persons Act (CRIPA)

Passed by Congress in 1980, the Act ensures that the rights of institutionalized persons are protected from unconstitutional conditions. Title 42 U.S.C. § 1997 *et seq*. permits the Attorney General to bring civil lawsuits against state institutions regarding the civil rights of those housed in the facility, including the conditions of their confinement and the use of excessive force. State institutions may include jails, prisons, and other correctional facilities (juvenile or adult), and other institutions that house the mentally impaired or chronically ill. CRIPA allows the DOJ to bring legal actions (similar to § 14141, discussed earlier) for declaratory or equitable relief for a pattern or practice of unconstitutional conditions of confinement.

From 1980 to 2004, the DOJ initiated CRIPA actions against 400 facilities, resulting in 120 consent decrees and settlements governing conditions of confinement. Examples of these consent decrees include the following (U.S. Dept. of State, 2005):

- The DOJ reached an out-of-court agreement with the Wicomico County Detention Center in Salisbury, Maryland, regarding systematic violations of prisoners' federally protected rights. The investigation showed that the Detention Center failed to provide required medical and mental health care, failed to provide adequate prisoner safety, and failed to provide sufficiently sanitary living conditions. Under the terms of the agreement the Detention Center will address and correct the deficiencies identified by the DOJ (July 2004).

- The Civil Rights Division of the DOJ filed a lawsuit challenging the conditions of confinement at the Terrell County Jail in Dawson, Georgia. The complaint alleged that the jail routinely violated federally protected rights, including failing to protect prisoner safely, and failing to provide required medical and mental health care (June 2004). A more detailed assessment of the trends of CRIPA is discussed in Chapter 8.

Discipline or Termination Under Administrative Liability

Criminal justice personnel in both state and federal agencies are bound by and subject to sanctions in their respective departments in accordance with agency rules, regulations, and policy and procedures manuals. These administrative rules and guidelines govern the conduct of employees. Violating them may expose the employee to liability and subject that employee to various forms of discipline up to and including termination. These rules are binding and may be enforced as long as they comport with constitutional requirements and do not violate the employee's rights.

Summary

In order to more fully understand civil liability, the foundations of liability have been presented. The differences between criminal law and civil law have been provided. It is important to understand that in civil law the injured party, not the state, brings an action before the court and seeks to be compensated through monetary awards. Intentional and negligent torts are two types of tort actions that are commonly brought against criminal justice personnel and often form the foundation of civil liability. Other categories of torts have been presented to further expose the reader to possible liability actions against criminal justice personnel and agencies. The primary method for filing civil lawsuits against public officers is through § 1983 for alleged violations of constitutional rights. The plaintiff seeks monetary damages against the officer or governmental entity for the alleged deprivation.

It is important to underscore that the standard of proof relied upon in civil litigation is much different than that in criminal proceedings. In civil cases, a preponderance of the evidence is all that is required for a plaintiff to prevail. This is a lower standard than "beyond a reasonable doubt." This means that a jury need only believe that there is sufficient evidence to tip the scale in favor of the plaintiff or defendant. The losing party may appeal a verdict in civil litigation, while in a criminal matter only the defendant may appeal a conviction.

Criminal justice personnel may be criminally and civilly responsible for their actions or failure to act when performing their duties. They may also be investigated by their own department and, as warranted, may be disciplined or terminated from employment.

An emerging trend that bears noting is the investigations performed by the DOJ under § 14141 into allegations of a pattern or practice of misconduct in police departments. The DOJ has implemented this section more frequently since 1999, resulting in greater use of five-year consent decrees. A similar trend is also emerging with investigations by the DOJ into institutional issues surrounding conditions of confinement under the CRIPA provision. These provisions are another subset of laws enforcing the civil rights of citizens and prisoners, enlarging the framework of accountability and responsibility of criminal justice practitioners. They have significant implications for police administrators and officers alike, and a more detailed discussion is provided in Chapter 8.

In the chapters that follow, each type of tort action will be thoroughly discussed. As each tort action is presented, the reader is encouraged to determine how each action may affect their own job responsibilities.

References

Detroit Free Press (1999). "Cop Who Hit Suspect Jailed for 27 Months." *Detroit Free Press* (August 27):1A, 3A.

del Carmen, R.V. (1991). *Civil Liabilities in American Policing: A Textbook for Law Enforcement Personnel*. Monterey, CA: Brady.

Gardner, T.J. & T.M. Anderson (2000). *Criminal Law*, Seventh Edition. Belmont, CA: Wadsworth Publishing Co.

Prosser, W.L. & R.E. Keeton (1984). *On Torts*, Fifth Edition. Minneapolis, MN: West Publishing.

Silver, I. (2005). *Police Civil Liability*. New York, NY: Matthew Bender & Co.

United States Department of State (2005). *Second Periodic Report of the United States of America to the Committee against Torture* (May). Washington, DC: U.S. Government Printing Office.

Chapter 3

Civil Liability Under State and Federal Tort Law

Allegations arising from public officials' misuse of authority may be filed in federal or state court. As was noted in Chapter 1, negligence and intentional torts form the foundation of civil liability. This chapter will examine liability actions brought against criminal justice personnel under both state and federal tort theories.

Negligence claims against criminal justice personnel are based on state tort law. Negligence definitions differ from state to state. Differences in definitions may be due to specific categories and definitions allowed under state law or court decisions. A citizen's right to sue a public entity is limited by the doctrine of sovereign immunity. Although in decline, this doctrine shields the government from being sued by citizens. Most states have constitutional or statutory provisions that delineate the extent of sovereign immunity. These acts are normally referred to as tort claims acts. These statutes should be consulted in order to determine whether a particular entity may be sued, and whether immunity exists. The type of negligence required to hold an officer civilly liable varies from state to state. Simple negligence may be the applicable standard in one state, while gross negligence may be required to establish liability in another state.

The standard applied in negligent torts is whether the officer's act or failure to act created an unreasonable risk of harm to another. Negligence occurs when a person acting unreasonably does not intend to harm another, but fails to exercise due care to prevent such harm (*Harris v. City of Compton*, 1985). More precisely, negligence can be defined as subjecting a person to an unreasonable risk of injury. When a police or correctional officer exercises control over an arrestee or prisoner, he or she has a duty to exercise reasonable care (*Wager v. Hasenkrug*, 1980; *Abraham v. Maes*, 1983). A person is in custody when he or she is arrested and later transported by the police or confined by detention officers. This means that the police have a legal duty to take reasonable precautions to protect the health and safety of prisoners in their custody, render medical assistance as needed, and treat arrestees humanely. This, however, does not imply that law enforcement or correctional officers are the absolute guarantors of the welfare of those in their custody.

Establishing negligence is difficult. In some negligence cases, an agency's own policies and procedures have been used to determine the level of care expected of criminal justice personnel when performing their duties. For example, in *Miller v. Smith* (1995), the wrongful death by suicide of an arrestee rose to a level of negligent conduct on the part of the chief. Failing to provide directives and guidelines in handcuffing or otherwise restraining an arrestee at the scene of a drunk driving arrest prior to the suicide caused liability to attach to the city. In *Clark v. District of Columbia* (1997), the violation of a suicide prevention policy was not negligence per se. The standard of care provided to prisoners in the facility exceeded a national standard, and liability did not attach.

To prove a state tort negligence claim, four elements must be established: (1) a legal duty, (2) the breach of that duty, (3) proximate causation, and (4) an actual injury. All of these elements must be proved by the plaintiff in order to prevail in a state tort claim of negligence. If any of the four elements is absent, there is no liability.

Duty

Negligence derives generally from common law concepts, and most courts have held that the defendant must violate a duty to the person injured (Silver, 2005). It may arise from laws, customs, judicial decisions, or agency regulations (Kappeler, Vaughn & del Carmen, 1991).

Negligence is based on two concepts: (1) the existence of a duty, and (2) fault, or the breach of that duty. Duty, as a matter of law, is to be determined by the court, while a jury examines fault from the perspective of a reasonable person.

Criminal justice personnel perform a variety of duties. The authority to perform these duties does not automatically create a legal duty to perform these functions or a duty to perform them with reasonable care. In State v. Hughes (1989), however, the court concluded that police officers have a duty to exercise reasonable care in their official dealings with citizens who may be injured by their actions. This concept also applies to correctional personnel. In *Davis v. City of Detroit* (1986), the court held that absence of a detoxification cell required by a jail rule was a defective condition in a public building. Further, in *Layton v. Quinn* (1982), the court held that prior court orders directing improvements within the jail were relevant to the issue of failing to comply and contributed to the suicide of a prisoner known to have mental problems.

In order to require an officer to act in accordance with certain standards or levels of care to avoid a risk of harm to another, there must be a legal duty. Determining whether a duty exists at all is essential. Where no duty exists, there is no liability. *Hurely v. Eddingfield* (1901) illustrates that our society continues to be reluctant to impose liability for inaction or to create too many duties to act. A classic example is the case of a drowning person. While there may be a moral duty to attempt a rescue, there is no legal duty to do so. The law of negligence is preoccupied with the notion that there is no legal duty to act in many situations where a moral duty exists (Silver, 2005). Although the outcome in *Nelson v. Trayer* (1966) might be different today under § 1983 cases, a deputy was held not negligent in arresting only a man for hitchhiking and not his wife, who was later struck and killed by a passing vehicle.

Statutes will frequently stipulate certain actions of a law enforcement or correctional officer when performing their duties. Legislatures have passed many laws that form the basis of negligence liability. A plaintiff may assert that the defendant officer violated a statute and that the violation caused his or her injury. For example, if a police officer fails to arrest a drunk driver, and that driver later causes an accident in which another person is injured or killed, that officer could be liable for failing to arrest the driver. In this example, the statute would require a sobriety test. If the driver fails the test, arrest would be required. The court could possibly conclude that the officer failed to follow a duty of adhering to departmental regulations and state law. Such failure could be construed as creating or causing the later accident, and liability would probably attach.

Breach of Duty

Identifying a legal duty owed to the plaintiff is insufficient on its own. The plaintiff must also prove that the officer failed to perform or breached the legal duty owed. Failing to perform a duty will be based on the factual situation of the incident. Police may have a duty to arrest drunk drivers, but this does not imply that if the police fail to arrest every drunk driver and an accident occurs that causes an injury or death, liability will attach (Kappeler, 1997).

Courts have recognized that criminal justice personnel are liable only to specific individuals and not the general public (*Harris v. District of Columbia*, 1991). For example, a police officer restrained a violent arrestee who was under the influence of PCP and locked him in a police van. Medical care was delayed because the emergency room physician required the officer to fill out certain forms that initially had been completed incorrectly. The arrestee subsequently died. The court determined that the officer did not breach a duty of care, because there was no clearly established obligation to provide general medical services nor to provide such services to those not formally committed.

In order to prevail, the plaintiff must show some special knowledge or circumstances that set him or her apart from the general public and show that a relationship exists between the officer and the plaintiff. For example, in *Azure v. City of Billings* (1979), officers were held liable for violating a statute requiring the police to transport intoxicated arrestees to a treatment facility. The arrestee had sustained injuries prior to arrest and was noticeably intoxicated. There were some signs that he had been assaulted, he was unsteady in his balance, and his speech was slurred. Rather than transport the arrestee to the medical facility, where his condition could have been treated, officers transported him to the local jail.

Proximate Cause

If the plaintiff is successful in establishing that there was a legal duty and that the officer breached that duty, he or she must show that the breach was the proximate cause of the injury. Proximate cause is the direct factual link between the act of negligence and the plaintiff's injury. Proximate cause is defined differently by many courts. For example, the Michigan Supreme Court in *Robinson v. City of Detroit* (2000) defined "proximate cause" as meaning the "one most immediate, efficient, and direct cause preceding an injury." It may be enough in one court to show that the officer's act or omission rose to a level that caused the plaintiff's injury, while other courts may rely on a higher standard of recklessness, wanton conduct, or gross negligence, rather than simple negligence.

A close causal link between the officer's negligent conduct and the harm to the plaintiff must be proven. This may be determined by asking, "But for the officer's conduct, would the plaintiff have sustained the injury, harm, or death?" An additional relevant question may be: "Was the officer acting recklessly?" The court in *Carlin v. Blanchard* (1988) held that a sheriff's deputy was negligent in the shooting of a fellow officer and was the proximate cause of the officer's injuries, despite the fact that the officer's own conduct contributed to his injuries.

Occurrence of Actual Injury

The final element required in state tort actions is that of actual injury or damage to the plaintiff. The plaintiff must prove that actual damage occurred as a result of the officer's negligent conduct. Absent a showing of an actual injury, a plaintiff will not prevail. The injury or damage does not have to be physical. Emotional distress is sufficient for recovery in a tort action. Because the police are part of a public agency and are accountable to the public, they have a duty to report their activities in a reasonable manner. A false message that a prisoner died in custody was actionable on a theory of intentional infliction of emotional distress (*Texas Dept. of Corrections v. Winters*, 1989).

Special Duty and Foreseeability

Courts have established that police and correctional personnel may owe a special duty when they have reason to believe that an arrestee presents a danger to him or herself (*Thomas v. Williams*, 1962). A special duty of care may arise when a particular arrestee is recognized to have a diminished ability to prevent self-injury or cannot exercise judgment with the same level of caution as an ordinary arrestee. Two types of individuals fall into these two categories: (1) the mentally disabled, who have diminished capacity for self-protection, and (2) those who are impaired by drugs or alcohol. When it is evident that a particular arrestee has a diminished capacity or cannot exercise the same level of care as an ordinary person because of mental illness or intoxication, police officers must ensure that reasonable measures are taken to care for that individual while he or she is in their custody.

The concept of special duty lacks precise definition but can be based on two factors: (1) the officer's knowledge of the arrestee's mental state, and (2) the extent to which the arrestee's condition renders him or her unable to exercise ordinary care. If it is foreseeable that an arrestee's condition creates a hazard in the given circumstances (if there is a reasonable anticipation that injury or damage is likely to occur as a result of an act or omission), a general duty of care can be required of the police. A combination of several factors must exist in order to indicate foreseeability, such as: (1) a level of knowledge of the arrestee's condition by the officer, (2) condition and history of the arrestee, (3) known propensities of the arrestee, etc. As these factors increase in severity, a court may be more likely to hold that a special duty existed. This may lead to liability if the duty is breached.

A special duty stems from a specific mandate (i.e., such as a statute) rather than from situational relationships (del Carmen, 1991). If an officer possesses sufficient knowledge of an arrestee's mental or intoxicated condition and the prisoner is rendered helpless, a special duty to render care may exist. A special duty of care creates a higher level of responsibility for officers. Other examples of a special duty include securing accident scenes, protecting witnesses and informants, suicidal prisoners in detention facilities, prisoner-on-prisoner assaults, failing to follow departmental rules, and operating equipment negligently.

In *Govea v. City of Norcross* (2004), the elements of negligence and foreseeability are illustrated. Officer Heiberger was specially trained to work with youths in the city and used his relationships to gather information for criminal investigations. While performing his duties for the Norcross Police Department, Heiberger was reprimanded for several safety infractions, including leaving his duty weapon unattended on the front seat of his patrol car, damaging a police radio by spilling a beverage on it, backing his patrol vehicle into a tree, and failing to submit investigative reports. His supervisor cited him for these infractions and Heiberger also received citations for excessive use of sick leave, failure to complete time sheets, failing to complete accident reports, and tardiness. The chief of police allowed him to resign rather than terminate his employment so that he could retain his police certification in Georgia. The chief also agreed not to disclose his poor performance to any hiring agency.

Heiberger was hired by the city of Chamblee and during his field training, he was cited for failing to discover a knife in the back seat of his patrol car, operating his patrol car erratically, and improperly applying handcuffs on a an arrestee. Officer Heiberger resigned from the force but requested to be re-hired within two weeks. The city of Chamblee rehired him but did not provide additional training for him. He again began working with youths in the community and a boy fatally shot himself with Heiberger's duty weapon when he was allowed him to handle it. The boy's parents filed a lawsuit against the cities of Chamblee and Norcross claiming that Heiberger's position as a police officer and employment created a relationship with the boy, and that the relationship caused the circumstances that created the fatality. The lower court decided against the parents, stating that the state did allow such a lawsuit. The parents appealed. The appellate court agreed with the parents and allowed them to pursue their negligence claims.

The appellate court stated that it was wrong for the lower court to decide that negligence did not cause the boy's death. The court noted that the city of Norcross should have "foreseen" that Heiberger would obtain future employment as a police officer. Further, given Heiberger's history of carelessness and inattentiveness, Norcross should have known he would commit some safety infraction that could lead to serious injury or death. Norcross negligently breached its duty to fully and accurately report Heiberger's employment history. Additionally, the court held that the city of Chamblee could not foresee that officer Heiberger's tendencies would cause the boy's death; however, they had access to the Norcross Police Department's personnel file and knew that supervisors in Chamblee observed him in the performance of his duties where he continued a pattern of inactiveness and carelessness.

This case illustrates what a plaintiff needs in order to prevail in a claim of negligence. Both employing agencies had a duty to ensure that Heiberger performed his duties properly. The chief of police of Norcross failed to inform Chamblee's police chief about Heiberger's tendencies and breached his duty, which ultimately became the proximate cause of harm in the boy's death. In this case the link of what was known by Norcross became the proximate cause of the harm sustained by the youth. The concept of foreseeability is evidenced by the fact that Heiberger's poor performance was known, he continued his negligent performance, and it became highly predictable that his actions would injure another. The cities of Norcross and Chamblee possessed such knowledge and their failure to act on that knowledge was the proximate cause of the boy's death.

Areas of Potential Negligence in Criminal Justice

Police and correctional personnel come into contact with a variety of individual—from the violent, the intoxicated, and the mentally impaired, to the sober and sane. They provide a myriad of functions by virtue of their 24-hour operational availability. Statutes may mandate a certain police or correctional response to such individuals. A selection of examples of potential negligence are discussed below.

Negligent Operation of Emergency Vehicles

A majority of police work involves vehicle patrol. Patrol officers regularly respond to emergency calls. State statutes authorize the use of police vehicles in emergency situations and limit how police officers may use their vehicles. Police must follow the same traffic laws as ordinary citizens. Police are obligated to operate their vehicles in a safe and reasonable manner in accordance with the law.

Even if police violate the emergency statute by pursuing an individual and the pursuit ends in an accident, the officer may not necessarily have been negligent. For example, police officers were not liable for damages in a collision that occurred after they chased an intoxicated motorist through a red light (*Reenders v. City of Ontario*, 1977). The court determined that there was no reason to believe that the motorist would not have run the red light absent the pursuit, because he was intoxicated and unaware that the police were pursuing him. In *State v. McGeorge* (1996), the court held that an officer was not negligent for engaging in a high-speed pursuit of a fleeing vehicle that collided with an oncoming car. The court held that reasonable minds could differ as to whether a continued high-speed pursuit was justifiable.

Many courts require a higher standard than mere negligence in pursuit cases. The court in a Maryland case held that gross negligence was the standard required when reviewing police conduct (*Boyer v. State*, 1991). The court determined that although the trooper may have driven at high speeds on a road with heavy traffic in an effort to apprehend an intoxicated person, he did not act with wanton and reckless disregard for the safety of others. In North Carolina, the standard for liability in police pursuits is gross or wanton negligence in cases in which the fleeing vehicle injures another (*Parish v. Hill*, 1999). An officer engaged in a high-speed pursuit that lasted for 10 miles in the early morning during light traffic. The officer did not force the car off the road, nor did he attempt to overtake it, therefore he was not grossly negligent. In *Morris v. Leaf* (1995), the Iowa Supreme Court ruled that liability for injuries to motorists caused by a collision with a pursued vehicle can only be based on reckless conduct by police in pursuits, not mere negligence. Neither the officer nor the city was liable when the pursued vehicle had already been in a hit-and-run accident and when pursuit of the already speeding car was designed to prevent further harm.

Consider, however, *City of San Antonio v. Schneider* (1990), in which the court ruled that "reckless disregard" meant something between ordinary and gross negligence. The court held that the officer acted with reckless disregard when he was speeding on a seemingly non-emergency call, knowing that a street was dangerous when wet, filled with stranded cars, and that he would have insufficient time to stop.

The Michigan Supreme Court, in *Robinson v. City of Detroit* (2000), ruled on the issue of whether police officers in vehicle pursuits face civil liability for injuries sustained by passengers in vehicles fleeing from the police when the fleeing car causes an accident. A 15-year-old boy was being brought home from work by a friend when his friend (the driver) began weaving from one lane to another. Police officers who saw this activated their overhead lights, and the driver sped off with the police officers in pursuit. The pursuit ended when the driver struck another vehicle. The 15-year-old passenger was killed in the collision. His estate sued the city of Detroit and the officers. The court held that the police first owe a duty to innocent passengers and pedestrians, but owe no duty to passengers who themselves are law violators, whether they help bring about the pursuit or encourage flight. The city of Detroit was entitled to judgment without trial, because it was not reasonable to conclude that the officers' pursuit caused the youth's death. The police vehicle did not hit the fleeing car, did not physically cause another car or object to hit the fleeing car, nor did it physically force the fleeing car off the road or into another vehicle or object. The individual officers were entitled to immunity, because their actions were not the proximate cause of the victim's injuries. The court concluded that "innocent persons who are injured as the result of police chases may sue an individual police officer only if the officer is 'the proximate cause' of the accident." The plaintiff did not have a cause of action against the others.

Wrongful Death

Wrongful death torts are acknowledged in every state and usually are the result of allegations of unjustified actions by an officer. Generally, when a death occurs during police intervention, transport, or custody, a wrongful death case is likely to result. The lawsuit is filed on behalf of the deceased by the estate, surviving family members, or a guardian. This type of liability action alleges that the government entity was intentionally or grossly negligent to the needs of the deceased. In wrongful death actions against police officers, the plaintiff generally asserts that the officers' actions or the department's customs and policies (or lack thereof) were the proximate cause of the death. These lawsuits attempt to recover damages for conscious pain and suffering; loss of financial support; loss of comfort, society, and companionship; and funeral expenses. The lawsuit may also claim that the criminal justice agency conspired to cause the death of the deceased and/or covered up the death with an inadequate internal investigation. Each case will obviously be comprised of numerous variables for the plaintiff to attack.

The claim must be based on an established tort theory. Examples include deaths from lethal force incidents, fatal vehicle pursuits, in-custody suicides, restraint deaths after a use-of-force altercation, and claims arising from delay or denial of medical care for an arrestee or prisoner. In *Fruge v. City of New Orleans* (1993), the estate of a diabetic arrestee who died while in police custody brought a wrongful death claim against the city. When arrested, the prisoner appeared intoxicated and was placed in an isolation cell, where he later was observed foaming at the mouth. He was transported to the hospital and died several hours later. The attending physician stated that he had a moderately enlarged liver, which can cause sudden death. The court found the officers to be negligent in their decision to incarcerate, because they owed a duty to the prisoner to protect him from harm and preserve his safety. The court concluded that the city had failed in its responsibility (breached its duty) by not ascertaining the arrestee's medical condition and transporting him to a hospital. The arrestee's intoxication triggered the need for a higher level of care by the police.

An emerging area of liability that is occasionally addressed in state court are unexpected deaths in police custody after restraints and varying levels of force have been used to control the violent person. In *McCrumb v. Kent County et al.* (2002), the estate of a mentally impaired man filed state tort claims for gross negligence and assault and battery after he was restrained by eight officers and died. McCrumb was being admitted into a private mental health facility for treatment for bipolar disorder and began hallucinating. He assaulted two security personnel and began destroying offices and threatening nurses, physicians, and other staff of the facility. Two Kent County deputies responded to a 911 call and initially attempted to control McCrumb in the hallway of the facility by talking to him. He charged the deputies and one sprayed two bursts of pepper spray at him, which were ineffective. McCrumb fled back into the facility and more deputies and two other agencies dispatched officers. In total, the county sent two more deputies and a lieutenant, while three other officers responded from the two other agencies.

After planning a response, five of the officers and the lieutenant entered the facility as McCrumb began advancing toward an office where staff of the facility had barricaded themselves. The officers engaged McCrumb and two other officers applied three short bursts of pepper spray to McCrumb. The spray was ineffective and he charged the officers, striking two of them in the chest and head. The officers used control holds and their weight to subdue him. The officers placed McCrumb on the ground, two officers held his legs, two other officers controlled his arms, while another officer controlled his head, as he attempted to bite the officers. Only one officer had partial weight on his back and the officers were able to restrain his hands with two sets of handcuffs. McCrumb struggled and a belt was secured around his ankles. He began to calm down and a nurse left to retrieve an injection for him. Within a few seconds, the officers noticed that McCrumb had become unresponsive, radioed for emergency medical care, removed the restraints and belt, and initiated life-saving procedures. Emergency medical personnel responded, rendered medical care, and transported him to the hospital where he died 15 minutes later.

The family filed a lawsuit and the court, seven years later, issued summary judgment for the all of the officers. The court ruled that the officers had a duty to take McCrumb into custody for mental health treatment and had the right to use reasonable force to accomplish the task. The court stated that the officers also had the right to protect themselves and that the force they used was not excessive and was consistent with the degree of resistance they encountered. There was a need to control McCrumb and a need to protect the staff of the facility from McCrumb. The court further opined that officers did not act recklessly as to demonstrate a substantial lack of concern for the welfare of McCrumb. In fact, the officers had done the "exact opposite," the court noted, and held that the officers' conduct did not amount to gross negligence.

A more common wrongful death action brought against police officers involves police shootings. In *Mathieu v. Imperial Toy Corp.* (1994), the Louisiana Supreme Court overturned a $4 million award against the city for officers' shooting of a mentally impaired individual. The individual had pointed a realistic toy gun at officers and they responded by shooting him. The estate brought a wrongful death and excessive force action against the officers, claiming that the officers should have known the gun was a toy. In another case, the jury awarded $3.6 million in damages to the estate of a man who was shot and killed by a police officer during a traffic stop (*Bodan v. DeMartin*, 1994). The family argued that the deceased had placed his hands on the steering wheel when the officer stopped him, while the officer stated that the driver had reached under the front seat, causing the officer to believe that the driver was reaching for a weapon and causing him to fear for his life. A more detailed discussion on excessive force claims arising out of lethal and less-than-lethal force incidents will be provided in Chapter 7.

A recurring theme of wrongful death claims emerges from police pursuits. These claims not only allege negligence of the police officers performing the pursuit, but allege that such performance by the police created the proximate cause of death of the person in the fleeing vehicle or an innocent bystander. Some allegations claim that if the police had not initiated the pursuit the person would have never eluded the police and that the pursuit was recklessly performed, which led to the death of that person or third party.

In *City of Jackson v. Perry* (2003), a bank employee summoned Jackson, Mississippi, police to report that a woman attempted to pass a forged check. Although the bank employee attempted to stall her, the woman ran outside to her car. Police arrived and observed the woman run to the only car in the parking lot and quickly drive away. A rookie and his field training officer followed the woman and a second patrol car joined in the pursuit. The woman sped through highly populated neighborhoods at speeds in excess of 80 miles per hour and on one occasion ran a red light. The patrol cars followed at 55 miles per hour. The officers in the first patrol car stated that they had stopped chasing her but continued to follow only to obtain her license plate number. Within one minute of the pursuit, the woman crashed into another person's car, killing them. While trying to flee on foot, the officers subdued the woman and arrested her.

Perry's estate filed a wrongful death lawsuit against the city and the woman. The family alleged that the officers acted in reckless disregard of public safety and violated departmental policy, which authorized a pursuit only when an officer knew a felony had been committed. At trial the judge ruled in favor of the estate, finding that the officers acted with reckless disregard for public safety and awarded $1 million in compensation to the family. The judge allocated 50 percent fault for the accident to the city and the remaining 50 percent to the woman, who ultimately settled with the estate. The judge later reduced the award against the city to $250,000, the limits of the city's insurance.

The city appealed the decision. The state appellate court affirmed the lower court's verdict, holding that the city was not immune under state law that protected police activities "unless the employee acted in reckless disregard of the safety and well-being of any person not engaged in criminal activity at the time of the injury." The court determined that the officers could have parked their patrol car behind the woman's car when they first entered the parking lot, thereby blocking her exit. The court also determined that the officers could have obtained her license plate number but instead engaged in a high-speed chase without knowing the amount of the check and not knowing whether she had committed a felony, thereby violating the department's policy. The court held that the officers performed the chase in a reckless manner by speeding through highly populated residential areas.

Suicides in lockups, jails, and prisons have spawned numerous wrongful death actions under negligence theories. In *Title v. Mahan* (1991), the estates of two deceased pretrial detainees brought a wrongful death claim under state law. The two had committed suicide in the jail, and the claim asserted that jail personnel failed to prevent the suicides. The court determined that jail personnel were liable for failing to provide adequate supervision for the detainees. In *Moore v. City of Troy* (1992), a jail detainee hanged himself with his own T-shirt shortly after being jailed. His belt, shoelaces, outer shirt, and pants were removed. Jail personnel had documented security checks and had made such a check 11 minutes prior to the suicide. The court determined that jail personnel had complied with all procedures and did not impose liability. In *De Sanchez v. Michigan Department of Mental Health* (1997), a defense of proper supervision did not defeat the "public building" exception to immunity when a suicide was facilitated by the dangerous design of a public restroom. The main liability issues of the case centered on negligent supervision and design of the building. The plaintiff argued that the bathroom was poorly designed because it contained "open" structures in which people could hang themselves. The court did not rule on the issue of whether a true defect existed.

After a suicide in a detention facility, the estate of the deceased filed a lawsuit against the county and jail officers in *Gray v. Tunica County, Mississippi* (2003). The detainee committed suicide in a holding cell by tearing a portion of his jumpsuit into several strips. The estate alleged that that the detention officers failed to perform their security checks as required by policy when the detainee was placed on a suicide watch, and that such inaction was the proximate cause of the detainee's death. The court granted summary judgment to the county, holding that the policy was not related to the suicide of the detainee, who was placed in a new cell designed for medical and suicide watch purposes. The court ruled that the policy involving intermittent checks were reasonably related to the legitimate purpose of protecting detainees from harm. The detention officer had checked on the detainee about an hour after he was placed in the new holding cell and the officer returned 30 minutes later to discover the detainee unconscious in the cell. The court reasoned that the suicide was unforeseeable and that it was doubtful that the detainee could have been helped, even if the officer had entered the cell immediately upon noticing that the detainee had altered his jumpsuit and was lying on the floor.

Failure to Protect

There is no general civil duty to prevent a crime, even in high-crime areas (*Calogrides v. City of Mobile*, 1985). This means that police are not liable for failing to protect the victim of a crime. This is in accord with the public duty doctrine. The doctrine was established by the United States Supreme Court in *South v. Maryland* (1896). An individual who was victimized by a mob requested protection from the sheriff's office. The sheriff refused, and the individual was seriously injured and filed a lawsuit against the sheriff. The Court held that the sheriff committed no misfeasance or nonfeasance to the person injured and liability failed to attach. Most states recognize this doctrine, and there is no liability for harm or injury when the police fail to protect the general public. The public duty doctrine insulates police from liability when members of the general public are harmed or injured and desire to file a lawsuit against the police for failure to protect. This helps to enhance discretionary decisionmaking on the part of the police and helps in reducing the risk of lawsuits for these types of actions.

Generally, police and correctional personnel have a duty to protect those under their control and custody. Numerous lawsuits have emerged from this "special relationship" doctrine. States define a "special relationship" in varying ways, but the concept basically means that criminal justice personnel owe a duty to the particular individual in their custody, rather than to the general public. Factors that create a special relationship include actual knowledge of a dangerous condition or situation (foreseeability); and any statute, rule, or policy that requires officers to perform and that can be reasonably said to be for the protection of the members of society. Common examples include failing to respond to a call, failing to arrest in domestic violence situations, failing to protect a witness or informant, failure to obtain medical assistance for an arrestee or prisoner, failure to arrest a drunk driver, delayed response to a call, failing to summon assistance, and failing to protect prisoners from themselves and other prisoners.

Liability did not attach against the city in *Hamseed v. Brown* (1995) for the stabbing of a woman by her boyfriend. The boyfriend had escaped from an officer who was attempting to arrest him for violating a no-contact domestic violence order. The officer allowed him to go upstairs to get some clothes, and he fled out a window. The boyfriend later found his girlfriend and stabbed her several times. The boyfriend was not under the officer's control at the time of the stabbing. In *State v. Powell* (1991), merely receiving a subpoena to testify in court did not create an affirmative duty to provide protection. A woman was subpoenaed to testify against her ex-husband in a child abuse case. He poured gasoline on her and set her on fire. She sued the state, claiming that it had a duty to protect her from him and failed in that duty. The court concluded that there was no special relationship. Conversely, in *Doe v. Calumet* (1994), the court ruled that a police officer's failure to rescue a minor girl from being raped resulted in failure to protect liability. The mother of the child ran into the street yelling for help while her daughter was being raped. The officer's refusal to intervene constituted a willful and wanton disregard for the safety of the child.

In *Mills v. City of Overland Park, Kansas* (1992), officers did not have a duty to take an intoxicated person without a jacket into protective custody in winter weather. He came into contact with the police after he was escorted out of a bar where there had been a disturbance. He walked away from the bar and was found frozen to death the next morning in a field near the bar. A state statute that allowed (but did not require) emergency detention of intoxicated persons was also not a basis for liability. In *Kerr v. Alaska* (1996), the state of Alaska was found liable for negligent failure to prevent two prisoners from planning and carrying out, with the help of others, the mail bombing of a house where an informant who helped to convict them was living. The court awarded $11.85 million to the individual who lost his father in the explosion, which also severely injured his mother.

Occasionally a plaintiff will file a claim that the officer's failure to protect an arrestee in his or her custody was the direct cause of the harm sustained and that such failure amounted to gross negligence. This is a high standard to prove and many courts give deference to police officers when warranted. In *Kruger v. White Lake Twp.* (2002), police took a woman into custody pursuant to her mother's request, fearing that she posed a danger to herself and others due to her level of intoxication. Responding to the call, the police learned that the woman had an outstanding warrant issued for her arrest by a neighboring township. The police arrested her and transported her to the White Lake Police Department to wait for her transfer to the adjacent township. Lacking a vacant holding cell, the woman was left unattended in the booking room, where she was able to free herself from the handcuffs and escaped. As she fled from the station, she ran into traffic and was struck and killed by an unidentified vehicle. The decedent's family filed a lawsuit alleging gross negligence on the part of White Lake Township's officers. The lower court dismissed the claim and the estate appealed. The appellate court affirmed the lower court's decision, noting that the officers' actions were not grossly negligent and that the more direct cause of the woman's death was her escaping from the police station, running into traffic, and being struck by the car.

False Arrest and Imprisonment

False arrest is the imposition of unlawful restraint upon another's freedom of movement. The elements of an action for false imprisonment are the detention of a person and the detention is unlawful. The detention may be accomplished by actual or apparent barriers, physical force, a threat of physical force, or the assertion of legal authority. Plaintiffs prevailing in false imprisonment cases have shown an intent to confine, acts resulting in confinement, and knowledge of the confinement or harm (*Brown v. Bryan County, Oklahoma*, 1995). False arrest can occur when an officer arrests a person other than the one named in a warrant and, if the warrant is illegal, providing false information to a magistrate. Liability is created when the officer obtains a warrant with malice, knowing there is no probable cause (*Malley v. Briggs*, 1986).

Numerous lawsuits have been filed under state tort law for false arrest and false imprisonment. In *Byrd v. New York Transit Authority* (1991), an award of $250,000 in compensatory and $125,000 in punitive damages was granted to the plaintiff. He had sustained injuries as a result of false arrest, malicious prosecution, and assault by transit officers during arrest. In *Marshall v. District Court* (1992), police officers assisted medical personnel in restraining the plaintiff while an emergency mental health evaluation was performed. The officers had advised her that she would be forcibly detained if she did not cooperate. She sued, claiming that the officers had falsely imprisoned her. The officers were immune from liability, because under state law they were responding to a call for assistance and acted in the belief that she was mentally ill and in need of confinement. In *Diogaurdi v. City of New Rochelle* (1992), the existence of a domestic protective order as well as the wife's complaint that her husband was harassing her gave the police a defense in a false arrest claim filed by her husband after he was arrested for violating the order. Liability did not attach for the arrest.

Malicious Prosecution

Malicious prosecution claims are made by a plaintiff who alleges that he or she was illegally prosecuted in a criminal or civil proceeding that was instituted for an improper purpose and without probable cause. The plaintiff must show: (1) the institution or continuation of original judicial proceedings, either criminal, civil, or administrative; (2) by or at the request of the defendant, (3) the termination of such proceedings in the plaintiff's favor; and (4) the suffering of injury or damage as a result of the prosecution (Plitt, 1997). Proximate cause is also critical in malicious prosecution cases if the initiator of a criminal proceeding loses control of it due to the actions of a prosecutor or judge—actions that may be deemed to supersede the original complaint.

Malice is a core element of malicious prosecution and involves an intentional wrongful act done without legal justification. Malice may consist of any improper and wrongful motive for bringing a criminal proceeding and does not require hatred of, or ill will toward, the plaintiff (*Davis v. Muse*, 1992). Further, a lack of probable cause for the institution of the original proceeding must be shown. The court in *Stitle v. City of New York* (1991) ruled that a claim of malicious prosecution can arise only after an arraignment, indictment, or some other evaluation by a neutral body that the charges were warranted. The claim cannot arise from an arrest only.

In *Carver v. Hartville Police Department* (1992), police officers and the police department were held not liable for malicious prosecution of a woman for aiding and abetting her son in a drug distribution organization. There was no evidence of malice and there was probable cause for the arrest. The officers had made observations as well as controlled buys. *Strong v. Nicholson* (1991) allowed circumstantial evidence to show that a prosecution was brought with reckless disregard and to obtain property allegedly in dispute, especially when the defendants had been legally advised to bring a civil lawsuit. Thus, malice was proven.

Malicious prosecution actions are generally not subject to qualified immunity found in many states, particularly where "bad faith" or acting outside the scope of employment is involved (*Kapper v. Connick*, 1996). In *McDaniel v. City of Seattle* (1992), prosecutorial immunity was not applicable to immunize a city against malicious prosecution by police officers, especially where false representations may have been made to the prosecutor.

Frequently a plaintiff may combine claims of false arrest and malicious prosecution in one lawsuit. In *Wilder v. Village of Amityville* (2003), the plaintiff Wilder and others protested the removal of a tree in the village. Citing pro-tree environmental and religious concerns, she allegedly attempted to block municipal workers from cutting the tree down by standing in the way. A police sergeant ordered her to move on three occasions and she refused to move. The sergeant arrested her for obstructing a governmental function in the second degree. Wilder filed a lawsuit and claimed that the sergeant used excessive force when he tightly applied handcuffs on her wrists, resulting in inflammation and soreness to her wrists. She claimed the sergeant denied her medical attention. She also filed claims of false arrest, malicious prosecution, and interference with her free speech rights.

The court granted judgment to the village and the sergeant, noting that the plaintiff's claim of excessive force failed because her allegation of sore, yet uninjured, wrists was not enough to be considered unlawful conduct in the lawful arrest situation. Further, the court noted that the sergeant made the arrest based on probable cause and that her false arrest and malicious prosecution claims failed as well. The court ruled that the law prohibited a person from intentionally preventing public servants from performing an official function. Finally, the court held that the plaintiff failed to prove that the village or the sergeant prevented her from expressing her pro-environmental or religious views through police brutality or abuse of the legal process.

Assault and Battery

Many civil actions arise from claims of assault and battery, because the use of force is inherent in police and correctional work. Such claims may arise from an arrest, because physical force is always necessary to take custody of the arrestee. In correctional facilities, some physical force is used to move prisoners, search prisoners, or prevent prisoners from harming themselves or others.

Assault is an intentional attempt to physically injure another, coupled with the present ability to complete the intention. There must be an intent to cause harmful contact, or the fear thereof, with the person of another. Acting recklessly or wantonly is generally not sufficient for an assault. Generally, words alone are insufficient to constitute an assault.

Battery is a voluntary act that results in harmful or offensive contact with another. It is not necessary that the offensive or unpermitted touching actually cause physical harm; it is sufficient if the contact is offensive. Under this definition, every time an officer uses force to control an arrestee or prisoner, there is the potential for this claim to be made when the force used is unjustified. The distinction between assault and battery is that assault is conduct that results in an individual fearing an imminent battery, while battery pertains to unlawful, offensive, unwarranted touching, even if slight (del Carmen, 1991). The two terms are normally applied together, because as in many jurisdictions assault is an attempted battery (*Johnson v. Suffolk County*, 1997).

In *Jackson v. North Carolina Dept. of Crime Control* (1991), liability attached when an officer used a blackjack (a short, leather-covered piece of lead) on an intoxicated, handcuffed arrestee. The arrestee was restrained and cooperative, and using force in this manner was regarded as negligent. Using a weapon in an unreasonable manner may give rise to liability. In *Moody v. Ferguson* (1989), a state trooper was found to be liable for assault under South Carolina law. The plaintiff was stopped by a state trooper, and when asked for his driver's license, he placed the car in reverse and fled from the trooper. The trooper unholstered his weapon and ran after the driver. The driver moved the car toward the trooper, and the trooper fired his weapon, hitting the rim of the tire. The court concluded that the trooper used his weapon in a negligent, unreasonable manner, and was liable for assault. In *Baker v. Chaplin* (1994), the court concluded that hitting a political demonstrator with an impact weapon while he was complying with police instructions and not resisting was not only excessive, but was deadly force. The impact weapon was thrust into the chest of the demonstrator, and the court determined that this constituted deadly force and violated state law and § 1983.

The estate of a detainee confined in a county jail filed a lawsuit under the state tort claims act and §1983, claiming that the detainee was beaten to death by detention officers, in *Pizzuto v. County of Nassau* (2003). The family sued the officers, the supervisors, and the county. The detainee had been sentenced to 90 days for driving under the influence of methadone, a misdemeanor. While in a holding cell, the detainee boisterously complained that he needed treatment for his narcotic addiction and a heated argument ensued between the officers and the detainee. The supervisor directed the officers to enter the cell to control the detainee. The officers entered the cell and punched and kicked the detainee in his face, legs, and torso for several minutes. An extensive cover-up followed and two days later the detainee collapsed in his cell. He was transported to the hospital where he died from his injuries several days later.

The officers pleaded guilty to assault and conspiracy and were convicted. The court ruled in favor of the estate's claims and liability attached against the officers and the other officers who stood by and watched and failed to intervene. The court held that the supervisor was also liable for his personal involvement and for the acts of the officers. A more complete discussion of liability issues surrounding claims of excessive force will be presented in Chapter 7.

Federal Tort Claims Act

As discussed above, tort actions asserting misconduct on the part of police officers or correctional personnel are brought under state tort law. An individual bringing an action against a federal agent, however, cannot file an action under state tort law theories, but must file a claim in accordance with the Federal Tort Claims Act (28 U.S.C. § 1346 [b] and §§ 2671-2680). The FTCA waives the immunity of the federal government but not its employees. Federal employees are responsible for ensuring that the rights of individuals are protected just as their state and local counterparts are; however, they may not be sued under state tort law or § 1983. A plaintiff suing a federal officer must base his or her action on a complaint arising out of the scope of the federal officer's employment (*Simmons v. United States*, 1986) and must file his or her complaint in accordance with the FTCA. The FTCA authorizes the partial waiver of sovereign immunity from the federal government. A lawsuit filed under the FTCA cannot be based on a constitutional violation, but must be based on tort claims (del Carmen, 1991).

Plaintiffs filing claims against federal employees do so under provisions set forth in the United States Supreme Court's decision in *Bivens v. Six Unknown Federal Narcotics Agents* (1971). Bivens was restrained with handcuffs, searched, and arrested on drug charges while federal agents searched his apartment for evidence of drug violations. The search was conducted without a warrant or probable cause, thereby violating his Fourth Amendment rights. Bivens sued the agents, claiming mental suffering and damages from the invasion of his privacy. The Supreme Court agreed with Bivens and concluded that the agents were acting within the scope of their employment, giving rise to a cause of action.

A *Bivens* action may only be brought against federal employees—not the federal government (*Federal Deposit Insurance Corp. v. Meyer*, 1994). Plaintiffs filing an FTCA claim must do so within two years after the violation (28 U.S.C. § 2675 [a]). The Supreme Court has specifically upheld the bringing of *Bivens* actions for violations of the Fifth Amendment's due process clause (*Davis v. Passman*, 1979), and for federal prisoners claiming Eighth Amendment violations (*Carlson v. Green*, 1980; *Farmer v. Brennan*, 1994).

In *Papa v. United States* (2002), the widow and children of an alien who been killed by another detainee while being held by the Immigration and Naturalization Services (INS) brought *Bivens* and Federal Tort Claims Act claims against the INS. The district court granted the defendant's motion to dismiss and the plaintiff's appealed. The appeals court reversed the lower court's decision, holding that the officers knowingly placed the alien in danger in disregard of, or with deliberate indifference to, his due process rights, which supported a valid *Bivens* claim. The appeals court further noted that a limited right under the due process clause extends to detained aliens.

The estate of a federal prisoner who was killed by his cellmate brought a claim under the Federal Tort Claims Act (FTCA) and also brought a *Bivens* action against the correctional officials, in *Alfrey v. United States* (2002). The district court dismissed the *Bivens* claim and granted summary judgment for the defendants based on the discretionary function exception to the FTCA. The estate appealed and the appeals court held that plaintiff failed to state a *Bivens* claim and that the discretionary function exception barred an FTCA claim based on the officers' response to the report of the cellmate's threat. The appeals court, however, ruled that that the federal officers had a nondiscretionary duty to perform a prisoner monitoring assessment of the prisoner, who was to be held at a federal facility pending trial on a federal charge, before assigning the prisoner to share a cell with a federal prisoner, precluding summary judgment on the FTCA claim.

Questions have surfaced regarding whether a private corporation could be successfully sued under *Bivens*. Like many correctional entities, federal correctional entities have turned to private corporations to provide operational and medical responsibilities for confined detainees. This question was addressed in *Sarro v. Cornell Corrections, Inc.* (2003). A federal pretrial detainee brought a *Bivens* action against the private operator of a prison facility, officers employed by the operator, and others. A federal magistrate recommended that summary judgment be entered for the defendants and the prisoner objected. The district court held that the prisoner could maintain a *Bivens* claim against the officers employed by the private operator, but the private corporation that operated the facility could not be sued under *Bivens*. The court held that officers and operators were not subject to *Bivens* actions because they did act under color of law, because only federal prisoners were housed in the facility.

Defenses to Negligent Tort Actions

There are a number of defenses to tort actions. For purposes of this chapter, only three types will be discussed: contributory negligence, comparative negligence, and assumption of the risk. Defenses and immunity strategies will be presented in more detail in Chapter 11.

Contributory Negligence

Contributory negligence doctrine has a lengthy history. The first case to apply this legal concept was the English case of *Butterfield v. Forrester* (1809). It was later used in the United States in *Smith v. Smith* (1824). The concept has been used in both state and federal courts.

Contributory negligence is conduct on the part of the plaintiff that contributed, as a legal cause, to the injury sustained by the plaintiff (Prosser &

Keeton, 1984). The argument is that the plaintiff was partially at fault for his or her injuries (Silver, 2005). It may operate as a complete or partial defense for the defendant, thereby relieving the defendant of liability. If the defendant can show that the plaintiff's action caused his own injury, the defendant will not be liable.

The defendant must show that the unreasonable actions of the plaintiff, by a preponderance of evidence, contributed to his or her own injuries. This may be accomplished through discovery, outside evidence, or testimony from an expert witness (Franklin, 1993). If the defendant is successful in showing that the plaintiff contributed to his or her own injuries, the plaintiff will be unable to recover any damages.

In *Fruge v. City of New Orleans* (1993), a diabetic arrestee, wearing a medical notification bracelet, foamed at the mouth while confined for public intoxication. The court concluded that the officers were negligent in failing to provide timely medical care to the prisoner. The court also found that the prisoner contributed to his own injuries, because he had consumed a considerable amount of alcohol, which exacerbated his condition.

Most courts have not applied contributory negligence and assumption of the risk concepts to suicides in custody (*Saunders v. County of Steuben*, 1998). It appears that the duty of providing care outweighs contributory negligence on the part of the detainee. The court in *Miga v. City of Holyoke* (1986) found liability when the decedent was known to the police agency, prior to being stopped, for drunk driving from previous stops. Despite a desire to place her in protective custody and a regulation forbidding the placement of unconscious detainees in jail cells, the defendants made no effort to obtain background information on her or to call a detoxification center. The exception to this may be cases in which a suicide in custody was unforeseeable. In *Murdock v. City of Keene* (1993), the court concluded that liability will not attach unless a jailer has actual knowledge of facts indicating that the prisoner is likely to commit suicide. The prisoner's intentional act will preclude a finding that the jailer's breach of duty was the proximate cause of the prisoner's harm. This holding was also affirmed in *Thomas v. City of Parma* (1993).

Comparative Negligence

Most states have instituted the doctrine of comparative negligence (Silver, 2005). A jury must determine the portion of the injuries sustained by a plaintiff that they think is attributable to his or her negligence and the portion that is attributable to his or her adversary's negligent conduct. There are four categories in which a state's comparative negligence law may be classified:

1. pure comparative negligence, in which the plaintiff's recovery is never barred, unless his or her negligence caused 100 percent of the injuries;

2. fifty percent modified rule, which bars recovery when the plaintiff's negligence is greater than the defendant's negligence;

3. forty-nine percent modified rule, which bars recovery unless the plaintiff's negligence is less than the defendant's negligence; and

4. slight-gross-rule, which bars recovery unless the plaintiff's negligence was slight in comparison to the defendant's negligence (Minzer et al., 2002).

Comparative negligence compares the plaintiff's and the defendant's levels of negligence. It acknowledges that both parties may have contributed to the injury. Even though the plaintiff bears a percentage of the responsibility for causing his own injuries, he can still recover damages. It does not eliminate liability for the defendant, but rather mitigates the amount of the award. For example, an officer may be 25 percent at fault in causing harm to the plaintiff, while the plaintiff is 75 percent at fault. If the jury were to award $1,000, the plaintiff would recover $250. The comparative negligence doctrine allows the court to determine the degree of fault of both parties in a particular incident.

In *Del Tufo v. Township of Old Bridge* (1996), the estate of an arrestee who died from a cocaine overdose while in police custody brought a wrongful death action for negligence. The arrestee had not informed officers that he ingested cocaine prior to his arrest, when he had the ability to do so. Medical care was provided for him when he began to show signs of seizures. The individual died an hour later in the hospital from cardiac failure due to the cocaine. The New Jersey Supreme Court found that comparative negligence was a defense to an action for negligent failure to summon medical care for an arrestee. The court rejected the idea that drug abusers fall into the same category as the elderly and mentally impaired; they have a responsibility to advise the police that they have consumed drugs. Self-inflicted harm equals self-care responsibility. Although seemingly absurd, in *McRoy v. New Orleans Police Department* (1990), the court held that, even though the arresting officer used excessive force while handcuffing an arrestee, fracturing his wrist, the arrestee resisted the arrest. A reduction of 50 percent for comparative negligence resulted.

Assumption of the Risk

While in many jurisdictions the doctrines of contributory and comparative negligence prevail, assumption of the risk is still used by some courts in determining degree of responsibility. Assumption of the risk applies when a plaintiff knew or should have known of the existence of certain risks.

Thus, the plaintiff knowingly engaged in certain activities and was harmed. If the defendant can prove the elements of assumption of the risk, the plaintiff is precluded from recovering damages.

There are three elements the defendant must prove in asserting the defense of assumption of the risk. First, the defendant must show that the plaintiff knew or should have known of the risk involved, or had actual knowledge. Evidence such as the plaintiff's behavior prior to the injury may support this element. Second, the defendant must show that the plaintiff had the ability to recognize the risk associated with the activities (behavior and knowledge). Finally, the defendant must show that the plaintiff had the opportunity to disengage from the harmful activity, but failed. There would be no risk had there been an opportunity for the plaintiff to remove himself from it. The general principle is that the plaintiff knowingly placed himself in a dangerous situation and should therefore be liable for his actions. For example, a police officer responds to a silent alarm of a robbery at a local bank. As the officer exits his vehicle, the bank robber exits the bank, notices the officer, flees on foot, and runs into the street, where a truck strikes and severely injures him. The bank robber cannot anticipate recovering damages when he knowingly chose to commit the robbery and also chose to flee from the officer by running into a busy street. The robber assumed the risk of the activity and the officer would not be liable.

In *City of Jackson v. Perry* (2003), previously discussed in the wrongful death section, the court applied the three elements of assumption of risk theory to the woman who eluded the officers after attempting to pass a forged check. The court ruled that the woman shared in the liability of causing harm to the innocent victim through her risky behavior of operating her car at speeds in excess of 80 miles per hour in a highly populated residential area. The court further noted that the woman had knowledge that such behavior would and could cause harm to another in the residential area and failed to disengage from such harmful activity. The judge determined that the woman assumed the risk when she operated her vehicle in a reckless fashion and assessed an undisclosed amount against her. The woman settled her claim with the family.

Remedies in Tort Actions

As noted in Chapter 2, a plaintiff in a civil action files a claim to recover monetary damages for an injury. There are three primary types of monetary damage awards available to a prevailing plaintiff in tort actions: compensatory, punitive, and nominal.

Compensatory Damages

The cardinal principle of compensatory damages in Anglo-American law is that of compensation for the plaintiff's injury caused by the defendant's breach of duty (Harper & James, 1956). The plaintiff receives a monetary award for actual damages. This can include physical injury and pain and suffering. For example, a plaintiff prevailing in an excessive force case may assert that he sustained a fracture as a result of a blow to the head with the butt of a shotgun. He would be awarded money for the injury. He may also claim that he has endured mental anguish, pain and suffering, humiliation, loss of income, and incurred enormous debt in medical bills as a result of the officer's actions. Compensation could also be granted for these claims. The Pennsylvania Supreme Court in *Catalano v. Bujak* (1994) upheld compensatory damages of $1,543,440 for medical expenses on a claim that a police officer used excessive force in making an arrest. Catalano was stopped for speeding and arrested for disorderly conduct. He claimed the arresting officer forced him over the hood of his car in order to handcuff him, and in the process Catalano injured his wrists when he extended his arms to break the fall against the hood. Catalano later underwent surgery on his wrists, lost work due to the surgery, was no longer able to perform his job as a manager at a supermarket, experienced pain and suffering, and his future earnings were reduced. The jury returned a verdict in favor of the plaintiff, concluding that the officer had engaged in willful misconduct.

Also recall that in the *City of Jackson* pursuit case that the court awarded the estate $250,000 in compensation. The court noted that the officers' actions were reckless, proximately causing the death, and such actions violated the department's pursuit policy.

Punitive Damages

Punitive damages are assessed primarily to punish the errant officer and to send a message to others that the court will not tolerate such misconduct. They are awarded for particularly egregious misconduct, far outside the scope of the officer's authority. Punitive damages are normally awarded for reckless or intentional misconduct on the part of the officer. Generally, the award is proportional to the severity of the wrong committed by the officer, although it is difficult to predict the amount of the award when there has been blatant misconduct. Further, if punitive damages are assessed, it is the individual officer's responsibility to pay the plaintiff. In *Smith v. Wade* (1983), the Supreme Court ruled that punitive damages may be awarded against an officer for displaying reckless and callous indifference, as well as evil motive and intent toward the rights of the plaintiff. In this case, a prison classification officer was held liable for $5,000 in punitive damages for recklessly assigning a prisoner to a housing unit with the knowledge that he probably would be assaulted. Several days later, the prisoner was sexually assaulted by other prisoners.

In *Moore v. City of Philadelphia* (1990), a robbery suspect was punched, kicked, and racially insulted by officers who forced him to strip to the waist and placed him in a cold room in an attempt to elicit a confession. He was awarded $581,977 in compensatory damages and $100,000 in punitive damages.

Nominal Damages

Nominal damages are awarded as a symbolic gesture. The court may award nominal damages as a token, recognizing that the plaintiff prevailed in the civil action, but did not sustain an actual injury. Generally, nominal damages are quite small and frequently only $1.00 is awarded.

Summary

The primary thrust of this chapter has been a discussion of state tort claims and defenses. The distinction was made between state and federal tort claims. Tort actions arising out of the conduct of federal employees are filed as *Bivens* actions, although they are similar to state tort actions.

Figure 3.1
State Tort Negligence Components

Four Elements of Negligence	Definition
Legal duty	Existence of a duty
Breach of duty	Commission/Omission
Proximate cause	Causal link
Injury	Actual injury sustained
Special Duty	Sufficient knowledge
Foreseeability	Reasonable anticipation
Defenses	
Contributory negligence	Plaintiff caused his/her own injury
Comparative negligence	Plaintiff and defendant share liability
Assumption of the risk	Plaintiff willingly engaged in activity
Damages	Monetary awards
Compensatory	Actual/consequential damages
Punitive	To punish blameworthy conduct
Nominal	Symbolic

This chapter has highlighted the more common types of torts—intentional and negligent—with case examples, and was designed to present general principles of tort theories. Tort law varies from state to state and can be complex, because intentional torts and negligence may be defined by statute in varying ways. As illustrated in Figure 3.1, to prevail in a state tort claim, a plaintiff must prove four components: (1) a legal duty, (2) breach of that duty, (3) proximate causation, and (4) injury. An injury sustained by the plaintiff does not have to be a physical injury. A discussion of damages was presented with defenses to illustrate how the law is applied in varying circumstances.

The differences between state torts and federal court claims were addressed, with case examples. Defenses to these claims show that criminal justice personnel can defend against a state tort claim, but they must show that their actions did not breach duty to perform a certain action in regard to the plaintiff. Criminal justice personnel should become familiar with state tort actions, as the potential to be sued in state and federal court simultaneously is a possibility. Criminal justice personnel should also closely examine the various types of defenses that exist as this will assist in averting a civil action.

References

del Carmen, R.V. (1991). *Civil Liabilities in American Policing*. Englewood Cliffs, NJ: Prentice-Hall.

Franklin, C.J. (1993). *The Police Officer's Guide to Civil Liability*. Springfield, IL: Charles C Thomas.

Harper, F. & F. James (1956). *Law of Torts*. New York, NY: Matthew Bender.

Kappeler, V.E. (1997). *Critical Issues in Police Civil Liability*, Second Edition. Prospect Heights, IL: Waveland Press, Inc.

Minzer, M., J. Nates, C. Kimball, D. Axelrod & R. Goldstein (2002). *Negligence*. New York, NY: Matthew Bender & Co.

Plitt, E.A. (1997). *Police Civil Liability and the Defense of Citizen Misconduct Complaints Manual*. Chicago, IL: Americans for Effective Law Enforcement.

Prosser, W.L. & R.E. Keeton (1986). *Tort Law*, Fifth Edition. St. Paul, MN: West Publishing Co.

Silver, I. (2005). *Police Civil Liability*. New York, NY: Matthew Bender & Co.

Vaughn, M.S. & R.V. del Carmen (1991). "Death in Detention: An Analysis of Police Liability for Negligent Failure to Prevent Suicide." *Journal of Criminal Justice* 19:381-393.

Cases Cited

Abraham v. Maes, 436 So. 2d 1099 (La. Dist. Ct. App. 1983)

Alfrey v. United States, 276 F. 3d 557 (9th Cir. 2002)

Azure v. City of Billings, 596 P.2d 460 (Mont. 1979)

Baker v. Chaplin, 517 N.W.2d 911 (Minn. 1994)

Bivens v. Six Unknown Federal Narcotics Agents, 403 U.S. 388 (1971)

Bodan v. DeMartin, No. BCo25408 (L.A. Superior Court, 1994)

Boyer v. State, 322 Md. 558, 594 A.2d 121 (1991)

Brown v. Bryan County, Oklahoma, 1410 F.3d 1410 (5th Cir. 1995)

Butterfield v. Forrester, 103 Eng. Rep. 926 (1809)

Byrd v. New York Transit Authority, 568 N.YS.2d 628 (A.D. 1991)

Calogrides v. City of Mobile, 475 So. 2d 560 (Ala. 1985)

Carlin v. Blanchard, 537 So. 2d 303 (La. Dist. Ct. App. 1988)

Carlson v. Green, 446 U.S. 14 (1980)

Carver v. Hartville Police Department, 594 N.E.2d 92 (Ohio Ct. App. 1992)

Catalano v. Bujak, 642 A.2d 448 (Pa. 1994)

City of Jackson, Mississippi v. Perry, 764 So. 2d 490 (Miss. 2003)

City of San Antonio v. Schneider, 787 S.W.2d 459 (Tex. Ct. App. 1990)

Clark v. District of Columbia, 714 A.2d 768 (D.C. 1997)

Davis v. City of Detroit, 386 N.W. 2d 169 (Mich. Ct. App. 1986)

Davis v. Muse, 51 Md. App. 93, 441 A. 2d 1089 (1992)

Davis v. Passman, 442 U.S. 228 (1979)

DeSanchez v. Michigan Department of Mental Health, 455 Mich. 83, 565 N.W.2d 358 (1997)

Del Tufo v. Township of Old Bridge, 685 A.2d 1267 (N.J.1996)

Diogaurdi v. City of New Rochelle, 578 N.Y.S.2d 660 (A.D. 1992)

Doe v. Calumet, 641 N.E.2d 498 (Ill. 1994)

Farmer v. Brennan, 511 U.S. 825 (1994)

Federal Deposit Insurance Corp. v. Meyer, 510 U.S. 471 (1994)

Fruge v. City of New Orleans, 613 So. 2d 811 (La. Dist. Ct. App. 1993)

Govea v. City of Norcross, 271 Ga. App. 36, 608 S.E. 2d 677 (2004)

Gray v. Tunica County, Mississippi, 279 F. Supp. 2d 789 (N.D. Miss. 2003)

Hamseed v. Brown, 530 N.W.2d 1380 (Iowa 1995)

Harris v. City of Compton, 172 Cal. App. 3d 301 (1985)

Harris v. District of Columbia, 932 F.2d 10 (D.C. Cir. 1991)

Hurely v. Eddingfield, 59 N.E. 1058 (Ind. 1901)

Kapper v. Connick, 681 So. 944 (La. 1996)

Kerr v. Alaska, No. 3AN-93-06531 (Super. Ct. Alaska 1996)

Kruger v. White Lake Twp., 250 Mich. App. 622 N.W.2d 660 (2002)

Jackson v. North Carolina Dept. of Crime Control, 97 N.C. App. 425, 388 S.E. 770, *cert. denied,* 326 N.C. 596, 393 S.E. 2d 878 (1991)

Johnson v. Suffolk County P.D., 245 A.D. 2d 340 N.Y. 2d 440 (A.D. 1997)

Layton v. Quinn, 120 Mich. App. 708, 328 N.W. 2d 95 (1982)

Malley v. Briggs, 475 U.S. 335 (1986)

Marshall v. District Court, 836 P. 2d 47 (Nev. 1992)

Mathieu v. Imperial Toy Corp., 646 So. 2d 318 (La. 1994)

McCrumb v. Kent County, et al., No. 95-2039-NO (Mich. 2002) [unpublished opinion]

McDaniel v. City of Seattle, 65 Wash. App. 360, 828 P.2d 81 (1992)

McRoy v. New Orleans Police Department, 558 So. 2d 1332 (La. Ct. App. 1990)

Miga v. City of Holyoke, 497 N.E.2d 398 (Mass. 1986)

Mills v. City of Overland Park, Kansas, 837 P.2d 370 (Kan. 1992)

Miller v. Smith, 921 S.W.2d 39 (1995)

Moody v. Ferguson, 732 F. Supp. 627 (D.S.C. 1989)

Moore v. City of Philadelphia, 571 A.2d 518 (Pa. Commw. 1990)

Moore v. City of Troy, 577 N.Y.S.2d 969 (A.D. 1992)

Morris v. Leaf, 534 N.W.2d 388 (Iowa 1995)

Murdock v. City of Keene, 623 A.2d 755 (N.H. 1993)

Nelson v. Trayer, 188 So. 2d 65 (Fla. Dist. Ct. App. 1966)

Papa v. United States, 281 F. 3d 1004 (9th Cir. 2002)

Parish v. Hill, 350 N.C. 231, 513 S.E. 2d 547 (1999)

Pizzuto v. County of Nassau, 239 F. Supp. 2d 301 (E.D.N.Y. 2003)

Reenders v. City of Ontario, 68 Cal. App. 3d 1045, 137 Cal. Rptr. 736 (1977)

Robinson v. City of Detroit, 426 Mich. 439, 613 N.W.2d 307 (2000)

Sarro v. Cornell Corrections, Inc., 248 F. Supp. 2d 52 (D.R.I. 2003)

Saunders v. County of Steuben, 693 N.E.2d 16 (Ind. 1998)

Simmons v. United States, 805 F.2d 1363 (9th Cir. 1986)

Smith v. Smith, 19 Mass. 621 (1824)

Smith v. Wade, 461 U.S. 30 (1983)

South v. Maryland, 59 U.S. 396 (1896)

State v. McGeorge, 925 S.W.2d 105 (Tex. Ct. App. 1996)

State v. Hughes, 230 N.J. Super 223, 553 A.2d 349 (App. Div. 1989)

State v. Powell, 586 So. 2d 1180 (Fla. Dist. Ct. App. 1991)

Stitle v. City of New York, 569 N.Y.S.2d (A.D. 1991)

Strong v. Nicholson, 580 So. 2d 1288 (Miss. 1991)

Texas Dept. of Corrections v. Winters, 765 S.W.2d 531 (Tex. Ct. App. 1989)

Title v. Mahan, 583 N.E.2d 796 (Ind. 1991)

Thomas v. City of Parma, 624 N.E. 2d 337 (Ohio Ct. App.1993)

Thomas v. Williams, 124 S.E.2d 409 (Ga. Ct. App. 1962)

Wagar v. Hasenkrug, 486 F. Supp. 47 (D. Mont. 1980)

Wilder v. Village of Amityville, 288 F. Supp. 2d 341 (E.D.N.Y. 2003)

Chapter 4

Civil Liability and Federal Law: Section 1983 Litigation

Federal civil lawsuits arising out of allegations of deprivations of constitutional rights by local officials are filed in accordance with § 1983. It provides remedies for violations of federal rights. Section 1983 lawsuits may include claims of abuse of authority by police and correctional personnel with arrestees and prisoners, issues of school desegregation, and other institutional reform litigation. For 40 years, § 1983 litigation has made up the majority of civil litigation in the United States. This chapter will provide an overview of the historical and contemporary use of § 1983 and the methods that are used to bring a constitutional claim against criminal justice personnel.

History of § 1983

At the conclusion of the Civil War, Congress enacted the Civil Rights Act (Title 18 U.S. Code § 242 [1866]) to put an end to the lawless activities of the Ku Klux Klan. The Act provides federal criminal penalties for state and local officials who violate guaranteed rights of citizens (Eisenberg & Schwab, 1987; Gressman, 1992). In April 1871, Title 42 United States Code § 1983 was passed by Congress, and it provides a vehicle for citizens to sue for violations of constitutional rights. Section 1983 added civil remedies to the criminal penalties that were enacted in 1866.

Prior to the Reconstruction period, there were only a handful of constitutional provisions that gave protection against actions by state and federal governments. State courts and the common law were virtually the only protections for citizens' lives, liberty, and property. The conclusion of the Civil War changed this. Between 1866 and 1870, Congress enacted three constitutional amendments: the Thirteenth Amendment (abolishing slavery), the

Fourteenth Amendment (due process and equal protection clauses), and the Fifteenth Amendment (right to be free from discrimination in voting). In 1866, Congress enforced the Thirteenth Amendment by passing a civil rights statute guaranteeing rights to African-American citizens. In 1867, Congress enacted a habeas corpus statute that gave those held in state facilities the right to challenge the constitutionality of their incarceration in federal court. Section 1983 was enacted at the end of a five-year period during which Congress was moving quickly to pass and enforce laws to protect the constitutional rights of citizens and provide remedies for violations of those rights.

Prior to § 1983, the only option for redressing a violation of a constitutional right was through the common law, and those actions were heard in state court. Section 1983 allowed for these cases to be heard in federal court. From its enactment in 1871 until 1961, § 1983 lay virtually dormant—it was used in only 24 cases during this period. It has been argued that there are three reasons for its lack of use (Collins, 1997). First, § 1983 was rarely used because of a narrow interpretation and because the Bill of Rights did not apply to the states until the Warren Court of the 1950s and 1960s began in earnest the process of selective incorporation of rights through the Fourteenth Amendment's due process clause. Second, § 1983 was not used much because it was unclear whether actions of public officials that were not formally sanctioned by state law would amount to state action. Third, § 1983 may have been dormant due to a narrow application by the Supreme Court regarding the types of rights it was supposed to guarantee. For some time the Supreme Court held that common law liberty and property rights were secured by state law and not the Constitution (or § 1983). For example, a police chief in *Brawner v. Irvin* (1909) whipped an African-American woman primarily because of her race. The federal trial court held that the rights that were denied did not fall under § 1983, but rather under state law. The court also doubted seriously whether her rights had been denied under state law.

These three rationales seem to indicate the court's reluctance to realistically implement § 1983 for many years. There may have been other reasons for this reluctance as well. As a consequence, during its dormancy, citizens were primarily relegated to redressing their civil rights disputes against local officials in state court through state tort actions.

Resurrection of § 1983

Section 1983 was enacted by Congress for three main reasons: (1) to redress unconstitutional laws; (2) to provide a federal forum when there was no state court remedy on the books; and (3) to provide a federal remedy when the state court remedy was available in theory but not in fact. Section 1983 provides:

law enf. personnel

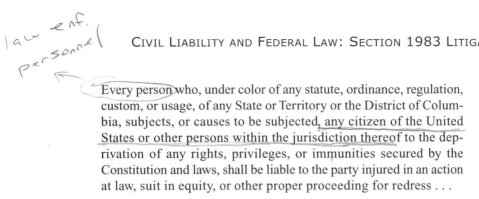

> Every person who, under color of any statute, ordinance, regulation, custom, or usage, of any State or Territory or the District of Columbia, subjects, or causes to be subjected, any citizen of the United States or other persons within the jurisdiction thereof to the deprivation of any rights, privileges, or immunities secured by the Constitution and laws, shall be liable to the party injured in an action at law, suit in equity, or other proper proceeding for redress . . .

This law has four important elements. First, a person filing suit must be a protected person within the meaning of the act. This means that anyone under the jurisdiction of the United States may bring suit under § 1983. Second, the defendant must have been acting under "color of law." This means the official must be acting within the scope of his or her authority at the time of the constitutional deprivation. Third, "every person" is interpreted to mean that every individual public official and governmental entity may be liable for constitutional deprivations. Finally, a constitutionally protected right must have been violated. In order to prevail, these elements must be established. These individual elements will be discussed in greater detail later in this chapter.

For 90 years, § 1983 lawsuits were rarely filed against government officials, because they were immune from suit. In two famous cases, however, the United States Supreme Court began to expand its interpretation of who could be sued under § 1983. In *United States v. Classic* (1941), the Supreme Court held that officials acting under color of law, as election officials were in Louisiana when they rigged an election, could be held liable for misuse of power possessed by virtue of state law. Interpretation of § 1983 expanded in *Screws v. United States* (1945), when the Court ruled that acting under color of law also meant acting under pretense of law. In *Screws*, Robert Hall, an African-American, was beaten to death by officers who had arrested him for theft. The officers were prosecuted under § 242 (criminal violation of civil rights) and the Court stated that "acts of officers who undertake to perform their official duties are included whether they hew to the line of their authority or overstep it."

The Supreme Court further expanded its interpretation of § 1983 in its landmark decision of *Monroe v. Pape* (1961). Prior to this decision, it was extremely difficult to hold criminal justice officials liable under § 1983 due to the requirement of acting under "color of law." *Monroe* broadened the language of this concept. Chicago police officers broke into Monroe's house in the early morning and rousted him and his family out of bed, made him stand naked in the living room, and ransacked the house. He was arrested and detained at the police department for 10 hours and later released. Monroe was never prosecuted, but did file a § 1983 lawsuit based on an illegal search and seizure and violation of his constitutional rights. The Court ruled that the officers' actions, which were clothed in state law, constituted acting under color of law, and that they misused their authority and power as police officers. The Court further concluded that Monroe did not have to exhaust alternative remedies available in state court prior to lodging his claim in federal court. In *Monroe* the Court dusted off the once-dormant law and opened the door for future litigation against the police and correctional personnel. This decision, however, did not include liability against government entities, but only against individual officers. Thus, the city of Chicago could not be sued (see Figure 4.1).

Figure 4.1
Monroe v. Pape (1961)

During early morning hours, 13 Chicago police officers broke into Monroe's house and ordered him and his six children out of bed and forced them to stand naked while they ransacked the house. He was then arrested and transported to the police station. He was held for 10 hours, not allowed to call an attorney, and was neither arraigned nor prosecuted. He filed a § 1983 lawsuit claiming that his Fourth Amendment protection against unreasonable search and seizure had been violated.

The United States Supreme Court granted certiorari to examine the issue of whether the Chicago police officers and the city should be liable under § 1983 for the officers' actions. The Court held that a plaintiff need not exhaust available state remedies prior to filing a § 1983 claim in federal court. The Court held that the officers' actions were "action under color of law" within the meaning of § 1983, even if what they did also happened to be in violation of state law. The Court concluded that the City of Chicago was not liable, because Congress did not intend to bring municipalities within the provisions of § 1983.

Justice Douglas's opinion was significant for several reasons. First, the decision dusted off the rarely used § 1983 after a lengthy period of disuse. Douglas stated that "Section 1983 makes a man responsible for the natural consequences of his actions." Prior to this decision, it was difficult to hold public officials liable for their actions under § 1983. Second, this is a seminal case because it literally opened up the floodgates of the courts, which have provided that citizens claiming that their constitutionally protected rights have been violated by a public officer's actions may now bring a civil suit against that officer. Third, the decision interprets the language in § 1983 that states: "every person acting under color of law, . . . may be held liable." Every person is defined as "every officer." When officers perform their sworn duties by virtue of state law and misuse their authority, they may be held liable for the abuse of such power. Liability will attach under § 1983 when an officer misuses his or her authority and violates an individual's constitutionally protected right.

Essential Elements of § 1983 Lawsuits

Monroe has become the cornerstone for police federal civil liability (Kappeler, 1997). The law itself does not create substantive rights or jurisdiction in the federal courts (*Chapman v. Houston Welfare Rights Organization*, 1979), and is therefore procedural. The plaintiff suing under § 1983 must specifically plead federal jurisdiction under the appropriate statute (*Monroe v. Pape*, 1961). Likewise, under *Monroe*, the plaintiff need not first bring separate actions under state and federal law. There are several essential elements in understanding the dynamics of § 1983 lawsuits.

How Is "Person" Defined?

In *Monroe* the Court defined "person" within the meaning of § 1983 as individual officers. A government employee may be sued for money damages in his or her individual capacity for acts performed while discharging those duties. A suit against a state employee acting in his or her official capacity imposes liability against the entity that the employee represents and cannot be brought, because the Eleventh Amendment prohibits lawsuits against the state (*Brandon v. Holt*, 1985).

Further, the Supreme Court ruled in *Will v. Michigan Department of State Police* (1989) that state officials cannot be sued under § 1983 when they act in their official capacity. The Court emphasized that Congress did not intend to include states or state agencies within the definition of "person" for purposes of § 1983 liability. Plaintiffs may, however, sue a state and state agencies for prospective injunctive relief under § 1983 (*Kentucky v. Graham*, 1985).

The Supreme Court further expanded the definition of "person" to include local governments and their employees in *Monell v. Department of Social Services of the City of New York* (1978). Prior to *Monell*, local governments were immune from § 1983 liability based on the rationale that they were not "persons" as defined by law. The Dictionary Act (enacted in 1871 and originally codified at 16 Stat. 431) allowed the word "person" to be applied to political bodies. Based on the history of § 1983 and relying on the Dictionary Act, the Supreme Court concluded in *Monell* that municipalities, as well as other governing bodies, are "persons" within the meaning of § 1983. The Court in *Monell* held that governmental bodies may be held liable when an officer acts pursuant to a custom or official policy of the agency and it violates an individual's constitutional rights. Plaintiffs may now sue and recover damages against county, city, municipal, and other units of local governments for the actions of their officers. A complete discussion of supervisory liability will be presented in Chapters 5 and 6.

How Is Acting Under "Color of Law" Defined?

For liability to attach, a person must be acting under "color of law." This phrase normally means that an officer or official misused his or her official powers granted by law in the office he or she was sworn to uphold (*Monroe v. Pape*, 1961). In *West v. Atkins* (1988), the United States Supreme Court further stated that employees who carry out their official responsibilities act under color of state law and are state actors even when they act in violation of state law. The courts have broadened this phrase to include actions taken under the auspices of state and local laws, ordinances, and agency rules. Actions that exceed the law and the scope of authority constitute acting under "color of law." For example, assaulting a prisoner after a prison disturbance would constitute action outside the scope of the officer's authority.

Actions taken under color of federal laws by federal employees are excluded. *Bivens* actions are not incorporated under § 1983. The off-duty actions of an officer cannot be the basis of litigation unless the officer uses police equipment or uses his or her authority as an "official" employee.

Inquiries by the courts to determine what constitutes acting under color of law require a determination of the "nature of the officer's act, not simply his duty status" (Vaughn & Coomes, 1995). Using the "totality of circumstances" analysis, courts determine whether an officer was acting under color of law by examining whether criminal justice personnel invoke power if they discharge duties routinely associated with their work, or if they use their authority to lure plaintiffs into compromising positions. Further, courts hold that officers act under color of law if they wear their uniforms, draw their firearms, identify themselves as law enforcement or correctional officers, place suspects under arrest, detain and confine them, file official reports, and otherwise hold themselves out as official personnel for a government agency (Vaughn & Coomes, 1995).

For example, in *Ousley v. Town of Lincoln* (2004), the court found that an off-duty officer was acting under color of law when he arrested a youth for assault and disorderly conduct and malicious damage of property. Officer Kevin Harty of the Lincoln Police Department was off duty when he stopped his personal vehicle after observing Ousley fighting with his girlfriend in the middle of the street. Ousley shouted "Go ahead and hit me!" and pounded on the hood of Harty's car with his fists. Harty, not in uniform, exited his car and an altercation occurred between Ousley and himself. Ousley claimed that Harty chased, beat, and strangled him. Witnesses claimed that they saw Harty chase Ousley, that they heard Harty yell that he was the police and that someone should call the police. Harty's version was that he had a brief "encounter" with Ousley and that he returned to his car and waited for the police. Prior to the police arriving, Harty called the Lincoln Police Department and requested backup.

Responding police observed an obvious altercation between Harty and Ousley. Harty's shirt was torn and he had abrasions on his body. Ousley was covered in blood. The police filed three criminal charges against Ousley. The judge dismissed all but the malicious damage of property charge, ruling that Harty was not a credible witness. Ousley filed a civil lawsuit, claiming that his constitutional rights had been violated.

At trial, the court ruled that, based on the "totality of circumstances," surrounding the incident, Harty acted under color of state law. The court examined the circumstances of this incident and noted that Harty did not wear police attire, did not use any type of police weapon, and the location of the incident, all of which pointed in his favor. The court, however, found that Ousley presented compelling evidence that Harty not only announced that he was a police officer, which several witnesses' testimony verified, but also that he was acting in his official capacity as an officer at the time of the altercation, and requested backup from the department. The court concluded that such evidence showed that Harty was acting as a "police officer" at the time of the incident and ruled in favor of Ousley.

What Is the Focus of the Complaint in a § 1983 Lawsuit?

The plaintiff must show that the conduct of the defendant resulted in the violation of a constitutional right or federal law that can be enforced in accordance with § 1983. Section 1983 creates no rights, but is a vehicle to redress violations of the Bill of Rights and certain federal statutes. Mere negligence is not actionable as a § 1983 claim—such claims must be brought in state court (*Daniels v. Williams*, 1986). Further, violations of city ordinances or state laws are not actionable under § 1983.

Figure 4.2 identifies the primary constitutional amendments that form the basis of § 1983 actions. Criminal justice personnel must be familiar with these amendments, because they regularly make decisions that involve rights that are protected by these amendments. Violating these rights can lead to civil liability. Officers' actions may also lead to litigation against their agency. Therefore, criminal justice officers need to know the law, their legal responsibilities, and their department's policy and procedure manual. They also must be aware of how these amendments apply to the status of offenders in the criminal justice system.

Figure 4.2
Selected Constitutional Amendments

First Amendment: "Congress shall make no law respecting an establishment of religion, or prohibiting the free exercise thereof; or abridging the freedom of speech, or of the press; or the right of the people peaceably to assemble, and to petition the government for a redress of grievances." If criminal justice personnel violate First Amendment rights in their official capacity, they are subject to § 1983 litigation (*Alliance to End Repression v. City of Chicago*, 1982; *Hutchings v. Corum*, 1980).

Fourth Amendment: "The right of the people to be secure in their persons, houses, papers, and effects, against unreasonable searches and seizures, shall not be violated, and no Warrants shall issue, but upon probable cause, supported by Oath or affirmation, and particularly describing the place to be searched, and the persons or things to be seized." This amendment restricts the state and its officers (*Wolf v. Colorado*, 1949).

Fifth Amendment: "Nor shall any person be subject for the same offense to be twice put in jeopardy of life or limb; nor shall be compelled in any criminal case to be a witness against himself, nor be deprived of life, liberty, or property, without due process of law; . . ." State and local officers must follow this requirement (*Benton v. Maryland*, 1969).

Sixth Amendment (in part): "In all criminal prosecutions, the accused shall enjoy the right . . . to have the assistance of Counsel for his defense." This provision binds the states, as do other requirements in this amendment (*Gideon v. Wainwright*, 1962).

Eighth Amendment: "Excessive bail shall not be required, . . . nor cruel and unusual punishments inflicted." Another restriction that is binding on the states (*Robinson v. California*, 1962).

The Fourteenth Amendment (in part): "No state shall make or enforce any law which shall abridge the privileges or immunities of citizens of the United States; nor shall any state deprive any person of life, liberty, or property, without due process of law; nor deny to any person within its jurisdiction the equal protection of the laws." This amendment, by its terms, applies to the states (*Powers v. Lightner*, 1987).

Remedies Under § 1983

Filing a § 1983 lawsuit allows the plaintiff a range of remedies should he or she prevail. A prevailing plaintiff may be awarded monetary damages and injunctive or declaratory relief. As ordered by a court, injunctive relief prohibits a certain practice that a government entity may be performing, which violates a constitutionally protected right of another. Declaratory relief, in the court's opinion, may determine that a regulation or practice is unconstitutional without necessarily requiring any remedial action.

Another benefit of filing a lawsuit in federal court is that the process of discovery (obtaining documents from the defendant) is more simplified than in state court. Plaintiffs filing a § 1983 lawsuit are not required to exhaust state remedies prior to filing in federal court. Since 1976, prevailing plaintiffs' attorneys may be awarded attorney's fees. These features make filing a § 1983 lawsuit attractive and more likely that plaintiffs and their attorneys will file § 1983 lawsuits against criminal justice personnel.

Section 1983 authorizes any citizen in the United States to file a federal civil lawsuit. Corporations are excluded. Section 1983 has also been interpreted to mean that aliens legally in the United States may also file suit under § 1983 (*Graham v. Richardson*, 1975). Some courts have extended the Fourteenth Amendment due process and equal protection clauses in § 1983 cases to apply to illegal aliens. Pretrial detainees, probationers, convicted prisoners, and parolees may also file § 1983 lawsuits.

A plaintiff may file a § 1983 lawsuit in either state or federal court simultaneously, although a majority are filed in federal court (*Maine v. Thiboutot*, 1980). Plaintiffs are subject to statutes of limitations when filing a § 1983 lawsuit. Statutes of limitation are laws that stipulate a certain period for the action to be filed in court from the date the incident giving rise to the action occurred. In *Wilson v. Garcia* (1985), the Supreme Court determined that § 1983 cases are "personal injury" cases, and that statutory periods used in state courts be used. Generally speaking, the statutory period is three years.

The same types of damages awarded in state tort claims are available in § 1983 litigation: nominal, compensatory, and punitive. Damages are awarded for injuries, pain and suffering, loss of earnings, emotional distress, medical expenses, and loss of property (*Carey v. Pipus*, 1978). Punitive damages may be awarded for particularly blameworthy conduct on the part of the defendant. In *Smith v. Wade* (1983), the Supreme Court held that actual malice is not necessary to recover punitive damages—reckless or callous indifference to constitutional rights is sufficient (see Figure 4.3).

In *King v. Marci* (1993), the court upheld a malicious prosecution award of $75,000 for two months in detention and emotional distress. Punitive damages for false arrest and excessive force were also proper. The court in *Franklin v. Aycock* (1986) assessed $5,000 each in punitive damages against three detention officers. They had repeatedly kicked a prisoner who was shackled in bed.

Plaintiffs filing § 1983 lawsuits may also seek declaratory and injunctive relief. When awarding a declaratory judgment, the court may declare that a state statute or regulation is unconstitutional. Declaratory relief in federal court is discretionary, as the court may award compensation for rights violations. For example, a court may examine a correctional department's use-of-force policy and declare it unconstitutional and require the department to rewrite it in accordance with constitutional provisions. When authorizing injunctive relief, a court goes further in providing redress to the plaintiff. The court could prohibit defendants from engaging in certain unconstitutional conduct in the future or require that they take certain steps to avoid further violations of the Constitution.

Figure 4.3
Smith v. Wade (1983)

Prisoner Wade was voluntarily placed in protective segregation in a youth correctional facility in Missouri because he complained of physical abuse by other prisoners. Classification Officer Smith placed Wade in a cell with another prisoner and later placed a third prisoner, who had a history of fighting, in the same cell. Smith was aware of the third prisoner's assaultive history, ignored it, and failed to determine whether other cells were available. Wade later was sexually assaulted and filed a § 1983 claim against Smith, other officers, and correctional officials, asserting that his Eighth Amendment rights were violated. Wade prevailed and was awarded $25,000 in compensatory damages and $5,000 in punitive damages. The appellate court affirmed the decision and Smith appealed the punitive damage award to the United States Supreme Court.

The Supreme Court examined the issue of whether a jury could award punitive damages against an officer who acts with reckless disregard of or indifference to the safety of a prisoner and his or her protected constitutional rights. The Court affirmed the decision. The Court concluded that a jury is permitted to assess punitive damages in a civil action in which an officer's action is motivated by malicious intent and if the defendant acted with callous indifference to, or reckless disregard of, a prisoner's rights. Punitive damages may be awarded for particularly egregious and blameworthy misconduct marked by evil intent or motive, as demonstrated by the defendant.

This case is significant because in awarding punitive damages, the jury is sending a message that such actions are outrageous and that it intends to punish the officer for such actions. Punitive damages may be awarded when a defendant's actions are motivated by malicious intent and when the defendant acted in a callous, reckless manner, without regard for the safety or rights of the prisoner. This decision makes it less difficult for a plaintiff to recover punitive damages.

Compensatory and punitive damages were awarded to a prisoner who sustained injuries after a use-of-force altercation with correction officers. In *Jackson v. Austin* (2003), officers instructed Jackson to stand in line for the prison medical clinic and Jackson attempted to explain that he was there for treatment his of knee. Jackson explained that he could not stand for long periods and needed to sit. The officer refused to examine the prisoner's medical restriction orders signed by a physician. He grabbed Jackson and pushed him to the floor and handcuffed him. A second officer on the scene did not participate in the action, but failed to intervene in the actions of the first officer.

Jackson filed a §1983 lawsuit and the court rejected a motion for qualified immunity from the officers. The court held that the prisoner did not have to prove that he sustained significant or permanent injuries and that the officers used excessive force in restraining him. The court ruled in favor of Jackson and assessed $15,000 in compensatory damages and $30,000 in punitive damages against both officers. The court also noted that the prisoner was 60 years old and that the officers were aware that he had a knee injury.

Injunctive relief may be granted in the form of a temporary restraining order, a preliminary injunction, or a permanent injunction. Courts can grant a broad range of injunctions in § 1983 cases. The Supreme Court in *Los Angeles v. Lyons* (1983) determined that the plaintiff could not sue for injunctive relief. The plaintiff, who had been a victim of a choke hold, sued, asking the court to enjoin the future use of choke holds by the Los Angeles Police Department. The choke hold had resulted in the deaths of 16 people, many of whom were African-American males like the plaintiff. The Court ruled that the plaintiff had not shown with certainty that he would have another encounter with the police. Even if he could make such a showing, he could not establish that the choke hold would be applied specifically to him. In an effort to limit federal court intrusion into the state's operation of prisons and jails after a finding of an unconstitutional conditions in a facility, the courts have normally given officials the opportunity to develop a plan to bring conditions into compliance with the Constitution (*Lewis v. Casey*, 1996).

Can Attorney's Fees Be Assessed?

Section 1983 does not on its face require the awarding of attorney's fees. Awarding of attorney's fees is discretionary on the part of the court. Congress modified the American rule in the Civil Rights Attorney's Fees Awards Act of 1976 (42 U.S.C. § 1988). The rule is a tradition at common law that each party pays his own attorney's fees, win or lose (*Alyeska Pipeline Service Co. v. Wilderness Society*, 1975). The statute provides a financial incentive to bring lawsuits that might not otherwise attract attorneys, either because only injunctive relief is sought, or because the likelihood of substantial damages is uncertain. The Attorney's Fees Act states in part:

> . . . the court, in its discretion, may allow the prevailing party, other than the United States, a reasonable attorney's fee as part of the costs, except that in any action brought against a judicial officer for an act or omission taken in such officer's judicial capacity such officer shall not be held liable for any costs, including attorney's fees, unless such action was clearly in excess of such officer's jurisdiction.

In order for an attorney to recover attorney's fees, the plaintiff must obtain at least some actual relief on the merits of his or her claim. Plaintiffs who proceed in a § 1983 lawsuit pro se (on their own behalf) are not entitled to attorney's fees even when they prevail. Further, the Supreme Court has held that prevailing plaintiffs, not prevailing defendants, sued under § 1983, should recover attorney's fees (*Hughes v. Rowe*, 1980). There does not have to be a trial in order to recover attorney's fees. In *Maher v. Gagne* (1980), the Supreme Court ruled that the plaintiffs were entitled to attorney's fees even though the case was settled through a consent decree agreement. This ruling is significant for conditions-of-confinement suits that are settled under a consent decree. This may also be of significance to law enforcement agencies that settle under consent decrees in the future.

In determining the appropriate amount to award an attorney under § 1988, the Supreme Court in *Hensley v. Eckerhart* (1983) established a figure known as the "lodestar." This figure is computed by multiplying the number of hours reasonably expended on the litigation by a reasonable hourly rate. This computation is completed at the end of the litigation. The following factors are normally considered in calculating the lodestar figure: (1) the time and labor required; (2) the novelty and difficulty of the questions presented by the case; (3) the skill required to perform the legal service properly; (4) the preclusion of other employment by the attorney due to acceptance of the case; (5) the customary fee for similar work; (6) whether the fee is fixed or contingent; (7) time limitations imposed by the client or the circumstances; (8) the amount in dispute and the results obtained; (9) the experience, reputation, and ability of the attorney; (10) the "undesirability" of the case; (11) the nature and length of the professional relationship with the client; and (12) awards in similar cases. In 1996, however, Congress placed a cap on the hourly rate used under § 1988 in prisoner rights litigation. In accordance with 42 U.S.C. § 1997e(d)(3), the hourly rate used in determining the fee by federal judicial courts cannot exceed $112.50.

In *Knopp v. Johnson* (1989), experienced attorneys sought fees up to $190 per hour. The 35-day trial in a prison conditions case led to attorney's fees of more than $200,000. In *Spell v. McDaniel* (1987), a particularly egregious case, the court assessed $900,000 for compensatory and punitive damages and $325,000 in attorney's fees. A police officer kicked a restrained and compliant arrestee in the groin. The injury required surgical removal of a testicle, which resulted in sterility.

Who Pays for the Damages?

Criminal justice personnel in a civil lawsuit usually have legal representation provided by their employing agency. Law or written policy in most state agencies provides for representation through the state attorney general's office. As long as the officer acted within the scope of his or her authority and was held liable, the state will pay part or all of the award.

Lawsuits against local law enforcement officers and county sheriff's departments are handled differently. The city or county attorney's office usually will defend a civil lawsuit filed against an officer or government agency. In many jurisdictions, local departments participate in a risk management pool and retain legal counsel through it. Still other departments retain their own attorneys to defend department personnel. Most agencies will provide an attorney for the officer, but it is a decision made by local administrators on a case-by-case basis. This may be addressed in the department's policy manual, and officers should be aware of the policy in their department. If the agency decides not to provide an attorney, it will be necessary for the officer to retain his or her own attorney.

Should an officer lose a civil lawsuit, generally his or her employing agency will pay the damage award. Many states provide indemnification for state employees, although the amount varies. Most agencies will not indemnify blatant or outrageous actions outside the officer's authority. If the court awards more than the indemnification, the officer pays the difference. Indemnification also varies in local agencies. If punitive damages are awarded, the individual officer must pay them. Payment by the agency would be contrary to public policy. Criminal justice personnel should be aware of how their agency provides legal representation in the event of a civil lawsuit and how damages awards are paid should the officer be held liable.

Mechanics of a § 1983 Lawsuit

Figure 4.4 illustrates the mechanical framework of a § 1983 lawsuit. With some exceptions, this basic process is followed. All § 1983 lawsuits originate with an incident (i.e., arrest, search, pursuit, use of force) in which a criminal justice officer acts under color of law in the performance of his or her duties. Depending on the situation, the act may or may not be within the scope of the officer's duties. The plaintiff may allege that the officer violated his or her constitutional rights as a result of the incident. In the case of jails and prisons, a prisoner may file a § 1983 lawsuit alleging that a rule or regulation has violated his or her constitutional rights, in addition to filing a complaint about an incident in which an officer violated his or her protected rights. As previously discussed, the plaintiff must file the suit within the statute of limitations. The plaintiff may file the lawsuit with legal counsel or may act as his or her own attorney (pro se).

The plaintiff will usually name individual officers who were involved in the incident, and also those in the chain of command—supervisors, administrators, and government entities. This is known as the "deep pockets" theory (del Carmen, 1991). This theory encourages the plaintiff to name multiple defendants in the lawsuit in an effort to find culpability with as many as possible—the idea being the more defendants named within the hierarchy of the agency, the more likely the award will be higher should the plaintiff prevail. Officers may have only limited resources with which to pay, but the city or the county might be better able to pay the award.

The plaintiff files a complaint with the court, outlining and describing the nature of the constitutional rights that allegedly were violated. All involved parties are named, and the complaint describes each defendant's liability. Each defendant receives a copy of the complaint. The attorney for each defendant also receives a copy of the complaint. Counsel meets with the defendants to discuss the alleged incident. Pertinent documents, such as the officer's incident report, policies and regulations, as well as any evidence, are reviewed. Defense counsel normally files a written response to the court denying the allegations or claiming immunity from the lawsuit.

Shortly after receiving the complaint, the defense counsel may file a motion to dismiss the case. A motion to dismiss asks the court to throw out the plaintiff's lawsuit because it is without merit, is not founded in law, or fails to state a valid legal claim. The judge may agree and dismiss the case, or may allow the plaintiff to amend the complaint.

Figure 4.4
Mechanics of a Civil Lawsuit

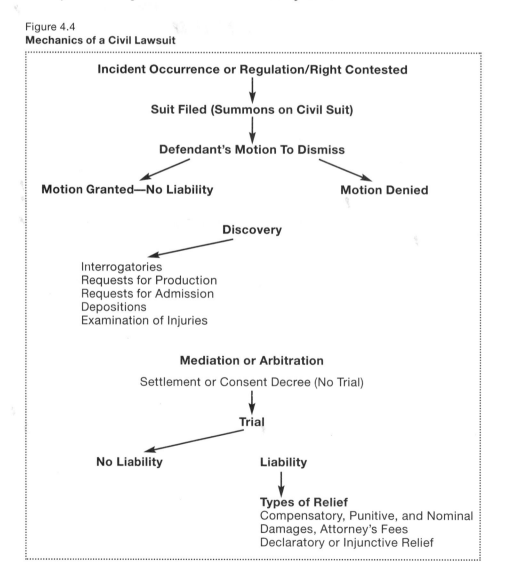

If the plaintiff's case survives the motion to dismiss, the discovery period begins. Discovery is a process by which one party gains information held by another party (Franklin, 1993). It is a period established by the court to allow the plaintiff and the defendant to explore one another's cases. Discovery provides for full disclosure prior to trial. It also allows the parties to examine evidence that may be useful in their case that may not be obtained through other means or sources. All jurisdictions provide for discovery.

There are five basic tools allowed in discovery:

1. Interrogatories
2. Requests for production
3. Requests for admission
4. Depositions
5. Examination of physical evidence

Interrogatories are written questions intended to solicit written or verbal responses. Interrogatories are commonly used and inexpensive. Under the Federal Rules of Civil Procedure, the number of questions is limited to 30. Named parties in the lawsuit sit down with their counsel and, under oath, answer each question. Second, documents known as requests for production are filed. This tool gives the requesting party the opportunity to obtain and examine physical evidence in the possession of the responding party. Documents may include departmental policies and procedures, incident reports, photos, audio and video recordings, drawings, personnel files, investigative reports, autopsy reports, and medical reports.

A third type of discovery tool is a request for admission. This document is a statement of fact under law asking the responding party to admit or deny the statement. If the issue in question is admitted to be true, it will be settled prior to trial. If the issue is contested it must be determined at trial. Both parties may use requests for admission. This can be helpful in settling issues prior to trial.

The fourth type of discovery tool is a deposition, which is out-of-court testimony given under oath and transcribed. This can be the most costly form of discovery. Both parties may take depositions of the other's clients. Although it is an informal questioning process in which the deponent answers verbally, rules of evidence still apply, and the responses are transcribed by a court reporter. Video and telephone depositions may be performed and used in conjunction with the transcribed document at trial. Deposition responses may be researched as to their accuracy and read to the jury at trial. Although used infrequently, the defendant may be asked to submit a written affidavit describing his or her actions in the incident. This, too, is taken under oath.

Finally, defense counsel will have the opportunity to examine the physical or mental injuries claimed by the plaintiff. This examination will be performed by a physician.

The discovery period is set by the court and may be extended at the court's discretion. Discovery may last as long as several months or years, depending on the complexity and magnitude of the lawsuit. At the conclusion of discovery, defense counsel may file a motion for summary judgment, asking the court to decide the case based on all evidence obtained through discovery. The court has several options: It can deny the motion; accept portions of the motion, requiring it to move to trial on those portions; or grant the motion. If the case involves both § 1983 claims and state tort actions, the federal court may dismiss the constitutional claims and remand the case to state court to deal with the remaining state issues.

If the defense counsel filed the motion for summary judgment, the plaintiff has the right to respond. The idea that each side is entitled to its "day in court" makes many courts reluctant to grant summary judgment. The court may hold that the issue is a matter for the jury to decide, and the case will move to trial. If the court grants summary judgment, the losing party has a right to appeal.

Due to the burgeoning court dockets across the country, many parties now attempt to find alternatives to going to trial. The predominant alternative methods are known as mediation and arbitration. Mediation is the more common of the two and involves the parties in dispute and a disinterested third person coming together in order to settle the case. The mediator does not have the authority to order the parties to settle the case. The mediator facilitates discussion and keeps the talks going in an attempt to work toward a resolution.

Arbitration, however, takes a more powerful judicial role in the dispute. The arbitrator listens to all the arguments from each side, weighs the evidence, and, based on the evidence, makes a recommendation. With mediation and arbitration, both parties must agree to the alternative method in reaching the resolution.

If the case goes to trial, jury selection begins. The judge and attorneys interview prospective jurors from a jury pool to determine who is qualified to serve as a juror. Individuals who cannot participate in an impartial manner are excused from duty. Once the jury is empaneled, the trial begins. The trial starts with opening statements, which provide an overview of the facts from the plaintiff and the defendant. Because the plaintiff has the burden of proof, his or her case is presented first. Once the plaintiff presents their witnesses and evidence, the defense presents their case. When both parties are finished presenting their evidence and witnesses, they make closing arguments to the jury. Both parties attempt to persuade the jury to find in favor of their client.

After closing arguments, the judge will instruct the jury about the law and their deliberations. The jury will take a period of time to deliberate the outcome of the case. The standard of proof used in civil cases is a preponderance of the evidence. The losing party may appeal the verdict. Should the jury find in favor of the plaintiff, the judge could issue a directed verdict in favor of the defendant officers. The plaintiff may still appeal such a verdict. If the plaintiff prevails, he or she would recover damages as discussed earlier and may be awarded attorney's fees.

This brief description of the mechanics of a § 1983 lawsuit is provided in order to illustrate the normal path of a civil case. Depending on the complexity and legal issues of the case, it can take years to complete. It will take even longer if the verdict is appealed. Many of the original complaints and allegations may never make it to court, due to rulings by the court and motions made by both parties. Prolonging the case with extensions and motions is sometimes a strategy in an effort for evidence to be lost, memories to fade, and witnesses to retire or die. Civil litigation is costly and highly stressful for those involved.

Summary

Section 1983 lawsuits are the most common type of litigation filed against criminal justice personnel. Students and practitioners alike should be aware of their potential liability under its provisions. Since the early 1960s, the courts have been inundated with civil rights cases. Section 1983 cannot be used by citizens or prisoners seeking to hold federal officials liable. It allows citizens, pretrial detainees, prisoners, and legal or illegal aliens to seek redress in federal court for alleged constitutional rights violations by officers acting under color of law. Commonly, acting "under color of law" is interpreted as meaning that the officer acted outside the scope of his or her sworn authority. Such actions taken by an officer may be while on duty or off duty, depending on the "totality of circumstances." Criminal justice personnel are encouraged to review their agencies' policies regarding conduct while off duty.

The mechanics of a § 1983 case and the process for working its way through the court system were provided. Discovery has significant importance to the criminal justice officer being named in the lawsuit. Discovery allows counsel of the plaintiff and the defendant to obtain information relevant to the litigation. Criminal justice practitioners should be prepared to respond to a variety of legal requests that indicate their knowledge or participation in the case. Defendants should also be prepared for a potentially lengthy process that can be disruptive to personal and job-related activities. Officers and supervisors named in a lawsuit are encouraged to meet with their legal counsel early in the proceedings. Moreover, defendants should be prepared to answer numerous questions at depositions or at trial by meeting with their attorney in advance of these proceedings.

During discovery the officer may have to complete interrogatories, give a deposition, and perhaps complete a written affidavit. Section 1983 lawsuits may be filed simultaneously in state and federal courts. Plaintiffs using § 1983 seek to hold state and local criminal justice personnel liable for causing a violation of constitutional rights and may be awarded compensatory and punitive damages, as well as attorney's fees. However, the fact that a § 1983 lawsuit has been filed does not necessarily mean that an officer's conduct was improper.

References

Collins, M.G. (1997). *Section 1983 Litigation*. Egan, MN: West Publishing.

del Carmen, R.V. (1991). *Civil Liabilities in American Policing: A Text for Law Enforcement Personnel*. Englewood Cliffs, NJ: Prentice-Hall.

Eisenberg, T. & S. Schwab (1987). "The Reality of Constitutional Tort Liability." *Cornell Law Review* 72:641-695.

Franklin, C.J. (1993). *The Police Officer's Guide to Civil Liability*. Springfield, IL: Charles C Thomas.

Gressman, E. (1992). "The Unhappy History of Civil Rights Legislation." *Michigan Law Review* 50:1323-1358.

Kappeler, V.E. (1997). *Critical Issues in Police Civil Liability*, Second Edition. Prospect Heights, IL: Waveland Press, Inc.

Vaughn, M.S. & L.F. Coomes (1995). "Police Civil Liability Under Section 1983: When Do Police Officers Act Under Color of Law?" *Journal of Criminal Justice* 23:395-415.

Cases Cited

Alliance to End Repression v. City of Chicago, 561 F. Supp. 537 (N.D. Ill. 1982)

Alyeska Pipeline Service Co. v. Wilderness Society, 421 U.S. 240 (1975)

Benton v. Maryland, 395 U.S. 784 (1969)

Brandon v. Holt, 469 U.S. 464 (1985)

Brawner v. Irvin, 169 F. 694 (C.D. Ga. 1909)

Carey v. Pipus, 435 U.S. 247 (1978)

Chapman v. Houston Welfare Rights Organization, 441 U.S. 600 (1979)

Daniels v. Williams, 474 U.S. 327 (1986)

Franklin v. Aycock, 795 F.2d 1253 (6th Cir. 1986)

Gideon v. Wainwright, 372 U.S. 335 (1962)

Graham v. Richardson, 403 U.S. 365 (1975)

Hensley v. Eckerhart, 461 U.S. 424 (1983)

Hughes v. Rowe, 449 U.S. 5 (1980)

Hutchings v. Corum, 501 F. Supp. 1276 (W.D. Mo. 1980)

Jackson v. Austin, 241 F. Supp. 2d 1313 (D. Kan. 2003)

Kentucky v. Graham, 473 U.S. 159 (1985)

King v. Marci, 993 F.2d 975 (2d Cir. 1993)

Knopp v. Johnson, 712 F. Supp. 571 (W.D. Mich. 1989)

Lewis v. Casey, 518 U.S. 343 (1996)

Los Angeles v. Lyons, 461 U.S. 95 (1983)

Maher v. Gagne, 448 U.S. 122 (1980)

Maine v. Thiboutot, 448 U.S. 1 (1980)

Monell v. Department of Social Services, 436 U.S. 658 (1978)

Monroe v. Pape, 365 U.S. 167 (1961)

Ousley v. Town of Lincoln, 313 F. Supp. 2d 78 (D.R.I. 2004)

Powers v. Lightner, 820 F.2d 818 (7th Cir. 1987)

Screws v. United States, 325 U.S. 91 (1945)

Smith v. Wade, 461 U.S. 30 (1983)

Spell v. McDaniel, 824 F.2d 1380 (4th Cir. 1987)

Robinson v. California, 370 U.S. 660 (1962)

United States v. Classic, 313 U.S. 299 (1941)

West v. Atkins, 108 U.S. 2250 (1988)

Will v. Michigan Department of State Police, 491 U.S. 58 (1989)

Wilson v. Garcia, 471 U.S. 261 (1985)

Wolf v. Colorado, 338 U.S. 25 (1949)

Chapter 5

Defenses to Civil Litigation and Risk Management

The procedures for filing civil litigation against criminal justice personnel have been discussed. Plaintiffs may file civil actions either in state court under state tort law or § 1983 and in federal court under § 1983. In this chapter, the legal concepts of immunities and defenses will be presented. The chapter will conclude with a discussion of reducing liability exposure by examining basic principles of risk management. It is critical that criminal justice personnel understand the defenses available, as well as their implications. Defenses in both state and federal court will be addressed, including official immunities and the good faith defense.

Official Immunity

A state cannot be a defendant under § 1983. States are not "persons" within the meaning of § 1983. The doctrine of sovereign immunity associated with the Eleventh Amendment prohibits private individuals from filing a lawsuit in federal court against a state without its consent. States, therefore, cannot be sued in federal or state court under § 1983. This, however, does not mean that an individual cannot sue an appropriate state official in order to compel the official's compliance with constitutional requirements. Moreover, sovereign immunity and statutory prohibitions on suing states apply only to the state itself and not to state agencies. Local governments, such as cities, counties, and other political subdivisions do not possess sovereign immunity. State officers are not protected by sovereign immunity when performing duties in their official capacity.

Sovereign Immunity

The origin of the doctrine of sovereign immunity is debatable. The doctrine has roots in both Roman and English common law and is based on the concept that the "king can do no wrong." The doctrine has shielded the government from being sued by a citizen. It was considered inappropriate for a citizen to file a lawsuit against the one who created and performed duties within the government. The legal effect of this doctrine is to prohibit a citizen from filing a lawsuit against the state or one of its subdivisions for an injury sustained by that person that was caused by the state, unless the state consents to the suit (Robinson, 1992). If consent is granted, it would normally take the form of a statute, defining the type of claim that may be filed.

In order to avoid citizens filing lawsuits against the states, Congress passed the Eleventh Amendment to the Constitution. Ratified in 1795, it states:

> The judicial power of the United States shall not be construed to extend to any suit in law or equity, commenced or prosecuted against one of the United States by citizens of another state, or citizens or subjects of any foreign state.

The effect of this amendment was to eliminate the use of federal courts as an entity through which individuals could file claims against the states. Moreover, in *United States v. Clarke* (1834), the Supreme Court held that sovereign immunity also applied to the federal government. The concern was about the prospect of hindering public service and safety should the state be sued by citizens.

The United States Supreme Court ruled in *Hans v. Louisiana* (1890) that in accordance with the Eleventh Amendment and Article III of the Constitution, sovereign immunity of the states barred lawsuits from being brought by individuals against the states in federal court without their consent. Hans attempted to sue the state of Louisiana for not making good on interest payments on state-issued bonds. The Supreme Court held that sovereign immunity prohibited such lawsuits in the federal courts.

The Supreme Court, however, did not conclude that constitutional provisions were unenforceable against states and their officials. In *Ex parte Young* (1908), the Court emphasized that state officials threatening the enforcement or implementation of unconstitutional statutes and actions could be enjoined in federal court without running contrary to the Eleventh Amendment. In *Young,* the attorney general of Minnesota was sued in his official capacity for allegedly enforcing unconstitutional statutes involving railroad rate schedules. The Court stated that Young was an individual threatening to engage in tort-like behavior who could be enjoined without regard to sovereign immunity. The Court found that although it was improper to sue a state's attorney general for monetary damages, it was proper to enjoin his actions because he was acting unconstitutionally. The Court reasoned that the actions of the attorney general were carried out in his official capacity, and such an illegal act could be enjoined.

Types of Immunity

Because citizens are barred from suing the government due to sovereign immunity, the only legal recourse for individuals is to sue the government official responsible for their injury. Government actions are carried out by government employees, and the courts recognizing this have established some protections, as long as employees are acting within the scope of their authority. At issue are what types of immunities or defenses are available to criminal justice personnel and what degree of immunity they possess.

State Tort Law Immunity

State tort law immunity originates in common law principles. Officers are protected from liability if sued under state tort law. Today only a small number of states maintain sovereign immunity under state tort law. Because of the Eleventh Amendment immunity provision, a state cannot be sued under § 1983. Most states have waived state tort immunity. A state official can be sued, however, and he or she can be held liable for his or her actions in office.

Absolute Immunity

Immunity doctrine originates from late nineteenth-century common law. Immunity in civil rights litigation is a defense in damages actions, but not in suits seeking equitable relief. In reality, absolute immunity means no liability at all. A lawsuit would be dismissed by the court.

The United States Supreme Court in *Cleavinger v. Saxner* (1985) reiterated that absolute immunity flows not from rank or title or "location within the Government," but from the nature of the responsibilities of the individual official. The Court denied absolute immunity to a prison disciplinary board that had punished a prisoner for violating prison rules, because they lacked attributes of the judiciary (see Figure 5.1).

In theory, absolute immunity examines the degree of discretion that the official has in policymaking and implementing action. The higher the level of the official, the higher the degree of immunity (*Bradley v. Fisher*, 1872). Thus, absolute immunity is available to judges, legislators, prosecutors, and members of the parole board. Absolute immunity has been reserved primarily for those involved in the judicial process. In *Pierson v. Ray* (1967), the Supreme Court held that absolute immunity shielded a municipal judge who was sued under § 1983 by clergymen who asserted that he had convicted them unconstitutionally for a peaceful protest against racial segregation. The Court emphasized that such immunity was critical to protect the integrity of the judicial process. The Court also held that absolute immunity did not apply to the arresting police officers.

Figure 5.1
Cleavinger v. Saxner (1985)

Prisoners from a Federal Bureau of Prisons facility filed a *Bivens* action against three members of a disciplinary committee who had found them guilty of violating prison regulations. The prisoners claimed that their rights under the Fifth Amendment were violated, and they were awarded $4,500 each in compensatory damages. An appellate court affirmed, and the United States Supreme Court granted certiorari to examine whether the members of the disciplinary committee were entitled to absolute or qualified immunity.

The Court held that the disciplinary committee members possessed qualified immunity. The Court identified the positions that are granted absolute immunity: judges, the president, parole board, and prosecutors. The Court reasoned that past case decisions have demonstrated that immunity analysis rests on functional categories, not on the status of the defendant. Absolute immunity flows not from rank or title or "location within the government," but from the "nature of the responsibilities of the individual official." The Court further held that they did not perceive the committee's function to be a "classic" adjudicatory function.

This case is significant because the Court identifies the criteria that distinguish absolute and qualified immunity. The Court ruled that members of the committee were not professional hearing officers, nor independent like a judge or administrative judge, as they worked for the warden. Thus, they were entitled to only qualified immunity. This decision applies to all public officers and officials, such as police officers, correctional officers, probation and parole officers, juvenile officers, and supervisory and administrative personnel.

There are three reasons American courts have supported absolute immunity for judicial, legislative, and executive duties: (1) public officials have a duty to the public to make complex decisions about matters pertaining to society, and mistakes are inevitable and it would be unfair to hold them liable; (2) the threat of liability poses a two-pronged consequence—it would discourage decisionmaking and discourage individuals from seeking public office; and (3) defending against lawsuits by public officials would severely deplete their time, energy, and money, rather than performing their official duties (*Harlow v. Fitzgerald*, 1982). The courts, therefore, have continued their support for immunity, not from a legal or historical philosophy, but more from a practical standpoint in operating the government.

Absolute immunity, however, is only a defense to damages actions and not claims for equitable relief (Silver, 2004). Even judges may be successfully sued for injunctive or declaratory relief, and attorney's fees will be available to prevailing plaintiffs (*Supreme Court of Virginia v. Consumers Union of the United States*, 1980). The Supreme Court, however, ruled in *Forrester v. White* (1998) that under the functional approach, a judge's employment decisions are administrative acts that are not protected by absolute judicial immunity.

Generally, law enforcement officers do not possess absolute immunity. At times, police officers may be protected by absolute immunity when they are carrying out court orders, because they are performing an essential judicial function (*Apostol v. Landau*, 1992). In this case, officers who were merely present during the service of a court order, which was valid, were immune, even on a claim of illegal execution. Police officers in *Jacobs v. Dujmovic* (1990), who executed a valid writ based on a landlord's lien, were absolutely immune, regardless of whether the writ was obtained correctly. In *Conner v. Alston* (1988), absolute immunity attached to a parole officer's adjudicative duties involving the parole revocation of a parolee arrested and charged with robbery.

Courts have granted absolute immunity on one occasion to police officers (and perhaps correctional personnel). In *Brisco v. Lahue* (1983), the Supreme Court determined that police officers could not be sued under § 1983 for giving perjured testimony against a defendant in a state criminal trial. Under common law, trial participants, such as judges, prosecutors, and witnesses, were granted absolute immunity for actions related to the trial. Police officers therefore possess absolute immunity when testifying, even though it may constitute perjury. A word of caution is needed here. Should the officer's testimony be false, the prosecutor may criminally charge and prosecute that officer for perjury.

Qualified Immunity

Criminal justice personnel in general are granted a different form of immunity, known as *qualified immunity*. Qualified immunity is based on the performance of discretionary acts. Discretionary acts are activities that require deliberation or judgment. This includes numerous tasks, but the courts determine the functions in which officers possess immunity. Discretionary actions, for example, may include the decision to arrest a drunk driver or cite a speeding motorist. In most situations, discretionary actions are applied to an agency administrator, who is responsible for policy decisions and implementation.

Criminal justice personnel are not immune from acts that involve ministerial duties. These duties amount to job functions in which the officer has no discretion. For example, in many jurisdictions, an officer who responds to a domestic violence disturbance and observes evidence of assault does not have the discretion to deliberate about whether an arrest is mandatory. In these types of cases, and in most jurisdictions, the officer must make an arrest.

There are two reasons for granting qualified immunity. First, without such immunity there would be a disincentive for officers to act in areas of constitutional uncertainty, even though their acts may later be judged constitutionally permissible. Fear of boldly crossing an ambiguous legal line would hinder officers in aggressively enforcing the law. Granting qualified immunity encourages reasonable officers to enforce the law vigorously within constitutional boundaries. Of course, acting outside the boundaries of the constitution de-immunizes the officer.

Second, immunity for criminal justice personnel is provided to avoid trial and even discovery in some cases. This is premised on the philosophy that immunity issues should be resolved prior to trial. The problem that frequently emerges, however, is whether an officer's actions were reasonable under the circumstances, or if they violated the plaintiff's constitutional rights. For example, whether a search is reasonable or unreasonable under the circumstances, and a reasonable officer would know that it is unreasonable, may influence the court to allow a jury to determine the issue at trial.

In *Scheuer v. Rhodes* (1974), the issue of immunity for a state governor and ultimately, high-level executives, emerged. The issue arose from Ohio's governor dispatching the Ohio National Guard onto the campus of Kent State University during student protests and disturbances regarding the United States' role in the Vietnam conflict. Soldiers opened fire and killed four unarmed students. The estates of the deceased students filed a lawsuit against the governor and he claimed absolute immunity from the lawsuit. The Supreme Court had previously opined that the *Young* decision allowed the state to invoke its sovereign immunity protection. But in *Scheuer* the Court concluded that neither sovereign immunity nor absolute immunity applied and that the governor and high-level executives could claim only qualified immunity. The Court reasoned that qualified immunity would apply according to the scope of the discretion exercised, the responsibility of the office, and the circumstances as they reasonably appeared at the time of the action in question.

A government official performing discretionary functions is entitled to qualified immunity in his or her individual capacity if his or her conduct does not violate constitutional standards in light of clearly established law at the time of the alleged violation. Qualified immunity is a government official's entitlement to not stand trial or face the other burdens of litigation as long as his or her conduct conforms to the law at the time. Implicit in the doctrine of qualified immunity is the recognition that police and correction officers, acting reasonably, may err (*Scheuer v. Rhodes*, 1974).

After *Scheuer,* the United States Supreme Court concluded in *Procunier v. Navarette* (1978) that state prison officials who were sued under § 1983 for alleged unconstitutional interference with a prisoner's mail could assert the qualified immunity defense. Prison officials may prevail on such a defense unless they violate "clearly established statutory or constitutional rights of which a reasonable person would have known."

The precedent-setting case that gives qualified immunity to criminal justice personnel is *Harlow v. Fitzgerald* (1982). The Supreme Court determined that the sole inquiry into whether an officer would be entitled to qualified immunity is whether the officer knew or should have known that he was violating the constitutional rights of the plaintiff (Figure 5.2).

Figure 5.2
Harlow v. Fitzgerald (1982)

Senior aides to President Nixon—Harlow and Butterfield—were accused of violating Fitzgerald's constitutional rights by having him dismissed from the Air Force. Fitzgerald asserted that they conspired to remove him from his post in retaliation for his blowing the whistle on purchasing practices within the Air Force. The lower court and the appellate court denied summary judgment to the two aides and they appealed. The United States Supreme Court granted certiorari to examine the issue of the type of immunity the two aides may possess as advisors to the president when acting in their official capacity.

The Court ruled that the two aides performed discretionary functions and when governmental officials perform such actions they are entitled to qualified immunity as long as their conduct did not violate an individual's constitutional rights.

This case is significant because it established new guidelines for determining how to assert a defense for "acting in good faith." To assert a good faith defense, the defendants must show that they were acting in accordance with the law at the time of their actions, based on training and experience. Acting in good faith is an affirmative defense and must be firmly supported by the defendant by showing that he or she did not violate constitutional rights of which a reasonable person would have known. The decision applies to § 1983 civil lawsuits and pertains to all criminal justice officials, such as police officers, correctional/detention officers, probation/parole officers, juvenile officers, and supervisors and administrators.

The Court stated:
> . . . we conclude today that bare allegations of malice should not suffice . . . We, therefore, hold that government officials performing discretionary functions generally are shielded from liability for civil damages insofar as their conduct does not violate clearly established statutory or constitutional rights of which a reasonable person would have known.

> With this decision, qualified immunity is provided to protect public officers in decisions in which the parameters of a person's constitutional rights are unclear. This may occur when: (1) a decision is made, and it is not clearly established that a constitutional right exists; or (2) the right was clearly established but the officer could not reasonably know that this decision or conduct was unlawful, thereby violating the constitutional rights of the plaintiff. Based on these two fundamental issues, the court must determine whether the officer is immune from civil liability. If the court concludes that the law was not clearly established and that the officer acted reasonably, the officer would be granted immunity.

Determining the reasonableness of an officer's actions can be problematic. This issue was answered in *Anderson v. Creighton* (1987). In *Anderson,* police officers and a Federal Bureau of Investigation agent conducted a warrantless search of the plaintiff's house. Although mistaken, the officers believed that a bank robbery suspect was hiding in the home. The officers entered the home with firearms drawn, assaulted the plaintiff's daughter, and knocked the plaintiff to the ground. The plaintiff was arrested and detained overnight in jail, although no charges were filed. The plaintiff filed suit and the FBI agent filed a motion for summary judgment based on probable cause to enter the home. The lower court granted summary judgment, but on appeal, the Court of Appeals reversed, holding that Anderson was not eligible for summary judgment. The Supreme Court reversed the appellate court's decision and held that Anderson was entitled to qualified immunity. In a 6-to-3 decision, the Court held that the principles of qualified immunity require that Anderson be permitted to argue that he is entitled to summary judgment if in light of the clearly established principles governing warrantless searches, he could, as a matter of law, reasonably have believed that the search of the Creighton's home was lawful. It should first be determined whether the alleged actions are actions that a reasonable officer could have believed lawful. If they are, then dismissal prior to discovery is required. If they are not, and if the actions Anderson claims he took are different from those alleged and are not reasonable, then limited discovery may be necessary.

The *Anderson* decision is important because it underscored the test of the "reasonable" officer developed in *Malley v. Briggs* (1986). In *Malley,* the plaintiff claimed in his § 1983 suit that his constitutional rights were violated when a state trooper obtained a warrant to arrest him based on an intercepted phone conversation that was part of a drug investigation. The charges were dropped and the plaintiff sued for unlawful arrest. The trooper claimed that he was entitled to absolute immunity. The Court rejected this defense, determining that the officer was entitled to qualified immunity. The Court examined whether a reasonable officer could believe entry into the home was justified by assessing the officer's actions in accordance with "objective reasonableness," and took into account the specifics of the law and the facts known to the officer. The standard used by the courts is "whether a reasonably well-trained officer in the same position would have known that his affidavit failed to establish probable cause and that he should not have applied for the warrant." When an arrest warrant lacks probable cause, liability is proper in accordance with the *Harlow* decision.

The principle of "reasonableness" is illustrated in *Tarantino v. Baker* (1987). Baker, a detective in a North Carolina sheriff's department, received an anonymous tip that Tarantino was growing marijuana in the general store. Baker went to the store at night and found a padlock on the front door and the windows covered. He went to the back door and knocked and did not receive a response. Baker shined his flashlight into a crack of the door, based on the "plain view doctrine," and observed marijuana plants inside the store. Tarantino was later arrested. At trial, the evidence was suppressed, as the court determined that Baker had exceeded the scope of a permissible "plain view" search. Tarantino filed a lawsuit claiming that his Fourth Amendment rights had been violated. The Fourth Circuit Court of Appeals dismissed the lawsuit, finding that a reasonable officer in Baker's situation would not know that his conduct violated the plain view rule. From this decision, it appears that when an officer's actions are close to going over the constitutional line, the courts will not hinder an officer from performing his or her duties.

The United States Supreme Court further addressed the issue of qualified immunity for police officers in *Saucier v. Katz* (2001). Katz was protesting a speech of then-Vice President Al Gore at a military base. He was approaching the podium when two military police officers grabbed him and escorted him away and into a van. Katz complained that the officers used excessive force, although he sustained no injuries. He filed a civil rights claim, asserting that his Fourth Amendment rights had been violated. The officers asserted a defense of qualified immunity. The U.S. District Court for the Northern District of California granted summary judgment, but on appeal the Ninth Circuit Court of Appeals denied qualified immunity for the officers. The Ninth Circuit held that qualified immunity and a constitutional violation issue should be treated as one issue before the trier of fact. The Supreme Court granted certiorari to address the requisite analysis in determining qualified immunity in situations involving excessive force and reversed the appellate court's holding.

The Supreme Court re-emphasized that the doctrine of qualified immunity protects government officials performing discretionary functions from liability as long as their conduct does not violate the constitutional rights of another. The Court restated that qualified immunity is a defense, but added that a ruling for qualified immunity requires an analysis not susceptible of fusion with the question of whether unreasonable force was used in making an arrest. Issues centering on qualified immunity must be taken in proper sequence and based on the merits of each case.

The question of the appropriateness of qualified immunity is whether a reasonable officer understood his powers and responsibilities to be, when he acted, under clearly established standards. To address this question, the

Supreme Court in *Saucier* established a two-part test for determining whether qualified immunity applies. First, in the initial inquiry, the court must consider the "threshold question": taken in the light most favorable to the party asserting the injury, do the facts alleged show that the officer's conduct violated a constitutional right? If the facts as alleged by the plaintiff fail to establish a violation, then immunity applies. On the other hand, if the alleged facts sufficiently demonstrate a constitutional violation, the court must determine whether the right was clearly established. In making this determination, the court must assess whether the right claimed must be more than a merely a generalized right, it must be clearly established in a particularized sense so that a reasonable official in the defendant's position knows that his or her actions violate that right. If the court determines that these two components are met in a motion for summary judgment, the court will grant such a motion. If, however, the court finds questions regarding these two components, the court will deny the motion and the case may proceed to trial or may be settled out of court.

This decision further supported the Supreme Court's decision in *Anderson* (1987). The Court concluded that the officers' conduct did not violate Katz's constitutional rights, because they only used force to protect the Vice President's safety and were entitled to qualified immunity.

While the *Saucier* case sheds additional light on the legal principle of qualified immunity and requires a two-part test to determine how a court will assess an assertion, its application is often problematic and complicated. In an effort to further apply the tenets of *Saucier* and to provide further elaboration on what constitutes qualified immunity, the United States Supreme Court granted certiorari to review the facts in *Brosseau v. Haugen* (2004). Responding to a 911 call of two men fighting, officer Brosseau approached the two men. The officer's arrival caused a momentary distraction and Haugen attempted to flee the area. Brosseau requested backup and Haugen hid himself in the neighborhood. Back-up officers responded with a canine to help track Haugen. Brosseau also learned that Haugen was a suspected felon with a no-bail warrant out for his arrest. The man that Haugen was fighting and a third man were instructed by officer Brosseau to stay in a pickup truck parked in the driveway. Haugen's girlfriend, along with her three-old daughter, was also on the scene and the officers instructed her to remain in her car.

An officer who was looking for Haugen down the street radioed that a neighbor had seen Haugen in her backyard. As Brosseau approached the area, Haugen quickly appeared and ran toward the parked vehicles in a driveway. Brosseau chased Haugen, and Haugen jumped into a Jeep parked in the driveway. Believing that Haugen was going to retrieve a weapon, Brosseau unholstered her weapon, pointed it at him, and ordered him to get out of the vehicle. Haugen ignored her commands and started the vehicle. Brosseau tapped on the window with her gun several times and the window shattered. Brosseau attempted to grab the keys and struck Haugen on the head with her gun. Haugen placed the car in gear and began to move. Brosseau jumped back and to the left, and fearing for her safety and the safety of other officers, and citizens in the area, fired one shot through the rear of the driver's side window, hitting Haugen in the back.

Haugen proceeded down the street in the Jeep and after about a half a block realized that he had been shot and stopped the vehicle. He suffered a collapsed lung and was airlifted to a hospital. He survived the shooting and subsequently pleaded guilty to the felony of "eluding." He later filed a § 1983 action, claiming that officer Brosseau used excessive force. The District Court granted summary judgment to Brosseau after finding she was entitled to qualified immunity. Haugen appealed and the Ninth Circuit Court of Appeals reversed, holding that Brosseau had violated Haugen's Fourth Amendment right to be free from excessive force and that the right violated was clearly established and thus Brosseau was not entitled to qualified immunity. The United States Supreme Court reviewed the case to further assess the application of qualified immunity and not the issue of excessive force per se.

The Court reversed the appellate court's decision, finding that Brosseau's actions were reasonable within the "backdrop of the established law at the time of the conduct." If the law at the time did not clearly establish that the officer's conduct would violate the Constitution, the officer should not be subject to liability or, indeed, even the burdens of litigation. The inquiry must focus on the "specific context of the case, not as a broad general proposition."

In supporting their argument in opposition to qualified immunity, the plaintiff cited *Tennessee v. Garner* (1985), *Graham v. Connor* (1989), and several lower court decisions. While the Court acknowledged the standard for using reasonable force in their *Graham* decision, the Court noted that liability did not attach in any of the lower court cases, finding that, like Brosseau, the litigated officers had probable cause to believe deadly force was justified. The Court also noted that the "cases" cited by the plaintiff in support of his opposition to qualified immunity by no means clearly established that Brosseau's conduct violated the Fourth Amendment.

Brosseau is instructive as it further directs a lower court in determining the application of qualified immunity. The Court underscored the two-part test established in *Saucier* by noting that qualified immunity operates "to protect officers from liability." If an officer had fair notice that his or her conduct was unlawful and this was clearly established through case decisions, that conduct must be viewed within the context of the law and the facts and circumstances that faced the officer at the time of the conduct. If the law is not clearly established at the time of the officer's conduct, the officer should not be subject to liability. Thus, qualified immunity would be granted to the defendant officer or agency. The Court noted that while *Garner* and *Graham* provide standards of review when assessing claims of excessive force, the standard is general and may apply to varying circumstances. According to the Court, the shooting in the *Brosseau* case did not "clearly" underscore established law of shooting a "fleeing suspect in a vehicle" that would preclude granting qualified immunity. The Court held that the shooting is far from the obvious one where *Graham* and *Garner* offer a basis for such a decision. Because the plaintiff could only show a "handful" of cases relevant to the shooting, the Court held that the cases by no means "clearly established" that Brosseau's conduct violated Haugen's Fourth Amendment rights.

Good Faith Defense

The good faith defense is not authorized in state tort claims and is commonly used in civil liability lawsuits by defendant officers. The defense can be asserted by public officials, but not by government agencies, if the plaintiff can show that the injury can be linked to a policy or custom.

Good faith is an affirmative defense based on a subjective standard that is closely tied to the trial court's discretionary powers. The term has been mistakenly referred to as acting without intent to do wrong, or a lack of evil intention on the part of the officer. More precisely, asserting a good faith defense has nothing to do with the intentions of the officer, but asserts the actions of an officer to be "acting in good faith" in accordance with the law at the time of the incident. Linked to the *Harlow* decision, the standard that emerges is whether the officer, at the time the act was committed, violated a clearly established statutory right of which a reasonable person would have known. There are several factors the court will consider when scrutinizing the officer's actions: (1) whether the officer's actions were based on departmental policy and regulations; (2) whether the officer was acting pursuant to a valid law that was later invalidated by a court; (3) whether the officer was acting on the orders of a supervisor and believed the order to be valid; and (4) whether the officer was acting on the advice of legal counsel and believed the advice was valid (del Carmen, 1995).

The plaintiff bears the burden of pleading a good faith defense in § 1983 lawsuits (*Gomez v. Toledo*, 1980). Thus, the plaintiff need not assert in the complaint that the officer acted in bad faith. All the plaintiff needs to prove is that the injury resulted from a violation of constitutional rights or illegal acts. To establish this, the defendant officer must show that he was acting in good faith at the time. To put it differently, the officer must show that he acted in the reasonable good faith belief that the action taken was legal. It becomes imperative that police administrators keep their officers apprised of changes in the law and update their policies and regulations in accordance with these changes.

Aczel v. Labonia (2004) provides an example of how the court determines whether an officer's conduct merits qualified immunity through invoking a good faith defense. Acting on what they believed was probable cause, officers of Danbury, Connecticut, arrested Aczel for allegedly sexually assaulting female tenants in Aczel's apartment building. A witness observed the officers strike him in the head after he was handcuffed. The witness further stated that the officers caused Aczel to fall to the ground and heard him screaming afterward, although he did not personally observe the officers push him to the ground. The witness took a better position and observed Aczel on the ground in the fetal position, heard the officers yell at him to stop resisting, although he was just lying on the ground. He further observed the officers pepper-spray Aczel.

Aczel filed a §1983 lawsuit and the lower court concluded that there were questions of fact that needed to be determined before the officers were entitled to qualified immunity. The officers appealed and the appellate court denied their motion for qualified immunity. The court reasoned that the there were too many discrepancies between their story and the witnesses' and Aczel's accounts to grant qualified immunity. The court reasoned that the law was clearly established on what constitutes proper conduct when making an arrest. Further, the court ruled that the officers gave conflicting accounts as to who initiated the use of force, how much force was used, and whether Aczel was actually reaching for one of the officers' weapons. Moreover, the court noted that the officers on appeal did not show that they were acting in good faith as they failed to argue any independent reason why they should be entitled to qualified immunity. It is not enough to "merely" assert that the officers were acting in good faith, there must be supportive documentation that accompanies such an assertion.

Probable Cause and Qualified Immunity

This is a narrow defense arising out of alleged illegal searches and seizures, false arrests, and false imprisonment. It is available to officers in both state tort actions and § 1983 litigation asserting that their actions were taken in good faith in accordance with the law at the time. Plaintiffs claiming that officers violated their Fourth Amendment rights by conducting an illegal search or seizure must show that the officer lacked probable cause. Immunity can be given to the officer if he or she can show that he or she had probable cause at the time.

Recall that in *Malley* the Supreme Court held that immunity would be denied where no reasonable officer could have believed that he or she had probable cause to obtain a warrant. Defendants seeking immunity based on probable cause have followed the Supreme Court's decision in *Anderson* rather than *Malley*. In *Gooden v. Howard County, Maryland* (1992), officers were granted immunity when they investigated screaming coming from an apartment. The officers removed the plaintiff, who admitted that she had made a loud noise in order to receive a psychiatric consultation. Qualified immunity applied because the investigation was objectively reasonable. In *Chew v. Gates* (1990), using a dog to search, despite the fact that it bit the suspect, did not violate clearly established law. The action was objectively reasonable because the crime was serious and the officer's safety was in peril.

Limits to qualified immunity involving a search without probable cause arose in *Schwab v. Wood* (1991). Attempting to obtain identification although he observed no criminal activity, an officer met verbal resistance and profanity. Reasonable suspicion was absent and the subsequent search and arrest were illegal. The plaintiff was acquitted of the charge of resisting detention. The plaintiff was granted summary judgment because "no reasonable jury could determine that a reasonably well-trained officer would believe that his actions were lawful under the circumstances."

Searches under a warrant are often upheld in accordance with a good faith defense. Section 1983 lawsuits based on deficiencies in the warrant itself rarely prevail. *United States v. Cancelmo* (1995) provided a close question as to probable cause. Officers drew up a drug search warrant based on conversations interpreted as using "coded" drug language and other conjectural circumstances. One person was a known drug dealer who frequently used coded language. Based on this information, a warrant was obtained and a reliable informant purchased cocaine at the plaintiff's house. Additional drugs found at the scene were held to justify a search of the entire residence. The Supreme Court upheld the search and stated that "hindsight, always perfect, does not render a search reasonable or unreasonable." Officers' failure to discover drugs was irrelevant.

The United States Supreme Court further addressed qualified immunity and the issue of probable cause in *Groh v. Ramirez* (2004). Groh, an agent of the Bureau of Alcohol, Tobacco, and Firearms, applied for a warrant to search Ramirez's ranch, where it was reported by an informant that there was a stockpile of weapons on the ranch, including automatic weapons, grenades, a grenade launcher, and a rocket launcher. Groh applied for a warrant to a magistrate judge. In an affidavit supporting the application, Groh listed the weapons to be searched on the ranch and the court found probable cause for the search and signed the warrant. The application described the objects and items to be searched and seized, but the warrant did not. Groh was required to report those items but he failed to provide a description of the ranch. Neither the application nor the affidavit was attached to the warrant and the warrant did not incorporate either of those documents by reference.

Groh and other agents conducted the search at the ranch the next day. Ramirez was absent from the home but his wife and children were there. Groh informed Ramirez's wife that he had a warrant to search the premises and also spoke to Ramirez on the phone, informing him that he was going search his residence. The search was not fruitful and Groh left a copy of the warrant with Ramirez's wife, although he did not give her a copy of the application or affidavit. Later the police faxed a copy of the application to Ramirez's attorney. Ramirez sued Groh and the other officers, claiming that they had violated his Fourth Amendment rights. The trial court found in favor of Groh, holding that the warrant was valid and that even if it was invalid, he was entitled to qualified immunity. Ramirez appealed the decision and the appellate court reversed the decision. Groh appealed to the Untied States Supreme Court to address the issue of qualified immunity.

Groh argued that although the warrant lacked the requisite information, the search was reasonable because it did not exceed the scope contemplated in the warrant application. However, because the particular items described in the application were not included in the warrant, there was no written assurance the magistrate had actually found probable cause to search for and seize every item listed on the application. The Court found that the warrant was invalid because it did not describe with specificity the items to be seized. The warrant was deficient and Ramirez had been denied information that outlined the scope of the search.

The Court held that, under the Fourth Amendment, absent certain exigent circumstances (which did not apply in the present case), the police had to obtain a warrant before searching a person's home, and the warrant had to be unambiguous. The Court ruled that any reasonable officer would have known that the warrant to search the ranch was invalid. The Fourth Amendment provides for the right to be free from unreasonable searches and seizures and the Court regarded the search as "warrantless."

Groh had a duty to ensure that the warrant was properly construed. The duty was to ensure that the warrant conformed to the constitutional requirements, not to simply proofread the document. The Court denied qualified immunity to Groh, stating that such immunity applied when a reasonable officer could have believed the warrant plainly complied with the Fourth Amendment's particularity requirement. The existence of the ATF's policy on invalid warrants proved to be detrimental to Groh. The Court stated that he should have known that he could not execute a patently defective warrant. Even a cursory review would have revealed a glaring deficiency that any reasonable police officer would have known was unconstitutional. A law enforcement officer had no right to qualified immunity if it would have been clear to a reasonable officer that his conduct was unlawful.

Qualified immunity applies to the discretionary functions of officers and is available on an individual basis. It is an affirmative defense made by an officer through his her counsel. As these cases show, the court will make their decisions on a case-by-case basis. The key to being awarded qualified immunity includes being proactive prior to performing the duties of a police or correctional officer. When asserting a claim of qualified immunity, the officer must show that he or she was following the established law at the time of the incident. This suggests that officers actually are knowledgeable about state and constitutional law. Officers must show that their actions were reasonable under the circumstances and that a reasonably trained officer would know that the conduct was constitutional or unconstitutional, depending on the conduct. These factors should be addressed in agency policy and procedures, as demonstrated in the *Groh* decision. Officers need to be trained on a regular basis and evaluated in the performance of their duties to ensure they are complying with policy and that their conduct conforms to constitutional mandates. When performing their sworn duties, officers should clearly and completely document their actions and reasons for acting in a particular manner. Adhering to these few elements will assist in being granted qualified immunity with more success.

Other Strategies for Reducing the Risk of Civil Liability

Criminal justice personnel have been successful in asserting qualified immunity as a defense in civil lawsuits. Invoking qualified immunity is, however, a "reactive" approach. The focus of criminal justice administrators and officers alike in the future should be toward developing proactive strategies and protection from lawsuits in order to reduce their frequency. Lawsuits may never be totally eliminated. However, understanding and implementing key elements of risk management and risk control can help to design a system to control some of the risk and protect the agency and its personnel.

What Is Risk Management?

Methods for managing risks associated with law enforcement functions are a concern not only for insurance carriers. Risk management is a process that also includes basic managerial functions: planning, organizing, and leading, as well as controlling agency losses at a reasonable cost. It uses accepted managerial techniques in order to preserve the assets of an organization or entity (Ashley & Pearson, 1993) and helps to control risk while managing costs. Risk management is a process of identifying and analyzing potential hazards, exposures, and undesirable events and carrying out decisions that minimize, control, or eliminate their effects on an organization.

The risk management process is comprised of two important elements. Risk financing involves varying methods from which an agency can choose to pay for potential losses. This element is most likely beyond the control of agency administrators and left to government officials. The second area, risk control, is within the influence of administrators, supervisors, trainers, and agency personnel. It is both a managerial and line-level function, because it seeks to promote a proactive approach to efficient organizational operations and to decrease risk exposure. Risk control involves several key factors: (1) identifying potential risk exposures of the organization; (2) examining the alternatives available to either eliminating potential risks or mitigating the effects of those that cannot be eliminated; (3) selecting the best alternative or combination of alternatives to deal with each exposure; (4) implementing the chosen techniques; and (5) monitoring the process in order to alter or improve the program based on observed results. These factors can serve as multiple layers of protection.

Integrating these factors into an agency's operating system can reduce the risk of future litigation. They also assist in developing a systematic framework of protection against liability. Risk management is controlling the risks inherent in performing criminal justice agency functions, which produces a net outcome of managing liability. This is a full-time, ongoing responsibility of criminal justice administrators as well as line personnel, and not a one-time task.

Managing liability can be problematic, as it requires assessing, planning, forecasting, and monitoring. Managing and controlling risk can be associated with hurricane preparation, which has taken on new, sophisticated measures in recent years. States along the Gulf of Mexico and the Atlantic coast have experienced their share of destructive hurricanes. Hurricanes Andrew (1993) and Floyd (1999) wreaked havoc, costing billions in property damage and taking numerous lives. As a result, the National Weather Service has developed more sophisticated technology with which to forecast and warn of future hurricanes. However, despite new technology, it is still difficult to predict with pinpoint accuracy how many hurricanes may occur in a season and where they may strike. Yet this weather phenomenon is still somewhat predictable, as history reveals that they are likely to occur with some frequency between June and November. Therefore, based on this assessment, as well as forecasting, the weather service and residents living in these states must take proactive steps to prepare for the risk of a hurricane, knowing that a hurricane is likely to occur during this period.

Managing the risk of liability in a criminal justice agency is similar to predicting the occurrence of a hurricane. It is obvious that civil lawsuits are likely to be filed against criminal justice personnel for a variety of reasons, but it is difficult to predict with certainty. Because the risk of liability is foreseeable, personnel must take a proactive approach in assessing, forecasting, monitoring and, to the extent possible, controlling the degree of risk associated with the tasks and functions that are most likely to give rise to potential lawsuits. Like hurricanes, not all lawsuits can be predicted or eliminated. Yet criminal justice agencies must be prepared to defend against such risks. It requires administrative and line-level personnel to work together to implement risk-control practices. These practices should not be another fleeting "administrative program." Risk management requires building a system of protections that can reduce the number of lawsuits and more successfully defend those that will be filed.

Elements of Managing Risk

Job Assessment

The first layer of protection is to conduct a job assessment. Prior to working on reducing or controlling risks, a thorough assessment of job functions should be performed. A job task analysis is a formal study of the job and examines the functions of line officers and supervisors. The job assessment will identify the numerous tasks that personnel perform. Once the tasks are identified, they should be examined further in terms of their frequency of occurrence and "severity," or criticality (see Figure 5.3).

Figure 5.3
Risk Management in Criminal Justice Agencies

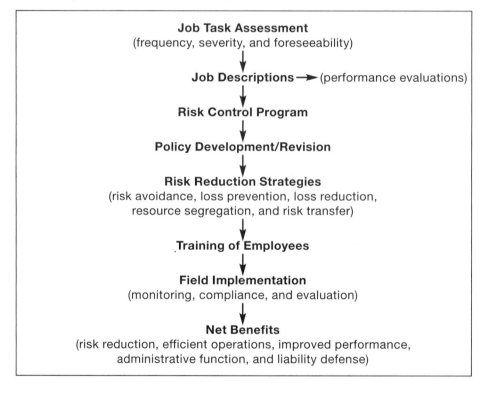

The National Weather Service predicts hurricanes based on past occurrences and present climatic conditions. Rating job tasks by their frequency and severity helps to evaluate past and present dimensions of the job in order to respond to future job tasks. By reviewing tasks in this fashion, it will become evident which functions are performed frequently and which tasks are severe or critical in nature.

Frequency can predict severity/criticality, and an inverse relationship usually exists between the two. Incidents that occur more frequently tend to be less severe in nature. Conversely, the most severe incidents occur with less frequency. Another important element to consider is that of foreseeability. A question to ask while assessing the frequency and severity/criticality of a task is "What is the foreseeability or likelihood of the officer performing the task as it relates to the frequency and severity of the task?" If the task or incident is foreseeable, occurs with some frequency, and is highly critical, then the task/incident should be addressed by a risk management program. For example, it is foreseeable that an officer may have to use his or her firearm in the line of duty. The severity or criticality of a police officer firing his or her duty weapon is extremely high, but the frequency of this occurring is generally low. Officers may go through their whole career without ever firing their weapon in the line of duty; yet due to the severity/criticality of firing a weapon, they must be fully prepared to know when to use lethal force, as well as being competent in using the firearm. Further, the frequency of riots occurring within a correctional institution is low, but when a riot occurs, history reveals that severity may be high. Correctional personnel may never experience a riot in their facility but must be prepared to respond, should the need arise.

A job assessment that examines the frequency and severity of core job tasks is the first step toward controlling risk. Other considerations in assessing job tasks are also helpful in determining critical dimensions of the job. In analyzing the nature of the job, other factors of frequency should be considered, such as citizen and prisoner complaints, officer incident reports, new equipment and technology, officer misconduct, internal/external investigations, officer accidents, workers' compensation claims, past financial losses (property/personnel), trends in past liability claims (department, region, state, etc.), calls for service, and costs in liability defense. In addition to the job assessment, these factors can be useful in pinpointing additional critical components of the job that can be used to strengthen the framework for risk control and, ultimately, liability reduction. Performing a job assessment can also be beneficial in providing information with which to update or create new job descriptions that can be essential in directing supervisors in more meaningful performance evaluations of employees. A job assessment forms the foundation for a risk control system within the agency.

Policy and Procedure Development

Once a job assessment has been conducted, the next step is to develop or revise policies and procedures for the foreseeable incidents officers encounter. Developing and revising policies and procedures is an administrative function and comports with legal requirements addressed in the Supreme Court's holding in *Monell v. Department of Social Services* (1978). Administrators can incur liability for failing to direct officers, which can be interpreted as a lack of direction and guidance through written policies and procedures.

It is acknowledged that not every situation an officer faces can be predicted, and therefore policies can never be developed that would cover all aspects of the job. Policies and procedures that target the frequent core tasks of the job should be developed in line with constitutional and state requirements. Policies clarify statutory and constitutional requirements for officers and should be written and updated to reflect recent changes in the law. They provide direction for responding to many situations the officer may encounter. Policies also help to keep personnel accountable for performing their duties in a reasonable and professional manner. Policies and procedures are at the core of the criminal justice agency and provide a layer of protection against assertions of liability for failure to direct. Policies and procedures should be reviewed annually and revised as the nature of the job changes and as the law changes.

Risk Control Strategies

Once the job assessment and policy development have been accomplished, the next step is to select a strategy or combination of strategies for controlling the risk of liability. The risk control strategies are: (1) avoidance; (2) prevention of losses; (3) reduction of losses; (4) segregation of resources; and (5) transference of risk. Depending on the foreseeability of an incident and its frequency and severity, the approach may be to use one or a combination of strategies. Many factors may emerge that will influence the selection of a strategy, such as number of department personnel, size of the jurisdiction, budget constraints, resources, facility constraints, legal requirements, and accreditation stipulations. These factors should be kept in mind when determining which strategy to use. Moreover, when considering a specific strategy, criminal justice personnel must consider their respective agency, available resources, and requirements that may preclude a particular strategy.

Risk Avoidance

The luxury of voluntarily avoiding a task or function regardless of its frequency is nonexistent in many jurisdictions. Providing 24-hour operations in corrections or policing is required. Thus, there is no option to avoid performing job duties. From the job assessment, however, some functions may emerge that can be curtailed or refined in order to decrease the frequency in participating in an activity. For example, some police departments have instituted a no-chase policy, based on the high degree of risk of property damage, injury, and death involving the officer and the public. Other police departments have instituted a practice of not providing escort services for funerals due to the risk of vehicle accidents and injuries. Some agencies limit the firing of a weapon from or at a moving vehicle unless the officer's life is in imminent peril. The practice in a majority of detention centers is to require medical clearance from a physician prior to admitting a prisoner with obvious physical injuries.

Loss Prevention

Loss prevention involves instituting measures prior to an incident. This is undertaken to prevent a loss from occurring. Examples include the creation and implementation of policies and procedures, in-service training, authorizing and issuing proper equipment, keeping equipment current and operational, equipping transport vehicles with screens, and facility design. The primary objective of loss prevention is to prevent the frequency of the loss-causing events.

Loss Reduction

Loss reduction is different from loss prevention in that it attempts to minimize the loss, rather than preventing the loss. In prisons or detention centers, physical and sexual assaults between prisoners sometimes occur. Instituting proper classification practices and regular personal security checks may not totally prevent such assaults, but may help to reduce the number of assaults within the facility. In policing, requiring a minimum of two officers to respond to domestic violence calls may help to reduce injuries to the officers and individuals involved. Additionally, some agencies permit only two vehicles to engage in high-speed pursuits and may also place a ceiling on the maximum speed of the police vehicles.

Segregation of Resources

Segregating resources consists of maintaining department resources in separate locations so that no single event significantly depreciates the use of equipment. This involves duplication of equipment (maintaining more than one), such as vehicles, back-up vehicles, spare equipment, restraints, facilities, and perhaps overlapping shifts during critical periods. It would also include separating resources or using multiple facilities, such as precincts or satellite centers, for overflow or efficiency purposes. Resource segregation is intended to reduce the severity of potential losses, because the agency will still be able to function.

Risk Transfer

Transferring risk involves strategies that move, or transfer, risk from one party to another. In policing this could mean a policy that requires officers to transport a mentally impaired person to a mental health facility in order to obtain psychiatric clearance prior to transporting him or her to a detention center. In a detention center this could involve requiring mental health professionals to evaluate a suicidal prisoner in the jail at initial reception or upon discovering suicidal behaviors. This strategy controls risks by identifying situations in which the officer or agency can transfer risk to another before incurring a loss. This is closely related to risk avoidance and loss prevention.

Training

Training is an essential managerial responsibility. The Supreme Court ruled in *City of Canton v. Harris* (1989) that training is to be provided for recurring job tasks. Thus, performing a job assessment not only identifies frequent and core job tasks, but also can be instrumental in directing training efforts.

All personnel should receive ongoing training commensurate with their duties and in the proper implementation of policy. High-profile or high-liability areas should be addressed regularly. For example, empty-hand control techniques are frequently used by police and correctional officers. Many lawsuits have been filed that assert that the officer used excessive force during arrest or when subduing a combative person. Subject control training should be provided regularly, along with training in the department's use-of-force policy. Personnel must be competent in deciding when and how much force to use in various situations, and must do so within the boundaries of policy and the law.

Training today is not a luxury. It must be the goal of each criminal justice executive to provide regular, ongoing training to all personnel. The nature of business in criminal justice agencies requires officers to have the latest information pertaining to the legal issues of performing their job. Training in legal and liability issues should be provided annually. Changes in societal conditions, offender characteristics, treatment strategies, crime prevention approaches, and improvements in technology require updated training for all personnel.

As new policies and procedures are developed or revised, all employees should receive a personal copy of the policies as well as training on the new policies. Testing employees' comprehension of policies is suggested. This strategy for disseminating policies and procedures can assist in proper implementation at the line level and illustrates that there is a level of understanding of how the policy is to be followed. Supervisors should also receive a copy of the policy and appropriate training as well. Administrators should seek many methods for training their personnel, such as classroom presentations, simulation training, roll-call training, on-the-job training (field training), agency videotapes of incidents, interactive computer-based training, seminars, conferences, and training through the Internet. Training and documentation of training are key elements in risk control and are required by the courts. They provide an important layer of protection against liability.

Field Implementation

It is an understatement to say that supervisory personnel are critical in any organization. Supervisors, as an extension of management, are an important component in reducing liability. There are two primary responsibilities of supervisors: (1) implementing policies and procedures, and (2) enforcing them. Historically, in many criminal justice agencies, supervisors received little attention in management training and the proper methods for implementing policy and personnel evaluations. Many organizational and liability problems can be corrected through proper training of supervisory personnel.

To avert and reduce liability, supervisors must be prepared to fulfill their responsibilities. The Field Training Officer (FTO) program in policing and corrections has provided new officers with a more efficient transition between the training academy and assuming the roles and responsibilities of an officer. Criminal justice administrators should also consider adopting or creating a similar program for newly promoted supervisors. After successfully completing such a program, administrators must remain committed to providing ongoing training for supervisors. Supervisors need to be trained in management philosophies, strategies for dealing with a diverse work group, legal and liability issues of management, administrative law, criminal law updates, policies and procedures updates, planning and goal setting, leadership skills, motivating the contemporary employee, managing stress, and evaluating employee performance. Maintaining a commitment to providing training to supervisors provides another layer of liability protection for the agency and all personnel.

Supervisors must also understand the disciplinary process within their departments. When personnel have violated policy, supervisors must respond appropriately based on the situation. They are the overseers and enforcers of policy and must ensure that personnel perform their duties in a professional and legal matter. Where there is a cavalier discipline philosophy, allegations of failure to supervise expose the department to litigation. As a matter of course, supervisors must be familiar with disciplinary procedures and the legal issues surrounding their responsibilities.

Administrators are encouraged to consider maintaining close contact with their risk management provider if they are a member of a risk management pool. A myriad of services are routinely provided by these entities, which can assist an agency in averting the risk of lawsuits and increasing officer safety. For example, risk management providers can provide agency risk assessments, audits of policies and procedures, model policies, training for agency personnel, and training videos on high-liability areas. The Michigan Municipal Risk Management Authority provides risk management services for law enforcement and detention agencies in Michigan. During the last 20 years they have performed liability assessments for their constituents in which they have developed model policies, training videos, and training on a variety of legal and officer safety issues, which have assisted in reducing the number of lawsuits and effectively defending cases that are litigated.

Similarly, the Legal and Liability Risk Management Institute (LLRMI) provides training, legal publications, and services for law enforcement and correctional agencies. Underscoring the importance of policy and procedure and officer performance in the field, they have assembled a *Quick Reference Legal Guide for Law Enforcement* (Ryan, 2005), which provides a brief overview of United States Supreme Court and lower court decisions. Highlights of each decision are noted, providing easy access to the focus of the decision, which can underscore agency policy and serve as guidance for officers in the field when they are faced with making decisions on various matters. Further, they have designed decision-making checklists for officers of frequently performed tasks that are addressed by policy and case decisions. For example, vehicle searches are performed with some frequency and carry the potential of a high risk of civil liability. Based on several United States Supreme Court decisions underscoring the Fourth Amendment and vehicle searches, LLRMI has designed a checklist that officers may refer to which incorporates policy, case law, and focus points to consider prior to conducting a search. The checklist includes components to developing probable cause, ordering occupants out of the vehicle, search incident to an arrest, and an inventory search, just to mention a few. These checklists embody significant sections of a working policy, can be used in training, and are used in the field when performing a task.

These two illustrations provide examples of how agencies can access their risk management provider, who can assist in risk control through the integration of case law, policy, and training through the design of checklists. These checklists provide a tool that can guide an officer in decisionmaking in high-liability areas. They represent a framework with which to assess an incident, make a decision, and later provide an explanation to justify the decision. Such assistance to officers assists in controlling risk in decisionmaking and can avert cases of liability. Even if an agency is not a member of a formal risk management program, an agency may replicate the process by researching high-liability areas and applicable case decisions, develop or revise policy accordingly, develop the checklists, and provide training for their officers. Such endeavors underscore proactive risk management techniques and illustrate risk control techniques.

Monitoring and Evaluating Risk Control

Once these risk control procedures have been instituted, supervisory personnel should monitor them. Policies that create new programs should be monitored to ensure proper implementation. Monitoring the process is essential in successful implementation and can ensure accountability with all personnel. Supervisory personnel are responsible for working closely with line personnel as they integrate policy with action. When problems emerge in implementing the policy, supervisors need to evaluate the problem and work toward its resolution. Rather than ignoring problems or resorting to old methods, a quick response to emerging problems will provide for more efficient line operations and decrease the risk of liability.

After a reasonable period of monitoring a policy, program, or new activity, constructive evaluation should occur. Line officers and supervisors should collectively evaluate the successes and problems associated with the activity. Modifications in responsibilities of personnel may result and should be worked out accordingly. Evaluation helps to measure the success and impact of the policy. Many criminal justice agencies embark on new programs or systems and do little or nothing to monitor and evaluate the outcome. Evaluation is necessary to determine the future activities of those who are participating so that changes may be made as warranted. Identifying problems early can help make needed changes, assist in reducing risk, and possibly reduce liability.

Net Benefits

Although adopting and developing risk management strategies can create more work for all employees in an organization, it has several positive management and line-level benefits. First, one of the primary goals of all employees is to work toward reducing the exposure of risk to personnel or property loss. Officer safety issues in corrections and law enforcement should be of utmost concern to administrators and line officers. An ongoing commitment to achieving this can be accomplished through risk management approaches. Second, developing and maintaining risk management techniques will create more efficient agency operations and simultaneously improve performance of all personnel. Street-level and cell block management efforts can be significantly improved. Work-related accidents can be decreased, as well as workers' compensation claims. Citizen and prisoner complaints can decrease as officers work to resolve problems at the root level. Analyzing the job can pinpoint revision or development of critical policies and procedures that will in turn help to focus ongoing training for all personnel. Third, developing and maintaining a risk management program are administrative functions. Risk management techniques are at the center of basic management. Management is responsible for the activities of the organization and how employees accomplish them. This can be achieved through planning, forecasting, controlling, communication, budgeting, staffing, supervising, training, and directing the tasks of all employees. All command personnel should work toward acceptable methods to achieve organizational goals by minimizing the risks associated with the job. Gaining the compliance of all personnel to work toward ways to reduce the risks of the job can also help keep employees accountable.

Finally, maintaining a risk management program will significantly assist in defending lawsuits that may arise. A risk management program should not be implemented primarily out of concern about being named as a defendant in a lawsuit. Establishing an ongoing process of risk management should be undertaken for the reasons listed above. By adhering to these risk management principles, an agency will place itself in a much better position to defend a lawsuit. Thus, a risk management program serves as a proactive management system that increases the ability of the organization to operate more efficiently, control foreseeable risks, direct employees in the performance of their duties, and work toward reducing identifiable job-related risks. In this way, should a lawsuit be filed against the department, management has a foundation on which to assert a legal defense. Adopting this proactive approach is preferable to attempting to build a reactive defense against a legal challenge after a high-profile incident. Maintaining a risk management system can show that the department and employees are acting in good faith in accordance with the law and professional industry practices. It also provides a mechanism whereby the agency can assert a more likely defense of qualified immunity. To successfully invoke a defense of qualified immunity, an agency must have a management system in place that illustrates that constitutional mandates are in place and are followed. Creating and maintaining such a system can be most helpful in persuading a court that the agency should be granted qualified immunity.

Summary

This chapter has explored two primary components for responding to civil lawsuits filed in accordance with § 1983. First, law enforcement officers do not have absolute immunity, but rather qualified immunity. They may assert such a defense by demonstrating that they should be immune from such liability because they were acting in good faith. In order to successfully prevail with such a claim, criminal justice personnel must show that they were acting in accordance with the current status of the law at the time, and within accepted training and policy provisions. Acting in good faith has been a successful defense in the past.

Second, in order to reduce litigation and provide a proactive approach to risk management, risk-control strategies were presented. Criminal justice agencies should strive to incorporate risk reduction strategies throughout the organization as identified through an ongoing process of risk assessment. This means that officers and supervisors participate together in identifying the frequency and severity of risks specific to job tasks that officers perform routinely. Once the risks have been identified, implementing elements of risk control should be considered in designing a risk control program so that managers and line-level employees may work toward more efficient agency operations in an effort to reduce the risk of liability in the future.

It is not possible to completely eliminate liability for police or correctional agencies. Therefore, criminal justice agencies must strive to be proactive in reducing such risks. Combining the two components of immunity and risk management can place the criminal justice agency in a viable position to defend future claims of liability. Criminal justice managers should closely examine these strategies and incorporate them as needed. Implementing risk management strategies remains one of the most important mechanisms in insulating a department from needless civil litigation. A majority of the consent decrees filed under § 14141 stipulate that police agencies undertake a system of risk management. Thus, managers should voluntarily incorporate these strategies into the overall operations of the department. In doing so, mangers show a good faith effort in taking proactive measures to perform their sworn duties within the framework of the law.

References

Ashley, S. & R. Pearson (1993). *Fundamentals of Risk Management*. Livonia, MI: Meadowbrook Insurance Group.

del Carmen, R.V. (1995). *Criminal Procedure for Law Enforcement Personnel*, Third Edition. Monterey, CA: Brooks/Cole.

Legal and Liability Risk Management Institute (2004). *Guide to Motor Vehicle Searches—Fourth Amendment*. Rochester, MN: Legal and Liability Risk Management Institute.

Robinson, C.D. (1992). *Legal Rights, Duties and Liabilities of Criminal Justice Personnel*, Second Edition. Springfield, IL: Charles C Thomas.

Ryan, J. (2004). *Quick Reference: Legal Guide for Law Enforcement*. Rochester, MN: Legal and Liability Risk Management Institute.

Silver, I. (2005). *Police Civil Liability*. New York, NY: Matthew Bender & Co.

Cases Cited

Aczel v. Labonia, No. 03-7414 (2d Cir. 2004)

Anderson v. Creighton, 483 U.S. 635 (1987)

Apostol v. Landau, 957 F.2d 339 (7th Cir. 1992)

Bradley v. Fisher, 80 U.S. 335 (1872)

Brisco v. Lahue, 460 U.S. 325 (1983)

Brosseau v. Haugen, 543 U.S. 194 (2004)

Chew v. Gates, 744 F. Supp. 952 (C.D. Cal. 1990)

Cleavinger v. Saxner, 474 U.S. 193 (1985)

Conner v. Alston, 701 F. Supp. 376 (E.D.N.Y. 1988)

Ex parte Young, 209 U.S. 123 (1908)

Forrester v. White, 484 U.S. 219 (1998)

Gomez v. Toledo, 446 U.S. 635 (1980)

Gooden v. Howard County, Maryland, 954 F.2d 960 (4th Cir. 1992)

Groh v. Ramirez, 540 U.S. 551 (2004)

Hans v. Louisiana, 134 U.S. 1 (1890)

Harlow v. Fitzgerald, 457 U.S. 800 (1982)

Jacobs v. Dujmovic, 752 F. Supp. 1516 (D. Colo. 1990)

Malley v. Briggs, 475 U.S. 335 (1986)

Monell v. Department of Social Services, 436 U.S. 658 (1978)

Pierson v. Ray, 386 U.S. 547 (1967)

Procunier v. Navarette, 434 U.S. 555 (1978)

Saucier v. Katz et al., 533 U.S. 194 (2001)

Schwab v. Wood, 767 F. Supp. 574 (D. Del. 1991)

Scheuer v. Rhodes, 416 U.S. 232 (1974)

Supreme Court of Virginia v. Consumers Union, 446 U.S. 719 (1980)

Tarantino v. Baker, 825 F.2d 772 (4th Cir. 1987)

United States v. Clarke, 33 U.S. (8 Pet.) 436 (1834)

United States v. Cancelmo, 64 F.3d 804 (2d Cir. (1995)

Chapter 6

Administrative and Supervisory Liability

Criminal justice administrators and supervisors, like other organizational executives, are responsible for planning, controlling, organizing, budgeting, staffing, directing, reporting, and supervising employees. Additional responsibilities include managing emergencies, establishing priorities, knowledge of day-to-day operations, community and institutional issues, technology, the political process, and managing people. One major area of concern is knowledge of legal and supervisory liability issues. The developing case law in this field strongly suggests that administrators and supervisors need to know the limits of their jobs and need to be aware of their subordinates' competence and performance.

Managing people is central to the effective operation of any organization. Criminal justice personnel exercise legal authority over citizens and prisoners. Therefore, they must exercise a high degree of skill in using their authority and discretion when executing department policy and enforcing the law. Legal actions against personnel frequently result from decisions in which they have implemented a specific policy that violated the constitutional rights of another. For example, a policy directs police officers to use a roadblock to stop a fleeing motorist and officers place a semi-truck with a trailer just over the crest of a hill at night. The fleeing motorist hits the roadblock with his car and dies. This could be considered an unwarranted use of excessive force. Other civil litigation may result from allegations of officers failing to perform their legally assigned duties, performing their duties negligently, misusing their authority, using excessive force, or depriving an individual of his or her constitutional rights.

The purpose of this chapter is to examine potential liability issues for the administrator in directing employees in criminal justice agencies. This chapter focuses specifically on federal § 1983 litigation that names administrators or supervisors as defendants for failing to properly fulfill administrative functions in directing, controlling, hiring, assigning, promoting, training, and disciplining employees. Case examples and strategies for reducing liability exposure are presented.

Administrative Liability

Criminal justice administrators and supervisors face potential liability that arises out of supervising their employees. Because administrators are responsible for many managerial functions, these duties frequently expose administrators to liability. Any employee action that allegedly deprives an individual of a protected right may in turn expose the administrator to liability. This often places administrators in a position to explain why they should not be held responsible for the employee's conduct. Such situations are often difficult to defend and make the administrative chain of command more vulnerable to liability, as well as heightening the potential for organizational liability.

Virtually every action taken by an administrator in dealing with citizens, prisoners, and employees involves potential liability and legal consequences. Administrators must manage within the context of legal supervisory responsibilities.

This does not suggest that managerial decisionmaking be impeded by paranoia—rather, it implies that the efficient operation of the contemporary criminal justice agency be maintained within working guidelines of potential supervisory liability issues. The duty of supervisors is to know their own potential for liability when they perform their basic managerial functions. Carrying out a supervisor's responsibilities requires not only developing the competency (directing, planning, budgeting, evaluating, etc.) to lead the organization, but also requires that administrators concomitantly continue to develop competency in hiring, training, supervising, and firing, to reduce their own risk as well as reducing the risk of the organization to litigation. A thorough understanding of the fundamental liability issues will equip the administrator to accomplish this objective.

Supervisory Liability Issues

Basis for Liability

Every criminal justice administrator and supervisor should be familiar with Title 42 United States Code § 1983 (see Chapter 3). Since 1978, this has been the primary vehicle by which administrators have been sued for violations of constitutional rights resulting from their management responsibilities. It is used to apply the rights guaranteed by the U.S. Constitution to the everyday decisions and policies of state and local government agencies. Administrators and supervisors must be familiar with the law and agency policies in order to avoid liability for violating an individual's constitutional rights.

Section 1983 lawsuits often name the supervisor along with the officer. This practice is based on the theory that the officer acts for the agency and, therefore, what is done reflects agency policy and practice. As a legal strategy, the plaintiff includes the agency and supervisors, because the higher a position the employee holds, the closer the plaintiff gets to the deep pockets of the county or state agency. Chances of monetary recovery are increased if supervisory personnel, by virtue of their position, are included in the lawsuit. Moreover, naming administrative and supervisory personnel may also create a conflict of interest in the legal strategy for the defense, thus strengthening the plaintiff's claim against one or more defendants.

Policymaker

The United States Supreme Court has held that supervisors can be held responsible for acts of their employees (*Monell v. Department of Social Services*, 1978). *Monell* expanded the meaning of the "every person" clause in § 1983 to include government entities. The supervisor is not liable because an employee violated the individual's constitutional rights, but may be liable for failing in his or her supervisory responsibilities when the failure results in a violation of constitutional rights (see Figure 6.1).

Under § 1983, the doctrine of *respondeat superior* (a Latin phrase meaning "let the master answer") does not form the basis of liability (*Polk County v. Dodson*, 1981). Under the common law doctrine of respondeat superior, the master is responsible for the actions of the servant. It does not, however, apply to public employment, because public officials are not the "masters" of their employees; they serve the government agency. This has been the case for much of our national history, as municipal and county employers of criminal justice agencies were not held liable on this theory. To attach liability would move into the realm of sovereign immunity. In addition, police officers acted as agents of the law sworn to uphold the law, not as employees of their agency. Respondeat superior only held an employer liable, not superior officers. Under other theories of liability, however, superior officers could be sued, for example, if they participated in or ratified the tortious actions of their subordinates (*Wilkins v. Whitaker*, 1983).

The *Monell* decision established governmental liability for the behavior of criminal justice personnel when they implement or execute promulgated or adopted policies or regulations, or conduct that results from a "custom" even though the custom has not received approval through formal channels. To establish governmental liability, the plaintiff must prove that a policy or custom existed, and that it was the moving force behind the officer's violation of a person's constitutional rights. The courts have not specifically defined the type of involvement that creates supervisory liability, but they have suggested several potential theories in which liability may be incurred under § 1983 against a supervisor, if the supervisor: **(1)** directly participated in the action; **(2)** after learning of the violation through a report or complaint, failed to remedy a wrong; **(3)** created a policy or custom under which unconstitutional practices occurred or allowed such a policy or custom to continue; and **(4)** was grossly negligent in managing the subordinates who caused the unlawful condition or event (del Carmen, 1991; Kappeler, 1997).

Figure 6.1
Monell v. Department of Social Services of the City of New York (1978)

Female employees of the New York Department of Social Services filed a § 1983 claim asserting that a policy requiring pregnant employees to take unpaid leaves of absence before they were medically necessary violated their constitutional rights. The claim sought injunctive relief and back pay. The department changed the policy prior to the decision and the lower court denied the request for back pay. The court of appeals affirmed and the employees appealed to the United States Supreme Court.

The Court granted certiorari to assess the issue of whether a municipality or local government entity could be held liable under § 1983 when the government's policy or custom violated a person's constitutional right. The Court rejected the idea that a government entity could be held liable under *respondeat superior*. The Court did state that a government entity could be held liable under § 1983 when an alleged unconstitutional action is the result of a policy or custom. The Court also expanded the "every person" language of § 1983 to include local governments.

This case is significant because local governments, along with their officers, can be held liable under § 1983 when their policy is the "moving force" that created a constitutional injury. Government entities are no longer immune from § 1983 litigation. *Monell* provides that the officer, the city, the county, and the government entity may be sued and held liable for monetary damages and injunctive and declaratory relief. Policies and procedures should be in writing and direct officers' actions within the preview of the law.

To prevail on a policy or custom issue, the plaintiff must actually establish that a policy existed and that executing it or failing to execute it caused the constitutional violation. For example, in *Jenkins v. Wood* (1996), liability did not attach against officials for alleged excessive use of force while search warrants for a residence were being executed, in the absence of evidence of a municipal custom or policy of encouraging or tolerating the use of excessive force while executing search warrants or the execution of illegal search warrants. Likewise, the plaintiff's claim in *Graham v. District of Columbia* (1992) that police officers used excessive force against him pursuant to official policy was dismissed. The plaintiff failed to identify any specific policy or any factual basis for a policy allowing excessive force. Conversely, in *McConney v. City of Houston* (1989), the municipality was held liable and paid out $25,000 for an unconstitutional policy of detaining a diabetic arrestee without a warrant for four hours even after determining he was not intoxicated.

The plaintiff must establish an affirmative causal link between a supervisor's inaction and the harm suffered (*Rizzo v. Goode*, 1976). In *Wilson v. City of North Little Rock* (1986), the court ruled that neither the chief nor other officials were liable for prior threats and harassment against a business catering to African-Americans. There was no evidence that linked the chief to actions of his officers, nor was there evidence that he knew of such threats or harassment. Generally, the issue consists of whether an action or omission of the supervisor caused an officer to violate the constitutional rights of another.

Official Policymaker

The question of who is considered an "official" policymaker arises frequently. Not all supervisors fall into this category. In *Monell* the Supreme Court stated that a policy can be created by those whose edicts or acts may fairly be said to represent official policy. On two occasions the Court has ruled on the issue of who is a policymaker for liability purposes. In *Pembaur v. City of Cincinnati* (1986), the Court held that public officials who have final policy-making authority can render an agency liable under § 1983. Acting at the direction of the county prosecutor, sheriff's deputies entered a medical clinic and arrested two individuals not named on the arrest warrant. The owner of the clinic, a doctor, sued under § 1983 and the Court found the county liable under *Monell*. This decision underscored *Monell* in that policy could be made by those who may fairly be said to represent "official policy," as the prosecutor in this case did.

In *City of St. Louis v. Praprotnik* (1988), the Supreme Court held that a government entity may be held liable where authorized policymakers "approve a subordinate's decision and the basis for it." The Court further added that the determination of who is the official policymaker for liability purposes is to be made by examining state law. Generally, criminal justice administrators would fall within this category. In *Marchese v. Lucas* (1985), the court found the sheriff to be the official agency policymaker and assessed $125,000 against him for failing to train and discipline correctional officers when they beat a prisoner. In *Ware v. Jackson County, Missouri* (1998), the jail director was determined to be the final policymaker as it related to the discipline of detention officers, even though other county officials could review and overturn his decisions. There was no systematic review process of his broad authority to discipline errant officers.

In determining who is the official policymaker in county law enforcement, the United States Supreme Court ruled, however, in *McMillian v. Monroe County, Alabama* (1997), that an Alabama sheriff, in his law enforcement capacity, was a state rather than a county official. In Alabama the governor and the attorney general normally have authority over the sheriff's office and not the county, because Monroe County had no law enforcement authority. Thus, when there is no authority to make policy in the area of law enforcement, no liability will attach.

Liability can be imposed against supervisors if they establish or enforce a policy or custom that causes a constitutional deprivation. But liability generally cannot be based on a single incident of misconduct. *In City of Oklahoma City v. Tuttle* (1985), the United States Supreme Court determined "that proof of a single incident of unconstitutional activity is not sufficient to impose liability. . . . unless it was caused by existing unconstitutional municipal policy, which can be attributed to a municipal policy maker." Generally, the plaintiff must establish that the deprivation was a result of continuing agency policy and that the policy was the moving force behind the deprivation.

Factors that may strengthen a plaintiff's claim of agency practices of constitutional abuses include:

1. Frequency of the violation;

2. The extent to which the practice was routinized by employees;

3. The extent to which the practice was accepted by supervisors;

4. The extent to which the action represented shared beliefs of employees;

5. Retention of, failure to discipline, or failure to investigate the violating employee;

6. Failure to prevent future violations (del Carmen & Kappeler, 1991).

Gaines v. Choctaw County Commissioners (2003) provides a prime example of how a sheriff's policy was actionable and how personal liability attached due to his participation in a constitutional violation. At the time of the arrest, the detainee was a patient in the hospital where he was being treated for acute renal failure and pneumonia. Over the protests of hospital physicians, the sheriff personally removed the detainee from the hospital and confined him at the jail. His condition deteriorated to the point where he was unable to walk or feed himself. On several visits the family of the detainee found his condition worsening and eventually paid other detainees to bathe and feed him. According to the family, detention officers refused to dispense medications to the detainee because the sheriff's policies did not require them to do so.

The sheriff did transport the detainee to a medical clinic and an attending physician recommended that he admitted to a hospital. The sheriff refused. The family contacted the state human resources agency, which intervened and caused the detainee to be admitted to the hospital. Upon admission he was found to be malnourished and dehydrated. He died two days later.

The estate of the detainee filed a lawsuit claiming that the sheriff and county denied the detainee medical care while confined. The court found no liability for failing to train the officers or the sheriff. The court also stated that the county did not have a duty to appoint a physician, but merely had the authority to do so; the county had the authority to act and its failure to do so could be construed as a county policy. The court agreed with the estate, holding that a Fourteenth Amendment violation was substantiated against the sheriff in his individual capacity, based upon on his direct participation and policies, which contributed to the death of the detainee.

Supervisors on the Scene or Commanding Officers Causing a Violation

Liability will attach for a supervisor on the scene who actually participates in or fails to prevent a violation from occurring. In *Masel v. Barrett* (1989), a sergeant who was supervising six officers monitoring a political demonstration was found liable when he stood by and watched the officers use excessive force on the demonstrators, as well as beating one of them. The claim of supervisory liability is valid unless the failure to intervene is proven to be negligent.

Liability can also attach even if the supervisor was not actually on the scene but directed or led the actions of the officer and it caused a violation. In some cases in which a supervisor decides to act or not act, or selects a tactic or type of equipment to use in an operation, it may increase the supervisor's liability. In *Morrison v. Washington County* (1983), a sheriff responsible for administering a jail was held liable because he was consulted about the decision to arrest an intoxicated individual (who later died in the jail) for public drunkenness. The sheriff had received information from officers in the field regarding the situation, and rather than being transported to the hospital, the arrestee was brought to the jail.

The Supreme Court in *Hudson v. McMillian* (1992) found two correctional officers and a prison lieutenant liable for the beating of a compliant restrained prisoner. The two officers were escorting the prisoner to a segregation cell and began hitting him in the face and kicking him in retaliation for an earlier argument. A lieutenant on the scene observed the beating but merely cautioned the two officers "not to have too much fun." The supervisor was held liable for failing to properly intervene, supervise, and control the officers.

For liability to attach against a supervisor, a plaintiff must establish a "causal connection" between the incident and the supervisors' failure. Generally, one incident does not show a practice of failing to intervene with officers. In *Warner v. City of New Orleans* (2004), Warner was arrested and claimed that the arresting officer used excessive force in violation of the department's policy on use of force and a policy regarding a special task force that was designed to actively patrol certain sections of the city. Warner filed a § 1983 lawsuit against the arresting officer for excessive force, against the Compass chief of police for failing to supervise his officers and promoting unconstitutional policies and procedures, although he was not on the scene at the time of the arrest.

The District Court found that the arresting officer did not use excessive force. The court ruled that the chief was not personally liable because there was no evidence that he had a legal duty to prevent an officer's misdeeds or that his failure to prevent such conduct amounted to a violation of Warner's constitutional rights. Further, the court stated that the chief's official duty was to make departmental policy and that the plaintiff failed to show evidence of any "persistent widespread practice of tolerating either false arrest or excessive force, or any failure to properly supervise the officers in the department. The court noted that the chief was not on the arrest scene at the time and was not involved in the incident. Thus, the plaintiff failed to establish evidence that would show that the alleged chief's failures as a supervisor were connected to Warner's alleged rights violations. The court further stated that the chief had taken proactive measures to lead his department and such measures were not "unwanted, wanton, or otherwise unconstitutional."

Theories of Supervisory Liability

Deliberate Indifference

Some ambiguity exists among federal courts regarding the level of culpability required for finding liability with supervisors under § 1983. The courts have used the standard of gross negligence on occasion but more commonly use the standard of deliberate indifference.

This standard was first established in *Estelle v. Gamble* (1976), when a prisoner sued correctional officials for denial of medical treatment and improper medical treatment of a back injury he sustained while working on the prison farm. The Court stated in *Estelle* that deliberate indifference involves a conscious intentional decision or choice to inflict unnecessary and wanton pain on a prisoner. In *Stokes v. Delcambre* (1983), the court upheld an award of $250,000 against a sheriff, $105,000 in punitive damages against a correctional officer, and $70,000 in compensatory damages against both defendants for ignoring repeated screams from a prisoner who was being sexually assaulted by other prisoners. The court determined that there was sufficient evidence to support deliberate indifference to the safety of the prisoner and that the officers were wanton and oppressive in their actions toward the prisoner.

The concept of deliberate indifference has been expanded over the years by the United States Supreme Court in several correctional cases (*City of Canton v. Harris*, 1989; *Wilson v. Seiter*, 1991; *Farmer v. Brennan*, 1994). The standard has not been specifically defined, but applied on a case-by-case basis. It generally means that the actor disregarded a known or obvious consequence of his or her actions, consciously chose a course of action with disregard for the harmful outcome, and disregarded a risk of harm of which he was aware. The Court in *Farmer* stated that officials must possess knowledge that a substantial risk of harm existed by evidence of their actions or failures to act.

Deliberate indifference may be demonstrated by either actual intent or reckless disregard. An administrator acts recklessly by "disregarding" a substantial risk of danger that is either known to the administrator or that would be apparent to a reasonable person in the administrator's position. Mere negligence is insufficient to support a § 1983 claim. Administrators are not liable if they can show that they responded reasonably to known risks.

There are many forms of administrative actions that in their totality may create evidence of deliberate indifference to constitutionally protected rights. Case law reveals seven general theories from which potential administrative liability emerges: (1) negligent hiring, (2) negligent assignment, (3) negligent entrustment, (4) failure to direct, (5) failure to supervise, (6) failure to discipline, and (7) failure to train. These theories are not mutually exclusive, meaning that the plaintiff may allege several theories in the lawsuit against the administrator. For example, it is not uncommon for the plaintiff in an excessive force claim against an officer to assert a failure by the administrator in directing, supervising, and training the officer. A discussion of each theory will follow, with the exception of failure to train, which will be addressed in Chapter 7.

Negligent Hiring

An emerging area of administrative liability is negligent hiring. Claims citing this deficiency generally assert that the constitutional violation would not have occurred had the administrator properly performed a thorough screening of the errant officer prior to hiring him or her. Liability stems from claims that the administrator failed to conduct a complete background investigation of the employee prior to employment. Liability emerges when an employee is unfit for appointment, such unfitness was known to the employer or should have been known through a background check, and the employee's act was foreseeable.

Hiring deficiencies led to liability in *Jones v. Wittenburg* (1977) and the sheriff was ordered by the court to train and psychologically test the staff. In *Brown v. Benton* (1978), the court found that termination of an officer was reasonable based on results of background checks. Liability attached in *Parker v. Williams* (1988) when evidence supported the plaintiff's claim against a sheriff for promoting a policy or custom of not conducting reasonable background checks on prospective employees. A former prisoner had been kidnapped and raped by the chief jailer. In *Benavides v. County of Wilson* (1992), the court concluded that the sheriff had complied with state requirements when hiring candidates for the position of correctional officer. Allegations of deliberate indifference for improper screening of employees were not supported, even though the prisoner sustained an injury during his confinement.

There is potential for administrative liability in failing to test and evaluate officer candidates for psychological deficiencies. The plaintiff in *Bell v. City of Miami* (1990) prevailed in a § 1983 action brought against the municipality for failing to adequately screen police officer candidates prior to employment. Allegations of an illegal entry and excessive force were upheld pursuant to a policy of failing to psychologically test police officer candidates and a failure to review complaints. A widespread pattern and practice of this failure was established. In *Stokes v. Bullins* (1988), the court held that a failure to use the National Crime Information Center (NCIC) by a small-town police department to check the background of a police officer candidate was not actionable. Even when the candidate had admitted to being arrested for a minor crime and a further check would have revealed 15 prior arrests, some including offenses involving violence, it failed to rise to a level of gross negligence. The candidate had lived in the community for many years, had not posed a problem, and the admitted arrests were investigated.

The United States Supreme Court decided a case involving hiring practices in law enforcement for the first time when it reviewed *Board of Commissioners of Bryan County v. Brown* (1997). This case involved an excessive force claim made against a deputy after he engaged in a pursuit. The plaintiff alleged that the sheriff was deliberately indifferent to the constitutional rights of citizens because he ignored an alleged violent history of the deputy and, therefore, the hiring practices were unconstitutional. The deputy had one misdemeanor arrest while in college, several years prior to employment, for an assault that occurred during a fight. The plaintiff asserted that this incident, of which the sheriff was aware, should have placed the sheriff on notice of the deputy's proclivity toward violence.

The Court ruled in favor of the sheriff, stating that the hiring policy was not the moving force behind the incident or the plaintiff's injury. While the Court did state that one incident could trigger liability, they were reluctant to impose liability for one isolated incident involving the hiring process. Emphasizing this reluctance, the Court noted, "every injury suffered at the hands of a municipal employee can be traced to a hiring decision in the 'but for' sense: but for the hiring of the employee, the plaintiff would not have suffered the injury. A court must carefully test the link between the policy maker's inadequate decision and the particular injury alleged."

The Court further stated:

> . . . a finding of culpability simply cannot depend on the mere probability that any officer inadequately screened will inflict any constitutional injury. Rather, it must depend on a finding that this officer was highly likely to inflict the particular injury suffered by the plaintiff. The connection between the background of the particular applicant and the particular constitutional injury must be strong.

Figure 6.2
Board of Commissioners of Bryan County v. Brown (1997)

Respondent Jill Brown and her husband drove from Texas into Oklahoma, and soon after crossing the state line they noticed a police checkpoint. Mr. Brown turned his vehicle around, and a deputy and a reserve deputy pursued the Browns' vehicle at high speeds. The Browns finally stopped and the deputies approached their vehicle. The reserve deputy approached the passenger side and ordered Mrs. Brown out. She refused and he used an "arm bar," pulling her from the vehicle and forcing her to the ground. Mrs. Brown sustained a knee injury and underwent corrective surgery. She sued under § 1983, claiming excessive force and that the sheriff improperly hired the reserve deputy by ignoring his background of misdemeanor charges for assault and battery, resisting arrest, and traffic charges. The District Court found in favor of Mrs. Brown and the county appealed. The appellate court affirmed.

The United States Supreme Court granted certiorari to determine the issue of whether the county was properly held liable for the respondent's injuries based on the sheriff's decision to hire. In a 6 to 3 decision, the Court found in favor of the sheriff's decision to hire the reserve deputy. Mrs. Brown asserted the "but for" test, claiming that the sheriff ignored the deputy's past and, but for a more thorough review, he would not have hired him. The Court rejected that theory and stated that a court must test the link between a policymaker's decision and a particular injury. The plaintiff must prove a deliberate indifference to the risk that a violation of the constitution will follow that decision. Only when the policymaker deliberately ignores "painfully obvious" information in the background of an applicant and makes a decision to hire where a constitutional right has been violated can the plaintiff claim deliberate indifference. In Oklahoma, a history of misdemeanors does not preclude one from being hired into law enforcement.

This decision is important because it was the first time the Court applied the deliberate indifference standard to hiring decisions. Applying the standard of deliberate indifference to hiring decisions creates a high barrier for a plaintiff to overcome. It is recommended that administrators develop and adhere to adequate hiring procedures, continue to conduct thorough and complete background checks, and require psychological examinations when making hiring decisions.

The Supreme Court opined that the deputy's background did not make his use of excessive force in making the arrest a plainly obvious consequence of the hiring decision. "Only where adequate scrutiny of the applicant's background would lead a reasonable policy maker to conclude that the plainly obvious consequence of the decision to hire the applicant would be the deprivation of a third party's federally protected right can the official's failure to adequately scrutinize the applicant's background constitute 'deliberate indifference'."

The implication of this decision is that administrators should ensure that they conduct adequate background investigations and use psychological examinations prior to hiring employees. There is no magic legal formula for hiring prospective employees, but failing to institute adequate measures and take reasonable steps in employee selection or ignoring information regarding the unfitness of a candidate can increase the risk of liability. Hiring procedures must be instituted, state standards must be met, and the law must be followed. In these cases the Supreme Court has created a high barrier for the plaintiff to overcome. The plaintiff must show that the employee's background made the specific constitutional violation a "painfully obvious consequence" of his or her being hired.

In *Morris v. Crawford County* (2002), a claim that the sheriff failed to properly conduct an adequate hiring investigation was dismissed by the court and the appellate court affirmed. A detainee confined in the jail claimed that, during booking, an officer assaulted him after he refused to take a Breathalyzer test. The detainee was arrested and confined in jail for disorderly conduct and driving while intoxicated. The detainee began banging on his cell and four officers responded. The detainee claimed that the officers dragged him out of his cell, beat him, and one officer used a knee drop on him that severed his intestine. The detainee claimed that this conduct violated his constitutional rights and that the sheriff knew of such violent tendencies at the time he hired the officer but ignored them, and that such knowledge was the direct cause of his injury.

The appellate court held that the detainee failed to show a strong causal connection between the officer's background and the specific constitutional violation. The court noted that the only violent act in the officer's background was an incident in which he slapped a detainee, although protective orders were obtained against the officer by his ex-wife and girlfriend. The court ruled that the sheriff and the county were not liable under § 1983 on the theory of deliberate indifference in the hiring of the officer.

Hiring an applicant is one of the most important decisions administrators must make. Failing to conduct a thorough and complete investigation can heighten the risk of civil liability in the future. Investigators need to be trained in how to perform background investigations in order to ensure that the most qualified person is hired. To ensure that background investigations are performed properly, consider the following recommendations (Brushway, 2004):

1. **Provide applicants with a personal history packet**. This packet should be distributed to applicants and should specify what forms need to be completed, by what date, and provide clear instructions. The packet should require all education and employment information, including names, addresses, phone numbers of supervisors, co-workers, and reference information.

2. **Obtain a notarized waiver**. Ensure that the language of the waiver allows the investigator the ability to access all aspects of the applicant's past. Records can show the character of the applicant. Make certain the waiver contains language that stipulates that negative information will remain confidential. Include a release of liability of the investigatory agency and a disclaimer that all information and materials are the property of the investigating agency.

3. **Conduct an "initial interview" to go through the personal history statement of the applicant.** Open-ended questions should be used to elicit information necessary for the investigator to begin the investigation. Creating a timeline can be helpful in cross-referencing information provided by the applicant with information the investigator discovers during the investigation.

4. **Follow up on reference information.** In addition to reviewing reference comments, follow up by making personal contacts with references and others who may have relevant information regarding the applicant. Avoid relying solely on reference letters, but rather speak with neighbors, friends, supervisors, past educators, military, etc.

5. **Learn from the past.** Avoid making the same mistakes that have occurred in other departments. Departmental investigators should be trained in all aspects of performing background checks and keep abreast of legal and liability issues affecting the hiring process in their state. Make certain to follow the required state hiring standards as well as the departmental policy on hiring candidates. The use of psychological assessments by trained and qualified individuals should be considered and used if required by the state.

These components can assist in performing adequate hiring investigations. They will be very useful in defending against claims that the hiring agency failed to conduct a less than thorough investigation or ignored information that should have been reviewed when making the hiring decision.

Negligent Assignment

Negligent assignment is assigning an employee to a job without ascertaining his or her competence, or retaining an employee on a job who is known to be incapable of performing the job. Examples include assigning a reckless driver to transport prisoners or assigning an officer who has in the past demonstrated mental or physical instabilities to a prison gun tower. The administrator has an affirmative duty not to assign a subordinate to, or leave in a position for which the subordinate is unfit. In *Moon v. Winfield* (1974), liability attached for failure to place a police officer who was unfit for his regular assignment into a non-sensitive position. The court held the supervisor liable because he had the authority to assign or suspend the officer, but failed to do so. The supervisor had received five separate misconduct reports within a two-week period, as well as a warning that the officer had been involved in a series of incidents that indicated mental instability.

In *L.W. v. Grubbs* (1992), an appellate court found supervisors liable when a prison nurse filed a claim for improperly assigning her to work with young violent prisoners when the supervisors knew of their previous violent histories. The court found that the supervisors created a dangerous situation when they assigned the nurse to work by herself with these prisoners, and, when left alone with them, she was raped by one prisoner.

An example of assigning an unfit person to perform the duties of a police officer is provided in *Grancid Camilo-Robles v. Diaz-Pagan* (1998). The plaintiff prevailed in an action against the superiors of a known mentally impaired police officer who was under psychological care for failing to remove him from assigned duties as a police officer. The plaintiff was arrested at gunpoint, slapped in the face, and held in a lockup by the officer for three hours for parking in unauthorized parking zone at the courthouse. The officer had a history of 18 disciplinary infractions for bizarre behavior and brandishing his weapon at citizens. He was committed to a psychiatric hospital after being diagnosed with schizophrenia and was released three months later. A police psychiatrist recommended that the officer be terminated, and the agency director discharged him. The officer appealed the decision and was reinstated. A psychiatrist reevaluated him, cleared him for full duty, and he returned to duty fully armed. One day later, he became engaged in a deadly force encounter and shot two people, killing one of them. He was assigned to desk duty, psychologically evaluated again, and again returned to regular duty by the department. He later threatened to kill a fellow officer, and the department terminated him. The officer eventually pleaded guilty to voluntary manslaughter and was sentenced to a prison term. In the subsequent civil action, the director was found liable for having foreknowledge of the officer's mental unfitness for duty and deliberate indifference to his condition by reassigning the officer to active duty, where a known and foreseeable harm and death occurred. The court maintained that the director acquiesced in his administrative capacity in assigning him duties for which he was clearly unfit. The court also held that the director failed to take preventive or training measures to control the known violent tendencies of the officer.

Administrators must pay careful attention to complaints and adverse reports against subordinates. They must be investigated and properly documented. Further, administrators must generally be aware of the strengths and weaknesses of subordinates and not assign them to perform tasks for which they lack skill or competence.

Negligent Entrustment

Negligent entrustment involves the supervisor's failure to properly supervise or control an employee's custody, use, or supervision of equipment or facilities entrusted to him or her (del Carmen, 1991). This theory of liability is different from negligent assignment in that negligent entrustment goes beyond employee incompetence in carrying out their duties to incompetence in the use of equipment entrusted to the employee. For example, legal claims may emerge for failing to direct the proper use of an impact weapon in a disturbance situation that later results in the serious injury or death of a prisoner. In *Roberts v. Williams* (1971), a county farm superintendent had given an untrained trustee guard a shotgun and the task of guarding a work crew. The supervisor was held liable because the shotgun went off, seriously wounding a prisoner.

In *Slaken v. Porter* (1984), a jury awarded a prisoner $32,000 when evidence supported a claim of excessive force by correctional officers after they used high-pressure hoses, tear gas, and billy clubs to subdue him while he was in a one-man cell. The officers and supervisory personnel were found to be deliberately indifferent to the prisoner's constitutional right to be free from a known risk of harm. Supervisors were found liable because they should have been aware of the officers' propensities and because they had the duty to ensure that instruments of control were not misused. In *Norris v. Detrick* (1996), the court found that prison officials properly administered two doses of chloracetaphenone (CN) gas when confronted by a prisoner with known martial arts skills who refused to return to his cell after numerous orders to do so. The court noted that whether the use of gas is constitutional depends on the totality of circumstances, including provocation, the amount of gas used, and the purposes for which the gas was used. In *Pereira-Gonzalez v. Lopez-Feliciano* (1990), police supervisors were held liable for failing to confiscate the duty weapon of an officer who had a history of spouse abuse. The officer shot his wife after asking supervisors to take the weapon.

Negligent entrustment need not only include the misuse of equipment or weapons. Sanctioning or condoning the misuse of physical force may also increase the risk of liability for superiors. A sheriff was liable in *Duckworth v. Whiesnant* (1996) for tacitly condoning the use of excessive force. The sheriff condoned the practice of kicking arrestees in the groin. In this case the deputy admitted to kicking the plaintiff in the groin while he was handcuffed. The court concluded that the county had "entrusted" this practice to officers and that it amounted to deliberate indifference.

The test of liability is that of deliberate indifference. The plaintiff must prove that the officer was incompetent, inexperienced, or reckless, and that the supervisor knew or had reason to know of this. The defense for the supervisor is that the use and custody of equipment were properly supervised, but despite adequate precautions, the incident still occurred.

Failure to Direct

A significant responsibility of any administrator is to develop and implement agency policies and procedures. Policies and procedures put into operation the statutory requirements of criminal justice personnel. They provide direction to officers in the proper performance of their duties. Policies guide officers in making decisions about how to legitimately respond in different situations, particularly when a supervisor is not immediately available.

Failing to direct refers to a failure to inform employees of the special requirements and limits of the job to be performed. This is frequently interpreted as the failure of an administrator to promulgate policies and procedures that direct personnel in the specific tasks of the job. In *Ford v. Brier* (1974), the court ruled that failing to establish adequate policies gives rise to civil liability. Examples include the supervisor failing to inform employees of the proper procedures for dispensing medication to prisoners or the limits of using force to restore order during a fight.

In police work some of the more obvious examples of failing to develop policies and guidelines include making arrests, using force, engaging in high-speed pursuits, performing searches on arrestees, and responding to the mentally impaired. For example, in *Garris v. Rowland* (1982), liability existed for failure to establish a policy of informing officers when an arrest warrant had been quashed. A practice of not informing officers of the status of arrest warrants had developed.

In *Rivas v. Freeman* (1991), liability attached against a sheriff for failing to develop sufficient and appropriate procedures and policies regarding identification of arrestees, warrantless searches, and computer checks for information. Although the sheriff was not personally involved in the arrest of the plaintiff, the court found that he formulated the policies and customs that resulted in the violations of the plaintiff's constitutional rights. The lack of established policies and procedures caused the plaintiff's arrest, his unnecessary six-day incarceration, and resulting humiliation. The evidence at trial supported a claim that the officer's actions showed that the sheriff failed to establish policies that would properly direct them in the performance of their duties.

In *Women Prisoners v. District of Columbia* (1994), the district court found prison officials liable for violating the rights of female prisoners who were subjected to sexual harassment. The court held that the harassment was the result of a government custom and practice and that officials failed to properly train employees in the area of sexual harassment. A federal district court in *Estep v. Dent* (1996) granted injunctive relief to a prisoner based on a claim that the prison policy that required him to cut his earlocks violated the Religious Freedom Restoration Act. Requiring the prisoner to cut his earlocks would substantially violate the tenets of his Jewish faith. The court found that prison officials were deliberately indifferent and failed to establish that the policy was the least restrictive means of furthering its interests in maintaining security.

A federal appellate court in *Vineyard v. County of Murray* (1993) found that the county was deliberately indifferent to the rights of prisoners who had been beaten by deputies. The court stated that the county's policy of condoning such behavior was the moving force behind the violation of the prisoner's constitutional rights. In *Valencia v. Wiggins* (1993), liability was assessed against jail officials who acted outside the boundaries of established policy. A prisoner was awarded $2,500 in damages and $27,000 in attorney's fees when the jury found that officers used excessive force against him in a jail disturbance. The officer struck a handcuffed, nonresisting prisoner and placed him in a choke hold. The jury found that the force and choke hold violated the jail's policy and constituted malicious and sadistic harm.

The best defensible position for administrators is to establish and maintain a current, comprehensive, and constitutional written policy manual. Policies should be reviewed and revised annually, in order to reflect the current status of the law. The written policy should reflect not only the theory, but also the actual practice of the department. Agency procedures should mirror written job descriptions. Employees should be trained and tested in their comprehension of policy content. Each employee should have an individual current copy of the policy manual and it should be inspected periodically. Supervisors must be familiar with and enforce all policies.

Failure to Supervise Subordinates

A fundamental responsibility of criminal justice supervisors is to provide adequate supervision and control over the activities of subordinates. Allegations of failing to supervise employees involve abdication of the responsibility to oversee employee activities. Failing to supervise employees properly can result in litigation for failing to know about employee behavior. Examples include tolerating a pattern of physical abuse of arrestees or prisoners, racial discrimination, and pervasive deprivation of individual rights and privileges.

Permitting unlawful activities in an agency may constitute deliberate indifference, giving rise to liability. The key issue relates to a policy or custom of inadequate supervision of employees. The plaintiff must show that the agency failed to supervise its personnel or that such failures resulted in deliberate indifference. The usual standard is whether the supervisor knew of a pattern of behavior but failed to act on it. The question becomes "What constitutes knowledge of a pattern of behavior among employees?" Many courts have established that actual knowledge is required, while other courts state that knowledge can be inferred if a history of violations is established and the administrator had direct and close supervisory control over the employee committing the violation. In *Johnson v. Cannon* (1996), the court found a sheriff liable for failure to provide proper supervision and control of a deputy. Over a period of several months, a deputy had stopped female motorists for traffic violations and forced them to have sexual intercourse with him. The failure to properly supervise the deputy rose to a level of deliberate indifference.

Courts hold that a supervisor must be "causally linked" to the pattern of constitutional violations by showing knowledge of it, and that this failure to act amounts to approval and thus tacit encouragement for the pattern to continue. In *Shaw v. Stroud* (1994), the estate of the deceased failed to connect an alleged failure to supervise with a North Carolina state trooper's history of excessive force claims in a situation in which he used deadly force. The trooper stopped a motorist in front of his house and attempted to arrest him for driving while impaired. During the arrest a struggle ensued, and the driver took the trooper's metal flashlight and struck him on the head. The driver came at the trooper again and struck him a second time, and on a third attempt the trooper fired his duty weapon several times, killing the driver.

The trooper, his sergeant at the time, and a former sergeant were sued by the family. The former sergeant had supervised the trooper for approximately five years but had transferred 18 months prior to the shooting. The trooper had accumulated more than 25 complaints from citizens alleging excessive force. A district court judge had also voiced concern to the trooper's supervisor regarding the number of "injured" defendants who appeared in his courtroom after being arrested by this trooper. The Fourth Circuit Court of Appeals dismissed the claim of inadequate supervision against the current supervisor because he had responded to complaints by sending other supervisors to monitor court cases and by riding with the trooper to evaluate his conduct during arrests. The court, however, remanded the case to the lower court with regard to the first supervisor's inaction, because the court held that he failed to investigate the many complaints lodged against the trooper, constituting a failure to supervise. The jury in the lower court found that the trooper responded correctly by shooting the motorist. Therefore, because the jury found in favor of the trooper, the supervisor could not be held liable.

The severity of an employee's constitutional violation must be sufficient in order to justify a verdict of failing to properly supervise an employee. In *Atchinson v. District of Columbia* (1996), a police officer confronted a man carrying a machete on the street. The officer shouted "Freeze!" one time and did not give another warning before using deadly force. The appellate court ruled that even a single incident of such use of force was adequate to support a complaint of inadequate supervision and training of police in the use of force. Conversely, in *Singleton v. McDougall* (1996), a sheriff was not liable for alleged inadequate supervision when an officer used deadly force in an arrest situation. The evidence showed that there had been "numerous" (although the number was not specified) incidents in which deputies had previously used deadly force. The plaintiff's contention was that such incidents proved that the sheriff failed to supervise his subordinates in the proper use of firearms and thus was deliberately indifferent to the rights of the citizenry. Despite previous lawsuits alleging the use of excessive force or wrongful use of deadly force by deputies, there had been no single case in which the courts had ruled that department personnel had violated a clearly established right in this area. The court concluded that the sheriff was entitled to qualified immunity, as the evidence failed to show that a reasonable person in the sheriff's position would know that the unresolved lawsuits established a right requiring corrective action.

In *Williams v. White* (1990), the Eighth Circuit Court of Appeals found that a prison superintendent may be liable for operating a prison with unsanitary and inhumane conditions and may be directly liable when he fails to train, supervise, or control his subordinates. In *Treadwell v. Murray* (1995), a prisoner asserted that correctional officials failed to oversee officers and medical personnel when the officials deprived him of an unsafe rehabilitative environment and initial inappropriate medical classification. The prisoner claimed that the physician's improper classification prevented him from being eligible for "different types of incarceration," such as halfway houses, work-release programs, or road camps. According to the prisoner, the director of corrections abdicated his supervisory responsibility by failing to oversee the actions of his employees, which ultimately resulted in a constitutional deprivation. The court found that the prisoner failed to state a claim of deliberate indifference under § 1983 based on supervisory liability. The court further concluded that the prisoner failed to substantiate any wanton, obdurate, or offensive acts by the director of corrections in his supervisory capacity, nor could he point to any single incident, or isolated incident, in which the director created any pervasive risk of harm that deprived the prisoner of a constitutionally protected right.

In *Giroux v. Sherman* (1992), a prisoner was awarded $36,000 in punitive damages, claiming on four occasions that at least eight correctional officers beat and tormented him without provocation. Due to the beatings, he aggravated an old injury, which required hospitalization. While in the hospital, he was also beaten and sustained kidney and throat injuries. Supervisory liability was also found when the court stated that supervisors failed to identify and correct their behavior.

In *Campbell v. City of New York* (2004), the court found that supervisors of an arresting officer were liable for failing to supervise and failing to discipline officer misconduct. Campbell requested police assistance when he was assaulted by his ex-wife's son. Officer Buckley responded, but did not arrest the son. The police received a second call from Campbell six months later, asking for assistance in enforcing a restraining order that allowed him to visit his children, who were in his ex-wife's custody. Officer Buckley responded and learned that Campbell's ex-wife had a protection order against him, and Campbell was arrested. Campbell served time in jail but the charges were later dropped. Campbell filed a citizen complaint for false arrest. Detectives investigated the complaint and informed Campbell that his ex-wife had called the NYPD reporting that he had threatened to kill her. Campbell's ex-wife signed an affidavit stating that Campbell made threats to her and he was arrested a second time. These charges were later dropped and Campbell filed a lawsuit claiming that supervisors of the NYPD failed to adequately supervise and discipline the officers involved in the case.

The court ruled in favor of Campbell, holding that the officers caused a formation of a custom, practice, and policy that was detrimental to Campbell's rights. The court found that supervisors failed to adequately supervise the involved officers and allowed a practice of officer misconduct. The court agreed with Campbell's claim that failing to supervise officers ostensibly encouraged other officers to retaliate against citizens who filed complaints. The court, however, dismissed the false arrest claim filed regarding the first arrest as there was a lawful protection order against him.

This decision not only questions the officer's decision-making ability, but questions a department's level of supervision with their officers. Supervisors can insulate themselves from allegations for failure to supervise by ensuring that officers follow through with all investigations in a timely manner and reminding investigators of the importance of remaining impartial in their review of citizen complaints. In addition, supervisors must show that they have taken proactive measures to properly supervise their officers when misconduct occurs. For example, supervisors were held liable in *Neris v. Vivoni* (2003) when it was shown that the supervisors had actual knowledge of employees' unconstitutional conduct and took no steps to remedy the situation. Failure to take remedial intervention measures in the face of such knowledge rose to a level of supervisory deliberate indifference.

It is imperative that administrators not shut their eyes to, or tolerate, improper employee conduct. Performance should be evaluated periodically, as well as informal appraisals of employee conduct to encourage proper conduct. Supervisors should review employee performance firsthand and review all incident reports. All complaints of improper conduct by officers must be investigated and appropriate discipline should be provided. Remedial correction of unsatisfactory employee performance should be documented, and employees who chronically fall below the accepted standard should be put on notice that employment is based on adherence to policy and proper conduct in the workplace. This strategy can assist in reducing potential supervisory liability.

Negligent Failure to Discipline/Negligent Retention

Failure to discipline involves the administrator's failure to investigate complaints about employees and take appropriate action as warranted. Allegations can also result from the supervisor failing to take action against an employee in the form of suspension, transfer, or termination when the employee has demonstrated unsuitability for the job. Claims of retaining errant officers after they have repeatedly engaged in misconduct can also result in supervisory liability.

The supervisor has an affirmative duty to take all necessary and proper steps to discipline or terminate a subordinate who is obviously unfit for employment. Unfitness may be determined either from acts of prior gross misconduct or from a series of prior acts of lesser misconduct that indicate a pattern (del Carmen, 1991). Courts have imposed liability for inaction when a supervisor had actual knowledge that the employee had previously engaged in unlawful conduct and did nothing to correct the behavior. In *Hogan v. Franco* (1995), the chief was found liable for failing to discipline, supervise, and train errant officers in the proper use of force. In this case the plaintiff sustained major nerve damage to his arm, wrist, and back from the improper use of handcuffs and misapplication of an impact weapon (a baton) by the arresting officer. Evidence was confirmed that the chief knew of a history of officers physically abusing prisoners or mishandling arrest situations. Trial testimony confirmed more than 10 successful lawsuits won by plaintiffs for similar complaints made against the department. The chief was aware of at least one officer who had a propensity for violence and beating arrestees. The chief was held liable for tolerating the failure to investigate, discipline, or correct violations, which suggested the adoption of a policy supporting such violations. Such persistent failure to discipline amounted to an inference of an unlawful policy of ratification of unconstitutional conduct within the meaning of *Monell* and rose to a level of deliberate indifference. The plaintiff was awarded $200,000 in compensatory damages against the chief and the officer.

The *Hogan* case illustrates how the courts make a connection between official policy and a failure to discipline in cases of known officer misconduct. In essence, failing to identify officer misconduct or tolerating known misconduct creates a de facto policy creating liability on the part of the administrator as the official policymaker of the department. It can rise to a level of deliberate indifference if the administrator or supervisor was aware of the misconduct and chose to ignore the misconduct or did not take measures to prevent it. In *Diaz v. Martinez* (1997), summary judgment was denied because the chief failed to discipline and maintain accurate records about a rogue officer or recommend remedial training. This demonstrated supervisory indifference. Moreover, in emphasizing the association between failing to discipline and official policy, the court held in *Grandstaff v. City of Borger* (1985) that the police chief was the sole policymaker, and therefore his failure to discipline several officers involved in an egregious shooting, in which a person was killed, was evidence of a municipal policy of ignoring constitutional rights violations.

In *Vann v. City of New York* (1995), the court determined that deliberate indifference was evidenced by an abusive officer who had been the subject of numerous complaints, disciplined several times, and placed on restricted duty. He was returned to regular duty and committed additional assaults. Prior to his return to regular duty, a psychological evaluation noted that the officer had a personality problem that escalated minor situations into violent incidents. In returning him to regular duty, the chief failed to monitor the problem officer's conduct despite prior "red flag" incidents of violent behavior. After his return to regular duty, the officer continued to receive citizen abuse complaints that were not investigated by the chief. Deliberate indifference was determined by a pattern of ignoring complaints in which the need to discipline was obvious.

A fundamental requirement of all supervisors is to enforce their own legitimate regulations and follow through with appropriate discipline as necessary. A correctional officer's rights were not violated when the department of corrections required him to wear an American flag patch on his uniform shirt (*Troster v. Pennsylvania State Department of Corrections*, 1995). In *Flynn v. Sandahl* (1995), the warden did not violate a correctional officer's due process rights by ordering him to submit to a psychiatric examination after co-workers complained that he had threatened them with physical harm. Any privacy interest of the officer was outweighed by requirements of maintaining a stable prison workforce.

In several cases, supervisors have been held liable for promulgating policies that discourage investigation of police misconduct, and failing to discipline, which encourage constitutional violations. In *Bastia v. Rodriguez* (1983), the court ruled that the persistent failure to discipline subordinates who violate constitutional rights could give rise to an inference of ratification. In *Skevofilax v. Quigley* (1984), a police chief was held liable for continually failing to discipline or control subordinates in the face of knowledge of their propensity to use force improperly. This created an official custom or de facto policy that was actionable under § 1983. In *Haynes v. Marshall* (1989), a prisoner brought a valid claim against a prison superintendent for having a policy of using force against prisoners to enforce rules.

In *Beck v. City of Pittsburgh* (1996), a "custom" of failing to discipline officers created liability for the police chief. It was determined that investigative policies requiring a complainant to produce evidence other than his or her word, not considering prior complaints against an officer, not having a tracking system for prior complaints and dispositions, eschewing standards for reporting patterns, and a practice of not reviewing recommendations for no discipline, were sufficient to establish deliberate indifference. Also, in *Nolin v. Town of Springville* (1999), the court found sufficient evidence of deliberate indifference on the part of the chief for failing to discipline and train officers. In a five-person department, numerous cases involving claims of excessive force had been settled out of court during a relatively short period. It was determined that all members of the department, including the chief, would have known of such claims. After each claim, the chief neither disciplined the officer nor required retraining. This pattern of settling claims in a small department, without disciplinary action being taken, or requiring retraining of officers in the use of appropriate force, rose to a level of deliberate indifference and liability attached.

Administrative liability will be avoided when supervisors fulfill their basic functions of properly enforcing security practices and institutional policies. A prison official's termination of a correctional officer found sleeping on the job after taking medication for an arthritic knee was not found to be arbitrary or capricious (*Nebraska Department of Correctional Services v. Hansen*, 1991). Correctional officials were not liable when they took prompt effective disciplinary action after a female employee complained of alleged sexual harassment by a correctional officer (*Hirschfeld v. New Mexico Corrections Department*, 1990).

If the agency's disciplinary system is deficient, supervisory liability may attach. In *Gutierrez-Rodriguez v. Cartagena* (1989), the court held the police administrator personally liable, as it found the disciplinary system to be grossly deficient, reflecting a reckless and callous indifference to the rights of citizens. Several officers in the department had accumulated numerous civilian complaints that had gone uninvestigated. Additionally, supervisors exhibited a pattern of failing to discipline officers. In this case the plaintiff was shot by four officers. They had approached his vehicle with guns drawn and the plaintiff, noticing the four in plain clothes, attempted to speed away. The plaintiff was parked off the road with his girlfriend and was not a "wanted" person. One round hit him in the back, causing him to drive into a ditch. The car landed on its side and the plaintiff sustained a back injury, leaving him a paraplegic.

The chief knew the histories of these officers but failed to take remedial or preventive measures. Failing to do so amounted to deliberate indifference and, as a result, the incident above occurred. The chief was found liable and the plaintiff was awarded $4.5 million. The disciplinary system existed in name only. The court found the following procedures inadequate:

1. Officers investigated could refuse to testify or give a statement.

2. The agency did not have any provision for remedial training as one of the disciplinary options.

3. The withdrawal of a complaint closed the internal investigation without the agency doing anything about it.

4. The immediate supervisors of the officers were not involved in the disciplinary process.

In another case the disciplinary system was so faulty that the court awarded summary judgment to the plaintiff. In *Cox v. District of Columbia* (1993), the civilian review board (which exclusively ruled on excessive force allegations) chronically delayed decisions and ignored statutory deadlines. The court considered that these "flagrant" violations deprived citizens of their constitutional rights and amounted to deliberate indifference on the part of the administration.

Properly following departmental procedures when considering discipline or termination of an employee are important in defending a claim that an officer was wrongfully discharged. Documenting past occasions of discipline is critical in justifying a supervisor's decision to pursue more severe sanctions or termination of the employee. In *Peterson v. Civil Service Commission of Cedar Rapids* (2005), the appellate court upheld the decision of the chief of police of Cedar Rapids, Iowa, when he terminated an officer for an incident of excessive force. Officer Peterson attempted to stop a motorist for speeding. Peterson activated his lights and siren as the motorist exited the highway, but the motorist ignored them. The motorist proceeded to his residence and pulled in the driveway. Peterson stopped behind him and activated his in-car video camera. The motorist exited his car and ignored Peterson's commands to stop and keep back from the car. Peterson was joined by several back-up officers and informed the motorist that he was under arrest. The motorist resisted arrest and the officers forced him to the ground to control and handcuff him. Two of the responding officers informed a supervisor that Peterson used excessive force during the confrontation by kneeing him in the head as they pinned him to the ground. Peterson informed a lieutenant that he only used his knee to pin the motorist's shoulder for control purposes, which was an authorized technique. The lieutenant, however, informed Peterson that he thought discipline was warranted. After an internal affairs investigation and an administrative hearing, the chief fired Peterson for excessive use of force. Peterson appealed the decision and the civil service commission upheld the termination.

Peterson filed a lawsuit and the court overturned the termination, holding that the videotape of the incident did not support chief's decision to fire him. The court ruled that the use of force was inadvertent and not excessive, and ordered that Peterson be reinstated. The civil service commission appealed the decision. The appellate court reviewed the videotape, witness statements, and the officers' testimony, and found that Peterson had used excessive force in response to the motorist's behavior. The court also examined Peterson's personnel file and noted that he had a prior suspension for a similar traffic stop. In that incident, Peterson pointed his firearm and taunted a driver for failing to follow his commands. The court noted that the department had implemented policy and practices for responding to employee misconduct and had followed them in the past. Thus, the court ruled that the chief had the authority to suspend, demote, or fire for misconduct that was detrimental to the public interest. Given the prior suspension, the severity of the sanction was appropriate as the next step in progressive discipline.

Clearly, administrators and supervisors must have workable disciplinary procedures that are adequate and legal. They must protect the rights of both the employee and the complainant. Steps of progressive discipline must be outlined and employees must be made aware of the consequences of misconduct. Supervisors must be trained in implementing appropriate disciplinary procedures in order to remediate or correct employee performance. Complaints about employees should be investigated, and proper procedures for conducting the investigation should be implemented. Supervisory documentation of the investigation and the results should be kept in the employee's personnel file. Steps toward termination should be followed as policy and investigation warrant as noted in the *Peterson* case.

In *Castagna v. City of Seal Beach* (2005), supervisors prevailed in a lawsuit when an officer claimed he was fired contrary to department policy and law. Officer Castagna became involved in a probate matter and forged a document. The conduct came to the attention of the department captain and he began an investigation. The investigation revealed that officer Castagna introduced a forged document, lied under oath, and lied to investigators, although the prosecutor declined to file charges. The department issued Castagna a "Notice of Intent to Discipline," advising him that the chief was considering terminating his employment. Officer Castagna was informed of his rights, notified of a pre-disciplinary hearing, and given copies of the forged documents. He was placed on administrative leave pending the results of the internal affairs investigation. Several months later, Castagna received a copy of the investigation's findings, concluding that he indeed engaged in misconduct. The notice did not specify any type of proposed discipline but did stipulate that he was to respond to the notice. Rather than respond he filed suit, claiming that the department failed to complete the investigation according to state law within one year and failed to outline any proposed discipline. He claimed wrongful discipline and requested a temporary order prohibiting the department from disciplining him. The officer was subsequently fired.

At trial the court refused the request for a temporary order and also held that the department followed the proper protocols for conducting an investigation and notifying him of such an investigation. The firing was also upheld by the court. Officer Castagna appealed and the appellate court affirmed the lower court's decision. The appellate court noted that the department followed the law and policy by conducting a timely investigation once they learned of the misconduct, that officer Castagna was properly notified, and afforded him with his rights while on administrative leave, and that the termination was lawful.

First Line of Defense

Critical components of administration include planning, controlling, directing, budgeting, and supervising subordinates. Administrators must also be concerned with the ever-present liability component, which may emerge from fulfilling their basic supervisory functions. The first line of defense against litigation begins with the administrator making a firm commitment and concerted effort to transform administrative functions into a proactive risk management program to minimize future lawsuits (as discussed in Chapter 5). Administrators and supervisors represent the best protection against liability, but the basics must be in place first.

Liability Risk Reduction

By integrating the fundamental components of management with risk reduction elements, administrators create a strategy that allows the organization to operate effectively and demonstrate a good faith effort toward reducing liability potential.

The basic elements of a risk reduction program include the following:

1. Performing an analysis of agency incidents, complaints, audits, and lawsuits in order to identify problems specific to agency needs. After an assessment has been conducted, supervisors should obtain the assistance of legal counsel to determine the latest court decisions (state and federal) that affect prisoner and employee rights.

2. Based on the outcome of the internal assessment, outdated policies should be revised and new policies should be developed. Revising existing policy and procedure manuals is essential to complying with court rulings and changes in the law. Once policies are revised or newly developed, administrators should keep supervisors updated on the revisions and the administrative interpretations of the revisions. This will ensure proper implementation and enforcement. It is recommended that agency policies be reviewed annually and revised accordingly. Correctional officials are encouraged to maintain up-to-date policies and procedures, developed in accordance with state and professional correctional standards.

3. All supervisors and employees should receive training in the policy manual on a regular basis. Moreover, all employees should be trained regularly in the legal dimensions of the job and in frequently performed tasks. All employees should receive regular competency-based training in the types of weapons and equipment that correspond to their duties.

4. Administrators and supervisors must provide proper direction, supervision, and reinforcement of training objectives to ensure that the mission of the agency is being carried out. Administrators must investigate complaints and follow established agency disciplinary procedures as necessary.

5. Written documentation of training, complaints, investigations, and employee disciplinary actions by administrators and supervisors is essential to corroborate management's role in supervising subordinates. Written documentation provides a record of events and incidents and establishes a process of reasonable actions taken. It will provide protection for the individual and the agency in civil litigation.

Summary

This chapter has examined the basis of supervisory liability under § 1983. While administrative liability under § 1983 started with the *Monell* decision, it is still developing, and has emerged as a primary source of litigation for supervisors. Case examples indicate that this area of litigation will continue, and it is incumbent upon administrators to keep abreast of the legal standards imposed upon them. Through court decisions, the days of unfettered supervisory discretion have been replaced with several theories of supervisory liability. Judicial intervention has created a mixed blessing for the administrator.

Management theories and practices indicate that administrators should be competent in directing the organization, as well as in planning, budgeting, staffing, decisionmaking, controlling staffing, reporting, and supervising employees. Since the *Monell* decision, administrators must also develop a new managerial competency in understanding that their actions or omissions may expose them to a heightened risk of liability under § 1983. This chapter examined six of the seven areas in which supervisors may be named as defendants for allegedly failing in their administrative functions: (1) negligent hiring, (2) negligent assignment, (3) negligent entrustment, (4) failure to direct, (5) failure to supervise, and (6) failure to discipline/negligent retention (failure to train is addressed in Chapter 7). The legal standard of review in these types of allegations is that of deliberate indifference, which is a high standard for the plaintiff to prove.

Court intervention relative to administrative functions has created a legal arena that requires administrators to be more proactive in working with employees and managing the operations of their organization. Court intervention, however, has also helped administrators to acquire more or new resources and facilities, which have improved overall operations and employee performance. Thus, administrators need to become more proactive in developing their knowledge of the law and the liability dimensions of their jobs. Developing and implementing risk reduction strategies as discussed in this chapter and Chapter 5 can assist administrators in operating an organization that works toward reducing the risk of supervisory liability, thus making it more efficient. Moreover, administrators should be committed to further educating their employees in the legal nature of their responsibilities. This combined approach will assist in reducing the number of lawsuits filed, as well as successfully defending lawsuits.

References

Bushway, S. (2004). "Background Investigations of Police Candidates: One of the Most Important Investigations You'll Ever Conduct." *Police Disciplinary Bulletin* 12:1-3.

del Carmen, R.V. (1991). *Civil Liability in American Policing: A Text for Law Enforcement Personnel*. Englewood, NJ: Prentice-Hall.

_____ & V.E. Kappeler (1991). "Municipal and Police Agencies as Defendants: Liability for Official Policy and Custom." *American Journal of Police* 10:1-17.

Kappeler, V.E. (1997). *Critical Issues in Police Civil Liability*, Second Edition. Prospect Heights, IL: Waveland Press, Inc.

Cases Cited

Atchinson v. D.C., 73 F.3d 418 (D.C. Cir. 1996)

Bastia v. Rodriguez, 702 F.2d 393 (2d Cir. 1983)

Beck v. City of Pittsburgh, 89 F.3d 966 (3d Cir. 1996)

Bell v. City of Miami, 733 F. Supp. 1475 (N.D. Fla. 1990)

Benavides v. County of Wilson, 955 F.2d 968 (5th Cir. 1992)

Board of County Commissioners of Bryan County v. Brown, 520 U.S. 397 (1997)

Brown v. Benton, 425 F. Supp. 28 (W.D. Okla. 1978)

Campbell v. City of New York, 2004 U.S. Dist. Lexis 7656 (S.D.N.Y.) [unpublished opinion]

Castagna v. City of Seal Beach, 2005 Lexis 7775 (Div. 3, 4th Cal. App.) [unpublished opinion]

City of Canton, Ohio v. Harris, 489 U.S. 378 (1989)

City of Oklahoma City v. Tuttle, 471 U.S. 808 (1985)

City of St. Louis v. Praprotnik, 485 U.S. 112 (1988)

Cox v. District of Columbia, 821 F. Supp. 1 (D.D.C. 1993)

Diaz v. Martinez, 112 F.3d 1 (1st Cir. 1997)

Duckworth v. Whiesnant, 97 F.3d 1393 (11th Cir. 1996)

Estelle v. Gamble, 429 U.S. 97 (1976)

Estep v. Dent, 914 F. Supp. 1462 (W.D. Ky. 1996)

Farmer v. Brennan, 114 S. Ct. 1970 (1994)

Ford v. Brier, 383 F. Supp. 505 (E.D. Wis. 1974)

Flynn v. Sandahl, 58 F.3d 283 (7th Cir. 1995)

Gaines v. Choctaw County Commissioners, 242 F. Supp. 2d 1153 (S.D. Ala. 2003)

Garris v. Rowland, 678 F.2d 1264 (5th Cir. 1982)

Giroux v. Sherman, 807 F. Supp. 1182 (E.D. Pa. 1992)

Grancid Camilo-Robles v. Diaz-Pagan, No. 97-2260061 (1st Cir. App. Ct. 1998)

Grandstaff v. City of Borger, 767 F.2d 161 (5th Cir. 1985)

Graham v. District of Columbia, 795 F. Supp. 24 (D.D.C. 1992)

Gutierrez-Rodriguez v. Cartagena, 882 F.2d 553 (1st Cir. 1989)

Haynes v. Marshall, 887 F.2d 700 (6th Cir. 1989)

Hirschfeld v. New Mexico Corrections Department, 916 F.2d 572 (10th Cir. 1990)

Hogan v. Franco, 896 F. Supp. 1313 (N.D.N.Y. 1995)

Hudson v. McMillian, 503 U.S. 1 (1992)

Jenkins v. Wood, 81 F.3d 988 (10th Cir. 1996)

Jones v. Wittenburg, 440 F. Supp. 60 (N.D. Ohio 1977)

Johnson v. Cannon, 947 F. Supp. 400 (M.D. Fla. 1996)

L.W. v. Grubbs, 974 F.2d 119 (9th Cir. 1992)

Marchese v. Lucas, 758 F.2d 181 (6th Cir. 1985)

Masel v. Barrett, 707 F. Supp. 4 (D.D.C. 1989)

McConney v. City of Houston, 863 F.2d 1180 (5th Cir. 1989)

McMillian v. Monroe County, Alabama, 520 U.S. 781 (1997)

Monell v. Department of Social Services, 436 U.S. 658 (1978)

Moon v. Winfield, 388 F. Supp. 31 (N.D. Ill. 1974)

Morris v. Crawford County, 299 F.3d 919 (8th Cir. 2002)

Morrison v. Washington County, 700 F.2d 678 (11th Cir. 1983)

Nebraska Department of Corrections v. Hansen, 470 N.W.2d 170 (1991)

Neris v. Vivoni, 249 F. Supp. 2d 146, 149-150 (D.P.R. 2003)

Nolin v. Town of Springville, 45 F. Supp. 894 (N.D. Ala. 1999)

Norris v. Detrick, 918 F. Supp. 977 (N.D. W. Va. 1996)

Parker v. Williams, 855 F.2d 763 (11th Cir. 1988)

Pembaur v. City of Cincinnati, 475 U.S. 469 (1986)

Pereira-Gonzalez v. Lopez-Feliciano, 731 F. Supp. 574 (D.P.R. 1990)

Peterson v. Civil Service Commission of Cedar Rapids, 697 N.W. 2d 127 (Iowa App. 2005)

Polk County v. Dodson, 454 U.S. 312 (1981)

Rivas v. Freeman, 940 F.2d 1491 (11th Cir. 1991)

Rizzo v. Goode, 423 U.S. 362, 96 S. Ct. 598, 46 L. Ed. 2d 561 (1976)

Roberts v. Williams, 456 F.2d 819 (5th Cir 1971)

Shaw v. Stroud, 13 F.3d 799 (4th Cir. 1994)

Singleton v. McDougall, 932 F. Supp. 1386 (M.D. Fla. 1996)

Skevofilax v. Quigley, 586 F. Supp. 532 (D.N.J. 1984)

Slaken v. Porter, 737 F.2d 368 (4th Cir 1984)

Stokes v. Bullins, 844 F.2d 269 (5th Cir. 1988)

Stokes v. Delcambre, 710 F.2d 1120 (5th Cir. 1983)

Treadwell v. Murray, 878 F. Supp. 49 (E.D. Va. 1995)

Troster v. Pennsylvania State Department of Corrections, 65 F.3d 1086 (3d Cir. 1995)

Valencia v. Wiggins, 981 F.2d 1440 (5th Cir. 1993)

Vann v. City of New York, 72 F.3d 1040 (2d Cir. 1995)

Vineyard v. County of Murray, Georgia, 990 F.2d 1207 (11th Cir. 1993)

Warner v. City of New Orleans, 2004 U.S. Dist. Lexis 7050 (E.D. La.)

Ware v. Jackson County, Missouri, 150 F.3d 873 (8th Cir. 1998)

Williams v. White, 897 F.2d 942 (8th Cir. 1990)

Wilkins v. Whitaker, 714 F.2d 4 (4th Cir. 1983)

Wilson v. City of North Little Rock, 801 F.2d 316 (8th Cir. 1986)

Wilson v. Seiter, 501 U.S. 294 (1991)

Women Prisoners v. District of Columbia, 877 F. Supp. 634 (D.D.C. 1994)

Chapter 7

Liability for Failure to Train

Since the United States Supreme Court decision in *City of Canton v. Harris* (1989), the plaintiff in the majority of civil lawsuits cites as a secondary claim that the errant officer was inadequately trained. Several scholars estimate that actions for failure to train and failure to supervise are the two most common types of claims brought against police administrators (Barrineau, 1994; Kappeler, 1997; del Carmen, 1991; Staff, 1990). Although tremendous strides have been made in mandating pre-service police training throughout the United States and the number of hours of in-service training for veteran officers is increasing (Flink, 1997), failure-to-train allegations are still a concern for the police administrator.

Because failure-to-train claims represent a majority of supervisory liability actions, this chapter addresses this critical managerial responsibility. Criminal justice administrators can be held liable if inadequate or improper training causes injury or the violation of an individual's constitutional rights. Ongoing training is critical for avoiding civil litigation (Gallagher, 1990) and in structuring a defense to legal assertions (Vaughn & Coomes, 1995).

Liability Framework for Failure to Train Under *Canton*

Supervisory Liability

Following *Monell v. New York City Department of Social Services* (1978), numerous § 1983 lawsuits have been filed against criminal justice departments on the basis that the incident involved misconduct that was motivated by the agency adopting a policy or custom of inadequate training or supervision of the officers. These cases generated considerable judicial disagreement regarding the appropriate standard with which to assess these actions. Standards applied ranged from ordinary negligence to willfulness.

Disagreement as to the type of evidence required to prove inadequate training produced a great deal of debate in the federal courts. Much of the uncertainty was resolved in the Supreme Court's 1989 decision in *Canton*.

Figure 7.1
City of Canton v. Harris (1989)

Harris was stopped for speeding and was arrested after she became uncooperative with the officer. She was transported to the police station in a patrol wagon and upon arrival was found sitting on the floor. She was brought inside for processing where she collapsed to the floor two times. The officers left her on the floor for approximately one hour during processing and failed to summon medical attention. Court testimony revealed that the shift commander was responsible for determining the medical care of arrestees but did not receive training with which to make medical decisions. She was released into the care of her family whereupon she was taken to a hospital by an ambulance summoned by her family. She was diagnosed as suffering from emotional stress reaction, anxiety, and depression. She was hospitalized for a week and received outpatient medical care for about one year. She sued the city for a variety of claims, but most notable were the claim of denial of medical care while in custody, and training deficiencies of officers in medical care for arrestees. Harris prevailed and was awarded $200,000 in damages. The city appealed to the Sixth Circuit Court of Appeals, which ruled that a municipality could be held liable for failure to train when a plaintiff could prove intentional, reckless, or gross negligence on the part of the municipality. An error was made by the court in explaining jury instructions and a retrial was ordered. Prior to retrial, the city sought review by the Supreme Court and they granted certiorari to determine the issue of whether a municipality could be held deliberately indifferent to the training needs of its officers.

The Court concluded that the standard with which to examine claims of failing to train is deliberate indifference. Deliberate indifference can mean a callous disregard of known risks and failing to take steps to abate it, or a conscious choice from among several alternatives. While the Court ruled that a municipality must provide ongoing training for recurring job tasks an officer encounters, the justices did not state how frequently training must be provided nor the duration of the training. On remand the appellate court reversed its former decision, based on deliberate indifference.

This case is significant because the Court has expanded the standard of deliberate indifference to claims against administrators for failing to train their officers. Deliberate indifference is a higher standard for a plaintiff to prove in court. Officers must receive realistic ongoing training to "obvious" recurring job functions. The decision also applies to correctional officials.

Expansion of the Deliberate Indifference Standard

The Supreme Court ruled that a local government can be held liable under § 1983 if an officer injures a person due to a deficiency in training. Inadequate training may serve as a basis for § 1983 liability where the failure to train amounts to "deliberate indifference" to the rights of persons with whom the police may come into contact. The degree of fault is fundamentally related to the policy requirement noted in *Monell* (Silver, 1996). Moreover, *Monell* will not be satisfied by a mere allegation that a training program represents a policy for which the city is responsible. The Court stated that "in light of the duties assigned to specific officers or employees, the need for more or different training is so obvious, and the inadequacy so likely to result in the violation of constitutional rights, the policy makers of the city can reasonably be said to have been deliberately indifferent to the need."

The former standard of gross negligence used by many lower federal courts was rejected by the Supreme Court, and the higher standard of deliberate indifference was adopted. This standard was first established in a Texas prison case, *Estelle v. Gamble* (1976). Deliberate indifference was expanded in *Canton* and requires proof of much more than negligence. Over the years, the Supreme Court has established that deliberate indifference resides on a continuum between "mere negligence and something less than acts or omissions for the very purpose of causing harm or with knowledge that harm will result" (Vaughn & del Carmen, 1995). "Deliberate" means that a particular course of action has been chosen from among several alternatives, and "indifferent" means there has been some conscious disregard for a person's rights (Plitt, 1997). Only where failure to train reflects a "deliberate" or conscious choice by a municipality can a city be liable for such a failure under § 1983. Liability may not attach for failure to train or improper training without some proof that the department was, or should have been, aware of the need and then made a deliberate choice not to provide training, or not to review and/or improve the training provided.

Factors Necessary to Establish Deliberate Indifference

The Court's opinion provides a framework for litigating failure to train under the deliberate indifference standard. Actionable cases of inadequate training rest with the plaintiff proving the following factors. First, it must be established whether a training program is adequate to the tasks that the particular employee must perform, and if it is not, whether such inadequate training can justifiably be said to represent "city policy." Second, the identified deficiency must be directly related to ultimate injury. The failure to train must have been the cause of harm. Third, it is not necessary for a policy regarding training to be unconstitutional in order for liability to attach. A valid policy may be unconstitutionally applied, and when the training in how to apply the policy is deliberately indifferent, liability may attach. Fourth, in general, one incident of improper training will not result in liability. A pattern or history of problems or incidents that can be related to improper training will normally be the key to liability. Fifth, the focus of training must address regular and ongoing tasks that officers routinely face. The Court noted that the use of deadly force is one such area requiring regular training. The plaintiff must prove that these known needs were left unattended by the municipality. Finally, the degree of training required need only be adequate to address a particular matter. The Court acknowledged the need for a department to evaluate its needs and allocate appropriate resources, but rejected the idea that training must be the most modern available. The standard established by the Court clearly makes it more difficult for plaintiffs to prevail in a § 1983 lawsuit.

Application of Deliberate Indifference

Although the Court resolved the long-debated controversy about inadequate training issues, it also created many questions regarding how lower courts should interpret and apply the deliberate indifference standard. Questions pertaining to failure-to-train issues include: (1) What constitutes a policy of inadequate training? (2) Can a municipality be liable for the single act of an officer? (3) Will liability attach for an occasional officer mistake? (4) Who has the responsibility to train officers? and (5) Who determines whether the training was adequate?

Answers to these questions are far from clear, but cases can provide general trends in how courts have applied the deliberate indifference standard in claims of deficient training. The mere fact that an incident occurred and a constitutional right may be involved does not automatically indicate that there is a training deficiency. The failure to train must first be linked to some specific policy relative to the training. In order for supervisory liability to attach, the burden of proof rests with the plaintiff to show that the policy was the moving force behind the constitutional violation (*Polk County v. Dodson*, 1981). A policy exists only when a course of action is established by the official responsible for final policy with respect to the subject matter involved (*Pembaur v. City of Cincinnati*, 1986). Application of these two Supreme Court cases is illustrated in *Vineyard v. Murray County of Georgia* (1993). The plaintiff brought claims of excessive force, failure to train, and failure to supervise against the sheriff. The claims arose from several deputies beating a restrained arrestee in a hospital bed. The deputies beat him repeatedly on the head and chest. He sustained a broken jaw and other injuries. Applying *Canton* to the policy and training issues, the federal district court found that the sheriff was deliberately indifferent to the needs of the arrestee. The Eleventh Circuit Court of Appeals determined that the county had inadequate polices for training, supervision, and discipline, as well as inadequate procedures for following up on citizen complaints. The manner in which the sheriff investigated the incident evidenced a policy of deliberate indifference and a manual of policies and procedures did not exist. The plaintiff was awarded $175,000 in compensatory damages and $60,000 in punitive damages. The court determined, however, in *Robinson v. City of St. Charles* (1992), that in order to prevail in a policy/training claim for excessive force, the plaintiff must show that the city had notice that its police training was inadequate and that it deliberately chose not to remedy the situation.

Can training liability be imposed for actions stemming from a single incident? The general answer to this question is no, but with an exception (*Oklahoma City v. Tuttle*, 1985). The Supreme Court, deciding a case about the fatal shooting of an unarmed individual, gave a qualified ruling, holding that claims of failure to train and supervise stemming from a single unconstitutional activity is insufficient to impose liability unless it was caused by an existing unconstitutional municipal policy, which policy can be attributed to a municipal policymaker. This holding is important because it rejects liability based on a single incident, but allows for an exception: if the incident was caused by an existing, unconstitutional policy (del Carmen, 1991). The exception was applied by the Court in *Pembaur v. City of Cincinnati* (1986). The county prosecutor was the "official policymaker" and directed officers to make a warrantless, forceful entry into a house with axes. The deputies were attempting to arrest two doctors who failed to attend a grand jury hearing. The Court ruled that the City of Cincinnati could be held liable on one occasion for a Fourth Amendment violation, because the prosecutor's decision to direct officers to enter the house constituted official policy or custom.

Liability was imposed in a single incident of failure to train and supervise in *Atchinson v. District of Columbia* (1996). The plaintiff, who was carrying a machete, was shot by an officer after receiving nothing more than a warning to "freeze," adequately asserted a claim against the District of Columbia for inadequately training and supervising officers in the use of deadly force. The federal appeals court held that even a single incident of such use of force was sufficient to support the complaint of inadequate training and supervision.

Determining the adequacy of a training program can be difficult. In *Canton*, the Court did not specify the subject matter or the number of hours required for officers to attend. In an effort to avoid federalism and to avoid second-guessing municipal training programs, the Court took the position that training be afforded to officers in order to "respond to usual and recurring situations with which they must deal." In resolving this question, the Court focused on the training program in relation to the tasks that the particular officers must perform. "That a particular officer may be unsatisfactorily trained will not alone suffice to attach liability on the city, for the officer's shortcomings may have resulted from factors other than a faulty training program." According to the Court, liability will not attach for a sound program that has been negligently administered. Neither will it suffice to impose liability for an officer making a mistake or avoiding an accident because he should have received more or better training—"[a]dequately trained officers can make mistakes." Liability can only attach when the city's failure to train reflects deliberate indifference to the constitutional rights of citizens. The deficiency must be closely related to the ultimate injury. Training should be designed to correspond directly to the recurring tasks of police work (*Jones v. City of Chicago*, 1989).

The nature of the police function is such that in all responsibly managed police officers are required to undergo training prior to being assigned patrol work. The court used the topic of lethal force as an example to demonstrate the need for adequate training. In *Zuchel v. City and County of Denver, Colorado* (1993), the city was found to be deliberately indifferent in regard to providing adequate training in the use of deadly force. The training consisted of only a lecture and a film and did not include "live" shoot/don't shoot practice training. In *Houck v. City of Prairie Village, Kansas* (1996), however, failure to have a detailed training program on problems of taking suicidal or mentally disturbed police officers into custody was not deliberate indifference to a known problem. The chief was not liable for failing to take custody of a suicidal officer who fired his gun within his residence. While not a deadly force case, the court in *Dorman v. District of Columbia* (1989) held that the need for specific training in suicide prevention, beyond what the officers had received, was not so obvious that the city's policy in not providing it could be characterized as deliberate indifference.

The standard of review in failure-to-train litigation is deliberate indifference. When analyzing assertions of inadequate training, the court will determine three critical components: (1) whether a constitutional right was violated; (2) whether there was a failure to train or the training was inadequate; and (3) whether there was deliberate indifference to the need for training.

In *Griffith v. Coburn* (2005), a federal district court of Michigan examined the question of whether officers should receive additional training beyond academy training. Officers attempted to serve an arrest warrant on Arthur Partee and met resistance in his house. Partee had exhibited bizarre behavior at home, had a history of mental impairment, and his mother asked that the police take him into custody. At the house, the officers met resistance as they attempted to take control of Partee. Partee lunged off of a couch at the officers and struggled with them. During the struggle, Partee managed to unsnap one of the safety snaps on an officer's holster and began to pry on it. The officer placed him in a lateral vascular neck restraint for about two to three seconds and they fell to the floor. Partee became unresponsive and resuscitation efforts by emergency medical personnel on scene failed to revive him.

Partee's estate filed a § 1983 lawsuit against the officers for excessive force. A claim was also filed against the chief of police for being deliberately indifferent to the training needs of the officers who used the neck restraint. The court granted summary judgment to the officers, finding that the neck restraint was not excessive force. The court assessed the failure to train claim within the framework of two components: "(1) 'failure to provide adequate training in light of foreseeable consequences that could result from the lack of instruction'; and (2) 'failure to act in response to repeated complaints of constitutional violations by its officers.'" Documentation was presented that showed that the officers received more than adequate training in the Pressure Point Control Tactics (PPCT) lateral neck restraint. Such training was approved by the state of Michigan's police training standards council.

The court ruled that the plaintiff failed to show that the need for post-academy training on the neck restraint was so obvious that the police department would be acting with deliberate indifference if they failed to conduct further training. The court also noted that the plaintiff failed to show evidence that the chief inadequately trained his officers and that the department was on notice by complaints from the community that officers misused the neck restraint. Absent such evidence the court granted summary judgment to the chief, concluding that the chief was not on notice that the training was inadequate.

Status of Failure to Train Liability

What has been the impact of the *Canton* decision on police training? In answering this question, Ross (2000) conducted a 10-year analysis of 1,500 published § 1983 federal court decisions citing the administrator for failure to train. Case analysis revealed that 64 percent of the litigation involved municipal police departments, 29 percent involved county sheriff's departments, five percent involved state police agencies, and two percent involved transit authority police agencies. All 1,500 cases arose from police officer actions, followed by claims of inadequate training (100%), failure to supervise (45%), failure to discipline (30%), and failure to direct (25%). Analysis indicates that failure to train and failure to supervise were combined as managerial liability issues in 54 percent of the cases. For example, an officer may have decided to engage in a high-speed pursuit and, as a result, the fleeing suspect killed an innocent third party. The estate of the deceased filed a § 1983 claim against the officer for deciding to pursue, and as a secondary claim filed a failure-to-train action against the administrator.

Figure 7.2
Top Ten Categories in Police Training Litigation since *Canton*

Topic	Plaintiff Prevailed		Police Prevailed		Average Award	Average Atty Fee
	%	(#)	%	(#)		
Nonlethal Force Physical (55%) Baton (20%) Restraints (17%) Aerosols (6%) Taser (2%)	44	(99)	55	(126)	$351,219	$79,592
False Arrest/ **Detention (n=185)**	37	(69)	63	(116)	$155,100	$35,300
Search and Seizure Residence (44%) Personal (23%) Vehicle (19%) Strip (14%)	35	(60)	65	(110)	$148,000	$34,800
Failure to Protect	38	(60)	62	(100)	$185,000	$39,400
Detainee Suicide	37	(57)	63	(96)	$231,000	$73,600
Lethal Force	42	(64)	58	(88)	$1,212,567	$96,100
Emergency Vehicle	39	(57)	61	(88)	$1,389,789	$95,900
Medical Care	38	(52)	62	(86)	$472,789	$100,500
Police as Plaintiff	19	(19)	81	(81)	Not reported	Not reported
Other	16	(15)	84	(82)	$289,678	Not reported
Total	36	(552)	64	(973)	$492,794	$60,680

Figure 7.2 identifies the 10 most frequently litigated training categories. Police administrators prevailed in slightly less than two-thirds of the litigation, or a two-to-one ratio. Nonlethal force and lethal force (i.e., excessive force claims) combine to be the most litigated areas asserting a failure to train officers (25%). Seventy-five percent of allegations asserting inadequate training in nonlethal force cases pertain primarily to physical force techniques and the use of equipment. Five of the categories (50%) involve issues of citizen deaths or injuries (lethal and nonlethal force, detainee suicide, pursuits, and medical care issues). Four of the categories (40%) involved high compensatory awards to the plaintiffs (pursuits, lethal/nonlethal force, and medical care issues). Three of the categories (30%) pertain to potential officer safety issues (nonlethal/lethal force and pursuits).

The data show that the standard of deliberate indifference is a high hurdle for the plaintiff to overcome when asserting a training deficiency. Despite this, the plaintiffs prevailed in approximately one-third of the cases overall, and the average award was significant, amounting to more than

$450,000. Lethal force and emergency vehicle operations categories skewed the average award due to claims that stemmed from wrongful death lawsuits. Claims asserting the denial of medical care and non-lethal force also account for high average awards granted to the plaintiff. Attorney's fees averaged slightly more than $60,000.

Determining accurate award trends in police civil liability cases is problematic. These figures must be read with caution, because the courts do not document the award or the amount of attorney's fees assessed in every published case. Moreover, the figures do not reflect the cost or the time that officers, administrators, or counsel spent in preparing to defend or try the case. Therefore, these figures are only presented to show limited trends in these categories and to reveal categories in which higher awards are more likely to occur, should the plaintiff prevail.

Implications of Failure-to-Train Litigation

Each litigated category in Figure 7.2 represents the most fundamental and critical tasks that police officers routinely perform, yet deficiency in training is frequently asserted. The prevailing ratio indicates two important factors of the deliberate indifference standard. First, the standard is difficult for plaintiffs to establish. Second, a majority of police departments appear to be providing training and successfully defending these allegations in a significant number of cases. Despite the prevailing record, the potential for liability still exists as the following discussion of cases illustrates.

Lethal and Nonlethal Force

These two categories represent critical issues for police agencies and exhibit high-risk areas for liability. Further, both categories represent high awards granted to prevailing plaintiffs. Police administrators are encouraged to ensure that their use-of-force policies reflect the *Graham v. Connor* (1989) and *Tennessee v. Garner* (1985) decisions, and provide ongoing refresher training for all officers in competently using their firearms, empty-hand control techniques, restraints, other control equipment, and the constitutional limits of using force. These two cases provide the standards for examining claims of excessive force by police officers. In *Davis v. Mason County* (1991), a jury awarded four plaintiffs $528,000 in compensatory damages, $225,000 in punitive damages, and $323,559 in attorney's fees in an excessive force case involving four deputies. For approximately four months these deputies had illegally stopped, beaten, and illegally arrested citizens. It was discovered that the deputies had little or no training, and at least one deputy did not attend a police academy. The court determined that the county exhibited deliberate indifference to the training needs of the deputies in the constitutional limits of force. In *Bordanaro v. McLeod* (1989), the plaintiff was awarded $5.3 million for deliberate indifference due to a "practice of breaking down" doors without a warrant. A lack of continuing training after the academy was found to have risen to a level of deliberate indifference involving deadly force, searches and seizures, and pursuits. The court found that the department was "ill-prepared and ill-equipped to perform the obvious and recurring duties of police officers." The department was operating under policies established in 1951 and no supervisory training was provided. The court in *Walsweer v. Harris County* (1990) awarded $6.3 million to a man rendered paraplegic after he was shot five times by the police. The county was held liable for inadequately training officers in the use of deadly force and maintaining deficient policies regarding force. Conversely, in *Mateyko v. Felix* (1990), the court held that providing three to four hours of training in the use of a Taser was adequate, even if officers did not know its full physical effects.

Frequently a plaintiff will automatically assume that an unreasonable use of force verdict will support a claim of failure to train. Such a presumption is not automatic, as the courts generally use the following criteria to review claims of failure to train: (1) the training program was adequate for preparing the officers to perform the tasks they encounter; (2) the training program was adequate in addressing the subject matter under question; and (3) whether the inadequacies of a training program contributed to or actually caused the injury.

In *Ciminillo v. City of Cincinnati* (2006), such an issue was appealed to the Sixth Circuit Court of Appeals. A crowd attending a party moved the "party" to the street and many of the participants became rowdy, by shouting, setting fires, and throwing bottles at other nearby residents. Officers responded wearing riot gear and the rowdy party crowd began throwing bottles at them. The plaintiff, who was not participating with the crowd, attempted to leave the area by exiting through the backyard of a nearby house. The homeowner stopped him in the yard and threatened him with a bat. As the plaintiff was moving away from the yard, he claimed that he observed a kneeling police officer firing "bean bags" at the crowd and he approached the officer with his hands raised, in a non-threatening and compliant manner. Ciminillo claimed that the officer discharged a bean bag at him, striking him in the chin and chest while he was attempting to leave the area at the request of the officer. He claimed that he sustained injuries to the chin and chest (requiring stitches in his chin), bruised lungs, and permanent facial scars.

The officer who fired the bean bag had a different version of the incident. The officer claimed that he gave several orders for Ciminillo to stop, but he kept advancing toward him while he was in the act of throwing an unknown object in his direction. Ciminillo filed a § 1983 lawsuit, claiming that the officer used excessive force in violation of his Fourth and Fourteenth Amendment rights, and also filed state tort claims for assault and battery. He also filed a claim against the city of Cincinnati for failing to adequately train the officer.

The lower court granted summary judgment on behalf of the officer and the city, and the plaintiff appealed the decision. The appellate court addressed the issue of whether the plaintiff was seized and how that may affect the use of force. The court ruled that the use of a bean bag resulting in an injury equates to a seizure. The court reasoned that a seizure occurs when a person becomes the deliberate object of an officer's exertion of the use of force. Using the criteria established in *Graham v. Connor* (1989), the court found that Ciminillo was attempting to comply with the officer, approached him with his hands up, was not threatening the officer, and was not committing a crime. The court reversed summary judgment on behalf of the officer, determining that shooting a non-threatening person with a less-than-lethal device was unreasonable force.

The appellate court affirmed the lower court's ruling that the city did not fail to adequately train the officer. According to the court, the plaintiff failed to provide evidence consistent with the three previously mentioned criteria. The plaintiff failed to show that there was a connection between the injuries sustained and a failure to train officers or an inadequacy in the training program. Further, the court held that the plaintiff could not produce evidence that revealed that the use of bean bags had not been misused on past occurrences. Summary judgment for the city was affirmed.

Failure to Protect

The police have a duty to exercise reasonable care toward arrestees. This duty commences at the time of arrest and continues until release from custody. The Supreme Court, however, in *DeShaney v. Winnebago County Department of Social Services* (1989) held that police generally are not liable for failure to protect individuals from harm inflicted by third parties, but may be liable for an injury inflicted by law enforcement officials (del Carmen, 1991). An increasing number of actions have been successful when the lawsuit has proven that there was actual failure to protect, and when there are facts and circumstances that make the harm or injury that occurred different from a risk faced by the general public. The plaintiff may claim that he is different from the public in general and that the police had knowledge of him and his situation. Training of police officers in this area is a policy concern for administrators, because liability may attach for the city when a lawsuit is filed for failing to protect an arrestee from himself or from actions by officers. Potential training and policy issues in this area include equal protection concerns of racial bias under the Fourteenth Amendment, domestic violence situations, and discrimination violations under the Americans with Disabilities Act (ADA). In *Barber v. Guay* (1995), a mentally impaired arrestee prevailed in a deliberate indifference claim to training under the ADA when he alleged that the arresting deputy denied him proper police protection and fair treatment due to his psychological and alcohol problem. The city of Chicago was liable for failing to protect a wife from domestic violence at the hands of her husband, who was a police officer in the department (*Czajkowski v. City of Chicago*, 1993). The husband's partner was found liable because he failed to intervene and assisted the officer in attempting to cover up the abusive incident. It was determined that the department had a custom of failing to take action and was deliberately indifferent to officer training.

Emergency Vehicle Operations

Of the 10 most commonly litigated training areas, police vehicle operation is the most frequently performed police function. This study reveals that these lawsuits represent the highest awards granted to prevailing plaintiffs. Researchers have documented the need for policy development and ongoing training in operating the police vehicle in emergency situations (Alpert, 1997; Beckman, 1987; Falcone et al., 1994; Gallagher, 1989; NIJ, 1998). Legal allegations that plaintiffs frequently assert include being deliberately indifferent in training to policy concerns; decisionmaking to pursue or to terminate; the use of spikes, roadblocks, and ramming; failure to use emergency equipment; improper use of the vehicle in a risky environment; and wrongful deaths of citizens. Based on a review of more than 250 pursuit-type cases, Kappeler (1997) found that generally one factor alone is insufficient to establish a valid claim, but as the number of factors increases, so does the likelihood of liability.

Past case rulings reveal conflicting trends in court decisions. In *Frye v. Town of Akron* (1991), a passenger was killed after a high-speed pursuit involving a motorcycle. The court held that police pursuits may violate due process and that failure to train in the mechanics of hot pursuit can be characterized as "deliberate indifference." In *Fulkerson v. City of Lancaster* (1992), the court determined that there was no "obvious need" for specialized training in high-speed pursuits beyond what was given in the academy. The court found that a single incident was insufficient to impose liability in a pursuit case where the city had not developed policy, but rather allowed the officer to use his discretion whether to pursue or not (*Dismukes v. Hackathorn*, 1992). According to the court, the pursuit was not objectively unreasonable and there was no evidence that the department had a history of pursuits that resulted in damage or injury.

The Supreme Court in *County of Sacramento v. Lewis* (1998) established that the standard for reviewing police actions in pursuits is "shocks the conscience." A deputy with the Sacramento County Sheriff's Department engaged in a high-speed pursuit of two youths on a motorcycle, at speeds of more than 90 miles per hour. Smith violated the department's policy by operating his vehicle in excess of 80 miles an hour. The chase ended after the motorcycle tipped over and Smith skidded into the motorcycle, causing the death of Lewis, a passenger on the bike. The District Court granted summary judgment to Smith and the Ninth Circuit Court of Appeals reversed. The United States Supreme Court reviewed the case in order to determine what standard should be applied in police pursuit cases.

Rejecting the deliberate indifference standard, the Court determined that conduct that shocks the conscience in accordance with the Fourteenth Amendment's the proper standard to apply in police pursuit situations. The Court reasoned that in the circumstances of a high-speed chase aimed at apprehending a suspected offender, where unforeseen circumstances demand an instant judgment on the part of the officer who feels the pulls of competing obligations, only a purpose to cause harm unrelated to the legitimate object of arrest will satisfy the "shocks the conscience" test. In chases in which there is no intent to harm an offender physically or to worsen their legal plight there is no liability.

Since the *Lewis* decision, the lower courts have had the opportunity to review legal actions surrounding police pursuits and training. In failure-to-train claims, the courts apply the *Monell* and *Canton* decisions in determining administrative liability. Generally, the *Lewis* decision has made it extremely difficult for a plaintiff in prevail in failure-to-train claim as the plaintiff must first show that the named officer intended to harm the suspect in the pursuit, which rises to a level of "shocking to the conscience." For example, the defendants in *Philebaum v. Myers, Ridenour v. City of Portland, Oregon* (2006), *McCoy v. City of Monticello* (2005), *Sanders v. City of Union Springs et al.* (2005), *Herman v. City of Shannon, Mississippi* (2004), and *Grazier v. City of Philadelphia* (2003) were granted summary judgment. Each case involved a pursuit that ended either in an injury or death to the suspect and claims were filed against the officer for violating their constitutional rights and against departmental supervisors for failure to train. Regardless of the jurisdiction, the courts consistently have ruled that a plaintiff must first prove the *Lewis* test. The courts agree that the plaintiff must show that the officer engaged in the pursuit with the intent to cause physical harm to the plaintiff or worsen their legal plight. Failing to do so does not give rise to liability. Absent such evidence, claims of failure to train fall. The courts consistently hold that police training must be so obviously inadequate that it amounts to deliberate indifference to the constitutional rights of citizens and that the inadequacy was the "moving force" behind the alleged constitutional violation. There must be a direct link between a failure to train and the alleged injury. The courts have maintained that comprehensive policies and training should be provided for officers who engage in pursuits, but until a plaintiff can successfully overcome the *Lewis* test, failure-to-train claims will normally fail.

False Arrest/Unlawful Detention

Taking a person into custody, charging him or her with a crime, and detaining him or her is certainly a recurring circumstance for police officers. It occurs more than 14 million times per year (BJS, 1998). False arrest and detention can be the basis for liability under § 1983. Both are considered intentional torts and the individual is restrained or deprived of freedom without legal justification (del Carmen, 1991). The plaintiff may allege that the administrator failed to properly instruct officers in the laws of arrest and detention or that the department practiced a custom of allegedly arresting and detaining people. In *Clipper v. Takoma Park, Maryland* (1989), the city was found liable for inadequate training in an improper arrest coordinated by the lieutenant who was in charge of the detective bureau and by the department's training coordinator. The investigating officer did not receive training materials giving typical examples of arrests properly based on probable cause. The arrestee was mistakenly arrested for a bank robber, who was videotaped. The court held that this evidence met the deliberate indifference standard and the plaintiff was awarded $304,355. In *Tilson v. Forrest City Police Department* (1994), the city was not held liable for failing to train regarding detention of arrestees. The arrestee was in a county jail for 14 months without being formally charged with a crime. The mere fact that the chief knew the plaintiff had been arrested and that written procedures for conducting criminal investigations were lacking illustrated insufficient grounds for imposing liability. In *Rivas v. Freeman* (1991), the sheriff was found liable for inadequately training deputies and detention officers in the mechanics of arrest and detention. The plaintiff sued for wrongful detention because he was misidentified as a probation violator and detained for six days. He was awarded $100,000.

Medical Care

The Supreme Court has ruled that the police do not specifically owe a duty of medical care to an individual citizen, absent a "special relationship" (*City of Revere v. Massachusetts General Hospital*, 1983). The due process clause of the Fourteenth Amendment requires a government agency to provide medical care to people who have been injured while being apprehended by the police. This is frequently a major allegation in excessive force claims, pursuits, arrests of intoxicated or mentally impaired individuals, and injuries sustained while in detention. The plaintiff will likely assert that the government entity was deliberately indifferent to the needs of the arrestee and failed to properly train officers in summoning medical care, observing symptoms of medical or psychological distress, and how to properly respond to such situations.

This study revealed the third highest award granted to plaintiffs in this category. In *Burkhart v. Washington Metro Area Transit Authority* (1996), the plaintiff was awarded $109,000 in damages, based on a claim that the transit authority inadequately trained officers in how to respond to disabled patrons, particularly the hearing impaired. The court in *Vine v. County of Ingham* (1995) held that the police agencies were not deliberately indifferent to the medical needs of arrestees. An arrestee who was under the influence of methyl alcohol died while in police custody. At booking in the city lockup, the intake officer placed the detainee in an observation cell, because he was belligerent and had attempted suicide during past confinements. The detainee passed out on the floor and was visually checked by officers periodically. Nearly six hours later officers noticed he was unresponsive and found he had choked on his mucus vomit. He was transported to the hospital and later died. The court determined that because deputies had received academy training and in-service training, despite not rendering medical treatment at booking, the sheriff was immune from liability.

The court underscored the fact that the police agency had provided minimal training in responding to the medical needs of arrestees, such as first aid and when to summon medical assistance. The officers were not required to have detailed training in medical treatment.

Arrestee/Detainee Suicide

Suicides and attempted suicides of arrestees present a significant problem for criminal justice practitioners. There has been a proliferation of cases brought against agencies and millions of dollars awarded to plaintiffs during the past 25 years. These actions normally allege that the agency and its employees failed to take steps to prevent a suicide attempt or a suicide, and allegations of inadequate training are typical of such cases. Under § 1983, plaintiffs allege that the city violated the constitutional rights of the person to be free from self-injury, failure to protect, and frequently for deficient building and policies. In *Farmer v. Brennan* (1994), the Supreme Court held that deliberate indifference must be established in prisoner safety and health cases, based on a showing that the official was subjectively aware of the risk and made no effort to reduce it. This still places some responsibility on administrators to ensure minimal safeguards when placing arrestees in detention. Legal standards require that policies and training be reasonably adequate to address the particular subject or problem. The courts in *Wallace v. Estate of Davis* (1994, $1.4 million awarded), *Hare v. City of Corinth, Mississippi* (1994), *Bragado v. City of Zion Police Department* (1993), *Elliot v. Chesire County* (1991), *Burns v. City of Galveston* (1990), and *Simmons v. City of Philadelphia* (1991) found the government entity to be deliberately indifferent to training methods, screening procedures, and the protection of suicidal arrestees. Each case dealt with deficiencies in minimum training guidelines and policies surrounding the foreseeable needs of arrestees exhibiting intoxication, mental impairment, and the stress associated with detention.

In *Harvey v. County of Ward* (2005), an arrestee committed suicide in the jail after he accumulated some of his medications. The decedent's estate claimed that jail officers had information (provided by the detainee's wife) that he was storing his medication so that he could later commit suicide. The family also filed a claim against the sheriff for failing to train his officers and implement policies that would lessen the likelihood of detainee suicide.

The court granted summary judgment for the sheriff and the officers in the absence of any evidence that either of them were aware of a conversation with the detainee's wife regarding his medication. The court also found that the sheriff's suicide prevention policy was reasonable and that the county was not deliberately indifferent to training its officers in suicide awareness. The fact that the policy had not been updated recently, and that the jail was not accredited by the American Correctional Association, did not alter the result when the policy contained a detailed listing of factors for the identification of possibly suicidal prisoners, procedures for screening detainees, and required that officers receive ongoing training in suicide intervention.

Compare, however, *Howard v. City of Atmore* (2004). A detainee committed suicide in a city lockup and his sister filed a civil lawsuit claiming that the officer failed to follow his training and policy in making security checks. The rules and policies of the facility required officers to make security checks twice an hour. Evidence revealed that the officer had not followed his training and policy, which led to the detainee's death. The court ruled that the officer was not entitled to summary judgment and liability attached. The chief of police however, was granted immunity by the court, as he had developed and implemented procedures, as well as training on the procedures concerning the identification and handling of potentially suicidal detainees.

Search and Seizure

Police officers frequently search and seize citizens' vehicles, property, dwellings, and businesses, as well as their persons. Plaintiffs alleging that the police improperly conducted a search and improperly seized property are more likely to file a lawsuit under § 1983 because they pertain to a violation of Fourth Amendment rights. Police administrators must ensure that officers routinely receive updated training that is commensurate with the law. A $6.1 million judgment was granted to the plaintiff in *Doe v. Calumet City* (1990) because the officers strip-searched females during traffic and misdemeanor arrests without probable cause. The city had adopted a policy that prohibited such searches, but failed to distribute it to officers and failed to conduct training explaining the policy. In *Hufford v. Rodgers* (1990), a sheriff was held liable for inadequate training and supervision of a deputy who seized a child from a mother pursuant to papers supplied by her former husband erroneously implying that he had a right to the child. The city of North Reading, Massachusetts, was held not deliberately indifferent to the rights of the plaintiff during a personal search in *Swain v. Spinney* (1997). During booking at the lockup, the plaintiff was strip-searched for possible drug possession and claimed emotional trauma after her eventual release. The city produced a policy and training manual developed by a statewide risk management group specifying when strip searches are warranted. The city had also provided training to officers. The plaintiff in *Wall v. Gwinnett County* (1993) settled out of court for $9.8 million relating to six site searches of his business and residence. More than 100 boxes of financial records were seized through the searches. The suit claimed that the search warrants were obtained by misrepresentation and that the searches were intended to damage the plaintiff's business. Allegations of inadequate training/supervision and emotional distress emerged.

The legality of a search poses critical concerns for police officers, and new cases are frequently decided. Like many other tasks, this requires administrators to conduct ongoing training. A case in point is the Supreme Court's decision in *Wyoming v. Houghton* (1999), which involved the search of a motor vehicle passenger's purse. The Court analyzed the situation as if the purse were a container in the car. The Court determined that when officers have probable cause to search a car, they may inspect a passenger's belongings found in the car if the container could conceal the object of the search.

Officer as Plaintiff

An emerging area of litigation is police officers as plaintiffs. They are filing claims against citizens for injuries or wrongs committed against them and the department for failing to train. In *Carlson v. City of Tonawanda* (1995), the deceased officer's estate prevailed when the deputy was fatally shot attempting to arrest a suspect. The estate sued the city on the basis of deficient policies and regulations and inadequate training policies, which created additional risks to those ordinarily faced by officers arresting a suspect. The court ruled in *Darrow v. Schumacher* (1993) that the mere failure to adopt a special training policy for special events could not be the basis of liability when there was no showing that any failure was the direct cause of an injury. The court held in *McCormick v. City of New York* (1991) that the city's failure to provide officers with a newer type of vest could not make the city liable for the shooting death of the officer, nor could a claim of failure to train be valid. In *Collins v. City of Harker Heights, Texas* (1992), the court ruled that federal civil rights law does not provide a remedy for a municipal employee fatally injured during employment because of the city's customary failure to train or warn its employees to know about hazards in the workplace.

Over the years, academy and in-service training instructors have moved to using more scenario-based training, in response to the Supreme Court's decisions for criminal justice agencies to provide realistic training. As such, the courts have begun accepting claims that allege an unsafe training environment. In *Cole v. State of Louisiana Department of Public Safety and Corrections* (2002), the court found in favor of a plaintiff correctional officer who sustained injuries requiring extensive hospitalization and treatment during an in-service scenario-based training exercise portraying a prison disturbance. The simulation training was designed for officers to role-play riotous prisoners so that the tactical unit of the prison could practice using techniques, equipment, and tactics to quell and control such a disturbance in the future. The simulation training called for five exercises and the morning exercises were conducted without incident. In the morning exercises, protective gear was worn by all personnel and those playing the role of officers used batons wrapped in foam. In the afternoon, Cole and other officers assumed the role of angry prisoners. The officers role-playing as "prisoners" wore helmets and the "officers" used unpadded batons. At trial, Cole testified that he had never participated in this type of role-play exercise in his previous seven years of employment and since being a member of the tactical unit. He stated that the training exercise turned into a "free for all." He reported that someone grabbed him and started hitting him on his left arm with full force several times. He yelled out "red," the code word which was supposed to stop the activity, but he continued to be struck with the unpadded batons. At some point the exercise was stopped and Cole was transported to a hospital. He sustained numerous injuries from being struck with the baton six times and being tackled to the ground, including a serious head injury resulting in brain damage, and general injuries to his neck, left shoulder, arm, and back.

Cole filed a lawsuit claiming that his injuries were sustained from an intentional tort of battery resulting from an unsafe training exercise conducted by his employer. At trial, a video was shown of the simulated training exercise. Photographs of Cole's injuries were also shown. The video showed that unpadded batons were used and that the helmet Cole wore came off while he was being struck. Administrators in charge of the training testified that tactical training is very physical, that officers could reasonably expect to get scuffed up and might incur bruises, but they would not sustain significant injuries. They also testified that they "try to avoid any significant injuries to the extent they can, but it is just a physical type of training."

After weighing the evidence and testimony, the trial court found that Cole had established that the Department of Corrections was liable for his injuries and awarded him $1.8 million, including $675,000 in general damages, $175,000 in future medical damages, $914,390 in lost wages, and $105,000 for loss of consortium to his family. The Department appealed the case and the Louisiana Supreme Court upheld the finding. The court held that striking someone with an unpadded baton is harmful or offensive conduct intending harm to result from such contact, and that Cole met the elements of proving an intentional tort. Further, the Court ruled that there was overwhelming evidence that the force used in the training was "unnecessary and unanticipated" in order to complete the goals of the training exercise. The Court upheld the damages awarded by the lower courts but reduced a portion of the medical compensation amount, without specification.

In *Hayes v. University of Southern Mississippi and Ted Socha* (2003), the court took occasion to assess the safety of training at a police academy. Hayes attended academy training in the Police Corps Academy at the University of Mississippi. The program was started by the United States Congress and gave oversight to the Department of Justice. During the fourth day of training during a 22-week course, Hayes participated in a mandated realistic, scenario-based training exercise that used various safety precautions. The exercise was performed in the gym on padded mats and the role-players as well as the training cadet officers wore protective gear, including headgear, mouthpiece, knee and leg protection, and groin protectors. Further, there were four academy personnel on-site, including a safety instructor who would oversee the exercise and stop it at the end of two minutes or if a problem occurred. The goal of the exercise was to assess the candidate's response to an unexpected physical reaction from a suspect who the candidate was questioning about suspicious behavior. The role-player was trained in what to do, what to say, and how far to take the scenario. During the exercise, Hayes was forced to the mat and rolled on her knee, sustaining an injury. The safety instructor immediately stopped the training, allowed Hayes to catch her breath, and escorted her off the mat. The instructor provided remedial medical attention to Hayes and then transported her to the hospital where she received treatment for an injured tendon in her knee. She returned to the academy and a month later, while completing a mandated test, was observed to be cheating by an instructor. After an investigation she was allowed to submit a letter of resignation. She filed a lawsuit claiming that the academy was indifferent in planning and operating an unsafe training exercise with unsafe conditions, assault, and delayed medical care, which directly led to her knee injuries. She requested payment of damages, compensation of medical bills which amounted to $43,000, and reinstatement into the academy.

At trial, academy personnel testified that the training scenario was planned out in advance and safety measures were implemented. As soon as an injury was observed the exercise was discontinued, and medical care was provided at the academy and at the hospital. The academy paid for the medical treatment at the hospital. An expert witness for the academy testified that the training exercise was properly planned and performed like other scenario-based training used across the United States and agreed that proper safety measures were in place and followed by academy instructors. The court agreed with the defendants and found the purpose of the training exercise was appropriate for the circumstances and in accordance with the Police Corps Academies and that the exercise was conducted with the degree of care ordinarily and customarily exercised in its performance.

The issue of an instructor providing safe and proper training was addressed in *Hamilton v. Martinelli & Associates* (2004). The plaintiff was a probation officer and her duties required her to restrain violent youthful offenders and that she receive commensurate subject control training. She was required to wear a uniform and carry pepper spray. During mandatory training, certified by the State Board of Corrections Standards and Training Commission, she sustained injuries to her neck and back while performing a physical control technique. She sued the instructor for negligence and an intentional tort. As a result of the injuries, she was not able to perform the job as a probation officer or police officer.

The lower court ruled against Hamilton, concluding that the doctrine of primary assumption of the risk barred her claim, and granted summary judgment to the instructor. She appealed and the appellate court affirmed. The appellate court concluded that Hamilton assumed the risk of her injuries in the training course. The court dismissed the fact that the instructor failed to provide a written disclaimer warning or consent form to students at the beginning of the training. The instructor did ask each participate to identify prior injuries and sensitive areas of their bodies by placing silver tape on the identified areas before the class started. The instructor also demonstrated the techniques to the participants before they practiced them. The court noted that this certified training enabled her to perform her employment duties and that by participating in an employer-required training course, she assumed the risk that she would be injured while attending training to restrain a violent youthful offender. The court finally concluded that she failed to offer evidence that the instructor exceeded the boundaries of the normal risks associated with this type of training.

Emerging Topics

Case analysis reveals additional areas that appear to be emerging as training concerns for administrators. Police officers are frequently asked to respond or to intervene with individuals suffering from alcohol and drug dependence or mental illness. A litigation trend has emerged as plaintiffs or estates of deceased individuals assert that the police responded improperly due to policy and training deficiencies. Intervention with this special needs population can heighten the liability risk for the officer and the local government. In *Young v. City of Atlanta* (1995), the court found the city liable for inadequately training officers in the city lockup to recognize arrestees with mental problems and dispensing prescribed medication during detention. In *Russo v. City of Cincinnati* (1992), the city was held liable for failing to train officers in how to respond to "disturbed individuals." Officers shot and killed a schizophrenic man who was in possession of two knives when he charged at them. An investigation revealed that the training of new and in-service officers was virtually nonexistent regarding the handling of mentally disturbed individuals. The court held the chief liable in *Roy v. Inhabitants of Lewiston* (1994) on the grounds that he failed to adequately train officers in nonlethal alternatives for subduing dangerous but intoxicated persons.

Issues of custodial deaths after a violent struggle and restraint with individuals under the influence of a chemical substance or suffering from mental impairment are emerging as a training concern, as the courts have recognized that these interventions occur with some frequency for police officers (*Brown v. Gray*, 2000). In the cases of *Cruz v. City of Laramie, Wyoming* (2001), *Johnson v. City of Cincinnati* (1999), *Gutierrez v. City of San Antonio et al.* (1998), *Kinneer v. Gall* (1996), *Animashaun v. O'Donnell* (1995), and *Elmes v. Hart* (1994), officers were forced to restrain highly combative individuals who were under high levels of intoxicants or were exhibiting signs of psychosis. After restraint, the subject suddenly died in police custody. The government entities were all found liable for inadequate policies and training in directing officers in how to respond to, restrain, and provide medical care to arrestees. Conversely, no liability attached in *Harris v. District of Columbia* (1991), *Estate of Phillips v. City of Milwaukee* (1996), *Cottrell v. Caldwell* (1996), *Melendez v. Howard County Government* (1997), *Guseman v. Martinez* (1998), and *Young v. City of Mount Ranier* (2001) for claims of inadequate policy or training in the restraint of intoxicated or mentally impaired individuals. All of these entities had provided policy direction and training for their officers in how to properly intervene and control such persons.

In *Lewis v. Board of Sedgwick County Commissioners* (2001), a detainee brought an action against the county alleging that jail officers used excessive force against him and that the county failed to adequately train its officers. The detainee became disruptive and detention officers used pressure point control tactics to control and subdue him, and then secured him in a restraint chair. The detainee alleged that such use of force violated his due process rights. A jury returned a verdict in favor of the detainee and awarded him $500,000 and the county requested a new trial or judgment as a matter of law. The court agreed and found that there was no evidence that the officers used excessive force or that the county was deliberately indifferent to the training needs of their officers. The court held that the county provided training on use-of-force techniques at the correctional academy and on the job. The county provided a training manual and policies outlining their force techniques and under what circumstances they authorized these techniques. The court noted that the county had encountered only 22 complaints of excessive force in its jail from approximately 90,000 detainees who were admitted into the jail.

Contrast, however, the decision in *Swans v. City of Lansing* (1998). After assaulting an arresting officer and assaulting a sergeant in the detention facility, a violent schizophrenic arrestee was "maximally" restrained and placed in a cell for observation. The arrestee unexpectedly died in custody. The estate filed suit and claimed a failure on the part of the police chief to train officers in the proper use of restraints. The jury found in favor of the plaintiff. The judge noted a policy and custom of using maximum restraint and that the officers were not trained regarding the manufacturers' warnings about the dangers of using the restraint system. The estate was awarded $12.9 million and the city later settled for $10 million. This area and the many variables associated with it, such as issues of force, restraints, responding to special needs populations, medical/psychological care, and transportation concerns, suggest considerations for training and potential policy revision.

An emerging trend in failure to train claims directed at criminal justice agencies are allegations that question how officers have been trained to respond to the mentally impaired. Police response to the mentally ill has been an ongoing complex societal issue since the 1970s, due to the closing of many mental health facilities and the increased usage of antipsychotic medications. In some communities, police contact with the mentally impaired may be increasing, necessitating varying response strategies and training. Plaintiffs' attorneys have begun to bring § 1983 actions against police departments based on the Americans with Disabilities Act (ADA, 1990). Title II § 12132 of the ADA provides that "no qualified individual with a disability shall, by reason or such disability, be excluded, or be subjected to discrimination by any such entity." In passing the Act, Congress's main purpose was to eliminate discrimination against individuals with disabilities. The Act applies to governmental entities such as criminal justice agencies, and it guarantees disabled persons full access to all of the "services, programs, or activities of a public entity." The Act applies to "all" core functions of government, including the lawful exercise of police powers, including the proper use of force by officers acting under color of law. The ADA is a remedial statute, designed to eliminate discrimination against the disabled in all facets in society. The question emerges as to whether police administrators have enacted policies and training that prepare their officers to respond to the mentally impaired or other disabled persons in accordance with the ADA.

This question was addressed in *Schorr v. Borough of Lemoyne, Pennsylvania* (2003). Schorr had been diagnosed with bipolar disorder. His condition deteriorated and his family was granted a request for an involuntary commitment order under the Pennsylvania Mental Health Procedures Act. A crisis intervention worker of the hospital issued the order and requested that the police assist in executing the commitment order. Two officers responded, placed him custody, and transported him to the hospital. He was placed in a "high security room" to wait for an evaluation. He escaped from the hospital when a crisis intervention worker entered the room. Schorr fled to his apartment and at the request of the family, two officers responded. A violent confrontation occurred and Schorr was shot and killed by one of the responding officers. The family filed a § 1983 lawsuit, claiming excessive force in violation of the Fourth Amendment. They also filed allegations of unconstitutional policies and procedures for dealing with mentally ill persons and failing to train officers to properly respond to the mentally ill under the provisions of the ADA. The District Court granted judgment in favor of the plaintiffs. The court reasoned that while the ADA does not apply to "on the street exigent circumstances decisions" facing the safety of officers or others, it does apply to claims of failure to train. The court ruled that the ADA applies in cases in which the agency failed to properly train their officers in properly responding to situations involving the mentally impaired. The court determined that non-compliance with the requirements of the ADA occurred well before the encounter with Schorr. Such a failure occurred when the policymakers of the department failed to institute policies to accommodate disabled individuals such as Schorr by giving officers the tools and resources to handle the situation peacefully.

While not binding on other federal court jurisdictions, this decision is instructive. In light of the *Schorr* decision, police administrators should review their procedures and revise them accordingly and provide their officers with appropriate training when interacting with disabled persons. Persons with disabilities can include a number of conditions and such procedures should be established to properly address the requirements. In *Miami-Dade County v. Walker* (2002), the county successfully defended such a claim. Officers attempted to arrest Walker, who had been diagnosed with schizophrenia. Walker was seriously injured in a violent struggle with the officers and the family filed a § 1983 lawsuit alleging that the county failed to train its officers. The court granted summary judgment to the county, holding that it did provide training for its officers as outlined in its policies and in a training document titled *How to Handle the Mentally Ill*. The court concluded that the county was not deliberately indifferent to the rights of the mentally ill.

Claims for failing to properly train police officers in properly responding to the mentally impaired were lodged against the chief in *Estate of Sowards v City of Trenton* (2005). Neighbors of Sowards saw him threaten another man with a knife and called the police. Sowards was diagnosed with paranoia schizophrenia but the responding officers were unaware of this fact. After speaking with the victim, two officers went to Sowards' apartment door, but Sowards refused to open it. He began yelling and cursing the officers, informing them that he had a surprise for them. The officers summoned back-up and a corporal and other officers responded. Unable to persuade Sowards to exit the apartment after some time, the corporal decided to use force. The corporal did not have a warrant, nor did he know that the occupant in the apartment was indeed Sowards, or whether he possessed a weapon. The officers kicked the door and dislodged it about a foot. The officers observed the barrel of a gun pointed at them and one officer yelled "gun." The officers dove for cover and called for an ambulance. Simultaneously, one officer began firing at Sowards through the door and the corporal also began firing. Other officers began firing and 39 rounds were fired in total. The Special Response Team also responded and the team entered the apartment and found Sowards dead on the floor. An investigation was performed and it was discovered that Sowards had not fired any rounds.

The estate filed a § 1983 lawsuit under the Fourth and Fourteenth Amendments, claiming excessive force, entering the apartment without a warrant, and also sued the city for failing to adequately train the officers on handling a barricaded gunman/hostage situation and failing to train officers to properly respond to the mentally impaired. The district court granted summary judgment and the Sixth Circuit Court of Appeals affirmed. The appellate court concluded that the officers' use of force was consistent with criteria set forth in the *Graham* decision and that entry into the apartment was necessary given the totality of circumstances, despite the outcome and that Sowards suffered from a mental illness. The court also ruled that the training of the officers was not the proximate cause of the shooting or the entry into the apartment, and summary judgment was also granted on claims of failure to train in responding to persons with a mental illness, as the officers had received such training.

Failure to Train in Corrections

Lawsuits alleging a constitutional injury resulting from a department's policy of failing to provide training to correctional employees are common. Prior to the *Canton* decision, several cases ordered jail and prison administrators to train their personnel or improve their training programs, *Jones v. Wittenburg* (1971), *Miller v. Carson* (1975), and *Owens v. Haas* (1979). In *Owens,* the Second Circuit Court of Appeals held that while a county may not be liable for merely failing to train employees, it could be liable if its failure was so severe as to reach the level of gross negligence or deliberate indifference. In *Hays v. Jefferson County* (1982), the Sixth Circuit Court of Appeals ruled that a supervisor may be held liable "only where there is essentially a complete failure to train. . . . or training was so reckless or grossly negligent that future misconduct is almost inevitable, or would be characterized as substantially certain to result."

Since *Canton,* several correctional administrators have been found liable in lawsuits alleging a failure to train. Using the deliberate indifference standard, a federal district court in *Coleman v. Wilson* (1995) determined that custodial staff were inadequately trained in signs and symptoms of mental illness, which supported allegations that disciplinary and behavior control measures were used inappropriately against mentally ill prisoners. The three-hour training course attended by all new officers and additional in-service training at the institutional level was insufficient to prevent some officers from using punitive measures to control prisoners' behavior without regard to cause of the behavior.

The Ninth Circuit Court of Appeals ruled in favor of prisoners in *Madrid v. Gomez* (1995) on several issues, including failure to train, excessive force, constitutionally inadequate mental health services, and deficient medical care. The court held that staffing levels were insufficient, training and supervision of medical staff were almost nonexistent, and screening for communicable diseases was poorly implemented. Prisoners frequently experienced significant delays in receiving treatment, there were no protocols or training programs dealing with emergencies or trauma, and there were no procedures for managing chronic illness. Prisoners established prison administrators' deliberate indifference, showing that they knew that unnecessary and grossly excessive force was routinely being used against prisoners by officers and that these practices posed a substantial risk of harm to prisoners. The court also held that prison officials had actual subjective knowledge that conditions of isolation presented a substantial excessive risk of harm for mentally ill and other vulnerable prisoners and that the officials acted wantonly in violation of the Eighth Amendment.

Prison officials were found liable in *Gilbert v. Selsky* (1994) when they failed to train hearing officers in prison disciplinary proceedings. The district court found that prison supervisory personnel were personally involved with violations of prisoners' constitutional rights.

Conducting regular training of correctional personnel and fully documenting that training can assist in defending against allegations of inadequate training. In *Vine v. County of Ingham* (1995), the district court held that the sheriff and the county were not deliberately indifferent to a prisoner who died in their custody after consuming methyl alcohol prior to arrest. The court ruled that the sheriff had provided the necessary training to his officers commensurate with state law, and they had also received substantial in-service training. The court noted that such claims would apply only if the conduct represents usual or recurring situations officers must deal with.

Prison officials successfully defended a failure to train claim in *Tucker v. Evans* (2002). A prisoner was attacked and killed by a fellow prisoner. The estate of the deceased prisoner brought a § 1983 action, claiming that prison officers failed to protect the prisoner and that they failed to properly train correctional officers. The district court denied summary judgment and on appeal the appellate court reversed the decision. The court reasoned that correctional officers had no prior warning that the prisoner was at risk because he did not know about an argument between the two prisoners. The court found that correctional officials did not show callous indifference to the prisoner and were entitled to qualified immunity because they did not violate the Eighth Amendment by failing to train their officers. According to the court, correctional officials provided officers with six weeks' training at the state's correctional academy and they also provided subsequent on-the-job training.

In some failure-to-train claims, the plaintiff has attempted to hold the governmental entity to national standards developed by associations regarding suggestions for training. In *Smith v. Board of County Commissioners of County of Lyon* (2002), county officials successfully defended such a claim. A county jail detainee brought a § 1983 lawsuit, claiming under the Eighth Amendment that he failed to receive adequate medical care for a spinal cord injury that he sustained during a fall at the jail. He also claimed that officials had failed to adequately train correctional officers. The detainee alleged that officers failed to provide treatment for his injuries and failed to provide clean bedding and clothing to him as he suffered from incontinence on five occasions.

The court granted summary judgment for the officers as they presented evidence that once they were aware that the detainee required medical attention they immediately took him to the jail medical unit for treatment. The detainee alleged that there were systemic and gross deficiencies in training detention officers. He claimed that county officials failed to follow certain national training standards, but failed to show that the county had any duty to follow the standards. The court granted summary judgment for the county on the training claims as well, holding that the minimum standards for the operation of county jails are established in state law, rather than by national standards.

Summary

Case review reveals that deliberate indifference is a difficult standard for plaintiffs to establish in asserting claims of inadequate training. The trends and the margin for winning civil lawsuits by the police illustrate this point. As several case examples have shown, police administrators should note specific training categories that may apply to their respective departments. Administrators are encouraged to review the following recommendations in an effort to shore up potential agency deficiencies to insulate the agency, supervisors, and officers from civil liability.

First, each administrator should conduct an internal assessment of routine and recurring tasks that officers and supervisors perform. Incident reports, calls for service, citizen/prisoner complaints, disciplinary actions, and changes in job requirements spanning a three-year period should be assessed based on the criticality and frequency of the activity. As changes in the law affect job functions, appropriate training should be developed. Based on this assessment, regularly scheduled training should be provided to all officers and supervisors in those activities. At a minimum, each category identified in this study should be a priority addressed on a recurring basis.

Second, once a training assessment has been finalized, administrators are encouraged to revise the policies and procedures that parallel training topics. For example, the use-of-force policy should be reviewed annually and revised to accompany the training. As use-of-force laws and authorized restraint techniques and equipment change, training that addresses the policy change should be performed. Moreover, a policy of annual/biannual training that outlines the topics to be covered and by what time interval the training will be conducted should be established by the administrator. It is recommended that training in high-liability areas requiring physical skills and competency be provided on an annual basis. Minimally, this would include lethal and nonlethal force (and equipment), emergency vehicle operations, arrest, and search and seizure laws. Officers should be provided with realistic, incident-based training in these areas. Training for officers in their constitutional requirements in these high-liability areas is also suggested. In the past 30 years, search and seizure laws and laws of arrest have been most likely to change. This affects officers' and supervisors' Fourth Amendment duties; therefore, annual training is recommended in these areas. Administrators are encouraged to provide training that comports with the standards as specified by the training and standards council for their respective states. Correctional administrators should likewise address training issues surrounding the First, Fourth, Eighth, and Fourteenth Amendments.

Third, to avert future failure-to-train liability and to maintain occupational professionalism, supervisory training should be instituted. This should include pre- and post-promotion training, conducted at least biannually, concentrating on supervisory duties and including policy interpretation, implementation, and enforcement, as well as performance evaluation of subordinates. Supervisors should also receive regular training that emphasizes managerial responsibilities in risk management and the reduction of administrative liability. A commitment to ongoing training for supervisors is essential for the efficient operation of the department.

Fourth, it is critical that all training be documented and accurate training records be maintained. Several computer programs have been designed to track training, and administrators should use the programs that are appropriate for their needs. Training records for each officer and administrator should be maintained and inspected at least twice a year to ensure their completeness. Administrators should monitor and evaluate current and future training needs annually. It is also recommended that police administrators review their Field Training Officer (FTO) program in light of the research findings. Training scenarios for FTOs could be developed from these high-liability areas, placing the new officer in positions in which he or she will be evaluated. This would be most beneficial in reinforcing appropriate decisionmaking and future behavior. Administrators are encouraged to enlarge their roll-call training with documentation and consider providing training through teleconferencing, interactive computer-based training, and training available via the Internet.

Scenario-based training has become popular with many criminal justice departments as well as training academies. Such training frequently utilizes contextual learning components. Contextualization is a style of adult learning that seeks to tie in new information with existing knowledge and real-life situations. It acknowledges that skills and knowledge are integrated into actual field applications. Using such training methodologies underscores the central component in the *Canton* decision, which addressed providing "realistic" training for officers. As agencies provide more scenario-based training, they should ensure that the scenarios are designed to meet the types of encounters that officers routinely face, that the scenarios are scripted out in advance, that all role-players are pre-trained, and that measures are taken to reduce the risk of injury to all participants, provide safety equipment for all participants, video tape the training, and thoroughly document the training. Such training can assist in defending the next allegation of failing to train.

Section 12132 under the Americans with Disabilities Act is emerging as component of legal actions filed against the criminal justice administrator. The criminal justice agency's response to the mentally ill should be coordinated with professionals from the courts, mental health, police, and detention facilities in order to provide a comprehensive approach to addressing the associated societal issues. Administrators should develop and/or revise policies and procedures, and provide training to officers consistent with state standards. This will go a long way toward defending allegations that the department was deliberately indifferent to the needs of the mentally impaired.

Since the *Canton* decision, police and correctional personnel have prevailed in a majority of civil lawsuits, and continued strides are being made toward providing regular training for police personnel. Administrators must continue to maintain the commitment to providing and expanding regular training in order to avert future lawsuits alleging inadequate training.

References

Alpert, G.P. (1997). "Pursuit Driving: Planning Policies and Action from Agency, Officer, and Public Information." *Police Forum* 7:1-12.

Barrineau, H.E. (1994). *Civil Liability in Criminal Justice*, Second Edition. Cincinnati, OH: Anderson Publishing Co.

Beckman, E. (1987). "Identifying Issues in Police Pursuits: The First Research Findings." *Police Chief* (July):57-63.

Bureau of Justice Statistics (1998). *Sourcebook of Criminal Justice Statistics—1998*. Washington, DC: U.S. Department of Justice.

del Carmen, R.V. (1987). *Criminal Procedure for Law Enforcement Personnel*. Monterey, CA: Brooks/Cole.

————— (1991). *Civil Liabilities in American Policing: A Text for Law Enforcement Personnel*. Monterey, CA: Brady.

Falcone, D.N., M.T. Charles & E. Wells (1994). "A Study of Pursuits in Illinois." *The Police Chief* (July):59-64.

Flink, W.L. (1997). *1997 Executive Summary of the Sourcebook*. Phoenix, AZ: International Association of Directors of Law Enforcement Standards and Training.

Gallagher, G.P. (1989). "Managing the Risks of Police Pursuits." *Governmental Risk Management Reports* (December):1-6.

————— (1990). "Risk Management and Police Administrators." *The Police Chief* 57:18-29.

Kappeler, V.E. (1997). *Critical Issues in Police Civil Liability,* Second Edition. Prospect Heights, IL: Waveland Press, Inc.

National Institute of Justice (1998). *Pursuit Management Task Force.* Washington, DC: U.S. Department of Justice.

Plitt, E.A. (1997). "Failure to Train Liability." *Americans for Effective Law Enforcement Police Civil Liability Manual.* Chicago, IL: AELE.

Ross, D.L. (2000). "Emerging Trends in Police Failure to Train Liability." *Policing: An International Journal of Police Strategies and Management* 23:169-193.

Silver, I. (1996). *Police Civil Liability.* New York, NY: Matthew Bender & Co.

Staff, H. (1990). "*Canton v. Harris* Determines Standard for Training Liability Cases." *The Police Chief* 57:37.

Vaughn, M.S. & L.F. Coomes (1995). "The Liability of Moonlighting: Are Police Officers Employed as Security Guards Acting Under Color of Law?" *Police Liability Review* 6:6-9.

Vaughn, M.S. & R.V. del Carmen (1995). "Civil Liability Against Prison Officials for Inmate-on-Inmate Assault: Where Are We and Where Have We Been?" *Prison Journal* 75:69-89.

Cases Cited

Atchinson v. District of Columbia, 73 F.3d 418 (D.C. Cir. 1996)

Animashaun v. O'Donnell, 1995 U.S. Dist. LEXIS 2074 (N.D. Ill.)

Barber v. Guay, 910 F. Supp. 790 (D. Md. 1995)

Bordanaro v. McLeod, 871 F.2d 1151 (1st Cir. 1989)

Bragado v. City of Zion Police Department, 839 F. Supp. 551 (N.D. Ill. 1993)

Brown v. Gray, 227 F.3d 1278 (10th Cir. 2000)

Burkhart v. Washington Metro Area Transit Authority, 11196 Dist. Lexis 1875 D.D.C. (1996)

Burns v. City of Galveston, 905 F.2d 100 (5th Cir. 1990)

Carlson v. City of Tonawanda, 635 N.Y.S.2d 365 (A.D. 1995)

Ciminillo v. City of Cincinnati, 434 F.3d 461 (6th Cir. 2006)

City of Canton v. Harris, 489 U.S. 378 (1989)

City of Oklahoma City v. Tuttle, 471 U.S. 808 (1985)

City of Revere v. Massachusetts General Hospital, 463 U.S. 239 (1983)

Clipper v. Takoma Park, Maryland, 876 F.2d 17 (4th Cir. 1989)

Cole v. State of Louisiana, Department of Public Safety and Corrections, 825 So. 2d 1134 (La. 2002)

Coleman v. Wilson, 912 F. Supp. 1282 (E.D. Cal. 1995)

Collins v. City of Harker Heights, Texas, 503 U.S. 115 (1992)

Cottrell v. Caldwell, 85 F.3d 1480 (11th Cir. 1996)

County of Sacramento v. Lewis, 523 U.S. 833 (1998)

Cruz v. City of Laramie, Wyoming, 239 F.3d 1183 (10th Cir. 2001)

Czajkowski v. City of Chicago, 810 F. Supp. 1428 (N.D. Ill. 1993)

Davis v. Mason County, 927 F.2d 1473 (9th Cir. 1991)

Darrow v. Schumaker, 495 N.W.2d 511 (S.D. 1993)

DeShaney v. Winnebago County Department of Social Services, 489 U.S. 189 (1989)

Dismukes v. Hackathorn, 802 F. Supp. 1442 (N.D. Miss. 1992)

Doe v. Calumet City, 754 F. Supp. 1211 (N.D. Ill. 1990)

Dorman v. District of Columbia, 888 F.2d 159 (D.C. Cir. 1989)

Elliot v. Chesire County, 940 F.2d 7 (1st Cir. 1991)

Elmes v. Hart, 1994 Tenn. App. LEXIS 278 (Tenn. Ct. App.)

Estate of Phillips v. City of Milwaukee, 928 F. Supp. 817 (E.D. Wis. 1996)

Estate of Sowards v. City of Trenton, 125 Fed. Appx. 31 (6th Cir. 2005)

Estelle v. Gamble, 429 U.S. 97 (1976)

Farmer v. Brennan, 511 U.S. 825 (1994)

Frye v. Town of Akron, 759 F. Supp. 1320 (N.D. Ind. 1991)

Fulkerson v. City of Lancaster, 801 F. Supp. 1476 (E.D. Pa. 1992)

Gilbert v. Selsky, 867 F. Supp. 159 (S.D.N.Y. 1994)

Graham v. Connor, 490 U.S. 386 (1989)

Grazier v. City of Philadelphia, 328 F.3d 120 (3d Cir. 2003)

Griffith v. Coburn, 408 F. Supp. 2d 491 (W.D. Mich. 2005)

Gutierrez v. City of San Antonio et al., 139 F.3d 441 (5th Cir. 1998)

Guseman v. Martinez, 1 F. Supp. 2d 1240 (D. Kan. 1998)

Hamilton v. Martinelli & Associates et al., 110 Cal. App. 4th 1012 (2003)

Hare v. City of Corinth, 814 F. Supp. 1312 (N.D. Miss. 1994)

Harris v. District of Columbia, 932 F.2d 10 (D.C. Cir. 1991)

Harvey v. County of Ward, 352 F. Supp. 2d 1003 (D.N.D. 2005)

Hays v. Jefferson County, 673 F.2d 152 (6th Cir. 1982)

Herman v. City of Shannon, Mississippi, 296 F. Supp. 2d 709 (E.D. Miss. 2004)

Houck v. City of Prairie Village, Kansas, 950 F. Supp. 312 (D. Kan. 1996)

LIABILITY FOR FAILURE TO TRAIN   **167**

Howard v. City of Atmore, 887 So. 2d 201 (Ala. 2003)

Hufford v. Rodgers, 912 F.2d 1388 (11th Cir. 1990)

Johnson v. City of Cincinnati, 39 F. Supp. 2d 1013 (S.D. Ohio 1999)

Jones v. City of Chicago, 711 F. Supp. 1465 (S.D. Ill. 1989)

Jones v. Wittenburg, 300 F. Supp. 707 (N.D. Ohio 1971)

Kinnneer v. Gall, No. C2-95-504 (S.D. Ohio 1996)

Lewis v. Board of Sedgwick County Commissioners, 140 F. Supp. 2d 1125 (D. Kan. 2001)

Madrid v. Gomez, 889 F. Supp. 1146 (N.D. Cal. 1995)

Mateyko v. Felix, 924 F.2d 824 (9th Cir. 1990)

Melendez v. Howard County Government, 121 F.3d 699 (4th Cir. 1997)

McCoy v. City of Monticello, 411 F. 3d 920 (8th Cir. 2005)

McCormick v. City of New York, 568 F.2d 365 (A.D. 1991)

Miami-Dade County v. Walker, 837 So. 2d 1049 (Fla. Dist. Ct. App. 2002)

Miller v. Carson, 401 F. Supp. 835 (M.D. Fla. 1975)

Monell v. New York City of Department of Social Services, 436 U.S. 658 (1978)

Owens v. Haas, 601 F.2d 1242 (2d Cir. 1979)

Pembauer v. City of Cincinnati, 475 U.S. 469 (1986)

Philebaum v. Meyers, Ridenour & City of Portland, Indiana, U.S. Dist. Lexis 8779 (Ind. 2006)

Polk County v. Dodson, 454 U.S. 312 (1981)

Rivas v. Freeman, 940 F.2d 1491 (11th Cir. 1991)

Robinson v. City of St. Charles, 972 F. 2d 974 (9th Cir. 1992)

Roy v. Inhabitants of City of Lewiston, 42 F.3d 691 (1st Cir. 1994)

Russo v. City of Cincinnati, 953 F.2d 1036 (6th Cir. 1992)

Sanders v. City of Union Springs et al., 405 F. Supp. 2d 1358 (N.D. Ala. 2005)

Schorr v. Borough of Lemoyne, Pennsylvania, 243 F. Supp. 2d 232 (M.D. Pa. 2003)

Simmons v. City of Philadelphia, 947 F.2d 1042 (3d Cir. 1991)

Smith v. Board of County Commissioners of County of Lyon, 216 F. Supp. 2d 1209 (D. Kan. 2002)

Swain v. Spinney, 117 F.3d 1 (1st Cir. 1997)

Swans v. City of Lansing, 65 F. Supp. 2d 625 (W.D. Mich. 1998).

Tennessee v. Garner, 471 U.S. 1 (1985)

Tilson v. Forrest City Police Department, 28 F.3d 802 (8th Cir. 1994)

Tucker v. Evans, 276 F.3d 999 (8th Cir. 2000)

Vine v. County of Ingham, 884 F. Supp. 1153 (W.D. Mich. 1995)

Vineyard v. County of Murray Georgia, 990 F.2d 1207 (11th Cir. 1993)

Wall v. Gwinnett County, No. 90 CV-1345-JEC, U. S. Dist. Ct. N. D. (1993)

Wallace v. Estate of Davis, 676 N.E.2d 422 (Ind. Ct. App. 1994)

Walsweer v. Harris County, 796 F. Supp. 269 (5th Cir. 1990)

Wyoming v. Houghton, 526 U.S. 295 (1999)

Young v. City of Atlanta, Georgia, 59 F.3d 1160 (11th Cir. 1995)

Young v. City of Mount Ranier, 238 F.3d 567 (4th Cir. 2001)

Zuchel v. City and County of Denver, Colorado, 997 F.2d 730 (10th Cir. 1993)

Chapter 8

Operating Criminal Justice Agencies Under a Consent Decree

Beyond civil litigation filed by citizens or prisoners in state or federal courts, there are additional methods by which criminal justice personnel are scrutinized about performing their sworn duties. Congress has passed significant legislation authorizing the Department of Justice to initiate investigations and pursue litigation against correctional and police entities. In 1980, Congress passed the Civil Rights of Institutionalized Persons Act (CRIPA), 42 U.S.C. § 1997, which addresses investigations relating to conditions of confinement. In 1994, Congress promulgated Title 42 U.S.C. § 14141 as part of the Violent Crime Control and Law Enforcement Act, which prohibits government authorities or those acting on their behalf (including law enforcement officials) from engaging in a pattern or practice of conduct that deprives people of their constitutional rights.

The purpose of this chapter is to describe how these two pieces of legislation operate and affect criminal justice agencies. The issue of police misconduct and prisoner abuse is clearly a matter of social policy and legislation requiring assessment. These laws have had a significant impact on the criminal justice system and represent a major federal government intervention into the operations of criminal justice agencies. Legislation affects policy, and administrators and officers should be aware of the mechanics of these two statutes and address changes in their agency's operations as appropriate.

Section 14141

High-profile incidents, such as the Rodney King arrest (1991), the Amadou Diallo (1994) and Abner Loumia (1997) incidents in New York, and the riots in Cincinnati after a police officer shot and killed an African-American youth (2001) have raised concerns about how the police treat citizens. In addition, the 2000 Rampart precinct scandal in Los Angeles, where a veteran officer, Rafael Perez, stole one million dollars' worth of cocaine only serves to convince the public that police corruption is rampant as well. These, among other incidents, have become popular examples that police pundits point toward in order to prove their contention that the police are corrupt and require federal regulation (U.S. Commission on Civil Rights, 2000).

These and other examples are frequently cited by police critics who make sweeping indictments alleging that the police profession is corrupt, that it hides behind the "blue curtain" of cover-up, and that it chronically uses excessive force. There is no question that acts of police misconduct have occasionally occurred and that excessive force has been used in some circumstances. There is no empirical evidence, however, to support claims that excessive force or officer misconduct occurs with statistically significant frequency (Ross, 2005). In his analysis, Ross found in 65 published articles on the police use of force from 1968 to 2004, including two Department of Justice national studies (1996 and 2001) and an International of Association Chiefs of Police independent national study (2001), that the use of any type of force is rare in police contacts with citizens. Moreover, he found that excessive force accusations, in contrast to public perception, were even rarer.

The United States Supreme Court has addressed proper police conduct in a series of landmark cases since the 1960s. The Court's interpretation of the "due process" rights of citizens has played a significant role in shaping social policy. For example, the Court's decisions in *Mapp v. Ohio* (1961) (which established the exclusionary rule) and *Terry v. Ohio* (1968) (which established standards for investigatory detentions and weapons pat-downs) placed restrictions on police in conducting searches and seizing evidence, and required police officers to follow legal procedures. These procedures are intended to properly guide officers and curb police misconduct. As shown in previous chapters, since the 1960s, citizens have used Title 42 U.S.C. § 1983 as the primary civil remedy for asserting legal claims against the police for alleged constitutional violations (Kappeler et al., 1993; Vaughn & Coome, 1995; Worrall, 2001; Ross, 2003; Silver, 2005). While § 1983 remains a viable mechanism to redress alleged governmental intrusions on citizens' rights, some scholars argue that it has only been partially successful in deterring or curbing police abuse of authority (Silveria, 2004; Walker, 2003; Kim, 2002; Levenson, 2001; Livingston, 1999). This argument, however, has been considerably weakened after the Court's decision in *Groh v. Ramirez* (2004), when it denied qualified immunity to an officer who relied on an invalid warrant that he had prepared, even though it was approved by a magistrate. The decision further warns against police abuse of power and sends a message to the police community regarding judicial intolerance of such misconduct.

Despite police reforms and commission reports about police practices over the past 50 years, advances in police practices, and court decisions, police misconduct still occasionally occurs. Seeking to remedy the issue, Congress enacted § 14141 of Title 42 as part of the Violent Crime Control and Law Enforcement Act in 1994. Section 14141 grants authority to the Department of Justice (DOJ) to pursue equitable and declaratory relief against police engaged in a "pattern and practice" that deprives individuals of their constitutional rights. Section 14141 does not authorize compensatory damage awards to citizen complaints, but rather gives the DOJ the power to initiate police reform by essentially dictating future management practices in that police entity (Silveria, 2004). In an initial assessment of the application of § 14141, Livingston (1999) argued and agreed with some police scholars that police reform will be most effective when reform involves not only simple adherence to the rules, but also a wholehearted embrace of change in organizational values and systems.

Section 14141 specifically authorizes the DOJ to bring a lawsuit against a police organization rather than individual officers. Beginning in 1996, the DOJ, initiated investigations of 22 police departments, which have resulted in seven consent decrees and six memorandums of agreement. One investigation was dropped. The DOJ is currently investigating eight police departments (DOJ, 2006).

Background of § 14141

Provisions of the Act

As a result of the Rodney King incident, Congress passed the Violent Crime Control Act in 1994. As part of this legislation, Congress gave authority to the United States Attorney General to investigate allegations of "patterns and practices" of police misconduct. Section 14141 substantially enhances the Department of Justice's statutory basis for intervening into the affairs of police departments. This provision allows the Special Litigation Section of the Civil Rights Division to investigate and bring a civil lawsuit against a police department when the Attorney General believes that constitutional violations based on patterns and practices have occurred. The fundamental purpose of § 14141 is to remedy systemic police abuse.

In establishing a claim, § 14141 requires the DOJ to demonstrate that a municipality or police department engaged in a "pattern or practice" of conduct by law enforcement officers that has deprived individuals of their constitutionally protected rights. Congress provided no explicit guidance nor has there been any judicial interpretation of § 14141, and defining a "pattern or practice" of misconduct can be problematic. There are, however, two components that shed light on the interpretation. First, the United States Supreme Court suggested in developing Title VII language that the term "pattern and practice" can mean "denoting something more than the mere occurrence of isolated or accidental or sporadic unlawful acts" (*Int'l Brotherhood of Teamsters v. United States,* 1977). In the police context, this can mean that a "pattern or practice" of conduct by police officers that violates constitutional rights would likely show that such conduct is a practice or custom that occurs frequently or regularly (Livingston, 1999). With such regularity of occurrence, a court could conclude that such abusive conduct is the *regular* practice rather than the *unusual* practice. The Supreme Court has also ruled in *Hazelwood School District v. United States* (1977) (a case predating § 1414) that a plaintiff can make a prima facie case of "pattern or practice" of discrimination simply through the introduction of statistical evidence. Because statistical evidence was sufficient proof of a "pattern or practice" of discrimination (in an educational setting), a plaintiff need not prove any overt institutional practice to satisfy the definition.

Second, in the predecessor to § 14141, the Judicial Committee Report in 1991 suggested that establishing a "pattern or practice" need not be based on extensive evidence of systematic repeated violations (H.R. Rep. 102). The report cited acts or omissions that constituted patterns and practices in illustrating the potential applicability of § 14141 to situations in which relief was formerly unavailable. For example, the Committee cited the Ninth Circuit Appellate Court's holding in *Mason County v. Davis* (1991). Affirming the lower court's decision, the appellate court determined that a § 1983 claim was valid when four separate plaintiffs showed a pattern of excessive force stemming from unconstitutional traffic stops performed by deputies over a period of nine months. Such a pattern of abuse demonstrated the inadequacies of training provided by the department for its officers.

Consent Decree

Once allegations of constitutional violations emerge, the DOJ conducts a preliminary inquiry to determine the nature of the allegations. The DOJ may notify the agency or the municipality that it will be conducting a formal investigation. If the investigation reveals evidence of a pattern or practice of abuse, the DOJ may release a letter of general findings to announce its discovery, or it may simply walk away, stating that there is no evidence to support a claim.

There are several options available to the DOJ when a "pattern or practice" is established, in its opinion, under § 14141. First, the DOJ may file a lawsuit against the police agency, which may involve a lengthy litigation process. Second, a lawsuit maybe filed with the expectation that the city will settle the case through a consent decree or settle it through a memorandum of agreement (MOA). While both are settlements, there are distinctions between them. Consent decrees serve as a court-ordered and court-enforceable settlements. A federal judge provides oversight of the consent decree, which normally lasts five years (Livingston, 1999). When a MOA is used to settle the DOJ claim, there is no judicial oversight. A municipality agrees in writing to comply with recommendations made by the DOJ, which threatens a future consent decree or litigation if the agency fails to comply with the agreement. Ostensibly, a consent decree is an MOA with teeth (Silveria, 2004). A Special Monitor is appointed by the court to serve as an independent auditor in consent decrees and MOAs. The Special Monitor reports on each defendant's compliance on a quarterly basis.

Investigation Trends of § 14141

Ten-Year Trends

The trends of consent decrees and MOAs filed by the DOJ from 1996 to 2005 are shown in Table 8.1. The DOJ has conducted 22 investigations involving one state police agency, 18 municipalities, and two county sheriff's departments (DOJ Special Litigation Section, 2006). These investigations have resulted in seven consent decrees and six MOAs.

Considering the lack of congressional guidance on the definition of a "pattern or practice," policy patterns of § 14141 have differed significantly from the Clinton administration to the Bush administration. Under the Clinton administration, the first investigations occurred in 1996. Pittsburgh, Pennsylvania, and Steubenville, Ohio, were the first cities the DOJ investigated for practices and patterns of police misconduct. Both investigations resulted in five-year consent decrees commencing in 1997 and both cities successfully completed the period of judicial monitoring (Livingston, 1999). The third and final police agency placed under a consent decree during the Clinton administration was the New Jersey State Police in 1999. The consent decree specifically addressed racial profiling and methods to remedy such allegations (DOJ, 1999). Prior to 2001 and the George W. Bush administration, the DOJ had initiated an investigation of the Los Angeles Police Department (LAPD), but they were placed on a consent decree during the first year of the Bush administration.

During the first three years of the Bush administration, more § 14141 investigations were completed than in the six years after its passage under the Clinton administration. Section 14141 investigations by the DOJ have increased under the Bush presidency. From 2001 to 2005, the DOJ conducted 18 § 14141 investigations. As a result, four agencies agreed to consent decrees, six agreed to MOAs, eight are still under investigation or monitoring,

Table 8.1
Trends of Consent Decrees, MOA and Investigations: 1997-2005

City/Year	CD	MOA	Investigation	Case Dropped
Albany, NY (2003)			x	
Bakerfield, CA			x	
Beacon, NY (2002)			x	
Buffalo, NY (2002)			x	
Cincinnati, OH (2002)		x		
Cleveland, OH	x			
Columbus, OH (2002)				x
Detroit, MI (2003)	x			
Highland Park, IL (2000)		x		
Los Angeles, CA (2001)	x			
Miami, FL (2001)			x	
Mount Prospect, IL (2003)			x	
Nassau County, NY (2001)		x		
NJ State Police (1999)	x			
Pittsburgh, PA (1997)	x			
Portland, ME (2003)			x	
Prince George's County, MD (2004)			x	
Schenectady, NY (2003)			x	
Steubenville, OH (1997)	x			
Villa Rico, GA (2003)		x		
Virgin Islands (2003)			x	
Washington, D.C.		x		

and the DOJ dropped the lawsuit in the Columbus, Ohio, investigation (DOJ, 2006). Investigations are still being conducted in accordance with § 14141, but the trends show that under the Bush administration the investigations are slightly more likely to result in a MOA.

Thus far, Columbus, Ohio, is the first city to challenge a § 14141 action in court. The city filed a motion to dismiss the action, claiming that § 14141 constituted an abuse of the government's power to enforce the Fourteenth Amendment (*United States v. City of Columbus,* 2001). Denying the motion, the federal district court held that § 14141 creates Congressional oversight to prevent violations of the Fourteenth Amendment. The case continued to drag on for several more years and the DOJ decided to drop the case under the Bush administration. This decision is important because it demonstrates an aggressive, adversarial approach to § 14141 enforcement (Silveria, 2004). A review of the contents of the MOA suggests a more "cooperative" strategy and policy approach to the enforcement of § 14141.

Types of Allegations Made Under § 14141

Section 14141 allows the DOJ to file a lawsuit against a police entity for allegations of "pattern or practice" of police misconduct. The allegations must show that an individual's constitutional rights were violated. While such allegations may include a variety of claims, analysis of the consent decrees and MOAs reveal several levels of claims.

The first level of claims regarding police officer misconduct is a natural outgrowth of COP as it is the officer or officers who initiates the contact with the citizen. Common complaints typically include: using excessive force; false arrest and false imprisonment; and improper traffic stops, searches, and seizures of people. The second level of claims concerns practices condoned by departmental administrators. Common allegations may include: supervisors who condoned officer abuses; failed to implement or enforce policies; failed to train, supervise, and discipline officers; failed to investigate officer misconduct or citizen complaints; and failed to implement a risk management system that could assess officer practices of abuse.

Principal Components of § 14141 Consent Decrees

Each consent decree addresses unique and specific abuses identified by the DOJ investigation of a particular police entity, and forms the basis for the claim of a "pattern or practice" of police misconduct. While not every consent decree requires the police agency to address the same issue or the same number of issues, analysis of the six consent decrees reveals a total of 94 factors that have been addressed during the monitoring period. Many of these factors required by the DOJ during the duration of the consent decree were derived from the DOJ's report on *Good Policing* (DOJ, 2003).

Consent decrees mainly call for the revision or development of policies and procedures. Common policy areas generally include: use of force, citizen complaints, in-car video camera usage, conducting investigations, performing arrests, searching and obtaining warrants, conducting traffic stops, foot pursuits, and racial profiling.

The second general factor of each consent decree is the establishment of a data-driven information management system. These systems are designed to provide useful information about the activities of all officers and supervisors in the department in order to establish accountability measures. The data management system is comprised of six separate elements, including: a risk management database and analysis; officer and supervisor database; citizen complaints; and an early identification system for problem officers. A separate tracking system must be designed and maintained that documents: police and citizen contacts, police use of force, traffic stops, citizen arrests, police misconduct, and police response to the mentally impaired.

Each database requires an involved officer to complete and submit designated forms and reports documenting their actions in a given incident.

The use of a reporting system is a core component in the consent decree actions (Walker, 2003). It is integrated into the data-tracking/reporting system, the revised policy, the early identification system, investigation protocols, and the risk management assessment system. In many agencies this has meant a total revamping of their entire system.

The early identification system is designed to identify potential problem officers so supervisors can provide those officers with early intervention, normally through counseling or additional training by a supervisor. The system is integrated into the other database systems described above. The system provides supervisors with greater flexibility in addressing performance problems (Walker et al., 2000). The concept is supported by research that suggests that in any law enforcement agency a small number of officers are involved in a disproportionate percentage of problem incidents, such as citizen complaints, use-of-force incidents, civil lawsuits against the department, and other indicators of performance problems (Walker, 2001).

Another factor addresses establishing varying agency programs. Such programs can include: field officer training, in-service training, police response to the mentally impaired, community outreach, and employee assistance programs. Training is a core component in consent decrees and MOAs. Generally, the decrees do not stipulate the content of such training. Common training subject areas include: use of force; search and seizure laws; response to domestic violence, hostage and barricade situations; emotionally impaired persons; vehicle pursuits; communication skills; and training on racial, gender, and religious differences of community citizens. Supervisors must also attend the training.

Performing investigations represents the fourth major factor of the consent decree, and topic areas can include: criminal, civil, citizen complaints, disciplinary complaints, and internal affairs investigations. A majority of many of the decrees contain the requirement of performing use-of-force investigations. Citizen complaint investigations also must be addressed. After investigations are concluded, a report must be submitted that shows how the investigation was conducted and the evidentiary basis of the findings of the investigation. These provisions are designed to correct specific problems that are unique to a department's failure to conduct investigations or past failure to perform a thorough and complete investigation.

The fifth factor addresses administrative oversight of the entire consent decree. For each agency, an independent monitor is assigned by the court to provide quarterly monitoring progress of how the agency was complying with the components of the consent decree.

All reports must be entered into a database that tracks the unique components of each consent decree. Supervisors must dedicate time to analyze trends and patterns of officer activities that were identified in the previous sections. Supervisors must periodically monitor the documents that are to be part of the ongoing assessment of officers, including annual performance evaluations (Livingston, 1999). Quarterly reports must be prepared by supervisors documenting these assessments. Certain steps must be taken when an officer accumulates a number of use-of-force incidents, citizen complaints, or other incidents that may reveal conduct outside authorized policy requirements. For example, if an officer accumulates more than three citizen complaints within two years, he or she must be counseled and attend refresher training in the subject matter consistent with the complaint. More severe sanctions may be assessed depending upon the severity of the complaint. Documentation of the remediation must be entered into the early intervention system and the database. Supervisors must perform annual evaluations of every officer under their command.

Memorandum of Agreement

Since 2001, DOJ investigations have increasingly resulted in memorandums of agreement (MOAs). MOAs are more conciliatory than consent decrees. They do not involve judicial monitoring as do consent decrees. While stipulations from consent decrees and MOAs may be similar, MOAs are more likely to address three primary topic areas beyond officer training and developing an early intervention warning system with all officers: (1) Policy and Procedure; (2) Citizen Complaints; and (3) Data Collection.

The first area addressed in an MOA is policy and procedure for performing investigations within the police department. All of the departments are required to revise their policies pursuant to the findings of the DOJ investigation.

Perhaps the most fundamental difference in the MOA is a change in the use-of-force policy. While police agencies today provide their officers with a use-of-force policy, revisions may have to be made, such as restricting the use of certain force techniques or equipment, reporting procedures, or tracking and analyzing force incidents. The Washington, D.C., MOA required the department to completely overhaul their use-of-force policy and bring it into compliance with applicable law and professional standards (DOJ, 2003). The city of Cincinnati was required to develop policy language that limited the use of pepper spray, the use of canines, and the use of the choke hold (DOJ, 2001). The Cleveland Police Department was required to address their procedures for using detainee holding cells and was also required to revise its lethal force policy (DOJ, 2002).

Previous complaints have been made that police frequently do not enforce their departmental policies. The problem may be that the officer in question is being investigated by his or her immediate supervisor, resulting in a less than thorough investigation. Thus, investigations into officer actions contrary to the policy are required in all MOAs to ensure the integrity of, and public confidence in, the investigation. The subject matter of investigations generally includes: use of force, citizen complaints, traffic stops, and searches and seizures. In Cincinnati, the MOA requires an investigation when an officer uses force. The officer must first notify his immediate supervisor, the supervisor must respond to the scene, and an investigator from internal affairs must respond to the scene of "serious" force incidents. The investigator may neither ask leading questions nor show preference to statements made by the officer, nor may they disregard a witness's or the arrestee's statement of the incident.

Another major component addressed in most of the MOAs is the handling of citizen complaints. Modifications to complaint procedures are required. The goal is to enhance citizen satisfaction in the outcome of the complaint process by providing more transparency in the process. In many of the MOAs, officers are required to carry complaint forms in their patrol vehicles and are required to inform citizens that they have a right to file a complaint about the officer's response. Investigations of citizen complaints must be performed and documented, and a report of the nature of the disposition and description of the evidentiary grounds used to determine the outcome of the investigation must be completed.

Data collection is also addressed by most MOAs. Data is required to be collected, analyzed, and assessed in a variety of topic areas, but is focused on traffic stops. This requirement has emerged from allegations that police have engaged in racial profiling practices during traffic stops. When an officer makes a traffic stop, he or she is required to submit a lengthy form documenting the nature of the stop. That information is submitted to a supervisor for review. The information is then entered into the database system for further analysis and it is also entered into the early intervention database.

Civil Rights of Institutionalized Persons Act

The Civil Rights of Institutionalized Persons Act, 42 U.S.C. § 1997 et seq. (CRIPA) was passed by Congress in 1980 and is similar to § 14141. CRIPA authorizes the United States Attorney General to conduct investigations and litigation relating to conditions of confinement in state or locally operated institutions (excluding private facilities). Under the statute, the Special Section of the Civil Rights Section investigates covered facilities to determine whether there is a "pattern or practice" of violations of residents' federal rights (the Section is not authorized to represent individuals or to address specific individual cases). The intent of Congress in passing CRIPA, as identified in § 1997g, is to correct deplorable conditions and abuses of the use of force in institutions that amount to deprivations of rights protected by the United States Constitution.

Section 1997a grants discretionary authority to the Attorney General. Under this provision, whenever the Attorney General has reasonable cause to believe that any State or political subdivision of a State, official, employee, or agent thereof, or other person acting on behalf of a state or political sub-division of a State is subjecting persons residing in or confined to an insti-tution to egregious or flagrant conditions that deprive such persons of rights protected by the Constitution, or that causes that person harm, may institute an investigation or civil action in a federal district court for equi-table or declaratory relief. The legislation does not provide for monetary awards. Section 1997b stipulates that prior to performing an investigation at a facility, the Attorney General must provide notification in writing to the governor or chief executive officer that an investigation will be taking place. The announcement must also identify the allegations and supporting facts warranting the investigation.

Section 1997a of the Act defines *institution* as: "any facility or institu-tion which is owned, operated, or managed by, or provides services on behalf of any State or political subdivision of a State." There are five types of "institutions" addressed under CRIPA: (1) jails and prisons, (2) juvenile correctional facilities, (3) mental health facilities, (4) developmental disability facilities, and (5) nursing homes. In accordance with CRIPA, the DOJ reviews complaints, conducts investigations, litigates civil actions that demonstrate a "pattern and practice" of abuse, enforces and monitors court orders, and monitors the progress toward compliance in consent decrees and settlements. The discussion in this chapter only addresses issues pertinent to jails, prisons, and juvenile facilities.

Since CRIPA's enactment in 1980, the DOJ has initiated 409 investiga-tions, resulting in 120 consent decrees and settlements, involving about 240 facilities (Department of State, 2005). These investigations represent about 55 percent jails, prisons, and juvenile correctional facilities. CRIPA enforce-ment has been a priority with the DOJ since 1999 and there are 56 ongoing investigations. In 2004, 10 jails and six prisons were under consent decree and seven investigations of jails, prisons, and juvenile institutions were under way (DOJ, 2004).

Similar to § 14141, an investigation under CRIPA can result in a consent decree. Investigations into alleged "patterns or practices" that result in a con-sent decree generally address the following topics regarding prisoner rights: medical and mental health care (including suicide prevention); prisoner supervision and failure to protect (including population manage-ment); classification and prisoner discipline; policies and procedures; abuses of the use of force by officers/staff; food services; officer and supervisor training and performance evaluations; the process of conduct-ing investigations of prisoner complaints; and quality of administrative man-agement of the facility.

If an institution decides to enter into a consent decree after the DOJ inves-tigation, a federal court will oversee the stipulations of the agreement and monitor the progress of the compliance with the orders, like § 14141 actions. Many of the consent decrees include an array of the above-described factors that the correctional entity must change, which would be specific to that institution, based on the DOJ's investigation. Failure to comply with the consent decree can result in extending federal oversight for a period of time determined by the court. The DOJ may also bring a civil action against the entity in federal court. Special monitors are appointed, as in § 14141 actions, to monitor the progress toward completion of the stipulations. The institution must provide periodic progress reports.

Discussion

These two statutes address the ongoing challenges of reforming criminal justice entities. Reforms have been attempted numerous times over the years. Formally, there have been two primary methods that have addressed abuses and misconduct. First, there have been several commission reports since the 1960s. Typically, incidents of alleged misconduct or riots generate an investigation, followed by "blue ribbon panel" reports calling for sweeping changes in the criminal justice agency involved. These reports have been successful in highlighting abuses, but they have not been successful in providing lasting solutions.

The second reform attempt has come through the judicial system. Title 42 U.S.C. § 1983 created a remedy for citizens and prisoners to challenge alleged constitutional rights violations by an officer and his or her supervisor. The United States Supreme Court, beginning with their decisions in *Monroe v. Pape* (1961) and *Monell v. Department of Social Services* (1978) has upheld this remedy. Numerous lawsuits have been filed during the last 40 years and the results of these lawsuits show that plaintiffs have been modestly successful in prevailing in civil rights actions (Kappeler et al., 1996; Ross, 1997). Critics complain, however, that the judicial system has been inconsistent in awarding claims on behalf of plaintiffs and that state laws generally indemnify the officers in the majority of punitive damage awards (Levenson, 2001; Silveria, 2000). Such claims, however, are not fully supported. At least two studies have found that plaintiffs have prevailed in civil lawsuits against the police in 48 percent of cases (Kappeler et al., 1996; Ross, 1998) in 45 percent of cases in correctional litigation.

The courts have fashioned other remedies to curb or punish officer misconduct. The exclusionary rule, developed by the United States Supreme Court in *Mapp v. Ohio* (1961), requires that police officers comply with the requirements of the Fourth Amendment (search and seizure) as well as the Fifth and Sixth Amendments (self-incrimination). It provides that evidence obtained unlawfully by police officers may not be used in a criminal proceeding. The Court ruled that it is the law that sets a criminal free—nothing can destroy a government more quickly than its own failure to follow the law.

It has been argued that exceptions to the exclusionary rule have weakened its ability to deter police abuse (Livingston, 1999; Walker, 2003). This argument, however, has been shown to be misleading. Davies (1985) and Orfield (1987) conducted independent studies that concluded that the exclusion of evidence in cases involving murder, rape, and other violent crimes is exceedingly rare. Orfield also noted that the more serious the crime, the greater the officer's desire to follow the legal procedures, thereby showing the deterrence effect of the exclusionary rule. The American Bar Association (1998) found in a study of police officers and prosecutors that since the *Mapp* decision, police officers generally follow the procedures of the rule and that it has enhanced professionalism. Levenson (1999) observed that there is no evidence and no reason to believe that a police officer will be any less motivated to lie in an administrative hearing, where his reputation and job position are at risk, than in a criminal proceeding where the court threatens to exclude evidence.

There are a variety of laws on the books (i.e., obstruction, perjury, planting evidence, etc.) that allow criminal prosecution of officers who engage in misconduct that rises to the level of criminal behavior. For example, the United States Department of State (2005) chronicles a selection of 18 criminal prosecutions as examples of police and correctional officers sentenced for crimes of abuse from 1999 to 2005. While any law or court standard directing officer conduct can be violated, the ultimate responsibility lies with the individual officer, supervisors, prosecutors, and the courts to ensure that the rule is followed. Prosecutors have the absolute discretion to refuse to prosecute cases if they suspect police misconduct. *Brady v. Maryland* (1963) requires the prosecutor to disclose evidence that may exonerate a defendant and that could be used to impeach a government witness, so a prosecutor has greater motivation to "look behind the curtain." For more than 40 years, however, the exclusionary rule has generally served as a successful spur toward professionalizing the police and curbing abuse (Kamisar, 2003). For example, two officers were convicted and sentenced to prison on federal charges for the Rodney King beating (Levenson, 2001), even after acquittal on state charges. Officer Rafael Perez of the Rampart Precinct of the Los Angeles Police Department was also sentenced to state prison for his participation in the scandal (Boyer, 2001).

Undermining Democratic Accountability

Consent decrees in general, and operating a criminal justice agency by consent decree have a profound effect on public policy. "Policy, wrote Kaufan (1960) is enunciated in rhetoric, and is realized in action." With its passage of CRIPA and § 14141, Congress has ushered in a new model of attempting to curb abuses or misconduct without fully considering the consequences of their handiwork. Management by consent decree represents the new paradigm of attempting to address misconduct and accountability at a federal level, rather than at the local or state levels. There is no question that police and correctional officers are human and abuses have occurred. Officer misconduct cannot be condoned and guilty officers should be held accountable. But the question emerges as to whether § 14141 and CRIPA represent the appropriate social mechanism by which to address allegations of abuse. After years of DOJ investigations and consent decrees, it remains questionable as to whether such federal intervention is effective in bringing lasting reforms to criminal justice agencies. There are several reasons for caution and skepticism about forcing consent decrees on police and correctional agencies and whether it represents legitimate social policy.

One question that begs to be answered is whether every solution should be a federal solution in a country that is founded on the principle of federalism. Federalism is defined as a political system in which power is divided and shared between the national/central government and the states (regional units) in order to limit the power of government. Policing by decree undermines that accountability of government to its constituents and therefore it becomes less responsive (Sandler & Schoenbrod, 2003).

Consent decrees by their intrinsic nature are settlements negotiated behind closed doors, although they become public record upon filing in the court proceedings. It has been suggested that because a potential consent decree requires the cooperation of the police entity in crafting equitable relief, such an agreement does not implicate a "strong" degree of federalism (Kim, 2002). When such important policy decisions are made behind closed doors under threat of a major lawsuit by the federal government, officials become indebted to them and to a minority of community constituents. This represents a policy consequence that results in the government failing to represent the public as a whole. A major power shift occurs when policy-making responsibility is stripped from the local or state government and transferred to the federal government and to the federal courts. Such an action violates the principle of limited government and turns the judiciary into a super-legislature. Subsequently, this frequently leaves governments less capable of responding to the legitimate desires of the public and makes elected officials less accountable to the public. Rabkin (1997) suggests that "the more government is accountable to private litigants, the less it can be accountable to anyone else. Limiting the choices of government officials limits their responsibility, for they cannot be responsible for choices they are not allowed to make."

Entering into a consent decree shifts power from the affected government to the DOJ and the courts. Neither the United States Constitution nor state constitutions allow one legislative body to bind the next, by either contract or budgetary appropriation (McConnell, 1987). Governments may not contract away the power to change policy. Citizens who may have legitimate concerns with governmental policies are unable to approach employees of the DOJ and the federal judge, neither of which are elected officials. Moreover, a consent decree is shifted away from concerns of local voters to the specific concerns of technocrats (Sandler & Schoenbrod, 2003). Consent decree investigations can take years to conduct and conclude. Police agencies essentially lose their rights to a speedy judicial process. Once the contents of the decree are issued police executives are bound by the stipulations.

Undermining Police Executive Leadership

Consent decrees have been used as a remedy in the United States during the past 40 years in a majority of prison and jail condition cases in an attempt to reform the prison and jail system. Jails and prisons have been subject to consent decree accountability for longer than their police counterparts. It is debatable whether these decrees have brought lasting reforms to correctional institutions, because the decrees have not accomplished all of their objectives (Sandler & Schoenbrod, 2003). DiIulio (1990) observed in his review of prison consent decrees that successful accomplishments were accounted for by small incremental advances and compromises rather than full-scale assaults. What this means is that when judges act like legislatures, they are more likely to succeed. This, however, exceeds the boundaries of judicial responsibility and allows the judge to assume to the role of a super legislature. Ironically, Congress restricted the use of consent decrees in corrections and limited judicial intervention when it passed the Prison Litigation Reform Act (1996), which ostensibly reduces the filing of "frivolous" prisoner lawsuits and terminates existing consent decrees of correctional facilities. Yet despite the passage of the PLRA, the DOJ continues to pursue investigations into correctional institutions.

A major consequence of consent decrees is that they cannot ensure effective leadership within the agency that is necessary for ongoing reforms to be accomplished, and may even undercut opportunities for such leadership to emerge (Livingston, 1999; Walker, 2003). Glazer (1979) remarked that court orders that are aimed at restructuring public institutions normally result in a decline in staff morale, an increase in staff turnover, and an increase in the unruliness of clientele groups, which undermines police authority by the entire consent process. Wilson (1989) noted that consent decrees aggravate the unfortunate tendency of bureaucracies to focus on counting things rather than helping people. Such appears to be the case with the new paradigm of performing criminal justice responsibilities by decree.

In the only study conducted to date on the impact of police consent decrees, the Vera Institute of Justice (Davis et al., 2002) surveyed a sample of police officers, supervisors, and community leaders in the city of Pittsburgh regarding their perceptions about the outcome of the decree. Generally, community leaders (40%) perceived that the police treated citizens better than before the consent decree, that the decree was a useful tool in improving police practices and accountability, and that they had greater confidence in the police. Citizen complaints declined by 50 percent overall. Supervisors reported that community-oriented policing efforts were detrimentally affected. Their concern emerged from the fact that they were strapped with a great deal of paperwork that kept them from spending quality time with their officers and providing leadership. Although a majority of supervisors reported that the early warning intervention system assisted in identifying problem officers sooner, discipline of officers declined by 45 percent.

The most significant negative impact of the decree was felt by line officers. They commented that their morale had been detrimentally affected, that they were more reluctant to use force and reluctant to make traffic stops. While the use of sick time declined slightly, there was an increase in officers leaving the department. Generally, officers reported that they were less likely to engage in proactive policing strategies. During the five years, arrests declined by 40 percent, clearance rates of arrests declined by 35 percent, traffic summonses declined by 35 percent, and arrests of African-American suspects dropped by 15 percent. There was no noticeable change in the occurrence of Part I or Part II crimes.

Costs

Start-up and maintenance costs linked with successful compliance with consent decrees are enormous. It is estimated that the LAPD consent decree may cost between $30 and $50 million annually, meaning that over five years, they could pay out more than $250 million (Levenson, 2001). The Cincinnati consent decree cost approximately $13 million in start-up costs and more than $20 million annually to ensure compliance with the stipulations (Walker, 2003). Without financial assistance from either the state or the federal government, municipalities will be unable to implement or maintain the requirements of the consent decree. Correctional departments have experienced the same problem in funding the associated costs with making the necessary changes consistent with the consent decrees. State and county budgets have had to be realigned and other funding priorities have been neglected in order to comply with a consent decree.

The financial problem is a congressional one. Congress has repeatedly been criticized by state governors for creating unfunded mandates for the states. The United States Supreme Court determined in *Printz v. United States* (1997), in overturning a portion of the Brady Handgun Violence Prevention Act, that by requiring state governments to absorb the financial burden of implementing a federal regulatory program, Congress can take credit for solving problems without having to ask their constituents to pay for the solutions and without raising taxes. Even when the municipalities are not forced to absorb the implementation costs, they are still put in a position of taking the blame for its burdensome effects. Having shifted the blame to local and state officials, Congress is not compelled to consider the negative consequences of their mandate.

Conversely, it is costly for the DOJ to conduct investigations. Since the 1990s, conducting investigations into allegations of misconduct in criminal justice agencies has been a major priority of the DOJ (Department of State, 2005). While costs for conducting such investigations have not been published, the following questions arise: "Does it make sound public policy to spend millions in conducting these investigations?" and "Does it make good public policy for DOJ attorneys to spend their time and budget conducting these investigations?" Clearly these are important questions that require detailed assessment if future investigations are performed.

Response

It remains debatable whether operating correctional institutions or policing under a consent decree will prove to be effective in bringing about lasting reforms to the criminal justice system. As a matter of practice, patterns of police abuse of citizens or prisoners should not be condoned and an organizational culture that allows such misconduct should be held accountable. Police and correctional officers must be accountable for following the law and proper procedures in performing their duties. Governments cannot be above the law, but federal intervention fails to provide the appropriate social policy to bring about long-term and lasting reforms. The incremental gains are not justified by the immense costs and the long-term threat to our system of democracy.

There are lessons to be learned from the consent decrees, and criminal justice managers should take these lessons into consideration. Administrators are encouraged to voluntarily undertake the following proactive strategies in order to increase their accountability. These strategies align with risk-management principles discussed in Chapter 5 through Chapter 7.

Because consent decrees require a monitor to review the compliance and progress toward the stipulations, administrators should first create a compliance officer position to oversee departmental activities. The compliance officer should report to the chief executive of the department (Schmidt, 2005; Ross, 2003). This position could be a supervisor who would be responsible for ensuring that policies and practices are implemented properly and tracks and assesses pertinent departmental information. Second, administrators should consider instituting a data tracking system designed to record information about the performance of officers and supervisors. Systematically collecting and assessing data about calls for service, arrests, use of force, traffic stops, and pursuits can be instrumental in providing police supervisors with valuable information to use in leading the organization and provide early warning of marginal officer performance. The same type of system could be used to track pertinent information in correctional institutions as well.

Third, administrators should voluntarily review and revise policies and procedures on a regular basis. As the law changes, policies should also be changed in order for officers and supervisors to perform their duties within legal parameters. Fourth, intersecting the data tracking system with the early intervention system has the potential to transform the organizational culture and department. It can raise the standard of officer conduct and supervisory accountability in maintaining proper officer performance and identifying problem employees early. The system provides supervisors with more flexibility in addressing appropriate intervention strategies to keep officer conduct from progressing further thus requiring more severe sanctions. It serves to maintain accountability of officers and supervisors and assists in reducing allegations of failure to supervise or discipline officers.

Fifth, in compliance with the United States Supreme Court decision in *City of Canton v. Harris* (1989), administrators should endeavor to provide their officers with ongoing training commensurate with their duties and in accordance with state requirements. Training should be documented in the data tracking system and designed to address frequently occurring situations, agency policies, and high-profile topics, such as: use of force, pursuits, arrests with or without warrants, domestic violence calls, traffic stops, ethical behavior, and conducting felony arrests. Correctional agencies should also address high-profile subjects as: use of force, responding to special needs prisoners, searches, disturbance control, special threat group management, escapes, medical and psychological care issues of prisoners, transportation of prisoners, and security functions, to mention a few. Sixth, agencies should ensure that investigations into citizen and prisoner complaints and incidents of officer use of force are performed properly, pursuant to policy and the appropriate legal standard. Administrators should consider using an external agency to perform investigations when high-profile cases occur.

The compliance officer should perform regular inspections and audits to ensure that departmental regulations are being followed to prevent any patterns of abuse from occurring. Implementing and maintaining such a system provides a proactive framework with several benefits. Administrators as agency leaders must set the tone for proper conduct and create a department culture that protects constitutional rights of citizens. Public education about such efforts could help to improve public confidence in police and protect it from frivolous complaints. This assures the public that officers are adhering to departmental policies and that supervisors are enforcing them properly, underscoring accountability. It demonstrates to the community that the department has voluntarily undertaken a system of self-governance without being threatened by a lawsuit or judicial intervention.

A fundamental component of the criminal justice profession is that administrators have the responsibility and the right to manage their own departments as other professions do. Criminal justice agencies in the United States have made significant changes since the 1960s, but the new era of consent decrees overshadows and discounts these accomplishments. Rather than the decree stipulations becoming the "standard," leaders of criminal justice agencies will be well served to study the stipulations and work toward making appropriate changes in their department as warranted. Voluntarily incorporating these features and changing agency practices as needed exhibits a policy that underscores professionalism, proactive leadership, and ensures that the agency can be accountable without forced federal intervention.

References

Bayley, D.H. (1988). "Community Policing: A Report from the Devil's Advocate." In J.R. Green & S.D. Mastrofski (eds.), *Community Policing: Rhetoric or Reality?* New York, NY: Praeger.

Bayley, D.H. & C.D. Shearing (1996). "The Future of Policing." *Law and Society Review* 30:585-605.

Bentham. J. (1789; 1948). *The Principles of Morals and Legislation.* New York, NY: Hafner Publishing Company.

Boyer, P.J. (2001). "Testimony on Police Misconduct Ignited the Biggest Scandal in the History of L.A.P.D.: Is it the Real Story?" *The New Yorker* May 21:60.

Bracey, D. (1992). "Police Corruption and Community Relations: Community Policing." *Police Studies* 15:179-183.

Catialno, S.M. (2005). *Criminal Victimization: National Crime Victimization Survey.* Washington, DC: Bureau of Justice Statistics.

Civil Rights of Institutionalized Persons Act (1980), Title 42 U.S.C. § 1997.

Davies, T.Y. (1985). "A Hard Look at What We Know (and Still Need to Learn) About the Costs of the Exclusionary Rule: The NIJ Study and Other Studies of Lost Arrests." American Board Foundation Research 610-645.

DiIulio, J.J. Jr. (1990). *Courts, Corrections and the Constitution.* New York, NY: Oxford University Press.

Glazer, N. (1979). "The Judiciary and Social Policy." In L.J. Theberge (ed.), *The Judiciary in a Democratic Society.* Lexington, MA: Lexington Books.

Greenfeld, P.A. Langan & and S.K. Smith (1997). *Police Use of Force: Collection of National Data.* Washington, DC: U.S. Department of Justice.

H.R. Rep. No. 102-104, 102d Congress, 1st Session at 406, 1911 WL 206794, at 138-39 (1991).

International Association of Chiefs of Police (2001). *Police Use of Force in America.* Alexandria, VA: Author.

Kamisar, Y. (2003). "In Defense of the Search and Seizure Exclusionary Rule." *Harvard Journal of Law and Public Policy* 1:119-138.

Kappeler, V.E., S.F. Kappeler & R.V. del Carmen (1996). "A Content Analysis of Police Civil Liability Cases: Decisions of the Federal District Courts, 1978-1990." *Journal of Criminal Justice* 21:325-337.

Kaufman, H. (1960). *The Forest Ranger: A Study in Administrative Behavior.* Baltimore, MD: Johns Hopkins University Press.

Kim, E. (2002). "Vindicating Civil Rights Under 42 U.S.C. 14141: Guidance From Procedures in Complex Litigation." 29 *Hastings Constitutional Law Quarterly* 767:1-34.

Klockars, C.B. (1988). "The Rhetoric of Community Policing." In J.R. Green & S.D. Mastrofski (eds.), *Community-Oriented Policing: An Alternative Strategy.* Washington, DC: International City Managers Association.

Langham, P.A., L.A. Greenfeld, S.K. Smith, M.R. Duros & J.L. Levin (2001). *Contacts Between Police and the Public: Findings from the 1999 National Survey.* Washington, DC: U.S. Department of Justice.

Levenson, L.L. (2001). "Police Corruption and New Models for Reform." 35 *Suffolk University Law Review* 1:1-41.

Levenson, L.L. (1999). "Administrative Replacements: How Much Can They Do?" 26 *Pepperdine Law Review* 879-881.

Livingston, D. (1999). "Police Reform and the Department of Justice: An Essay on Accountability." *Buffalo Criminal Law Review* 2:817-859.

Longmeadow Press. (1981, originally published 1851). *The Works of Charles Dickens.* London, UK: Octopus Books Limited.

McConnell, M.W. (1987). "Why Hold Elections? Using Consent Decrees to Insulate Policies from Political Change." *University of Chicago Legal Forum* 295.

Nagel, R.F. (2001). *The Implosion of American Federalism.* Oxford, UK: Oxford University Press.

Orfield, Jr., M.W. (1987). "Comment: The Exclusionary Rule and Deterrence: An Empirical Study of Chicago Narcotics Officers." *54 University of Chicago Law Review* 1015-1055.

Prison Litigation Reform Act (1996). Public L. No. 104-134, Statute 1321, Codified at 18 U.S.C. § 3626.

Rabkin, J.A. (1989). *Judicial Compulsions: How Public Law Distorts Public Policy.* New York, NY: Basic Books.

Rosen, J. (1998). "Search and Seizure." *New Republic* March 27:10.

Ross, D.L. (2005). "A Content Analysis of the Emerging Trends in the Use of Non-Lethal Force Research in Policing." *Law Enforcement Executive Forum* 5:121-149.

Ross, D.L. (2003). *Civil Liability in Criminal Justice*, Third Edition. Cincinnati, OH: Anderson Publishing Co.

Ross, D.L. (2003). "Emerging Trends in Police Failure to Train Liability." *Policing: An International Journal of Police Strategies and Management* 2:169-193.

Ross, D.L. (1997). "Emerging Trends in Correctional Civil Liability Cases: A Content Analysis of Federal Court Decisions of Title 42 United States Code Section 1983: 1970-1994." *Journal of Criminal Justice* 25:501-515.

Sandler, D. & D. Schodendbrod (2003). *Democracy by Decree.* New Haven, CT: Yale University Press.

Schmidt, W. (2004). "Criminal Justice Compliance Officer." *Journal of Law Enforcement Executive Forum* 5:1-14.

Silver, I. (2005). *Police Civil Liability.* New York, NY: Matthew Bender & Co.

Silveria, M.J. (2004). "An Unexpected Application of 42 U.S.C. 14141: Using Investigative Findings for 1983." 52 *UCLA Law Review* 601:1-30.

U.S. Commission on Civil Rights (2000). *Revisiting Who Is Guarding the Guardians?: A Report on Police Practices & Civil Rights in America.* Washington, DC: Author.

United States Department of Justice Web site (2006). www.DOJ.gov. Civil Rights Special Litigation Division. html. Accessed February 2006.

United States Department of Justice (2003). *Principles of Good Policing: Avoiding Violence Between Police and Citizens.* Washington DC: United States Department of Justice.

United States Department of State (2005). *Second Periodic Report of the United States of America to the Committee Against Torture.* Washington, DC: U.S. Department of State.

Vaughn, M.S. and L.F. Coomes (1995). "Police Civil Liability Under Section 1983: When Do Police Officers Act Under Color of Law?" *Journal of Criminal Justice* 23:395-415.

Walker, S. (2003). "New Approaches to Ensuring the Legitimacy of Police Conduct: The New Paradigm of Police Accountability: The U.S. Justice Department 'Pattern or Practice' Suits in Context." 22 *Saint Louis University Public Law Review* 3:1-43.

Walker, S. (2001). "Early Warning Systems for Police: Responding to the Problem Police Officer." *Research in Brief.* Washington, DC: U.S. Department of Justice.

Walker, S., G.P. Alpert & D.J. Kenney (2000). "Early Warning Systems for Police: Concept, History, and Issues." *Police Quarterly* 2:132-152.

Wilson, J.Q. (1989). *Bureaucracy: What Government Agencies Do and Why They Do It.* New York, NY: Basic Books.

Wilson, J.Q. (1985). *Thinking About Crime.* New York, NY: Vintage Books.

Worrall, J.L. and O. Marenin (1998). "Emerging Liability Issues in the Implementation and Adoption of Community-Oriented Policing." *Policing: An International Journal of Police Strategies and Management* 1:1221-136.

Worrall, J.L. (2001). "Culpability Standards in Section 1983 Litigation against Criminal Justice Officials When and Why Mental State Matters." *Crime & Delinquency* 47:28-59.

Cases Cited

Brady v. Maryland, 373 U.S. 83 (1963)

City of Canton v. Harris, 489 U.S. 378 (1989)

Groh v. Ramirez, 540 U.S. 551 (2004)

Hazelwood School District v. United States, 433 U.S. 299 (1977)

International Brotherhood of Teamsters v. United States, 431 U.S. 324 (1977)

Mason County v. Davis, 927 F. 2d 1473 (9th Cir. 1991)

Mapp v. Ohio, 367 U.S. 643 (1961)

Monroe v. Pape, 365 U.S. 167 (1961)

Monell v. Department of Social Services of New York, 436 U.S. 658 (1978)

Printz v. United States, 512 U.S. 898 (1997)

Terry v. Ohio, 392 U.S. 1 (1968)

United States v. City of Columbus, No. CIV A. 2: 99CV1097 (S.D. Ohio 2000)

Chapter 9

Use of Force in Law Enforcement and Corrections

Law enforcement and correctional personnel have legal authority to use force in the performance of their duties. The police frequently use force to effect lawful arrests, in self-defense, and to overcome unlawful resistance. Correctional personnel frequently use force in self-defense, breaking up fights, maintaining security and order, and quelling disturbances or riots. When using force, criminal justice personnel must justify the type and degree of force used in any situation and are required to use force within a framework of legally prescribed guidelines. Agency procedures guide officers in their use of force. Using force outside these guidelines can give rise to civil liability if a citizen or prisoner alleges that the officer violated his or her constitutionally protected rights by using unreasonable force.

Use of force by criminal justice practitioners is one of the most controversial aspects of the legal authority granted to them. Frequently, in incidents in which force was used, claims of excessive force arise and numerous questions emerge, such as: What constitutes excessive force? What is reasonable force? Was the amount or type of force used by the officer appropriate and necessary? What is the appropriate standard with which to evaluate the use of force? Did the officer violate the constitutional rights of the plaintiff? These and many more questions will be raised by a plaintiff seeking to win monetary damages. This chapter examines the liability issues surrounding claims of excessive force in police and correctional work. This topic is of critical importance to officers, because they must be aware of how the courts have established standards with which to evaluate such claims. Moreover, supervisory personnel must understand their role in training officers in proper use-of-force decisionmaking and use-of-force procedures, developing policy guidelines for agency personnel, and investigating claims of excessive force. Allegations of excessive force and brutality will be addressed and legal precedents will be presented.

What Is Known About the Use of Force by Criminal Justice Personnel?

Studies on Police Use of Force

Research studies that evaluate police use of force as well as legal decisions were limited prior to the 1980s. Hopkins (1931) reported on a study of the New York Police Department and found in 166 cases (23% of the cases examined) that some type of physical force was used against citizens. Common methods of force used were strikes (67 cases), rubber hose (19 cases), blackjack (12 cases), and one suspect was hung out of a window. The Wickersham Commission (National Commission on Law Observance and Enforcement, 1931) also reported such police use-of-force practices.

More recently, however, police use-of-force measures have become fertile ground for scholarly research. Past researchers have focused their efforts on deadly force and firearms issues primarily because of their high profile and potential for liability, and because of more complete record-keeping, which makes data collection less problematic (Alpert, 1989; Binder & Fridell, 1984; Binder & Scharf, 1980; Bloomberg, 1982; Chevigny, 1969; Fridell, 1989; Fyfe, 1978, 1988; Geller, 1985; Horvath, 1987; Jacobs & Britt, 1979; Lester, 1984; Matulia, 1982; Milton et al., 1997; Pate & Fridell, 1993; Reiss, 1971; Schultz & Service, 1981; Waegel, 1984). In comparison, less research has been conducted on the nature and extent of nonlethal force used by police, although a body of research is emerging. Most empirical research on nonlethal force by police has been based on data collected through the observation of officers on patrol (Reiss, 1971; Friederich, 1980; Sykes & Brent, 1983; Bayley & Garofalo, 1989a). These studies indicate that force used by the officer is infrequent in citizen and police encounters and is generally a result of antagonistic behaviors of the citizen. Other studies have reviewed use-of-force reports filed by police (Croft, 1985; Croft & Austin, 1987; NIJ, 1999; Garner et al., 1996; Greenfeld et al., 1997; Greenleaf & Lanza-Kaduce, 1995; McLaughlin, 1992). These studies indicate that police use of force is a complex issue, frequently revolving around the changing situational dynamics of the arrest environment, and is rare in occurrence, given the number of citizen and police contacts and the number of arrests that are made annually. It is also recognized that continuing research on the situational dynamics of police-citizen encounters is needed to further improve our understanding of the police use of force (Mastrofski & Parks, 1990; Ross, 1999; Alpert & Dunham, 1999).

The Violent Crime Control and Law Enforcement Act of 1994 (VCCLEA) illustrates congressional concern about allegations of police use of excessive force. Part of the Act (§ 14141) authorizes the Civil Rights Division of the Department of Justice to initiate civil actions against police agencies when, among other conduct, their use of force reaches a level constituting a pattern or practice of depriving individuals of their constitutional rights.

Since 1999 the Department of Justice has performed 22 investigations of police departments. As a result of these investigations, seven police departments have entered into consent decrees, which stipulate federal intervention for five years. Memorandums of agreements have been entered into with six agencies and the DOJ is currently conducting investigations of nine police departments (DOJ, 2006).

Since the passage of the VCCLEA, the DOJ has twice conducted the largest national use-of-force survey (Greenfeld et al., 2001; Langham et al., 1997). Surveys were received from individuals over the age of 12 (21% of the population) who had police contact during the preceding 12 months. In 1996, 45 million people had a face-to-face contact with the police, while 44 million people had contact with the police in 1999. Survey findings estimate that in one percent of the contacts, police used or threatened the use of force. About 76 percent of the respondents indicated that the force used or threatened was "excessive"; 87 percent were male, 59 percent were white, and 38 percent were non-white. Comparisons of the two study periods are presented in Figure 9.1

Figure 9.1
Summary of the Police Use of Force National Data—1997/2001

Factor	1997 (%)	2001 (%)
Handcuffs applied	86	91
Physical control techniques	85	84
Pepper spray	5	12
Batons/Electrical devices	6	2
Firearms	5	5
Minor injury sustained	15	15
Under influence of any substance	30	30

Respondents further indicated that about 25 percent provoked the officer into using force, about eight percent were charged with resisting arrest, six percent were charged with drunk driving, and three percent were charged with assaulting the officer. A majority of the types of force used consisted of four circumstances: (1) traffic stops; (2) disturbance calls; (3) felony arrests; and (4) domestic calls. Officers encountered verbal resistance, resistance during searches and handcuffing, suspects running from the officer, physical assaults, and assaults threatening the use of a weapon. Respondents stated that at least two officers were present, only 20 percent of the contacts involved one officer, and the officers were predominately white males (85%).

The International Association of Chiefs of Police (IACP) has been studying the use of force by the police since 1991. Their published study (2001) reported that 564 police departments submitted incident report data regarding 45,913,161 calls for service, which included county, state, municipal, and federal agencies. These calls for service resulted in 177,215 use-of-force incidents and 8,082 citizen complaints. A baseline figure of the police use of force was 3.61 for every 10,000 dispatched calls for service. This resulted in a rate of the police using force in less than one percent. Arrests (39%) accounted for the most frequent circumstance in which force was used, followed by disturbance calls (21%), traffic stops (14%), domestic incidents (11%), drunk/disorderly calls (9%), and investigations (6%). The prevalence of excessive force was estimated by examining force incident complaints and the number sustained, equaling 0.42 percent of the time. Expressed differently, excessive force was *not* used in more than 99 percent of the incidents. Intoxication significantly influenced the use of force during traffic stops, as they reflect 46 percent of the force incidents. Male drivers were almost 10 times more likely to use multiple types of force against the officers in traffic stops, requiring officers to use physical and chemical force (52%). Subjects did not incur an injury in 60 percent of the incidents, minor injuries accounted for 38 percent, major reported injuries accounted for less than one percent and five subject deaths occurred. Officers sustained an injury in only 13 percent of the incidents, minor injuries were sustained in 12 percent, and in less than one percent of the incidents was an officer injured. Citizen complaints for the use of physical force generated the majority of complaints, followed by impact weapons, pepper spray, and firearms.

Ross (2005) performed a content analysis of 43 published police use-of-force studies in the United States from 1969 to 2003 in order to assess the trends and patterns of the studies' findings. He found that 15 studies used incident reports, 14 used surveys, 11 used field observations, and three used citizen complaints to study the police use of force. Highlights of the studies showed that the police used any force in about three percent of the arrests and excessive force was used in less than one percent of the arrests. The police primarily used any type of mechanical restraints and physical control techniques in 85 percent of the incidents, used pepper spray in about 10 percent and used multiple types of force techniques/equipment in 88 percent of the incidents. Subjects resisted the police efforts of arrest or control in 88 percent of the confrontations and used multiple types of physical and verbal resistance against the officer in 90 percent of the circumstances. The subject displayed behaviors consistent with intoxication of any substance in 65 percent and suspects used a weapon against the officer in four percent of the incidents. The police encountered resistance requiring the use of force in situations of: felony arrest (44%); traffic stop (24%); disturbance call (12%); and domestic calls (12%).

Although these studies reported that force used by the police is infrequent, use-of-force incidents have precipitated numerous civil litigation actions against the police for excessive force. Limited research has been conducted regarding the nature and trends of civil litigation relative to excessive force claims. A publication group (LRP, 1992) researched police shootings and found that plaintiffs prevailed in 63 percent of the cases and that the average award was $1,327,927. Kappeler et al. (1993, updated in 1996) conducted a content analysis of published § 1983 claims against the police from 1978 to 1994, and identified the 20 most prevalent topics of litigation filed against the police. They reported that excessive force claims ranked sixth out of 20 categories in which plaintiffs (56%) are likely to prevail in a § 1983 lawsuit. They also found that the average award in excessive force claims amounted to $178,878. Ross (2000) reported that from 1989 to 1999, claims for failing to train in nonlethal force is the most litigated topic area filed against administrators. Police prevailed in 57 percent of failure-to-train claims involving nonlethal force, and 60 percent in lethal force allegations.

Studies on Use of Force in Corrections

Physical encounters between prisoners and correctional personnel are intrinsic to the institutional environment. Working as a correctional officer can be a dangerous job, and deciding to use force is an extremely critical issue. The decision to use force in corrections has resulted in riots, disturbances, death and injury, property damage and, of course, civil liability.

Research studies specifically analyzing force used by correctional officers are virtually nonexistent. A handful of studies have examined prisoner assaults on correctional officers (Kratcoski, 1987; Light, 1991; Ross, 1996; Rowan, 1996). Camp and Camp (2002) reported that from 1994 to 2001, prisoner assaults averaged 14,000 annually against prison correctional officers and 4,000 annually against detention officers. The Department of Justice (2003) reported that prisoner assaults on officers increased more than 28 percent in prisons and 15 percent in jails from 1995 to 2001. Prior studies reveal that a majority of prisoner assaults occur while the officer is performing routine tasks, such as enforcing facility rules, breaking up fights, and supervising prisoners. These studies suggest that prisoner assaults on officers are often unprovoked and spontaneous, with prisoners losing control and lashing out at officers as the nearest symbol of authority.

Ross (1990) conducted a national examination of the status of use-of-force policies in state and federal adult institutions (41 states and Federal Bureau of Prisons). He reported that 90 percent of the respondents had a use-of-force policy that was written within three years of the survey. Hemmens and Atherton (1999) conducted a study on use of force in corrections for the American Correctional Association. They surveyed officials in state adult correctional institutions (46 states, two military prisons, and the Federal Bureau of Prisons), 30 jails, eight institutions in Canada, and 39 juvenile institutions. They reported that the American and Canadian prison systems have a written policy on the use of force, and 97 percent of the jails and juvenile institutions have written policies. All respondents were less likely (45%) to have a policy covering specialized applications of force (special response teams and use of specialized equipment and restraint techniques). More than 80 percent of the agencies allow officers to use chemical agents on prisoners in a variety of situations, and less than 45 percent allow the use of stun guns. Firearms use is authorized in more than two-thirds of U.S. correctional institutions and jails, and in only 17 percent of the Canadian institutions and 11 percent of the juvenile departments. Forty-three percent of respondents revealed that they did not sustain an "excessive force" incident in 1997. Approximately 51 percent, however, indicated they had incurred between one and 25 incidents of "excessive force," and 94 percent reported that they had disciplined the officer.

Ross (2004) conducted a use-of-force study in 11 county detention facilities for the Michigan Municipal Risk Management Authority (MMRMA). All of the agencies were insured by MMRMA and were dispersed throughout the state of Michigan, including the Upper Peninsula. He analyzed 549 use-of-force incidents between 2000 and 2003. A statistical review of the incidents where detainees resisted the officers, requiring a level of force, revealed that 40 percent of the incidents occurred in the booking area; that officers had to use force as result of performing a basic job function, such as a search, an escort, and supervising detainees; officers were three times more likely to encounter a use-of-force situation while conducting a personal search than in a self-defense situation; officers encountered a resistive detainee who was intoxicated in 32 percent of the incidents—18 percent were mentally impaired; detainees exhibited verbal and physical assault resistance more than other types of resistance, while lethal force used by detainees only accounted for five percent of the detainee assaults; in 35 percent of incidents, detainees wrestled with officers on the floor; detention officers primarily employed verbal control to dissuade detainees, but also used physical force measures more frequently than other forms of force; multiple officers generally responded to a use-of-force encounter as opposed to only one officer responding; and officers and prisoners rarely sustained injuries from these encounters.

This brief review of the use-of-force literature reveals the topic to be a paramount issue for the public and criminal justice personnel. In response, the United States Supreme Court has established guidelines for determining the components of excessive force and has established standards of review when considering allegations of excessive force (*Tennessee v. Garner*, 1985; *Whitley v. Albers*, 1986; *Graham v. Connor*, 1989; *Hudson v. McMillian*, 1992). While not easily defined, these standards outline how claims of excessive force in police work and corrections are examined. The United States Supreme Court has developed different standards for examining use of force, and the appropriate standard is based on the status of the individual. Therefore, the remaining discussion will describe how the courts specifically apply use-of-force standards in policing, in detention facilities, and in prisons.

Lower Court Use-of-Force Decisions

Claims alleging the use of excessive force by criminal justice personnel that violate the constitutional rights of an arrestee or prisoner may be filed in state court using state tort laws or in federal court under § 1983. The major distinction between the two court systems is the component of a constitutional deprivation. To be successful in a federal action, the plaintiff must prove that the officer's actions caused the deprivation of a constitutionally protected right (Kappeler, 1997). Excessive force lawsuits are filed in state court as torts for assault and battery or wrongful death. Existing tort law or statutes will govern the examination of such claims. Most claims of excessive force are filed in federal court under § 1983.

"Shocks the Conscience" Test (Fourteenth Amendment)

Prior to the United States Supreme Court's decisions on the use of force, lower courts (*Skinner v. Brooks*, 1944; *Stein v. State*, 1976; *Fobbs v. City of Los Angeles*, 1957; *Hostin v. United States*, 1983) had authorized criminal justice personnel to use reasonable and necessary force in the following circumstances: to effect an arrest and overcome unlawful resistance, in self-defense, in defense of a third party, and to prevent an individual from harming himself. Before the *Garner* (1985) and *Graham* (1989) decisions, there was considerable controversy in the lower federal courts about which doctrinal approach should be used in excessive force claims. Some courts held that excessive force claims should be viewed as deprivations of liberty without due process of law. This approach was premised upon the notion that individuals have a substantive due process right under the Fourteenth Amendment to be free from the unreasonable and unwarranted violation of their physical integrity by police officers, even in the course of an otherwise valid arrest (*Screws v. United States*, 1945; *Brazier v. Cherry*, 1961; *Monroe v. Pape*, 1961; *Johnson v. Glick*, 1973; *Shillingford v. Holmes*, 1981). For many years, a majority of courts used Judge Friendly's decision in *Johnson v. Glick* (1973), employing the "shocks the conscience" test. This "test" originated in *Rochin v. California* (1952), in which Justice Frankfurter stated that due process prohibits governmental actions that "shock the conscience." Under that formulation, the due process standard has generally been construed to incorporate subjective factors, such as the intent or motivation of the government actor. In use-of-force cases, the question usually turns on whether the type and degree of force was designed to "punish" an individual rather than to accomplish a legitimate law enforcement goal, such as maintaining or restoring control. Using Justice Frankfurter's "shocks the conscience" test, the court in *Glick* established four factors for evaluating the actions of the officer: (1) the need for the use of force; (2) the relationship between the amount of force needed and the amount that was used; (3) the severity of the injuries sustained by the plaintiff; and (4) whether force was applied in good faith or maliciously and sadistically for the purpose of causing harm.

Although the *Glick* standard originated from a use-of-force incident in a detention facility, it was applied by many courts to police and correctional situations. Uniform application of the "shocks the conscience" test was not universally accepted by the courts. The test created judicial disagreement as to what actions actually constitute significant bodily injury before the plaintiff could prevail in a § 1983 action. Some courts held that only "serious" or "severe" injuries are actionable under § 1983 (*Raley v. Fraser*, 1984; *Owens v. City of Atlanta*, 1985; *Gumz v. Morrissette*, 1985). These courts strictly applied the test, concluding that not every tort committed by a police officer violates a person's rights guaranteed by the Fourteenth Amendment. In *Raley*, a choke hold was placed on the plaintiff by a police officer four times during an encounter. His arms were bruised and his face was scraped, handcuffs on his wrists caused welts, and he suffered a sore throat and a hoarse voice for weeks following the incident. These injuries were not permanent, and although the plaintiff's resistance was minimal, the court concluded that the officer's use of "draconian measures" was not disproportionate between the officer's actions and the plaintiff's resistance. The court of appeals affirmed. In *Owens* an arrestee died from positional asphyxia as a result of being placed in a "stretch" hold position known as the "mosses crosses" in a jail cell. The court concluded that the method of restraint did not violate the decedent's constitutional rights.

Fourth Amendment Interpretation

Other courts, however, did not require a showing of a severe injury to prevail in the legal action. Some courts emphasized the second factor of the *Glick* test, using juries to determine whether the amount of force was justified given the facts (*Shillingford v. Holmes*, 1981; *Hall v. Tawney*, 1980). Moreover, during this period, other courts analyzed excessive force claims as Fourth Amendment violations if the incident resulted from an unreasonable search and seizure (*Kidd v. O'Neil*, 1985; *Gilmere v. City of Atlanta*, 1985: *Martin v. Gentile*, 1988). Judge Phillips' opinion in the *Kidd* case reveals the court's reasoning regarding principles of examining the use of force. He explained that the constitutionally protected interests that citizens have in personal security may be invaded in various contexts due to countervailing governmental interests. The issue is always what degree of force is justified by those interests in the circumstances of a particular case. The court emphasized that it is not the severity of the force used, standing alone, that is the measure of whether a constitutional violation has occurred.

Use-of-Force Standards Established by the Supreme Court

From 1985 to 1992, the United States Supreme Court developed several standards for evaluating claims of excessive force. These standards can be somewhat confusing and difficult to apply. The following case illustrates this point:

> After booking and fingerprinting an intoxicated arrestee, a police officer attempted to transport him to the county jail 20 miles away. The arrestee was handcuffed, with cuffs behind his back, and placed in the backseat of a patrol car (not seatbelted), which had a protective Plexiglas screen. Approximately five miles into the transport, the arrestee reached through the open window of the screen, threatened to kill the officer or himself, and grabbed the steering wheel, causing an accident. The arrestee crawled through the window into the front seat and choked the officer. The officer and arrestee exited the vehicle and the arrestee continued to choke the officer. The officer attempted to use his pepper spray, but accidentally sprayed himself, disabling him considerably. A passerby stopped and assisted the officer and placed the violently resisting arrestee in a "chokehold" on two separate occasions. After the second application, the arrestee appeared to submit, but became unresponsive and subsequently died on the way to the hospital in an ambulance. The estate filed a § 1983 claim of excessive force under the Fourth Amendment. The defendant filed for summary judgment under the Fourteenth Amendment, and the court granted summary judgment to the officer.

This case (*Proffitt v. City of Pana, Illinois*, 2000) illustrates the problem of which standard of review should apply in a use-of-force situation. The arrestee was legitimately arrested, booked, and transported to jail. However, he was not formally lodged in a detention facility. Should the Fourth or Fourteenth Amendment apply? The court, granting summary judgment, applied the Fourteenth Amendment ("shocks the conscience" test), because the arrestee had been booked and fingerprinted. This type of question emerges routinely, and Figure 9.2 illustrates the varying Supreme Court standards and their appropriate application. The following discussion provides an assessment of how the United States Supreme Court applies different standards to claims of excessive force.

Lethal Force

With the *Tennessee v. Garner* decision (1985), the Supreme Court provided its interpretation of the constitutional guidelines on the use of deadly force against a fleeing felon. Prior to this decision, the *Glick* standard was

Figure 9.2
U.S. Supreme Court Use of Force Case Law and Standards

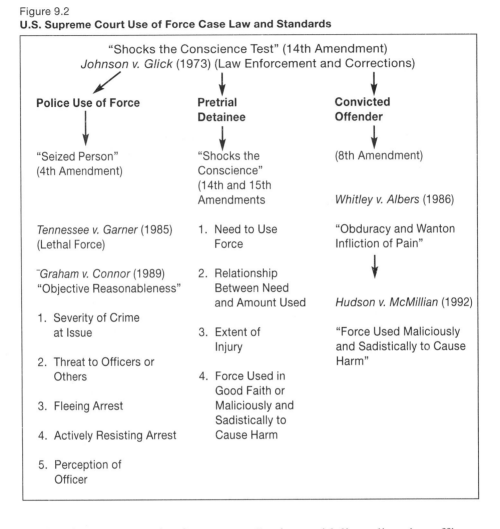

applied in most excessive force cases. Further, guidelines directing officers in the use of deadly force were found in state law or agency regulations. In *Garner,* the Supreme Court for the first time established a standard of review for evaluating claims of excessive force arising from deadly force incidents. This decision also initiated a separation for the evaluation of use-of-force cases in policing and in corrections, an issue lower courts had been struggling with for years.

The justification of using deadly force to prevent the escape of a suspect was first defined in *Tennessee v. Garner* (1985). Two Memphis police officers responded to a call about a prowler inside a building at 10:45 P.M. Once at the scene, the officers observed a 15-year-old burglar attempting to flee. One officer noticed the youth and believed he was unarmed, but shot him as he was scaling a fence to prevent him from escaping. The officer used deadly force in accordance with a state fleeing statute that authorized officers to use such force to prevent suspects from escaping.

The youth died and his father filed a § 1983 lawsuit for alleged violations of the Fourth, Fifth, Sixth, Eighth, and Fourteenth Amendments. The family petitioned the United States Supreme Court to review the "fleeing felon" deadly force rule. The Supreme Court held that the rule was unconstitutional and served no important governmental function. The Court held that it is not permissible to use deadly force to prevent the escape of a felony suspect under all circumstances.

Moreover, the Court maintained that "apprehension" by the use of deadly force constitutes a seizure subject to the Fourth Amendment's reasonableness requirement. Conversely, the Court stated that if an officer has "probable cause to believe that the suspect poses a threat of serious physical harm, either to the officer or to others, it is not unconstitutionally unreasonable to prevent escape by using deadly force." The police must have probable cause to believe that the suspect is dangerous.

The *Garner* decision is significant, because for the first time the U.S. Supreme Court applied the Fourth Amendment to claims of excessive force arising from a deadly force incident, not general principles of due process of law. The primary issue, therefore, in excessive force claims becomes the matter of seizure under the Fourth Amendment. A court must balance the need for the seizure against the nature and quality of the seizure to determine whether the seizure was reasonable. Obviously, not all seizures require the use of lethal force. Reasonableness depends on when a seizure is made and how it is performed. The decision in *Garner* therefore provides:

1. An officer must have probable cause to believe that the suspect poses a significant threat of death or serious injury to officers or citizens.

2. Lethal force may be warranted to prevent an escape or protect a citizen.

3. Lethal force may be used only when a felony has been committed. The felony must be dangerous, involving violence or the threat of violence.

4. A suspect is dangerous if he threatens the officer with a weapon or the officer has probable cause to believe the suspect committed an offense in which he inflicted or threatened to inflict serious physical injury.

5. When practical, an officer should give a warning prior to using lethal force.

Lethal Force Actions

Many cases hinge on the issue of whether the arrestee presented a clear threat of harm to the officer. Plaintiffs will most likely litigate such cases from the perspective of hindsight. This strategy ignores the fundamental holdings of both *Garner* and *Graham* in that the use of force will be judged at the moment it is required, from the perspective of the officer, and the rapidly evolving events of the situation—not from hindsight, regardless of the outcome. The use of lethal force by police underscores these principles as the following cases illustrate.

An officer in *Fraire v. City of Arlington* (1992) shot and killed the driver of a truck he was attempting to stop for driving while impaired. When the driver attempted to run over the officer, he fired one shot into the oncoming truck. The court held that the officer acted in self-defense because the driver placed him in imminent danger, and therefore the officer had used reasonable force. The court concluded that objective reasonableness is measured by the established law at the time of the incident.

Compare, however, a similar incident with a different decision by the court in *Smith v. Cupp* (2005). An officer arrested Smith for making several harassing phone calls from a Waffle House. The officer cuffed Smith, searched him, placed him in the back seat of the patrol car, and radioed for a tow truck. The officer's patrol car did not have a protective screen separating the front and back seats. The officer left the patrol car running, along with the air conditioning. As the officer met the tow truck operator, Smith climbed into the front seat of the patrol car, put the car in gear, and rapidly accelerated the car directly at the officer. The officer fired four rounds at the car as it came at him, barely missing him. Three of the rounds hit the car and one round hit Smith in the ear. The car travelled a few yards and collided with a tree. Smith died and his family filed a § 1983 action claiming excessive force.

The district court denied summary judgment, holding that the officer's use of deadly force was constitutionally unjustified. Anticipating that the officer would file an interlocutory appeal, Smith sought certification for an immediate appeal. The Sixth Circuit Court of Appeals affirmed the lower court's decision. The court reasoned that Smith had been compliant and arrested for a non-violent offense, and although there was some danger to the public from Smith's driving off in a stolen police car, the danger was not so grave as to justify the use of deadly force. The court further concluded that no person at the scene was ever in danger. According to the court, although Smith had possession of a dangerous "weapon," he was not threatening the lives of those around him when he was fatally shot. Finally, the court held that this type of situation did not present a "perceived serious threat of physical harm to the officers or others in the area from the perspective of a reasonable officer," and such deadly force was unconstitutional. This case is instructive as it applies to the facts of this situation. The decision does not alter the factor of the "perception of the officer" in examining the choice to use a level of force, but addresses the immediacy of the need to use force in self-defense.

Determining how the courts interpret the appropriate standard in lethal force shootings can be problematic. In *Gutierrez-Rodriguez v. Cartagena* (1989), the court held that four officers acted with "reckless and callous indifference" in firing their weapons and rendering the plaintiff a paraplegic when they shot him in the back. Four undercover officers approached the plaintiff's vehicle, in which he and his girlfriend were seated. Seeing the officers, the plaintiff began to drive away and the officers opened fire on the car. The jury awarded $4.5 million in compensatory and punitive damages, which was upheld by the court, agreeing that the officers deprived the plaintiff of his protected liberty interests.

Courts acknowledge that events occur rapidly during an arrest, and decisions pertaining to the degree of force must be made quickly and often occur under adverse conditions. In *Pittman v. Nelms* (1996), two officers stopped a vehicle driven by a suspected drug dealer. The officers approached the vehicle from opposite sides, and one officer leaned into the window on the driver's side. The driver quickly accelerated the car and the officer's arm became trapped inside. The car dragged the officer 25 to 30 feet. The officer's partner fired his weapon into the back seat as the car was dragging his partner. The round hit the driver and the vehicle stopped. The driver later filed suit for excessive force, claiming that the officer should not have shot, because his partner was thrown away from the car after traveling only 10 to 15 feet, he was not seriously hurt, and the incident lasted only a few seconds. The court ruled in favor of the officers, stating that the officer was in serious danger and the situation was tense, uncertain, and rapidly evolving. The officers did not use excessive force, as a reasonable officer faced with this type of danger could have believed his decision to fire was justified. The same standard of review was applied in *Nelson v. County of Wright* (1998); *Radecki v. Barlea* (1998); *Medeiros v. Town of Dracut* (1998); and *Colston v. Barnhart* (1997). In each of these cases, the officers were under immediate assault and in imminent personal danger during the arrest. The officers discharged their firearms but only wounded the arrestee. The confrontations lasted less than three minutes, were tense, and escalated rapidly. The court held that a reasonable officer could have believed that the use of deadly force would not be excessive or in violation of clearly established law, which required an objectively reasonable response.

It appears that there are divergent court decisions regarding lethal force and when it may violate departmental policy. In both *Sigman v. Town of Chapel Hill* (1998) and *McRae v. Tena* (1996), police fired their weapons and killed an arrestee who threatened the officers with a weapon. The court determined that reasonable force must be viewed by the perception of the officer at the moment it is required, despite the language of the department policy restricting the officer's use of force. The policy is irrelevant when officers are faced with immediate danger. In both *Wallace v. Estate of Davis* (1997) and *Russo v. City of Cincinnati* (1992), officers shot and killed a mentally impaired person who was suicidal and threatened officers with weapons. The court found that the officers acted unreasonably and violated their policy on dealing with the mentally impaired. The men had not actually pointed the weapons at the officers, and the courts concluded they did not pose a serious threat to the officer.

The court also concluded that the force was unreasonable, and therefore violated department policy, when an officer held a gun to the head of a nine-year-old child, threatening to pull the trigger during the search of her home (*McDonald v. Haskins*, 1992). The child posed no threat to the officer and did not resist, attempt to flee, or assault anyone. The facts in the case stated a valid excessive force claim. Lethal force will be evaluated on the likelihood that the officer perceived a serious risk of harm to himself, based on the circumstances at the time, and force must be tailored to its necessity. The court in *Mathieu v. Imperial Toy Company* (1994) held that the officers who shot nine times at a mentally impaired man who held a toy gun used unreasonable force under the circumstances. The court opined the officers approached the man in an open area, with no available cover or backup, and allowed for no alternative but deadly force if the individual made any movement.

The Ninth Circuit Court of Appeals (*Cruz v. Escondido*, 1997) and a U.S. District Court in Kansas (*Guseman v. Martinez*, 1998) have defined the parameters of lethal force. Neither of these cases involved officers using their weapons, but in *Cruz* a police dog was deployed to restrain the plaintiff, who sustained injuries that required lengthy hospitalization and surgery. In *Guseman* the plaintiff died as a result of positional asphyxiation due to her wrists and ankles being restrained. The question for the courts in these two cases focused on how likely death must be in order for the force used to be considered deadly force. In *Cruz* the court rejected the Model Penal Code definition of force that causes or creates a substantial risk of causing death or serious bodily injury. Rather, the court interpreted both *Garner* and *Graham* to mean that a plaintiff must present evidence that the force used, in the circumstances under which it was used, posed more than a remote possibility of death. The court concluded that lethal force is force that has a reasonable probability of causing death. In *Guseman* the court concurred with the Ninth Circuit's definition of lethal force, commenting that almost any force can cause death in aberrant circumstances. Deadly force under the Fourth Amendment applies only to that force that is reasonably likely to cause death. In both cases, officers were exonerated.

Officers responded to a silent alarm at a liquor store where a mentally impaired man threatened to harm two employees with a concealed axe in *Isom v. Town of Warren, Rhode Island* (2004). The employees were able to escape from the store and informed the responding officers that the suspect had an axe in his hands. Back-up officers responded, and entered the store taking various tactical positions, and began talking with Isom. He told the officers that he was going to die today and raised the axe slightly over his head. From positions of cover, the officers continued to talk with Isom but he became non-responsive. A detective entered the store and decided to spray Isom with pepper spray so that the other officers could subdue and control him. The detective instructed Isom to drop the axe and when he did not comply he sprayed him. The spray did not affect him and Isom turned, raised the axe above his head, and charged the officers. From about 10 feet away from Isom, two officers fired their weapons. He fell to the floor and later died. The department's use-of-force policy authorized officers to use force in self-defense or defense of another, to preserve the peace, to overcome resistance, to perform searches, to prevent self-injury or suicide, and to prevent an escape from custody. The policy authorized the use of pepper spray to protect an officer or another, to subdue a person resisting arrest, or to deter persons engaged in riotous conduct.

Isom's estate filed a § 1983 lawsuit alleging that the officers used excessive force in violation of the Fourth Amendment and also filed claims of a wrongful death. The lower court granted summary judgment for the officers and the estate appealed. The appellate court affirmed the decision, ruling that the officer acted within his discretion when he decided to use the pepper spray and did not breach his duty of care. The court held that there was no evidence that the officers acted unreasonably and framed their assessment of the officers' actions within the criteria established by the United States Supreme Court in *Graham*. The court ruled that the situation was "fraught with hazard," as Isom was committing a crime, posed an immediate threat to the safety of the officers and others, and was actively resisting arrest. The claim of wrongful death also failed, as the court ruled that the officers followed the department's use-of-force policy, which gave them broad discretion when using force.

In conjunction with § 12131 of the Americans with Disabilities Act (1990) and allegations that an officer used excessive force in the shooting of a family member, in *Sudac v. Hoang* the family brought a legal action under the Fourth Amendment (2005). Sudac was diagnosed with bipolar disorder. His condition worsened and he began tearing up the house and threatened his mother and sister with a knife. Fearing that they would be killed, his mother and sister left the house, retreated to a neighbor's house, and called the police. Sudac left the house and threatened a neighbor with the knife as two officers from the Kansas City, Kansas, Police Department responded. As the officers exited their patrol vehicles, Sudac fled down an alley and the officers followed him. Sudac stopped and the officers maintained a distance of about 10 to 15 yards, drew their weapons, and asked him to drop the knife. Sudac began walking backward down the alley and the officers followed him. Sudac abruptly stopped and one officer sprayed him with pepper spray, which had no effect. Sudac continued walking backward as the officers followed and occasionally he would extend his hand with the knife at the officers. The officers had their weapons pointed at him and instructed him to stop and to drop the knife, but he ignored their requests. While Sudac was walking, the officers noticed that a couple was getting out of a car and, fearing that they would be harmed, closed the gap between themselves and Sudac to about eight feet. Sudac stopped, raised the weapon above his head and quickly lunged at one of the officers. The officer fired four rounds, killing Sudac.

Sudac's mother filed suit, claiming that the officer deprived her son of his Fourth Amendment right to free from an excessive use of lethal force. She also claimed that the officer used force without recognizing that her son was a mentally disabled person in violation of his constitutional rights. The district court granted summary judgment to the officer, holding that the officer properly perceived that there was probable cause to believe that his life was in immediate jeopardy. The court stated that the law does not require an officer to utilize "alternative, less intrusive means if their conduct is objectively reasonable," even though they did attempt other means to control Sudac. Officers may use deadly force in self-defense and it is not constitutionally unreasonable. Finally, the court ruled that under the totality of circumstances, the officer used objectively reasonable force and was entitled to summary judgment. Claims alleging that the officers violated the ADA also failed.

The *Graham* Decision and Objectively Reasonable Force

Objective Reasonableness Standard

With its decision in *Graham v. Connor* (1989) (see Figure 9.3), the United States Supreme Court put to rest the debate about how to examine claims of excessive force during an arrest. *Graham* applies only to persons at liberty. The Court established that excessive force claims arising out of arrests, investigatory stops, or other seizures of "free citizens" are properly analyzed under the Fourth Amendment's objective reasonableness standard. Deciding whether the force used in a given instance is "reasonable" under the Fourth Amendment requires a careful balancing of the nature and quality of the intrusion on the arrestee's Fourth Amendment interests against the countervailing governmental interests. The Court emphasized that the overriding function of the Fourth Amendment is to protect an individual's personal privacy and dignity against unwarranted intrusion by the state. This principle parallels the *Terry v. Ohio* (1968) decision, in which Justice Warren broadly characterized the personal security and privacy interests protected by the Fourth Amendment.

Figure 9.3
Graham v. Connor **(1989)**

Graham, a diabetic, asked his friend Berry to drive him to a convenience store to purchase orange juice to counteract the onset of an insulin reaction. Once in the store, he observed a long line at the checkout counter, decided to put the juice container down, and ran out of the store. Graham requested that his friend drive him to another friend's house for assistance.

Officer Connor of the Charlotte, North Carolina, police department observed Graham hurriedly exiting the store and conducted an investigatory stop. During the stop, Berry informed the officer of Graham's condition, and the officer ordered Berry to wait while he performed a check and summoned backup. During the check, Graham exited the vehicle, ran around it twice, and passed out. Several officers responded, and one rolled the unconscious Graham over and secured him with handcuffs. Berry attempted to explain that Graham was experiencing an insulin reaction, but officers ignored him. One officer thought Graham was drunk and needed to be locked up, while another officer stated "ain't nothing wrong with him, I've seen a lot of diabetics that never acted like this." The officers picked Graham up and slammed him headfirst into the hood of the car. The officers shoved him into the police car, where he sustained a broken foot, cuts on his wrists, a bruised forehead, and an injured shoulder. Berry attempted to give some orange juice to Graham while in the squad car, but the officers refused to let him have it. Later, Officer Connor returned to the store and found that no crime had taken place and the officers drove Graham home.

Graham filed suit, claiming that the officers used excessive force during the arrest. Relying on the *Glick* test, officers prevailed at trial and the Fourth Circuit Court of Appeals affirmed. The Supreme Court granted certiorari and found that the lower courts had improperly applied the appropriate standard in determining the excessive force claim. The Court remanded the claim to the district court for reconsideration under the Fourth Amendment standard. The jury, using the Fourth Amendment reasonableness standard, found in favor of Graham. The officers' use of force was unreasonable, because Graham was unconscious when apprehended. This was further compounded by his medical condition, as officers failed to acknowledge warnings by Berry that Graham was experiencing an insulin reaction.

This case is significant because the Court ruled that the appropriate standard of review of excessive force claims arising from an arrest is "objective reasonableness" in accordance with the Fourth Amendment. The Court established the following factors of legal review: the severity of the crime at issue, whether the suspect is actively resisting arrest, whether the suspect is attempting to evade the arrest by flight, and whether the suspect is an immediate threat to the officer or others. The Court noted that officers are often forced to make split-second decisions regarding force and that the reasonableness of such decisions must be based on the perception of the officer and not through hindsight. Determining whether reasonable force was used will be made by courts on a case-by-case basis, in light of the facts and circumstances the officer faced at the time force was required.

The Court held that the Fourth Amendment governs all use of force against persons at liberty, and this corresponds with its former decision in *Garner*. The Court also extended this principle beyond deadly force cases to all excessive force cases in which the person is a "free" citizen. *Graham* would suggest that the use of any significant force against an unresisting arrestee is unreasonable.

Equally important, the Court stressed that the government's primary interest is in the apprehension of criminal suspects as it relates to excessive force claims. That interest is jeopardized whenever a suspect forcibly resists arrest or attempts to avoid detention by fleeing. The government is also concerned about the health and safety of police officers confronted by an armed or otherwise dangerous suspect during the course of an arrest or investigatory stop. In *Chimel v. California* (1969), the Court stated that it is entirely reasonable for a police officer to "search the person in order to remove any weapons that the arrestee might seek to use in order to resist arrest or effect his escape." Otherwise, the officer's safety might be endangered, and the arrest itself frustrated. Moreover, the government has an interest in preventing arrestees from concealing or destroying evanescent evidence during arrest. In *Graham* the Court recognized that the right to make an arrest or investigatory stop necessarily carries with it the right to use some degree of physical coercion or threat to effect it. The Court's deference to varying degrees of physical coercive police conduct derives from and comports with the common law tort principle that police officers are privileged in making forcible arrests.

The Court established several criteria with which to evaluate excessive force claims. Noting that there is no precise or mechanical application possible for this test of reasonableness, the Court requires that careful attention be paid to the facts and circumstances of each case, including the severity of the crime at issue, whether the suspect poses an immediate threat to the safety of the officers or others, and whether the suspect is actively resisting arrest or attempting to evade arrest by flight. The Court emphasized that reasonableness must be judged from the perspective of a reasonable officer on the scene, not hindsight, and should take into account the fact that police officers are often forced to make split-second decisions about the degree of force to use in a particular situation. The Court also noted that an assessment of an excessive force claim will be judged on the totality of circumstances. The Court endorses a "reasonableness at the moment" standard that requires fact finders, when assessing the reasonableness of a particular seizure, to take into account the unpredictable and rapidly evolving dynamics of the arrest environment. The question in each case is whether the officers' actions are objectively reasonable in light of the facts and circumstances confronting them, without regard to their underlying intent or motivation (Klotter, 1999).

For example, in *Smith v. Freland* (1992), a police officer acted reasonably when he shot and killed a motorist who had fled from him at speeds in excess of 90 miles per hour when the officer reasonably believed he was in imminent danger or citizens were imminent danger. The motorist attempted to run the officer down and went through a roadblock. When the officer had him cornered in a cul-de-sac, he turned around on a lawn and drove right at the officer, at which point the officer fired his duty weapon. The officer's use of deadly force was measured against the facts at the time the force was used, as opposed to what may have been done or what was possible by way of hindsight. The court concluded that the officer fired in self-defense and prevention of the motorist's escape, as it presented a threat to others.

It therefore follows that when the crime is minor and the individual neither resists nor attempts to flee, the use of force may be constitutionally excessive, depending upon the facts of the incident. If the person peacefully submits to an arrest, only the amount of force required to secure that person in handcuffs would be appropriately reasonable. Even minimally physically intrusive police conduct may offend a person's Fourth Amendment rights when the government's interests are not justified under the circumstances. This may occur after a suspect has been subdued and is restrained and compliant, and an officer uses unnecessary physical force.

This point was illustrated in *Hogan v. Franco* (1995), in which the jury returned a verdict in favor of the plaintiff for excessive force on the part of three officers. The plaintiff was arrested after resisting the confiscation of alcohol at a public fireworks display. After he was handcuffed, an officer threw him against a fence so forcefully that the handcuffs tightened around his wrists. During transport to the station in a police van, the officer drove in a reckless manner, causing the arrestee to be thrown about. At the station, an officer beat the restrained arrestee with a baton before placing him, injured, in a holding cell. The plaintiff requested medical attention but was denied, and an unidentified officer struck him with a baton. The next day, the plaintiff was taken to the emergency room at the local hospital and was treated for lacerations of the leg and severe bruising of the head and chest from the baton strikes. He also sustained severe nerve damage to his wrist and lower back from being handcuffed.

The court concluded that the actions of the arrestee were nonviolent and the arrest was for an ordinance violation (open container), not a misdemeanor. The plaintiff was not a threat to any officer, no officer was ever in danger, and he was not a flight risk. Because there was no reasonable explanation for his injuries, the officers were held liable. The plaintiff was awarded compensatory damages amounting to $200,000.

Application of *Graham*

Ross (2002) conducted a 10-year study of the lower court's application of the *Graham* standard. Using a content analysis methodology, he took a random sample of 1,200 cases from 4,800 published § 1983 cases (25%) from 1989 to 1999. These cases represent legal actions litigated in court claiming excessive force on the part of law enforcement officers. Four force categories and prevailing trends emerged from the analysis: (1) the use of empty-hand control techniques accounted for 36 percent of the cases (including wrist locks, pressure points, control holds, takedown techniques, and neck restraints) with officers prevailing in 65 percent of the actions; (2) the use of mechanical restraints accounted for 27 of the cases and officers prevailed in 68 percent of the claims; (3) lethal force actions represented 18 percent and officers won 80 percent of the time; (4) use-of-equipment claims accounted for 19 percent; and (5) officers prevailed in 83 percent of the lawsuits.

While the study reveals that officers prevail on average in slightly more than 70 percent of the claims that are litigated in court, there is a divergent perspective of how the lower courts apply the standard of "objective reasonableness." Generally, the majority of the lower courts interpret objectively reasonable force based on the manner of the officer's intrusion, the scope of the intrusion, the need to perform official duties, justification of the intrusion, facts and circumstances of each situation, and the degree of resistance the officer encountered, including the threat and/or the use of weapons. The lawfulness of the officer's decision to use force will turn on the facts and circumstances known to the officer at the time the force was used. What was determined or discovered after the force was used cannot be used to justify the use of force and would not normally be admissible evidence. This trend is underscored by the generally held principle known as the "one plus one theory" of control in which, generally, officers may use one level of force higher than the level of resistance they encounter (Silver, 2005). The officer's use of force does not have to be the least intrusive amount available. Courts have permitted the police to use somewhat greater amounts of force that inflicted or threatened to effect an arrest, because such force may be required to subdue the assailant.

Other courts, however, have attached additional criteria in assessing claims of excessive force by requiring a plaintiff to prove that he sustained: (1) a significant injury that (2) resulted directly and only from a use of force that was clearly excessive and (3) the excessiveness was objectively unreasonable. The injury must be significant—minor harms and transient distress do not constitute significant injuries. The fact that the force may have been excessive does nor allow recovery for injuries that would have occurred absent the excessive nature of the force. A few courts, in contradiction of the *Graham* standard, have added that the injury sustained from the use of force must be severe and that the officer's actions were initiated with "malicious intent" (*Ortega v. Schram*, 1991).

Although the decision in *Graham* established the standard by which to review claims of excessive force arising out of arrests, a lack of uniform application of the standard exists within the courts. In this section, several use-of-force topics are discussed, illustrating how the courts have applied the objective reasonableness standard.

Restraint Equipment Claims

The common law has recognized, and the *Graham* case emphasized, that an officer need not retreat when confronted with resistance to a lawful arrest. Police officers are entitled to use "objectively reasonable" force to overcome resistance in effecting an arrest. Applying the reasonableness standard to use-of-force situations, however, can be problematic and is open to interpretation.

Although the Supreme Court held in *Graham* that a "severe" injury resulting from an application of force was not an element required in determining reasonable force, the Fifth Circuit Court of Appeals has created a seemingly hybrid standard by combining components of the Fourth and the Fourteenth Amendments. In *Johnson v. Morel* (1989), the court, sitting en banc, held that in order to prevail on an excessive force claim under § 1983, a plaintiff must prove that he sustained a significant injury, which resulted from force disproportionate to the need, and the excessiveness of which was objectively unreasonable. Johnson (an African-American) was driving across a bridge with other African-American passengers when his car stalled. A police officer happened by and began pushing the stalled vehicle with his squad car while shouting racial epithets. On the other side of the bridge, Johnson complied with an investigatory stop and exited his vehicle. The officer continued shouting at him and, after a check, discovered that Johnson's driver's license had expired. The officer arrested Johnson and handcuffed him so tightly that it caused severe lacerations on his wrists and left permanent scars. Johnson filed a § 1983 lawsuit and the district court found in favor of the officer. Johnson appealed and the appellate court concluded that an officer's use of excessive force does not give constitutional import to minor harms. The Fifth Circuit held that a jury must determine whether Johnson's injuries were constitutionally significant.

The Fifth Circuit Court of Appeals dismissed an excessive force claim against a deputy sheriff in *Wisniewski v. Kennard* (1990) on the grounds that the plaintiff had not sustained "significant injuries" during the arrest. The plaintiff had escaped custody while being transported to jail. Once the deputy found him, he handcuffed his wrists tightly, stuck his duty weapon in his mouth, threatened to blow his head off, and punched him three times in the stomach. The district court found in favor of the deputy, and the Fifth Circuit affirmed, concluding that the injuries were not significant. However, in *McCrory v. New Orleans* (1990), a district court found in favor of the plaintiff when an officer handcuffed his wrists, fracturing his hand. The officer had arrested the plaintiff for intoxication and for disturbing the peace. The plaintiff was uncooperative and attempted to pull his arm away during handcuffing. As a result, the plaintiff sustained a fractured hand and filed a lawsuit claiming that excessive force was used. The court found in favor of the plaintiff, but also stated that he contributed to his own injury in resisting being handcuffed.

Not all courts have followed the Fifth Circuit's interpretation of significant injury in handcuffing cases. The Second Circuit, underscoring *Graham*, held in *Calamia v. City of New York* (1989) that excessive force claims arising out of an arrest should be heard by a jury according to the Fourth Amendment standard. The plaintiff had been handcuffed during arrest, but no permanent injury was sustained. The plaintiff contended that the officer placed the handcuffs on too tightly and forced him to sit in an uncomfortable position for several hours. The court made no mention of a threshold of injury requirement. Similarly, in *DeGraff v. District of Columbia* (1997), *Bond v. Queen* (1999), *Trout v. Frega* (1996), *Smith v. Mattox* (1997), and *Taft v. Vine* (1995), the courts concluded that the use of handcuffs was reasonable, given that a valid arrest was made and that officers followed proper procedures during their application. There was no standard of a significant injury considered by the courts, despite the claim that officers fractured the plaintiff's wrist in *Trout*, and that an officer handcuffed a female plaintiff to a mailbox for a short period in *DeGraff*. The standard applied in these cases was that of objective reasonableness in accordance with *Graham*.

Empty-Hand Control Techniques

Police officers frequently must resort to an empty-hand control technique to control a resisting arrestee. These techniques may include joint locks, takedown tactics, control holds, pressure points, hand/leg strikes, and neck restraints. Claims in this category are filed more frequently because of their more common use during arrest.

The Ninth Circuit, in contrast to the Fifth Circuit, has maintained a framework of excessive force claims review by considering the totality of circumstances. In *Forrester v. City of San Diego* (1994), approximately 100 sit-in demonstrators refused to comply with verbal commands by officers to move as they were trespassing and blocking an entrance to a medical building. Demonstrators ignored warnings from the police that they would use pain compliance techniques to move them. The officers administered pain compliance to the wrists and arms of the demonstrators and moved them out of the way of the building. Complaints of injuries were asserted by the demonstrators, including bruising, pinched nerves, and one broken wrist. Several of the demonstrators filed suit, lost in district court, appealed, and the appellate court affirmed. The Ninth Circuit Court of Appeals concluded that police officers are not required to use the least intrusive degree of force possible. Rather, the question is whether the force used was reasonable in effecting a particular seizure. The court found that the officers' application of pain compliance techniques was not excessive.

Other circuits appear to follow this same line of analysis. In *Wallace v. City of Shelby* (1997), a federal district court determined that the use of a leg sweep to control a resisting arrestee during handcuffing was reasonable force.

The plaintiff repeatedly refused to place her hands behind her back during an arrest for domestic violence. After the plaintiff disobeyed several verbal instructions by the officer to cooperate, the officer used an authorized leg sweep, which caused him to lose his footing on the ice, and he and the arrestee fell to the ground. The plaintiff's face was injured and she filed suit. The court reviewed the circumstances and ruled that the officer did not violate the plaintiff's rights. The facts supported the case, and the court held that the officer's motive in applying force was irrelevant. The Fourth Circuit Court of Appeals in *Hart v. Rogers* (1998) held that the use of a bear hug to control a resisting and intoxicated arrestee did not violate his constitutional rights, despite a minor head injury. As the officer was attempting to place the plaintiff in the patrol car, he pushed the officer and began to run from the officer. Being intoxicated, he stumbled and the officer placed his arms around his upper torso. The plaintiff resisted and they fell to the ground, slightly injuring the plaintiff's head. A lawsuit was filed and the lower court found in favor of the officer. The appellate court affirmed. The appellate court held that the officer encountered a larger, intoxicated, resisting citizen, who shoved the officer and was attempting to flee. In light of the circumstances, wrapping his arms around the plaintiff and taking him to the ground was objectively reasonable.

In *Mahone v. Palazzo* (1999), the court ruled that the use of a wristlock was reasonable despite the fact that the resisting plaintiff suffered a fractured wrist. It was unclear whether the officer injured the wrist during controlling the plaintiff prior to handcuffing or whether the plaintiff injured it earlier during a fight with his wife when he had struck her in the face. The court reasoned that using a wristlock was necessary to remove the plaintiff from a residence, and had he not attempted to pull away from the officer during arrest, the officer would not have applied it. Likewise, in *Smith v. Mattox* (1997), the Eleventh Circuit Court of Appeals affirmed the use of an armlock in the course of effecting an arrest after the plaintiff had threatened the officer with a baseball bat. When confronted by the plaintiff with the bat, the officer ordered him at gunpoint to drop it. He complied, ran from the officer, and after a short time fell prone to the ground as instructed. The officer knelt on the plaintiff's lower back to handcuff him. The plaintiff resisted as the officer brought his hand back for handcuffing, and in so doing the plaintiff's arm was broken. The court concluded that the officer's use of force was reasonable because the arrestee had moments earlier posed a threat of safety to the officer by threatening him with a bat and attempting to flee.

The Tenth Circuit Court of Appeals, however, ruled in *Paul v. The City of Altus* (1998) that placing an officer's knee on the neck of a prone arrestee during handcuffing could be considered excessive force. The plaintiff was not resisting, and the officer had been trained not to place his knee on the neck during handcuffing. The court found in favor of the plaintiff because the officer was "deliberately indifferent" to the safety of citizens. Similarly, in *Matasic v. City of Campbell* (1997), the Sixth Circuit Court of Appeals

ruled that an allegation of placing a foot on the plaintiff's neck was not excessive. Officers attempted to stop the plaintiff's vehicle because they thought
he was stealing a car. The plaintiff attempted to elude the officers and a pursuit took place. Once the plaintiff stopped, the officers wrestled him to the
ground and handcuffed him. The plaintiff sustained a one-centimeter lac-
eration and some abrasions. The court concluded that the force used by the
officers was reasonable because the officers thought they faced a dangerous
fleeing felon.

Compare, however, the court's ruling *in Garcia v. City of Chicago*
(2003). While waiting to pick up his cousin at his uncle's restaurant, Garcia
noticed an officer drive by who had gang affiliations. The officer had
threatened to beat him up over a photo that showed the officer flashing gang
signs. The police department had a strict prohibition against officers affil-
iating with gangs. Two other officers joined the first officer and demanded
that Garcia turn over the picture. Garcia attempted to move away from the
officers but they pushed him on the ground and drug to the truck. The officers punched and kicked him numerous times, head butted him, and slapped
him in the face. Garcia sustained a broken nose, which caused disfigurement,
and incurred a tumour on his hip where he was kicked.

Garcia filed a lawsuit against the officers for excessive force. He also
alleged that the city had a custom and practice of not adequately investigating, disciplining, or prosecuting misconduct by officers. At trial, Garcia
produced 72 citizen complaints about police misconduct between 1999 and
2001. According to Garcia, these complaints supported his allegation of a
pattern and practice. The jury awarded Garcia $1 million in compensatory
damages and the city appealed. The court decided to lower the award to
$250,000. The court agreed that the attack was brutal and was borne out of
"passion and prejudice."

In *Feldman v. Community College of Allegheny* (2004), the court agreed
with arresting officers that they appropriately used a straight-armbar takedown technique. A student at the college had an ongoing dispute with a computer lab instructor and refused to leave the lab. The instructor called
security, who in turn summoned the police to remove him. Two officers
responded and directed the student to leave, but he refused and actively resisted their efforts of control. The student claimed that the officers wrestled him
to the ground and kicked him in the head. The officer's account was that one
officer used a trained straight-armbar technique and took him to the ground
because he refused to leave and resisted their efforts of control. The student
sued the college, the officers, and the city police department, alleging false
arrest and excessive force. The arrest charges were dropped. The court
granted summary judgment and the student appealed. The Third Circuit Court
of Appeals affirmed the lower court's decision, agreeing that the officers used
objectively reasonable force. The court agreed that the student needed to be
controlled before being placed in handcuffs and that the technique used was
proportionate to the resistance confronted.

Perhaps one of the most controversial empty-hand control techniques used by police officers is the neck restraint. Improper application of the technique has led to several deaths. Conversely, proper application has assisted in controlling violent suspects and reduced the need for the officer to use lethal force. A policy of using neck restraints was the subject of concern for the United States Supreme Court in *Los Angeles v. Lyons* (1983). During a traffic stop the plaintiff had been rendered unconscious as a result of a police "choke hold." He did not offer resistance. He sued for an injunction regarding the practice of using the neck restraint, because the hold had been used in similar situations and 15 deaths had occurred. The Court refused to issue an injunction, because Lyons could not prove that he would be subject to such a hold in the future.

The Fifth Circuit Court of Appeals concluded that an officer allegedly grabbing an arrestee around his throat on two separate occasions during an arrest, for suspicion of having cocaine in his mouth, failed to show evidence of an injury (Williams v. Bramer, 1999). The court concluded that a physical confrontation inevitably occurred when an officer searched the detainee. The plaintiff's alleged injuries of fleeting dizziness and temporary loss of breath and coughing were not cognizable injuries rising to the level of a constitutional violation.

In two neck-restraint cases decided in the Tenth Circuit, the courts found in favor of the plaintiffs (*DeCorte v. Robinson*, 1998; *Franklin v. City of Kansas City, Kansas*, 1997). The courts agreed that the officers' use of the "carotid hold" was unreasonable in light of the minimal resistance encountered during arrest. The Ninth Circuit, however, in *Nova v. City of Dublin* (1997), declined to order an injunction prohibiting the use of the neck restraint, which would force the police department to revise its policy on using neck restraints. In *Mosier v. Robinson* (1989), the court also concluded that using a choke hold on a restrained, intoxicated arrestee at the police station was excessive and unreasonable.

In *Coburn v. Benton Township et al.* (2005), a federal district court of Michigan examined the whether officers used excessive force when they applied a vascular neck restraint on an actively resisting person during arrest. Officers attempted to serve an arrest warrant on Griffith and met resistance. Griffith had exhibited bizarre behavior at home, had a history of mental impairment, and his mother requested that the police take him into custody. At the house the officers met resistance as they attempted to take control of Griffith. He lunged off of a couch at the officers and struggled with them. During the struggle Griffith managed to unsnap one of the officer's safety snaps on his holster and began to pry on it. The officer placed him in a lateral vascular neck restraint for about two to three seconds and they fell to the floor. Griffith became unresponsive and resuscitation efforts by emergency medical personnel on scene failed to revive him.

The family filed a § 1983 lawsuit against the officers for excessive force. They also filed a claim against the chief of police for being deliberately indifferent to the training needs of the officers who used the neck restraint. The court granted summary judgment on behalf of the officers, finding that the neck restraint was not excessive force. The court agreed that the officers are permitted to use a degree of force in effecting the arrest of an individual who is actively resisting arrest. The court determined that there was evidence to show that Griffith reached for the officer's weapon during the struggle. Such behavior, the court ruled, posed a threat of serious physical harm to the officer and to others, and his actions accordingly justified the use of deadly force. If the officer was justified in using deadly force, then he could certainly use the neck restraint, which the court ruled was not deadly force. Finally, the court held that the use of the vascular neck restraint under the circumstances was not objective unreasonable. Accordingly, the defendants were entitled to qualified immunity, thereby dismissing the excessive force claim.

Police Equipment

In an attempt to minimize the need for police to use lethal force, various types of equipment have been developed to help officers effect arrests. These types of weapons include impact weapons, Tasers, stun guns, and aerosol sprays. As officers have used these instruments, claims of excessive force have emerged.

The First Circuit's decision in *Bordanaro v. McLeod* (1989) found that officers from two police departments violated citizens' constitutional rights. Six police officers beat unarmed patrons in retaliation for a fight between an off-duty officer and a guest at a bar. The officers beat the patrons with clubs, bats, a fire axe, and nightsticks. As a result, one patron died. This unconstitutional practice of excessive and abusive use of weapons resulted in an award against the municipalities of more than $5,000,000. The Ninth Circuit Court of Appeals in *Davis v. Mason County* (1991) found that sheriff's deputies used excessive force on four separate occasions during illegal arrests. Three different deputies misused their stun guns and batons, and pointed weapons at compliant citizens while conducting traffic stops. The jury award against the individual deputies was $320,000. The court ruled that the deputies' conduct was driven by evil motives or intent and that they exhibited reckless and callous disregard for the constitutional rights of the citizens.

The question of the officer's objectively reasonable use of force is usually left for the jury to decide, but must be judged in light of the information and situation facing the officer at the time the force was used. A police officer need not suffer a brutal or serious injury prior to using serious force on a citizen. The force need only be reasonable under the circumstances. In *Cotton v. Busic* (1992), the officer got into a scuffle with an arrestee who had

earlier been throwing rocks at houses. During handcuffing, a second officer thought the arrestee was reaching for his partner's weapon and struck him
in the head with an impact weapon, while the first officer struck him in the
head with a flashlight. The arrestee sustained bumps, bruises, and lost one
eye. In light of the facts, the court determined that the force was reasonable.
In *Mathis v. Parks* (1990), an officer was attempting to persuade a drunk individual at a bar to leave with his brother, when an argument developed. The
officer retrieved his impact weapon as the drunk individual continued to
argue, and the officer then struck him in the head with the baton, causing cuts
and bruises. A second officer arrived on the scene and attempted to handcuff him. He resisted and the officer kneed him with full force in the stomach. As the officers were transporting him, they noticed that he was having
a heart attack, and he died prior to arriving at the hospital. The court ruled
on behalf of the plaintiff, stating that although he was drunk, he was only trespassing and not physically resisting or being aggressive.

In contrast to the above court decisions, in *Carver v. Bullock* (1999), the
Fourth Circuit Court of Appeals ruled in favor of an officer who struck an
arrestee as he attempted to run from him after a vehicle pursuit. Once the officer caught the citizen, the citizen began kicking the officer. The officer had
his flashlight in his left hand (the encounter took place at night) and struck
him one time on the head. The court concluded that the circumstances created a dangerous and tense situation and that the officer's use of force was
reasonable. In *Radecki v. Barlea* (1998), the Tenth Circuit Court of Appeals
used the "shocks the conscience" standard in evaluating another officer's use
of his flashlight as an impact weapon. During an arrest, the arrestee attempted
to grab the officer's weapon. A second officer yelled to the officer under
attack to hit him with his flashlight. The officer did, causing him to release
his grip on the weapon. The individual began to run from the scene, and the
second officer shot and killed him. The lower court determined that the
deputy's conduct did shock the conscience and found him liable for using
excessive force. The deputy appealed and the appellate court reversed the verdict, finding that he did not use force that shocked the conscience, because
he was confronted with an explosive emergency situation when the arrestee
suddenly grabbed for his weapon.

The use of electrical devices (Tasers) has become more prominent in
policing and corrections. Like other types of equipment, they have been the
subject of litigation. In *Mateyko v. Felix* (1991), a district court in California ruled against an officer's use of a Taser during an arrest. An officer had
stopped an individual for jaywalking. As the officer was issuing a citation,
the citizen resisted and the officer radioed for assistance. The responding officer used the Taser to restrain the arrestee, who later sued, claiming excessive force. The court held that the use of a Taser did not constitute deliberate
indifference to the arrestee's rights under § 1983. The court determined that
he resisted, was convicted of resisting arrest, and therefore the force used was
reasonable under the circumstances.

In *Draper v. Reynolds* (2004), the officer used a Taser during a traffic stop. Meeting Draper behind his truck, the officer asked that he retrieve documents from the cab five times, but he refused to comply. Draper became agitated, began yelling and cursing at the officer, stating that he was harassing him and blinding him with his flashlight. The officer used the Taser as a stun device one time and was able to control and handcuff Draper. Draper sued, claiming that the officer used excessive and disproportionate force.

The court granted summary judgment, agreeing with the officer that the arrest circumstance was tense, rapidly evolving, and uncertain. Because Draper continued to refuse the verbal commands of the officer, the court held that additional commands of arrest were not necessary, and had the officer attempted to handcuff him, an unnecessary struggle would have ensued, leading to serious injury. Based on the totality of the circumstances, the use of the Taser was proportional to the tense situation, and the officer did not violate Draper's constitutional rights.

Citing *Draper*, the court in *Stanley v. City of Baytown, Texas* (2005) granted summary judgment to the officer who used a Taser to effect an arrest. Officer Elizondo responded to assist paramedics and fire rescue personnel in controlling Stanley so that they could provide medical treatment for him. Stanley was highly agitated and combative, having previously taken steroids. Stanley was dressed in only boxer shorts, was sweating profusely, and actively resisting, making it difficult to control him. The paramedics and rescue personnel abandoned their efforts to treat Stanley, fearing for their safety. Stanley was unresponsive to their verbal attempts to calm him down. Elizondo arrived on the scene and spent several minutes trying to calm him down but was unsuccessful. Elizondo decided to use his Taser in the "push/stun mode," and applied a two-second application of the Taser. The Taser application was successful, Stewart calmed down, was treated by medical personnel, and did not receive any injuries. Stanley filed a lawsuit claiming that the officer used excessive force. The district court granted summary judgment for the officer, commenting that Elizondo's use of the Taser was not unreasonably disproportionate to the need to use force. In fact, the officer's decision to use the Taser may well have prevented much greater harm to Stanley and other people. Further, the court emphasized that the officer's intervention was reasonable and in keeping with his community caretaking function and therefore did not constitute an unlawful seizure.

Police have been using various forms of pepper spray when faced with arrestee resistance since the late 1980s. As the police have increasingly used these products, several claims citing excessive force have been filed. Most courts have ruled that the use of pepper spray is reasonable force. In *Darnell v. Carver* (1998), *Omokaro v. Whitemeyer* (1998), *Monday v. Oullette* (1997), *Sappington v. Bartee* (1999), *United States v. Holloway* (1995), and *Lester v. City of Rosedale* (1991), the courts agreed that in light of the circumstances during arrest and the degree of resistance offered by the arrestee, it was reasonable to use an aerosol in order to control the person.

In *Monday,* an officer sprayed a 300-pound mentally impaired man who was refusing to be transported to the hospital for admission. No injuries were sustained and the man was controlled and handcuffed. In *Holloway,* the court determined that it was reasonable and not outrageous to spray an arrestee in order to remove crack cocaine from his mouth.

In *Omokaro* (1998), the plaintiff resisted officers' efforts to control him. He would not comply with orders of arrest and officers sprayed him. He fell to the ground, but kept kicking and thrashing. The officers used their baton for pressure on the shin and applied pressure point techniques under his jaw. When these techniques failed, one officer was able to control him by applying a lateral vascular neck restraint. His hands and legs were restrained as he attempted to kick and bite the officers. Within a matter of minutes he was observed to be unconscious, CPR was administered, and Omokaro was revived and transported to a hospital. He sued, claiming excessive force, but judgment was granted in favor of the officers. The court stated that the officers used objectively reasonable force relative to the severity of the crime at issue, the threat posed by the arrestee, and how actively he resisted arrest.

Conversely, in *Lamb v. City of Decatur* (1996) and *McCartt v. Keyes* (1999), the courts held that the use of pepper spray was unreasonable force. In *McCartt,* the arrestee had allegedly been trespassing on a private beach. During arrest, the responding officer attempted to place handcuffs on the plaintiff, and he backed away. When the officer warned that he would be sprayed, the person was still defiant. The officer sprayed and immediately restrained him with handcuffs. A lawsuit was filed claiming use of excessive force. The lower court ruled in favor of the plaintiff, and the Sixth Circuit Court of Appeals affirmed. The court concluded that the plaintiff was illegally arrested, did not display any risk of aggression, was not attempting to flee, and was not a danger to officers. In *Lamb,* the plaintiff and other demonstrators filed a class action lawsuit alleging excessive force as the police sprayed them twice to break up a "peaceful" union protest. The court ruled that using force against people who were exercising their First Amendment rights of assembly and free speech was clearly unconstitutional, and declared the force unreasonable. The court also stated that there is no value in the First Amendment if demonstrators could be dispersed or intimidated by the unnecessary use of force.

Survivors of an arrestee who died during an altercation filed a § 1983 lawsuit in *Wagner v. Bay City, Texas* (2000), claiming excessive force and deliberate indifference to medical needs. The arrestee actively resisted arrest by striking officers with his fists. The officers sprayed the arrestee with pepper spray, placed him on the ground with one shin across his back, and handcuffed him. They transported him the jail and the arrestee was heard moaning. At the sally port (a secure jail entrance area), the officers found the arrestee to be unresponsive and summoned medical personnel, who attempted to treat him but were unsuccessful. The federal district court denied summary judgment for the officers and the appeals court reversed the decision, granting judgment for the officers. The court ruled that the officers were not deliberately indifferent to the medical needs of the arrestee, and used reasonable force to control him. The court also noted that decontamination of pepper spray could effectively be done in the jail and the officers believed the arrestee was still breathing during transport.

As indicated earlier, previous studies on police use of force show that officers use multiple types of force in about 88 percent of altercations. *Stewart v. Prince County* (2003) provides an example of how the courts review such cases. Employees of a Target store asked a customer, Stewart, to leave the store and not return, because he had threatened a female employee. He left but returned several times. Security called the police but they did not respond. Several hours later Stewart returned to the store and began throwing items at the cashier. An officer responded and found Stewart at a nearby store. Corroborated by a video camera, the officer walked Stewart to the store, side-by side, to apologize to the employee and warned him not to return to the store. Within several minutes, Stewart returned to the store a third time and security summoned the same officer, who responded. Again the videotape showed the officer speaking with Stewart, who became agitated, threatened the officer, and refused to leave. A struggle ensued and the officer radioed for backup. The tape showed another officer responding and the two officers wrestled with Stewart. The second officer sprayed Stewart with pepper spray several times and struck him with his collapsible baton several times. The officers were finally able to control him and placed him in handcuffs. As they escorted him out of the store, Stewart collapsed and died en route to the hospital of cardiac arrest.

Stewart's family filed a § 1983 lawsuit against the officers, the police department, and Target. The defendants requested summary judgment and the family demanded a trial. The court agreed that a trial was necessary and the defendants appealed. The Fourth Circuit Court of Appeals concluded that the defendants were entitled to summary judgment as they had used objectively reasonable force. The court determined that the officers correctly and appropriately escalated their use of force in response to Stewart's active resistance. The court further noted that Stewart was given ample opportunity to leave the store but became defiant and actively resisted efforts of arrest. The officers had used verbal control without success; and the use of pepper spray, batons, and handcuffs was not unconstitutionally unreasonable given the totality of circumstances. The videotape also showed that the officers used force proportionately in response to Stewart's behavior.

Officers sometimes use canines in effecting arrests and such cases have resulted in lawsuits claming excessive force. In *Jarrett v. Town of Yarmouth* (2003), officers engaged in a high-speed pursuit of Jarrett, who was observed to be speeding. Officers radioed for a canine officer as Jarrett crashed his vehicle and fled the area. For about 20 minutes the canine officer tracked Jarrett and spotted him in the middle of the road about 50 yards away. The officer yelled for Jarrett to stop or he would release the dog. Jarrett fled and the officer instructed his dog to locate Jarrett and hold him. The dog was trained in the "bite and hold" technique and within 30 seconds the dog found Jarrett. He bit Jarrett on the leg, held him until the officer instructed him to "release," and the dog complied. Jarrett was transported to the hospital by ambulance, treated for his injuries, received stitches, and was released from the hospital after two weeks. Jarrett was charged with two misdemeanor offenses. He filed a lawsuit claiming that the officers used excessive force by releasing the dog on him, alleging that such actions constituted deadly force.

The jury found in favor of Jarrett, awarding him $50,000 in punitive damages. The officers appealed and the appellate court reversed the verdict. The court concluded that the use of force must be assessed from the perspective of the officer on the scene. The court held that releasing the dog was not deadly force and that the "bite and hold" method was not unconstitutional. Further, the court held that the officer's decision to release the dog was objectively reasonable under the circumstances.

Post-Arrest Use of Force

As discussed, the *Graham* standard of using force applies to "free" citizens. The question then emerges of what standard applies to post-arrest situations and pretrial detainees. This question creates confusion about when the Fourth Amendment protection ends and due process protection under the Fourteenth Amendment begins. Additional questions arise as to when the Eighth Amendment prohibition against cruel and unusual punishment regarding the use of force applies. These questions are more than academic, because the status of the arrestee will help a court determine which amendment is appropriate and which standard will be applied in a use-of-excessive-force case. This becomes important, as the outcome of an excessive force case will depend on the standard used by the court. In *Henson v. Thezan* (1988), an arrestee who was charged with child molestation, rape, and attempted murder alleged that he was pushed down a flight of stairs, beaten during transport, and beaten at the police station. The court applied the Fourth Amendment because the arrestee had not yet appeared before a judicial officer.

The court in *Valencia v. Wiggins* (1993), however, found that a pretrial detainee's beating in a detention facility was not governed by the Fourth Amendment standard. Rather, the court applied the *Whitley* and *Hudson* (Eighth Amendment) standard, because it was impractical to draw a line between convicted prisoners and pretrial detainees for the purpose of maintaining security in the facility.

The standard generally applied to post-arrest force situations in detention facilities is the "shocks the conscience" standard previously discussed in the *Johnson v. Glick* case (1973) under the Fourteenth Amendment due process clause (see Figure 9.2). The evaluation of use-of-force claims under due process is fundamentally different from the objective reasonableness standard, in that it focuses on the state of mind or motivation of the officer. If it can be shown by the plaintiff that the force used by the officer was unnecessary, inflicted an injury, and was for sadistic and malicious purposes rather than to restore order, liability will most likely attach. Application of the "shocks the conscience" standard is applied on a case-by-case basis.

For example, in *McClanahan v. City of Moberly* (1998), a pretrial detainee alleged that she was the victim of excessive force in connection with her transfer from a police department to a county jail. The district court granted summary judgment for the defendants, finding that the detainee's allegations of being slapped three times, without any evidence of a resulting injury, was at most a slight injury that did not implicate the due process clause of the Fourteenth Amendment. In *Riley v. Durton* (1997), a pretrial detainee brought a § 1983 action and claimed that an officer used handcuffs, inserted the tip of a pen into the detainee's nose, threatened her, and slapped her across the face. The appeals court affirmed the lower court's summary judgment for the officer, finding that the Fourth Amendment did not extend protection from excessive force to pretrial detainees and the alleged use of force did not violate the Eighth Amendment. The court held that the officer's use of force did not violate due process where an injury suffered by the detainee was minimal.

The estate in *Brothers v. Klevenhagen* (1994) brought a § 1983 claim against the county and the sheriff, alleging the use of excessive force. The deceased, an unarmed pretrial detainee, attempted to escape during transport from one holding cell to another. The deputies fired at the detainee only as a last resort to prevent an escape, and he would have escaped if the deputies had not fired at him. The appeals court affirmed the lower court's summary judgment for the county. The court found that the due process clause of the Fourteenth Amendment, rather than the Fourth Amendment, provided the appropriate constitutional standard for evaluating the deputies' use of force. The sheriff's department policy allowed deadly force only when immediately necessary to prevent escape and was designed in a good faith effort to maintain or restore discipline, and not maliciously and sadistically for the purpose of causing harm.

Claims of brutality against detainees emerge within the context of excessive force. One particularly egregious example is illustrated by *Mathis v. Fries* (1996). While confined as a pretrial detainee, Mathis claimed that the facility's director of security sexually abused him. The district court entered summary judgment for the detainee, finding sufficient evidence to support claims that the director repeatedly sodomized the detainee while he was handcuffed to pipes in the security office. Finding that these acts violated the detainee's due process rights, the court rejected a petition for qualified immunity and awarded the detainee $250,000 in compensatory damages and $500,000 in punitive damages. The court called the director's action an outrageous abuse of power and authority. The court in *Casaburro v. Giuliani* (1997) found that egregious physical misconduct toward an arrestee may violate the Eighth Amendment if it was a punishment. An allegation of handcuffing a detainee for seven hours while in a holding cell would qualify, absent a legitimate reason. Tight handcuffing for the sole purpose of causing harm was actionable because it was "grossly disproportionate" to the need and the misdemeanor charge against the arrestee.

Post-Conviction Use of Force

The United States Supreme Court has established different standards of excessive force review when such claims originate in a prison setting. The explicit language of the Eighth Amendment prohibits the imposition of "cruel and unusual punishments." According to the Court, this language was designed to protect those convicted of crimes. The Court noted in *Ingraham v. Wright* (1977) that the clause applies after the state has complied with constitutional guarantees associated with criminal prosecution. Therefore, applying the Eighth Amendment standard to convicted persons should not be problematic.

Whitley v. Albers *(1986)*

Following the *Garner* (1985) decision, the Supreme Court in *Whitley v. Albers* (1986) reviewed a deadly force incident that occurred during a prison riot. The Court established how the Eighth Amendment prohibits cruel and unusual punishment, including allegations of excessive force asserted by prisoners. In *Whitley*, Oregon prison officials were confronted with a disturbance by prisoners who had killed another prisoner and taken a correctional officer hostage. Threats to kill the hostage and other prisoners were made by prisoners, should force be used by officials. Officials ultimately decided to use force to free the hostage and retake the cellblock. Prisoner Albers was shot in the left knee after several warnings to release the hostage had failed and after a warning shot had been ignored. He filed suit against prison officials, claiming that his Eighth and Fourteenth Amendment rights had been violated.

The Supreme Court reversed the appeals court's decision, which had found in favor of Albers. The Court ruled that the infliction of pain in the course of a prison security measure is only an Eighth Amendment violation if it is inflicted "unnecessarily and wantonly." The standard of deliberate indifference was rejected by the Court as not sufficiently broad enough to be used in analyzing deadly force claims associated with prison riots. The Court held that whether the force used inflicted unnecessary and wanton pain and suffering ultimately turns on whether the use of force was applied in a good faith effort to maintain or restore discipline, or whether it was applied maliciously and sadistically for the purpose of causing harm. This language is taken from the fourth component outlined in the *Glick* (1973) decision.

The Court held that liability would attach in deadly force situations if the prisoner could show that such force manifested "obduracy and wantonness." "Obdurate" can be defined as "hardened feelings," or "without remorse." "Wantonness" can be defined as "malicious," "without regard," "inhumane," or "merciless." For example, in *Austin v. Hopper* (1998), an onerous and barbaric "security" measure was condemned when it was determined that there was no immediate threat to security or an attempt to restore order was present. A practice of compelling prisoners to stand for hours shackled to a "hitching post," spread-eagled, without the ability to stretch or move in direct sunlight caused great pain, heat exhaustion, dehydration, and injury, for nondangerous rule infractions. This practice clearly violated the Eighth Amendment and exemplified the Court's definition of obduracy and wantonness.

The court in *Gravely v. Madden* (1998) found that a correctional officer who shot and killed an escaping prisoner did not act with obduracy and wantonness in violation of the Eighth Amendment. An appeals court reversed a lower court decision against the officer, because the court determined that he acted within the scope of his authority, the force was reasonable, and therefore he had qualified immunity. The prisoner had escaped from a minimum-security facility and was staying at a friend's residence. When the officer entered the house, the prisoner was twice instructed to stop and give up. The prisoner leaped off a porch and the officer fired one round, killing him.

Hudson v. McMillian *(1992)*

Using the *Whitley* standard, courts have ruled in favor of prison officials when the use of deadly force is warranted. This standard has mainly been applied to prisoner escapes and riot situations (*Duametef v. Fial*, 1996; *Kinney v. Indiana Youth Center*, 1991). The question emerges, however, of whether the *Whitley* standard applies to all use-of-force situations or cases involving only deadly force. For a time the courts were divided on this question. The Supreme Court's decision in *Hudson v. McMillian* (1992) resolved this controversy and held that all excessive force claims must show malice, sadism, and intent to cause harm (Figure 9.4). In establishing this standard of excessive force review in corrections, the Court underscored its earlier standard of review in the *Whitley* decision: whether force was applied in good faith, in an effort to maintain or restore discipline, or maliciously and sadistically for the purpose of causing harm.

The *Hudson* case arose out of an incident in an Angola, Louisiana, prison where two correctional officers beat a compliant and handcuffed prisoner during an escort to another cell. As the officer punched Hudson, a supervisor observed the beating and merely cautioned the officers "not to have too much fun." Hudson sustained minor bruises and swelling of his face, lip, and mouth. A punch to the face also cracked his dentures and loosened his teeth. He filed a civil action claiming excessive force. A federal district court found in favor of Hudson, but an appellate court reversed. The U.S. Supreme Court granted certiorari to answer the question of whether the use of excessive physical force by correctional officers against a prisoner constituted cruel and unusual punishment. The Court responded by saying "yes," holding that an injury to a prisoner does not have to be "serious" or "significant" to constitute cruel and unusual punishment in violation of the Eighth Amendment. The Court held that the officers' actions did indeed violate Hudson's constitutional rights, despite the fact that he sustained only minor injuries.

Figure 9.4
Hudson v. McMillian (1992)

After an earlier argument, two correctional officers at the state prison at Angola, Lousiana, handcuffed prisoner Hudson and removed him from his cell. While escorting Hudson to an administrative segregation cell, the officers punched and kicked him, even though he was compliant. The supervisor on duty observed the officers striking Hudson, but merely told them "not to have too much fun." The blows were strong enough to dislodge Hudson's dental plate, which broke when it hit the floor. Hudson also sustained minor bruises and swelling of his face, mouth, and lip. Hudson filed a § 1983 lawsuit, claiming excessive force in violation of his Eighth Amendment right to be free of cruel and unusual punishment. He prevailed in the lower court, winning $800.00. On appeal, the Fifth Circuit Court of Appeals reversed. Hudson appealed to the United States Supreme Court.

The Court examined the issue of whether the use of force against a prisoner constituted cruel and unsual punishment even if the prisoner did not sustain a serious injury. The Court held, in a 7 to 2 vote, that a prisoner does not have to sustain a serious injury in order to prevail in a civil action. A prisoner will prevail on a claim of excessive force when he can show that the officer used force "maliciously and sadistically" to cause harm. The severity of injury is not at issue. The Court estalished that the standard for the use of nonlethal force for correctional officers is whether the officer used force in a good faith effort to maintain or restore order, or maliciously and sadistically for the purpose of causing harm. The court concluded that the officers used force in a malicious and sadistic fashion, thereby violating Hudson's constitutional right to be free from cruel and unusual punishment. Hudson did not possess a weapon, was not threatening the officers, was secured in handcuffs, and was compliant.

The question to be asked in correctional use-of-force situations is: What level of force is needed and was the force used repugnant to the sensibilities? The standard established by the Court makes it easier for prisoners to prevail in excessive force actions.

For the first time, the Supreme Court held that in use-of-force cases, the extent of injuries sustained is irrelevant. The Court rejected the third component from the *Glick* decision (extent of injury sustained). The Court emphasized that when prison officials maliciously and sadistically use force to cause harm, contemporary standards of decency are violated, regardless of whether significant injury is evident. This clause becomes the standard to assess all excessive force claims—not just prison disturbances or riots. *Hudson* states that in order to establish a valid claim of excessive force under the Eighth Amendment, it must be shown that the defendant used force in a "malicious and sadistic manner for the purpose of causing harm."

The Court noted that not every push, shove, or injury leads to civil liability. They noted that the Eighth Amendment excludes from constitutional review *de minimis* (trifling) uses of physical force, provided that such force is not "repugnant to the conscience of mankind." A definitive meaning of this phrase remains unclear. Generally, the intent of the officer is examined along with the legitimate objective and rationale for the application of force. The standard is applied on a case-by-case basis depending on the circumstances of the incident.

For example, in *Samuels v. Hawkins* (1998), the court found that throwing a cup of water at a cuffed and shackled prisoner who had thrown a cup of urine at the correctional officer was not malicious and sadistic. Similarly, in *Stanley v. Hejiria* (1998), a videotaped cell extraction of a riot ringleader did not demonstrate sadistic or malicious conduct on the part of the response team and liability did not attach. Minor injuries were not constitutionally severe enough to be characterized as significant where force was reasonably necessary.

Moreover, in *Dennis v. Thurman* (1997), a prisoner brought a § 1983 claim alleging that 36 officers withheld water from him for 36 hours after a forced cell extraction. The prisoner had to be forcibly extracted from his cell in order for officers to search it, because they had learned he was planning to kill a correctional officer. Officers had to use a block gun, which shot rubber blocks at high velocity. The court held that the officers did not use excessive force against the prisoner in removing him from his cell. The court found that no officer acted maliciously or sadistically for the purpose of causing pain to the prisoner. Shutting off the water to his cell for an extended period did not violate his Eighth Amendment rights, because he had in the past used water to flood his cell, creating a dangerous condition for himself, other prisoners, and officers.

In *Campbell v. Sikes* (1999), an appellate court affirmed summary judgment for correctional officers and a doctor on a claim that the officers used excessive force by restraining a mentally impaired prisoner. The court found that using a straitjacket to restrain the prisoner failed to constitute excessive force, absent evidence that the force was applied maliciously and sadistically. The court noted that the prisoner posed a serious threat to herself and others, lesser restraints were ineffective, the restraints used caused no physical injury, and the prisoner's physical condition was carefully monitored.

Conversely, in *Giroux v. Sherman* (1992), a prisoner prevailed in an excessive force claim asserting that on four separate occasions eight officers beat and tormented him without provocation. For one beating, the prisoner was awarded $10,000. This beating was so severe that the prisoner was hospitalized with internal injuries. While in the hospital, other officers punched his kidneys, complicating his recovery. He was awarded additional damages amounting to $10,000 and punitive damages of $10,000. The prisoner was awarded additional damages resulting from two other attacks in which one correctional officer punched him in the throat and head without provocation, and another officer wantonly and without cause beat him in the kidneys, causing further injury and requiring surgery. The prisoner was awarded more than $38,000 in damages.

In *Madrid v. Gomez* (1995), the court found evidence of sadistic and malicious conduct of correctional officers who beat mentally impaired prisoners. Prisoners of the Pelican Bay State Prison in California brought a class action lawsuit citing numerous constitutional violations, including excessive force allegations. The court held that prisoners established that prison officials frequently used unnecessary and grossly excessive force against prisoners and that these practices posed a substantial risk of harm to prisoners. The court found that officials had an affirmative management strategy that permitted the use of excessive force for the purpose of punishment and deterrence. Such practices and actions of officers constituted wanton and malicious conduct in violation of the Eighth Amendment.

In *Estate of Davis by Ostenfeld v. Delo* (1997), a court held that officers, a supervisor, and the prison superintendent were liable for using excessive force when they forcibly removed a prisoner from his cell. The court found evidence to support the claim that the prisoner was struck in the face and head 20 to 25 times by several officers, while other officers held him down after he had complied with an order to lie face down. The prisoner sustained numerous injuries, and the court found that the officers used force maliciously and sadistically for the purpose of causing harm. After an investigation ordered by the superintendent, he failed to take corrective action against an officer who failed to submit a mandatory force report, was found to have sustained numerous complaints of excessive force in the past, and for whom recommendations were submitted for his termination. The superintendent was held liable, and the prisoner was awarded $70,000 in compensatory damages and $40,000 in punitive damages.

Assessment of Hudson v. McMillian

For more than 10 years the courts have applied the *Hudson* decision in prison use-of-force encounters in accordance with the Eighth Amendment. Ross (2004) conducted a content analysis of 4,010 published § 1983 cases filed against correction officers in prison to examine how the courts have applied the standard. A random sample of 1,025 (25%) cases decided from 1992 to 2002 was examined. As shown in Figure 9.5, the sample revealed five common use-of-force categories.

Figure 9.5
Trends of Use-of-Force Claims in Corrections by Type (1992 to 2002)

Claim Type	Number Studied (%)	Prisoner Prevailed (%)	Officer Prevailed (%)
Physical force	455 (44)	90 (20)	365 (80)
Restraints	355 (35)	77 (19)	278 (78)
Aerosols	110 (11)	26 (26)	84 (76)
Force devices	100 (9)	22 (22)	78 (78)
Lethal force	5 (1)	0	5 (100)
Total Number	1,025 (100)	215 (21)	810 (79)

As shown in Figure 9.5, correctional officers prevailed in each category and during the reporting period, officers prevailed in more than 75 percent of the prisoner claims. Claims of physical force accounted for 44 percent of the actions, and include empty-hand control techniques, such as control holds, wristlocks, takedowns, pressure point, hand/leg strikes, and neck restraints. The use of restraints included handcuffs, leg restraints, straitjackets, four-point restraints, and the restraint chair. The use of aerosols accounted for 11 percent of the claims and included chemical agents and pepper spray. Force devices included the use of batons, Tasers, stun guns, and sting ball grenades, and accounted for nine percent of the cases studied. The use of a firearm accounted for only one percent of the actions. Use-of-force claims involving combinations of the above categories accounted for 58 percent of the cases (excluding firearms).

Case analysis also revealed four plaintiffs' allegation levels in asserting a claim of excessive force. The first level alleged that the responding officers overreacted by using the degree of force he or she employed. Claims at this level generally asserted that the officers recklessly misused physical control techniques and/or force equipment, and failed to follow their training and the department's use-of-force policy. A frequent secondary claim alleged that the plaintiff suffered some type of injury as a result of the excessive force, and that timely and adequate medical care was denied or delayed. The third claim level asserted that supervisors failed to adequately train, supervise, and direct officers in the constitutional limits of force and failed to keep officers proficient in force tactics and equipment. The final level of allegations generally claimed that supervisory personnel failed to investigate excessive force claims and failed to discipline officers, thereby tolerating a "pattern and practice" of excessive force. The cases below provide examples of these levels of claims and how the lower courts have applied the *Hudson* standard.

In *Marquez v. Gutierrez* (2003), a prisoner brought a § 1983 lawsuit claiming that an officer's use of deadly force was excessive, in violation of his Eighth Amendment rights. While the plaintiff prisoner was assaulting another prisoner, the correctional officer assigned to a security tower shot the attacking prisoner in the leg, causing severe injury. The district court ruled that the officer used excessive force. It denied summary judgment and the officer appealed. The appellate court reversed the lower court's decision, concluding that a reasonable correctional officer could have believed that shooting one prisoner in the leg to stop an assault that could have resulted in a serious injury or death of another prisoner was a good faith effort to restore order, and was therefore lawful.

In *Jackson v. Austin* (2003), a prisoner who was severely beaten by correctional officers did not have to show that he sustained a significant or permanent injury in order to prevail. While waiting to see the prison physician, a prisoner with a knee condition sat down in the medical clinic. Officers ordered him to stand and the prisoner attempted to explain that he was permitted to sit because his knee injury prevented him from standing for long periods. Refusing to look at the prisoner's written medical restriction, the officers forcefully pushed him to the floor and handcuffed him. The prisoner did not sustain an injury and the court awarded the prisoner $15,000 in compensatory damages and $30,000 in punitive damages. The court also found liable an officer who did not participate in the altercation, but failed to intervene. The court noted that the prisoner was 60 years old and that the officers were aware that he had a knee injury.

As indicated in Figure 9.2, the use of restraints accounted for about one-third of the claims. The United States Supreme Court addressed a unique application of restraints in *Hope v. Pelzer* (2002). The Alabama prison system instituted a restraint process for disruptive prisoner conduct known as the "hitching post." As a punitive measure, a recalcitrant prisoner would be restrained to the post with his hands extended above shoulder level for several hours, usually outside in the sun. While restrained to the post a prisoner would have little mobility to move his arms, the handcuffs would cut into his wrists, causing pain. Frequently, the prisoner's ankles would also be shackled.

Prisoner Hope was restrained to the hitching post for fighting and disobeying orders to work on two occasions. During the first incident, Hope was restrained to the post for two hours, and was offered water and a bathroom break every 15 minutes. On the second occasion, Hope was restrained to the post for several hours without a shirt, provided with water but not permitted bathroom breaks. He claimed that one officer taunted him about his thirst. He filed a § 1983 lawsuit alleging excessive force against three officers. The district court granted summary judgment to the officers and Hope appealed. While the appellate court found that the hitching post constituted cruel and unusual punishment in violation of the Eighth Amendment, the court granted qualified immunity to the officers. Hope appealed to the United States Supreme Court and they agreed to review the case. Reversing the appellate court's decision, the Court determined that restraining a prisoner in such a manner established an Eighth Amendment claim and exhibited cruel and unusual punishment. The Court held that the restraint process constituted an "unnecessary and wanton" infliction of pain for reasons "totally without penological justification." Further, the Court stated that a reasonable officer would have known that using a "hitching post" as alleged by the prisoner was unlawful.

Aerosols are commonly used in prison in order to control a combative or insubordinate prisoner. Aerosols are considered a less-than-lethal use of force and have been successful in reducing the risk of injury to prisoners and the officers who are attempting to control prisoners. In *Treats v. Morgan* (2002), a prisoner brought a § 1983 action against the officers, alleging that officers used pepper spray excessively in violation of his Eighth Amendment right. The prisoner failed to obey the commands of correctional officers and did not threaten them or anyone else. An officer administered a burst from the canister in the prisoner's face and a supervisor placed him on the ground and handcuffed him. The court denied the officers' request for summary judgment and the appellate court affirmed. The appeals court ruled that the spraying a prisoner who only disobeyed an order and was not threatening prison security or other persons precluded summary judgment.

Summary

Several factors should be evident from this discussion. The use of force by police and correctional officers is a critical topic in civil liability and is of fundamental importance. Understanding how the courts examine claims of excessive force is essential. Officers can never justify their use of force for punishment or revenge rationales. Legitimate force used by officers must be within the framework of standards established by the United States Supreme Court. The Court has established three standards of review, depending on the status of the individual. The use of force in policing requires a Fourth Amendment review under the standard of "objective reasonableness" established in the *Graham* decision. The Court identified five factors for analyzing claims of excessive force.

Second, as an arrestee's status changes to that of a pretrial detainee, the courts use the "shocks the conscience" standard of review as articulated in the *Glick* decision. Examining allegations of excessive force in this category appears to create the most confusion as to when the Fourth Amendment applies, when the Fourteenth Amendment applies, and when to consider the Eighth Amendment. Generally, the Fourteenth Amendment due process clause applies to pretrial detainees, although from time to time courts have been known to apply the Eighth Amendment.

Third, the *Hudson* ruling underscores that the excessive force claims arising out of the prison context will be evaluated in accordance with the Eighth Amendment. The applicable standard of using force in good faith and not maliciously or sadistically for causing harm aligns with the cruel and unusual punishment clause of the Eighth Amendment. Severe or significant injury need not occur for a valid excessive force claim to be made.

While the general trend of contemporary rulings by the Supreme Court has been to substantively limit a plaintiff's ability to prevail in civil rights actions, the *Graham* and *Hudson* decisions have opened the door to increased § 1983 use-of-force litigation. Prior to *Graham*, under the Fourteenth Amendment standard, plaintiffs were protected from egregious police behavior that caused severe injuries (*Wise v. Bravo*, 1981). In contrast, the *Graham* standard of objective reasonableness is more restrictive, protecting individuals from police conduct that is objectively unreasonable (*Maynard v. Hopwood*, 1997).

The Fourth Amendment reasonableness assessment requires a fact finder to examine only one question: Was the force used by the police officer objectively reasonable based on the totality of the circumstances? An unreasonable seizure itself crosses the constitutional boundary of whether the plaintiff sustained severe injuries. Therefore, proper application of the Fourth Amendment should stress the reasonableness of a seizure rather than focusing on the extent of a plaintiff's physical injury.

In *Graham* the Supreme Court commented that there is no precise definition of objective reasonableness and cannot be mechanically applied, but must be evaluated by the totality of circumstances, the perspective of the officer, and within the framework of the five-part test. There is, however, divergent interpretation and application of these factors. Generally, it can be concluded that the majority of the lower courts primarily interpret "objectively reasonable force" as being based on the manner of the officer's intrusion, the scope of the intrusion, the need to perform official duties, justification of the intrusion, facts and circumstances of the situation, and the degree of resistance the officer encountered, including the threat or the use of weapons. The lawfulness of the officer's decision will turn on the facts and circumstances known to the officer at the time the force was used. What was determined or discovered after the force was used cannot be used to justify the use of force and would normally not be admissible evidence. An officer's motivation in using force is irrelevant, and evil intent does not make an otherwise reasonable use of force bad and, likewise, the absence of evil intent does not make an objectively unreasonable use of force appropriate.

Finally, studies performed on case trends by the lower courts when applying the standards from the *Graham* and *Hudson* decisions show that officers are prevailing in a significant number of litigated cases. This also shows that officers are generally receiving sufficient training in use-of-force decision-making, using force within the law and policy, and adhering to legal precedents. Officers should continue to receive regular training on civil liability cases pertinent to their job duties when employing force techniques and force equipment. They also have more equipment options at their disposal than in previous years, which gives them a greater range of options to use when encountering resistance

Correctional officers are reminded that a prisoner does not have to show that he sustained an injury in order to assert a legitimate claim. The court only needs to determine that the officer used force maliciously, with the intent to cause harm. Police and correctional officers must be able to articulate their perception as to why they chose a certain course of action in justifying the type and degree of force they used. Officers are encouraged to submit thorough and detailed reports after a force incident.

Administrators and trainers should continue to review court decisions in their jurisdictions across the nation in order to more effectively design guidelines that provide officers with a range of options regarding the appropriate level of force in a given situation (see Figure 9.6). Further, continuing training in the use of all equipment, including classroom training and practical application training, should be provided regularly. Supervisors should receive ongoing training in how to evaluate officers' incident reports

Figure 9.6
Use of Force Policy Considerations

- Policy Philosophy
- Definitions
    - Control
    - Resistance
    - Objectively reasonable force
    - Nonlethal force and lethal force
- Authority to use force
- Types of resistance (psychological intimidation, verbal, passive, defensive, active aggression, and aggravated active aggression)
- Levels of force
    - Officer presence
    - Verbal instructions
    - Empty-hand control (control holds, wristlocks, come-along holds, takedown tactics, pressure points, hand/leg strikes, stuns, and neck restraints)
    - Aerosols (pepper spray and other chemical agents)
    - Use of dogs
    - Impact Weapons (batons, flashlights, Tasers, stun guns, etc.)
    - Lethal force guidelines
- Description of authorized equipment (restraints, restraint chair, etc.)
- Escalation/de-escalation of force
- Medical considerations
- Force and restraint of "special needs" prisoners
- Transportation in restraints
- Reporting use of force
- Investigation of use-of-force incidents

on use of force and enforce departmental guidelines when unreasonable force is discovered. Supervisors play a significant role in determining whether reasonable force was used in arrest situations. A continued commitment on the part of police administrators, trainers, and officers will help in developing a balance between the rights of citizens to be free of unreasonable seizures and the interests of society in maintaining legitimate law enforcement, while protecting police officers.

References

Alpert, G. (1989). "Police Use of Deadly Force: The Miami Experience." In R.G. Dunham & G.P. Alpert (eds.), *Critical Issues in Policing: Contemporary Readings*. Prospect Heights, IL: Waveland Press, Inc.

———— & R. Dunham (1999). "The Force Factor: Measuring Police Use of Force Relative to Suspect Resistance." In *Police Use of Force*. Washington, DC: National Institute of Justice.

Bayley, D.H. & J. Garofalo (1989a). "The Management of Violence by Police Officers." *Criminology* 27:1-27.

———— (1989b). "Patrol Officer Effectiveness in Managing Conflict During Police-Citizen Contacts." In *Report to the New York State Commission Criminal Justice and the Use of Force* (Vol. III, May). Albany, NY: New York State Commission on Criminal Justice and the Use of Force.

Binder, A. & P. Scharf (1980). "The Violent Police-Citizen Encounter." *Annals of the American Academy of Political and Social Science* 452:111-121.

Binder, A. & L.A. Fridell (1984). "The Use of Firearms by Police Officers: The Impact of Individuals, Communities, and Race." Doctoral dissertation, State University of New York, Albany.

Bloomberg, M. (1982). "Issues and Controversies with Respect to the Use of Deadly Force by Police." In T. Barker & D.L. Carter (eds.), *Police Deviance*. Cincinnati, OH: Pilgrimage Press.

Bureau of Justice Statistics (2003). *Census of State and Federal Correctional Facilities in 2000*. Washington, DC: Department of Justice.

Bureau of Justice Statistics (1997). *Police Use of Force: Collection of National Data*. Washington, DC: U.S. Department of Justice.

Camp, C. & G. Camp (2003). "Prisoner Assaults on Correction Officers." *Corrections Yearbook*. Middletown CT: Criminal Justice Institute, Inc.

Chevigny, P.B. (1969). *Police Power: Police Abuse in New York City*. New York, NY: Vintage Books.

Croft, E.B. (1985). "Police Use of Force: An Empirical Analysis." Doctoral dissertation, State University of New York at Albany.

———— & B.A. Austin (1987). "Police Use of Force in Rochester and Syracuse, New York, 1984 and 1985." In *Report to the New York State Commission on Criminal Justice and the Use of Force* (Vol. III, May). Albany, NY: New York State Commission on Criminal Justice and the Use of Force.

Department of Justice (2006). *Consent Decrees*. Available at: www.usdoj.gov/crt/split/documents/ httm. Accessed January 4, 2006. Washington, DC: Special Litigation Section of the Civil Rights Division.

Fridell, L. (1989). "Justifiable Use of Force Measures in Research on Deadly Force." *Journal of Criminal Justice* 17:157-165.

Friederich, R.J. (1980). "Police Use of Force: Individuals, Situations and Organizations." *Annals of the American Academy of Political and Social Science* 425:82-97.

Fyfe, J.J. (1978). "Shots Fired: An Examination of New York City Police Firearms Discharges." Doctoral dissertation, State University of New York, Albany.

———— (1988). "Police Use of Deadly Force: Research and Reform." *Justice Quarterly* 5:165-205.

Garner, J., T. Buchanan, T. Schade & J. Hepburn (1996). *Executive Summary: Understanding the Use of Force by and Against the Police*. Washington, DC: National Institute of Justice.

Geller, W.A. (1985). "Officer Restraint in the Use of Deadly Force: The Next Frontier in Police Shooting Research." *Journal of Police Science and Administration* 13:153-171.

Greenfeld, P., A. Langham, S. Smith & R. Kaminski (1997). "Police Use of Force: Collection of National Data." *Research in Brief*. Washington, DC: Bureau of Justice Statistics.

Greenleaf, R.G. & L. Lanza-Kaduce (1995). "Sophistication, Organization, and Authority-Subject Conflict: Rediscovering and Unraveling Turk's Theory of Norm Resistance." *Criminology* 33:565-585.

Hemmens, C. & E. Atherton (1999). *Use of Force: Current Practice and Policy*. Lanham, MD: American Correctional Association.

Hopkins, E.J. (1931). *Our Lawless Police*. New York, NY: Viking Press.

Horvath, F. (1987). "The Police Use of Deadly Force: A Description of Selected Characteristics of Intrastate Incidents." *Journal of Police Science and Administration* 15:226-238.

International Association of Chiefs of Police (2001). *Police Use of Force in America*. Alexandria, VA: IACP.

Jacobs, D. & D. Britt (1979). "Inequality and Police Use of Deadly Force: An Empirical Assessment of a Conflict Hypothesis." *Social Problems* 24:401-411.

Kappeler, V. (1997). *Critical Issues in Police Civil Liability*, Second Edition. Prospect Heights, IL: Waveland Press, Inc.

————, S.F. Kappeler & R.V. del Carmen (1993, updated 1996). "A Content Analysis of Police Civil Liability Cases: Decisions of the Federal Courts, 1978-1990." *Journal of Criminal Justice* 21:325-337.

Klotter, J.C., J.T. Walker & C. Hemmens (2005). *Legal Guide for Police: Constitutional Issues*, Seventh Edition. Cincinnati, OH: Anderson Publishing Co.

Kratcoski, P. (1987). "The Implications of Research Explaining Prison Violence and Disruption." *Federal Probation* 52:27-32.

Langham, P.A., Greenfeld, L.A., Smith, S.L., Durose, M.R. and Levin, D.J. (2001). *Contacts Between Police and the Public: Findings From the 1999 National Survey*. Washington, DC: Bureau of Justice Statistics.

Lester, D. (1984). "The Use of Deadly Force by Police." *Police Journal* 57:170-171.

Light, S. (1991). "Assaults on Prison Officers: Interactional Themes." *Justice Quarterly* 8:243-261.

LRP Publications (1992). *Personal Injury Verdict Reviews*. Horsham, PA: Author.

Mastrofski, S. & R. Parks (1990). "Improving Observational Studies of Police." *Criminology* 28:475-496.

Matulia, K. (1982). *A Balance of Forces*. Gaithersburg, MD: International Association of Chiefs of Police.

McLaughlin, V. (1992). *Police and the Use of Force: The Savannah Study*. Westport, CT: Praeger Publishers.

Milton, C.H., J.W. Lardner & G.L. Albrecht (1997). "Police Use of Deadly Force." In H.W. More, Jr. (ed.), *Critical Issues in Law Enforcement*, Fourth Edition. Cincinnati, OH: Anderson Publishing Co.

National Commission on Law Observance and Enforcement (Wickersham Commission) (1931). *Report on Lawlessness in Law Enforcement*. Washington. DC: U.S. Government Printing Office.

National Institute of Justice (1999). *Use of Force by Police*. Washington, DC: U.S. Department of Justice.

Pate, A. & L. Fridell (1993). *Police Use of Force: Official Reports, Citizen Complaints, and Legal Consequences*. Washington, DC: Police Foundation.

Reiss, A. (1971). *The Police and the Public*. New Haven, CT: Yale University Press.

Ross, D.L. (2005). "A Content Analysis of the Emerging Trends in the Use of Non-Lethal Force Research in Policing." *Journal of Law Enforcement Executive Forum* 5:121-148.

———— (2004). "An Analysis *of Hudson v. McMillian*: Ten Years Later." *Criminal Law Bulletin* 6:15-48.

———— (2004). *An Analysis of Detainee Resistance and Detention Officer Use of Force in Michigan Jails: 2000-2003*. An unpublished Technical Report prepared for the Michigan Municipal Risk Management Authority, Livonia, MI.

———— (2002). "An Assessment of the *Graham v. Connor*, Ten Years Later." *Policing: An International Journal of Strategies and Management* 2:294-318.

———— (1990). "Study Examines Non-Deadly Physical Force Policies." *Corrections Today* (July):64-66.

———— (1996). "A National Assessment of Prisoner Assaults on Correction Officers." *Corrections Compendium* 25:1-8.

———— (1999). "Analyzing Patterns of Citizen Resistance During Police Arrest." *FBI Law Enforcement Bulletin* (June):22-28.

———— (2000). "Emerging Trends in Police Failure to Train Liability." *Policing: An International Journal of Police Strategies and Management* 23:169-193.

Rowan, J.R. (1996). "Who is Safer in Male Maximum Prisons?" *Corrections Today* 58:2-4.

Schultz, D. & J. Service (1981). *The Police Use of Force*. Springfield, IL: Charles C Thomas.

Sykes, R.E. & E.E. Brent (1983). *Policing: A Social Behaviorist Perspective*. Brunswick, NJ: New Rutgers University Press.

U.S. Department of Justice (1999). *Use of Force by Police*. Washington, DC: National Institute of Justice.

———— (1997). *Use of Force: Collection of National Data*. Washington, DC: Bureau of Justice Statistics.

Waegel, W.B. (1984). "The Use of Lethal Force by Police: The Complaint." *Journal of Police Science and Administration* 8:247-252.

Cases Cited

Austin v. Hopper, 15 F. Supp. 2d 1210 (M.D. Ala. 1998)

Bond v. Queen, 71 F.3d 1151 (1st Cir. 1999)

Bordanaro v. McLeod, 871 F.2d 1151 (1st Cir. 1989)

Brazier v. Cherry, 293 F.2d 401 (5th Cir. 1961)

Brothers v. Klevenhagen, 28 F.3d 345 (5th Cir. 1994)

Calamia v. City of New York, 879 F.2d 1025 (2d Cir. 1989)

Campbell v. Sikes, 169 F.3d 1353 (11th Cir. 1999)

Carver v. Bullock, 168 F.3d 481 (4th Cir. 1999)

Casaburro v. Giuliani, 986 F. Supp. 176 (S.D.N.Y. 1997)

Chimel v. California, 395 U.S. 752 (1969)

Colston v. Barnhart, 130 F.3d 96 (5th Cir. 1997)

Cotton v. Busic, 793 F. Supp. 191 (S.D. Ind. 1992)

Cruz v. Escondido, 126 F.3d 1214 (10th Cir. 1997)

Darnell v. Caver, 156 F.3d 1229 (6th Cir. 1998)

Davis v. Mason County, 927 F.2d 1473 (9th Cir. 1991)

De Corte v. Robinson, 969 F.2d 358 (5th Cir. 1998)

DeGraff v. District of Columbia, 120 F.3d 298 (D.C. Cir. 1997)

Dennis v. Thurman, 959 F. Supp. 1253 (C.D. Cal. 1997)

Draper v. Reynolds, 369 F.3d 1270 (11th Cir. 2004)

Duametef v. Fial, 922 F. Supp. 807 (W.D. N.Y. 1996)

Estate of Davis by Ostenfeld v. Delo, 115 F.3d 1388 (8th Cir. 1997)

Fobbs v. City of Los Angeles, 316 P.2d 668 (Cal. Ct. App.1957)

Forrester v. City of San Diego, 25 F.3d 804 (9th Cir. 1994)

Fraire v. City of Arlington, 957 F.2d 1268 (5th Cir. 1992)

Franklin v. City of Kansas City, Kansas, 959 F. Supp. 1380 (D. Kan. 1997)

Garcia v. City of Chicago, 2003 U.S. Dist. Lexis 16564 (E.D. Ill.)

Gilmere v. City of Atlanta, 774 F.2d 1495 (11th Cir. 1985)

Giroux v. Sherman, 807 F. Supp. 1182 (E.D. Pa. 1992)

Graham v. Connor, 490 U.S. 386 (1989)

Gravely v. Madden, 142 F.3d 345 (6th Cir. 1998)

Gutierrez-Rodriquez v. Cartagena, 882 F.2d 553 (1st Cir. 1989)

Guseman v. Martinez, 1 F. Supp. 2d 1240 (D. Kan. 1998)

Gumz v. Morrissette, 772 F.2d 1395 (7th Cir. 1985)

Hall v. Tawney, 621 F.2d 607 (4th Cir. 1980)

Hart v. Rogers, 148 F.3d 1168 (4th Cir. 1998)

Hensen v. Thezan, 698 F. Supp. 150 (N.D. Ill. 1988)

Hogan v. Franco, 896 F. Supp. 1313 (N.D.N.Y. 1995)

Hope v. Pelzer, 536 U.S. 730 (2002)

Hostin v. United States, 566 F. Supp. 1125 (D.D.C. 1983)

Hudson v. McMillian, 503 U.S. 1 (1992)

Ingraham v. Wright, 430 U.S. 651 (1977)

Isom v. Town of Warren, Rhode Island, 360 F.3d 7 (1st Cir. 2004)

Jarrett v. Town of Yarmouth, 331 F.3d 140 (1st Cir. 2003)

Johnson v. Glick, 481 F.2d 1028 (2d Cir. 1973)

Johnson v. Morel, 876 F.2d 477 (5th Cir. 1989)

Kidd v. O'Neil, 774 F.2d 1252 (4th Cir. 1985)

Kinney v. Indiana Youth Center, 950 F.2d 462 (7th Cir. 1991)

Lamb v. City of Decatur, 947 F. Supp. 1261 (C. D. Ill. 1996)

Lester v. City of Rosedale, 757 F. Supp. 741 (N.D. Miss.1991)

Los Angeles v. Lyons, 461 U.S. 95 (1983)

Madrid v. Gomez, 889 F. Supp. 1146 (N.D. Cal. 1995)

Mahone v. Palazzo, 98-C-6020 (N.D. Ill. 1999)

Martin v. Gentile, 897 F.2d 863 (D.C. Cir. 1988)

Matasic v. City of Campbell, 954 F. Supp. 150 (N.D. Ohio 1997)

Mateyko v. Felix, 824 F.2d 824 (9th Cir. 1990)

Mathieu v. Imperial Toy Company, 646 So. 2d 318 (La. 1994)

Mathis v. Parks, 741 F. Supp. 567 (E.D.N.C. 1990)

Mathis v. Fries, 935 F. Supp. 1284 (E.D. N.Y. 1996)

Maynard v. Hopwood, 105 F.3d 1226 (8th Cir. 1997)

Medeiros v. Town of Dracut, 21 F. Supp. 2d 82 (4th Cir. 1998)

McCartt v. Keyes, 194 F.3d 1313 (6th Cir. 1999)

McClanahan v. City of Moberly, 35 F. Supp. 2d 744 (E.D. Mo. 1998)

McCrory v. New Orleans, 558 So. 2d 1322 (La. Ct. App. 1990)

McDonald v. Haskins, 966 F.2d 292 (7th Cir. 1992)

McRae v. Tena, 113 F.3d 1241 (9th Cir. 1996)

Monday v. Oullette, 118 F.3d 1099 (6th Cir. 1997)

Monroe v. Pape, 365 U.S. 167 (1961)

Mosier v. Robinson, 722 F. Supp. 555 (W.D. Ark.1989)

Nelson v. County of Wright, 162 F.3d 986 (8th Cir. 1998)

Nova v. City of Dublin, 121 F.3d 453 (9th Cir. 1997)

Omokaro v. Whitemeyer, 205 F.3d 1338 (5th Cir. 1998)

Ortega v. Schramm, 922 F.2d 684 (11th Cir. 1991)

Owens v. City of Atlanta, 780 F.2d 1564 (11th Cir. 1985)

Palmer v. Marion County, 327 F.3d 588 (7th Cir. 2003)

Paul v. City of Altus, 172 F.3d 879 (10th Cir. 1998)

Pittman v. Nelms, 87 F.3d 116 (4th Cir. 1996)

Proffit v. City of Pana, Illinois, No. 98-3182 (C.D. Ill. 2000)

Radecki v. Barlea, 146 F.3d 1227 (10th Cir. 1998)

Raley v. Fraser, 747 F.2d 287 (5th Cir. 1984)

Riley v. Durton, 115 F.3d 1159 (4th Cir. 1997)

Rochin v. California, 342 U.S. 165 (1952)

Russo v. City of Cincinnati, 953 F.2d 1036 (6th Cir. 1992)

Samuels v. Hawkins, 157 F.3d 557 (8th Cir. 1998)

Sappington v. Bartee, 195 F.3d 234 (5th Cir. 1999)

Screws v. United States, 325 U.S. 91 (1945)

Shillingford v. Holmes, 634 F.2d 363 (5th Cir. 1981)

Sigman v. Town of Chapel Hill, 161 F.3d 782 (4th Cir. 1998)

Skinner v. Brooks, 288 58 N.E.2d 697 (Ohio Ct. App.1994)

Smith v. Cupp, 430 F.3d 766 (6th Cir. 2005)

Smith v. Freland, 954 F.2d 343 (6th Cir. 1992)

Smith v. Mattox, 127 F.3d 1416 (11th Cir. 1997)

Stanley v. City of Baytown, Texas, WL 2757370 (S.D. Tex. 2005)

Stanely v. Hejiria, 134 F.3d 629 (4th Cir. 1998)

Stein v. State, 385 N.Y.S.2d 874 (1976)

Stewart v. Prince George's County, 75 Fed. Appx. 198 (2003)

Sudac v. Hoang, 378 F. Supp. 2d 1298 (D. Kan. 2005)

Taft v. Vine, 70 F.3d 304 (4th Cir. 1995)

Terry v. Ohio, 392 U.S. 1 (1968)

Tennessee v. Garner, 471 U.S. 1 (1985)

Treats v. Morgan, 308 F.3d 868 (8th Cir. 2002)

Trout v. Frega, 70 F.3d 304 (E.D. Ill. 1996)

United States v. Holloway, 906 F. Supp. 1437 (D. Kan. 1995)

Valencia v. Wiggins, 981 F.2d 1440 (5th Cir. 1993)

Wagner v. Bay City, Texas, 227 F.3d 316 (5th Cir. 2000)

Wallace v. City of Shelby, 968 F. Supp. 1204 (N.D. Ohio 1997)

Wallace v. Estate of Davis, 676 N.E.2d 422 (Ind. Ct. App. 1997)

Whitley v. Albers, 475 U.S. 312 (1986)

Williams v. Bramer, 186 F.3d 63 (5th Cir. 1999)

Wise v. Bravo, 666 F.2d 1328 (10th Cir. 1981)

Wisniewski v. Kennard, 901 F.2d 1276 (5th Cir. 1990)

Chapter 10

Section 1983 and Correctional Liability Issues

Justice White, writing for the United States Supreme Court in *Wolff v. McDonnell* (1974), stated that there is "no iron curtain drawn between the Constitution and prisons of this country, . . . a prisoner is not wholly stripped of constitutional protections when he is imprisoned for crime." Since the *Wolff* decision, prisoners have filed numerous lawsuits under § 1983, claiming deprivation of constitutional rights. Prisoners may file lawsuits in both federal and state courts under § 1983. Most prisoner litigation is filed in federal court *in forma pauperis* (Maahs & del Carmen, 1995; Ross, 1997). Section 1983 prisoner actions have included inadequate medical care, access to the courts, prison conditions, use of excessive force, failure to protect, and administrative deficiencies.

Prisoners commonly file § 1983 lawsuits seeking to gain some type of monetary award or equitable relief. In these lawsuits, the prisoner is generally complaining about the manner in which officials treated him or her, challenging the constitutionality of the treatment or conditions of confinement, or contesting a correctional practice or rule. Other prisoners may file lawsuits to break up the monotony of prison life. Frivolous lawsuits have been submitted to harass correctional officials or to seek an opportunity to leave the facility for a court appearance.

Court decisions concerning prisoner litigation have had a profound impact on the correctional system. Since the 1970s, court intervention through case decisions has directly affected a wide range of prison issues, including health care services, access to the courts, use of force, religious practices, disciplinary procedures, conditions of confinement, officer brutality, and administrative practices. As a result, both jail and prison operational policies and procedures have been significantly affected. This chapter will describe the liability issues most frequently raised by prisoners under § 1983 and examine the standard of review.

Application of the Deliberate Indifference Standard

The U.S. Supreme Court's holding in a particular case often results in establishing a standard or test with which to evaluate future claims. Arguably, one of the most common and far-reaching standards applied to correctional litigation developed by the Court is that of "deliberate indifference." This standard was established in the seminal case of *Estelle v. Gamble* (1976). In this Texas prison case, the prisoner sustained a back injury while on a work assignment and claimed that he was repeatedly denied or delayed medical care, despite 17 examinations by medical doctors, X rays, prescribed medication, and bed rest. The Supreme Court determined that the proper method for examining claims of denial of medical care under the Eighth Amendment is whether correctional officials were deliberately indifferent to the needs of the prisoner. The Court ruled that liability will attach when the actions of correctional personnel constitute cruel and unusual punishment in violation of the Eighth Amendment. In *Estelle* the Court found that the officials' response did not rise to a level of deliberate indifference.

Deliberate indifference is not easily defined and is difficult to apply. The Court distinguished deliberate indifference from "negligence." Since first enumerating this standard, the Court has held that deliberate indifference resides on a continuum between "mere negligence and something less than acts or omissions for the very purpose of causing harm" (*Farmer v. Brennan*, 1994). "Deliberate" means that a particular course of action has been chosen from among various alternatives, and "indifference" means that there has been some conscious disregard for a person's rights (Plitt, 1997).

Deliberate indifference requires certain duties: (1) serious medical complaints, especially of a continuing nature, should not be ignored (whether correctional personnel regard them as false or exaggerated); (2) medically trained personnel should make medical judgments; (3) serious, chronic symptoms should receive attention; and (4) neither a blind eye nor a deaf ear should be tolerated regarding a prisoner's complaint where, with proper care, a correctional officer could have known about the complaint (Silver, 2000). Under the deliberate indifference standard, there is a general expectation that "adequate" or "reasonable" care will be provided to prisoners under the control of correctional personnel. A system that provides adequate medical and mental health care to prisoners at intake and throughout incarceration must be in place. Most, if not all, detention and prison facilities have instituted health care services to prisoners, despite continued claims of inadequate medical care. Prisoners generally have no right to be treated by a private physician (*Hawley v. Evans*, 1989).

Deliberate indifference can be manifested in a number of ways. The refusal of correctional or medical personnel to provide care, or a delay in providing such care, may be actionable under the deliberate indifference standard. A series of incidents that, if viewed in isolation, appear to involve only negligence, may give rise to deliberate indifference. Problems caused by understaffing, a lack of or deficient equipment, substandard facilities, and a lack of procedures may be so egregious that the ensuing inability to render adequate medical care is so evident that the failure to redress these problems is tantamount to "deliberate indifference" (Krantz, 1997).

Actions emerging from a pretrial detainee's claims of being deprived of needed medical care are examined under the due process clauses of the Fifth and Fourteenth Amendments rather than the Eighth Amendment. The courts have agreed that the cruel and unusual punishment clause of the Eighth Amendment does not apply to pretrial detainees, but the due process clause protects them.

Over the years, the Supreme Court has expanded the standard of deliberate indifference beyond health care services. The Court has extended the standard to other prisoner claims, including conditions of confinement (*Wilson v. Seiter*, 1991), failure to protect (*DeShaney v. Winnebago County Department of Social Services*, 1989; *Farmer v. Brennan*, 1994), failure to train (*City of Canton v. Harris*, 1989), claims emerging from supervisory deficiencies, and claims resulting from custodial suicides. The following discussion illustrates how the courts have applied this standard to correctional situations.

Deliberate Indifference and Health Care

Providing health care services to pretrial detainees and state prisoners is a fundamental responsibility. Today's detention and prison facilities confine prisoners with a variety of medical and psychiatric problems ranging from diseases like HIV/AIDS to differing degrees of mental illness. Over the years, numerous types of civil liability claims alleging inadequate medical care have emerged. Ross (1997) found that in a 25-year analysis (1970 to 1994) of § 1983 litigation in jails and prisons, medical care claims were the most frequently filed by prisoners and correctional officials prevailed in approximately 55 percent of the cases.

In *Arnold v. Lewis* (1992), a prisoner filed a § 1983 claim against correctional officials for being deliberately indifferent to his mental health care needs. The district court ruled in favor of the prisoner, finding that the officials' actions constituted deliberate indifference to serious medical needs in violation of the Eighth Amendment. The officials had placed the prisoner in lockdown as a punishment for symptoms of her paranoid schizophrenia as an alternative to providing mental health care. The officials knew that the mental health program at the facility was deficient and were aware that the prisoner's mental condition deteriorated when she was locked down in a small cell without treatment, but failed to correct the grossly inadequate psychiatric care. Prison officials' actions warranted injunctive relief, ensuring that she would receive the appropriate treatment.

A lower district court granted summary judgment to correctional officials in a § 1983 action brought by a female prisoner in *Giron v. Corrections*

Corp. of America (1998). After being raped by a correctional officer, the plaintiff alleged that correctional officials deliberately disregarded a substantial risk of harm to her and denied her psychological care. The court concluded that the official's awareness of two prior incidents of sexual misconduct by other officers was insufficient to establish that the officials must have drawn the inference that a substantial risk of harm existed. The court held that she was not deprived of necessary medical care after the sexual assault. The plaintiff was seen by a psychiatrist 18 times and a psychologist at least 100 times during a six-month period.

In *Tucker v. Randall* (1993) a pretrial detainee alleged inadequate medical care by detention officers of a sheriff's department. The appeals court affirmed the lower court's holding that the officers did not act with deliberate indifference to the medical needs of the detainee, even when they failed to treat him with ice and aspirin as instructed by a doctor, or delayed more than two months in having the injuries reexamined. A reasonable person would not have viewed the detainee's injuries as life-threatening or serious. The detainee was transported to a hospital prior to booking and the hospital doctor did not treat the injuries as serious or life-threatening. Further, the detainee did not complain of injuries to the booking officer upon arrival.

The duty to provide medical care is a continuing one, and delay of such care either at the onset or continuation of serious medical symptoms may be actionable. In *Lancaster v. Monroe County, Alabama* (1997), a sheriff and several of his detention officers were found to be deliberately indifferent to the serious medical needs of an alcoholic pretrial detainee who died from seizures brought on by withdrawal symptoms. The detainee was jailed for driving under the influence of alcohol and placed on a top bunk in a holding cell, because lower bunks were occupied. Detention officers were notified twice by the detainee's wife that he was an alcoholic and suffered from delirium tremens. The officers acknowledged the condition and promised to watch him. The detainee's father notified the sheriff of his condition, and the sheriff informed the father that the detainee would be taken to the hospital if he had a seizure. During the night, several prisoners stated that the detainee suffered from the "shakes" and a headache. At mid-morning, the detainee sat up in his bunk, began shaking, and fell out of bed, landing on his head. He was transported to the hospital, where he died three days later due to the head injuries. The pathologist determined that the detainee was having a seizure when he fell out of his bed. The detainee's wife filed a § 1983 action for wrongful death and deliberate indifference to the deceased's serious medical condition. The court found in favor of the plaintiff and determined that his inebriated condition progressed into seizures, constituting a serious medical condition. The evidence showed that the condition would worsen with delay and that the sheriff failed to plan for medical care until after the detainee had a seizure. The officers knew the deceased's condition was serious, yet allowed him to remain in the top bunk and failed to plan to obtain medical attention until after the seizure.

In *Reed v. McBride* (1999), an appellate court found in favor of a prisoner's Eighth Amendment claim of withholding food and life-sustaining medication from him while incarcerated. The court found that the prisoner's medical condition progressively worsened, making it serious, and supporting his claim of deliberate indifference. The court found that depriving a prisoner of food may be so objectively serious as to support a claim of cruel and unusual punishment under the Eighth Amendment, when the amount and duration of the deprivation is considered. The prisoner suffered from a variety of ailments, including paralysis, heart disease, Hunt's syndrome, high blood pressure, rheumatoid arthritis, and other crippling diseases. In *Gutierrez v. Peters* (1997), however, the appellate court affirmed judgment in favor of prison officials when a prisoner claimed that he received inadequate medical treatment for an infected cyst on his eye. The court acknowledged that the cyst was a serious medical condition, but failed to find that the officials acted with deliberate indifference despite isolated delays in treatment. The court found that a six-day wait to see the physician was not an unreasonably long delay for the condition in view of the fact that the physician had seen the prisoner one week earlier and had concluded the cyst was not infected, and the physician promptly prescribed a course of treatment.

Delay in providing medical care in a detention facility was addressed in *Blackmore v. Kalamazoo County* (2004). The Sixth Circuit Court of Appeals reversed the lower court's provision for summary judgment when a detainee filed a lawsuit claiming delay in medical attention. Blackmore was admitted into the Kalamazoo County jail for driving under a suspended license. He was booked, placed in a cell, and within an hour he began complaining of abdominal pain. Detention officers gave him antacids but did secure further medical care. Two days later he again complained of extreme abdominal pains and requested immediate medical care. The officers placed him the observation cell as Blackmore was vomiting the antacids given earlier. Later that day, a nurse examined him and determined that he was suffering from appendicitis. He was transported to the hospital and an appendectomy was successfully performed. Blackmore filed a lawsuit claiming that the officers violated his constitutional rights by denying him prompt medical attention. He also alleged that the sheriff failed to implement policies and to train officers to adequately respond to detainee medical needs.

In reversing the lower court's decision granting qualified immunity to the officers, the appellate court ruled that Blackmore proved that the officers demonstrated a "culpable state of mind" by being aware that Blackmore had a serious medical condition and yet failing to seek medical care until two days after he made the complaint. To be liable, a detainee must show that his medical needs posed a "substantial risk of serious harm." The court ruled that a serious medical need is one that has been diagnosed by a physician as mandating treatment or one that is so obvious that even a layperson would easily recognize the necessity for medical care. The court reasoned that Blackmore complained over two days that he had abdominal pains, filed several sick call requests asking for medical care, was observed to be vomiting, and the officers placed him the observation cell. His condition was progressively deteriorating and officers were aware of his obvious need for medical care but did not seek medical attention until two days later. Thus, Blackmore sufficiently showed that his need for medical care was not addressed, violating his Eighth Amendment rights. The court also found that the county failed to implement policies on how to deal with prisoner illness and they also failed to adequately train the officers. Such failures supported a constitutional claim of deliberate indifference.

Deliberate Indifference and Psychological Care

The deliberate indifference standard also applies to the psychological needs of mentally impaired prisoners. Allegations generally revolve around appropriate treatment of the mentally impaired while incarcerated and involuntarily medicating a prisoner who manifests a mental defect. The United States Supreme Court has addressed this issue and the lower courts have on numerous occasions applied the standard of deliberate indifference.

In *Washington v. Harper* (1990), the United States Supreme Court ruled that involuntarily medicating a prisoner who has been diagnosed by a psychiatrist as suffering from a mental defect and who posed a significant risk of harm to himself and others did not violate the Fourteenth Amendment. Harper was diagnosed with bipolar disorder and refused to take his prescribed medication. In compliance with prison policy, two psychiatrists determined that he was "gravely disabled" and posed a danger to others and himself, and medicated him without his consent. He filed a § 1983 lawsuit challenging the decision to medicate him against his will.

The Court rejected his claim, holding that the state had a legitimate interest in the safety and security of the prison—for the safety of other prisoners, for Harper, and for the officers and staff in the institution. The Court ruled that involuntarily medicating a prisoner implies a due process component consistent with the Fourteenth Amendment and that a hearing must be conducted prior to administering medication without a prisoner's consent. Pursuant to the state of Washington's policy, such a hearing was in place and before involuntarily medicating Harper, he was provided with a hearing. The hearing outcome concluded that for the safety of Harper and the security of the institution, he be medicated without his consent. The Court ruled that such a policy and practice protected Harper's due process rights under the Fourteenth Amendment and affirmed the state of Washington's penological and therapeutic interest in medicating Harper against his will.

The nation was stunned in 1998 when a man walked into the Capitol building in Washington, D.C., and shot and killed two federal police officers when he was looking for "aliens" and the key to the innermost portions of the Capitol. In *United States v. Weston* (2002), the appellate court ruled that the Federal Bureau of Prisons could involuntarily medicate Weston. Prison psychiatrists concluded that Weston needed to be medicated, but he refused. His attorney filed a legal action requesting that officials be prohibited from medicating him without his consent. The appellate court affirmed the lower court's decision to involuntarily medicate Weston because the action was essential in order to render the prisoner non-dangerous, based on medical/safety concerns.

The United States Supreme Court has further expanded their decision in *Harper* by examining whether the government can medicate a mentally impaired prisoner against his will so that he can be rendered competent to stand trial. The Court addressed this issue in *Sell v. United States* (2003). A federal criminal defendant with a long history of mental illness was initially found competent to stand trial for a criminal charge of fraud. He was released on bail but was later denied bail because his condition deteriorated. His attorney requested a reconsideration of his competence. After an examination at a medical center for federal prisoners, the defendant was found incompetent to stand trial and was hospitalized to determine whether he would attain competency to allow his trial to proceed. The defendant refused to take his antipsychotic medication and, after a hearing, a psychiatrist authorized that he be medicated involuntarily. A U.S. magistrate judge issued an order forcing the administration of drugs. The district court found no evidence that the defendant was dangerous, but upheld the order, finding that the involuntary medication was the only viable hope of rendering the defendant competent to stand trial in order to obtain an adjudication of his guilt or innocence.

The appellate court affirmed and the United States Supreme Court ruled that the Constitution allows the government to administer psychiatric drugs even against the defendant's will, in limited circumstances. The Court held that in order to administer such medication against the will of the accused defendant for trial purposes, four criteria must be met: (1) there are important governmental interests at stake, such as timely prosecution, bringing the defendant to trial, assuring the trial is fair, and the court's evaluation of the facts of each case; (2) involuntary medication will significantly further such governmental interests that the administration of drugs will likely render the defendant competent to stand trial: (3) involuntary medication is necessary to further such interests and any alternative and less intrusive treatments are unlikely to produce the same results; and (4) the administration of drugs is medically appropriate—that is, in the defendant's best medical interests in light of the defendant's medical condition.

The *Sell* decision was applied to a prisoner serving a sentence on death row in *Singleton v. Norris* (2003). Singleton was serving his sentence on death row and was being forcibly medicated. He sought an order that would stop the treatment. The state court denied the request and he filed a habeas corpus petition seeking a stay of execution of his death sentence. The district court denied the petition and the prisoner appealed. The appellate court affirmed, holding that a state does not violate the Eighth Amendment or due process by executing a prisoner who has regained competency through forced medication that is part of appropriate medical care.

Deliberate Indifference, the Americans with Disabilities Act, and Prisoners

The Americans with Disabilities Act (ADA) was enacted in 1990 to protect qualified people with disabilities. The Act not only applies to free citizens but also applies to prisoners in state prisons and other correctional facilities (*Pennsylvania Dep't. of Corrections v. Yeskey*, 1998). In *Yeskey,* a prisoner who had been denied admission to a prison boot camp program due to his history of hypertension sued correctional officials under the ADA. The United States Supreme Court held that Title II of the ADA, prohibiting a "public entity" from discriminating against a "qualified individual with a disability," applied to prisoners in state prisons. As applied in the correctional environment, the ADA was instituted to protect disabled prisoners from discrimination under the Fourteenth Amendment and has primarily been applied to health care issues.

A district court let stand a jury verdict and monetary damages in the amount of $150,000 in a § 1983 action stemming from an ADA claim in *Beckford v. Irvin* (1999). The plaintiff prisoner had been confined to a wheelchair since 1984. In 1994 he was transferred from a psychiatric center to another correctional facility, where he was assigned to a Mental Health Observation Unit (MHOU). He was placed in the MHOU such that his wheelchair could fit within the cell. Shortly after the transfer, officials took away the wheelchair and denied him access to it for the majority of his time at the facility, despite his repeated requests. The jury concluded that the prisoner's rights had been violated because he was denied the use of his wheelchair, he was unable to participate in outdoor exercise or take a shower. The jury awarded damages against two supervisory officials for being deliberately indifferent to the prisoner's serious medical needs.

In *Hanson v. Sangamore County Sheriff's Dep't* (1998), failure to provide a known deaf arrestee with an interpreter or the physical means to make a telephone call was actionable under the ADA. A § 1983 claim based on a violation of the ADA was not defensible by qualified immunity. The district court rejected county officials' motion for summary judgment in *Roe v. County of Comm'n of Monongalia County* (1996), when a mental health patient brought an action under the ADA. The plaintiff was picked up on a mental health warrant and held in a padded cell, handcuffed, and shackled. He was not given proper treatment or a hearing and was not allowed to use a bathroom, change clothes, or eat without handcuffs. The court found that the prisoner stated a valid claim because he was unable to communicate with his family, was unable to attend to his personal hygiene, and was isolated in a manner that the ADA was designed to prevent.

Diabetic prisoners brought a class action under § 1983 against state correctional officials alleging violations of the Eighth Amendment and the ADA in *Rouse v. Plantier* (1998). The court denied summary judgment for the defendants on the issue of whether the prisoners' diabetes was a disability under the ADA. The court ruled that the prisoners might be substantially limited in the foods they could eat, in the exercise regime in which they could engage, and by numerous special complications that diabetes presented for them. If the prisoners' condition was considered without mitigating measures such as medicines, or assistive or prosthetic devices, the court found it was clear that they could be considered disabled.

Prisoners with disabilities have brought legal actions complaining that the use of restraints by correctional officers violates their constitutional rights. In *Williams-El v. McLemore* (2002), a prisoner sought equitable relief against a practice of using restraints on prisoners with disabilities. The prisoner alleged that correctional officers failed to provide him large handcuffs, rather than the standard handcuffs, for transportation purposes. The prisoner was diagnosed with a congenital deformity known as Kasabach Merrit Syndrome, which caused his right hand to be severely curled inward at the wrist and caused pain to his extremities when improperly positioned. The court barred summary judgment for the correctional officials, holding that they were deliberately indifferent to his disability needs by using handcuffs that did not accommodate his disability under the ADA, which caused him undue pain in violation of the Eighth Amendment.

The courts have also taken occasion to address ADA as it applies to parole decisions. In *Thompson v. Davis* (2002), a state prisoner who had a history of substance abuse brought a legal action against state parole board members, alleging a practice of denying parole to prisoners with substance abuse histories, in violation of the ADA. The lower court dismissed the case and the prisoner appealed. The appellate court found that, under the provisions of the ADA, a parole board may not categorically exclude a class of disabled people from consideration for parole because of their disabilities,. The court found that while the term "qualified individual with a disability" under the ADA does not include an individual who is currently engaging in the illegal use of drugs, the ADA protects individuals who have successfully completed, or are participating in, a supervised drug rehabilitation program and are no longer using illegal drugs.

Deliberate Indifference and AIDS

Since the 1980s, more prisoners entering correctional facilities have been diagnosed with HIV/AIDS. Between 1991 and 1995 (Maruschak, 1997) the number of HIV-positive prisoners grew at about the same rate (38%) as the overall prison population (36%). At year-end 1995, four percent of all female state prisoners were HIV positive, compared to 2.3 percent of male state prisoners. Detention facilities have also seen a steady increase in prisoners being admitted with AIDS or HIV. This has posed a significant problem for correctional officials in terms of classification, housing, providing medical care, and privacy concerns. Liability issues under the Eighth Amendment have also emerged for correctional officials.

Testing prisoners for AIDS has resulted in litigation based on the notion that testing is unconstitutional, or conversely, that failure to test was impermissible. *Harris v. Thigpen* (1991) held that testing and segregation of HIV-positive prisoners violated neither the Eighth nor Fourteenth Amendments. Providing medical care to HIV-positive prisoners was not deliberately indifferent. Assisting a terminally ill prisoner was seen as therapeutic and isolation involved no deprivation of any constitutional right to privacy because institutional concerns outweighed any prisoner rights. Conversely, failure to mandatorily test all prisoners infected with HIV and segregate carriers was not deliberately indifferent where extensive educational programs and some testing were in place (*Meyers v. Maryland Div. of Corrections*, 1992).

Expanding the disabilities associated with the Americans with Disabilities Act, the United States Supreme Court ruled in *Bragdon v. Abbott* (1999) that HIV infection is a "disability" under the ADA, even when the infection has not yet progressed to the so-called symptomatic phase, as a physical impairment that substantially limits the major life activity of reproduction. A patient infected with HIV brought an action under the ADA against a dentist who refused to treat her at his office. The court held that when assessing the risk associated with treating or accommodating a disabled person under the ADA, the risk assessment must be based on medical or other objective evidence and not simply on a person's good-faith belief that a significant risk existed.

In *Polanco v. Dworzack* (1998), an AIDS-infected prisoner brought an action against prison medical personnel, alleging deliberate indifference to his serious medical needs. The district court granted summary judgment to the defendants, holding that the failure of medical personnel to provide the prisoner with a specific, name-brand dietary supplement he had requested was not deliberately indifferent to his serious medical needs. The court further noted that a prisoner does not have the right to the medical treatment of his choice, and therefore a mere disagreement with a doctor's professional judgment is not a constitutional violation. The prisoner had been maintaining steady weight, was given daily supplementary snacks, and medical personnel met with him whenever he requested a sick call.

The district court in *McNally v. Prison Health Care Services, Inc.* (1998) found that a pretrial detainee stated a valid claim that his constitutional rights were violated when he was denied his HIV medication. The court found that the jail's failure to provide him with medication was deliberately indifferent to his medical needs, causing him to suffer significant harm. The detainee was arrested by police and injured by arresting officers. The police took him to a hospital for treatment of cuts on his nose and a blackened eye prior to transporting him to the jail. Once at the jail, the detainee informed booking personnel that he had been diagnosed with HIV and was on a strict regimen of medication and needed his medication immediately because he had missed a dose earlier in the day. The detainee's physician confirmed this, but the detainee was denied his medication during his three-day confinement. Upon release from the jail, he was hospitalized for several days as a result of being deprived of his medication.

In *Rivera v. Alvarado* (2003), a prisoner's mother brought legal action claiming that correctional officials and doctors failed to adequately treat and provide medical care to her son in violation of the Eighth Amendment. Her son was diagnosed with AIDS and she claimed that the officials and doctors were aware of his serious medical needs and failed to provide proper treatment, which contributed to his death. The court dismissed the lawsuit, finding that the doctors were not deliberately indifferent to the health care needs of the prisoner. The court noted that the prisoner was admitted to the hospital in a timely manner, where the medical staff took X rays and administered antibiotics, and that the doctors, a first-year resident and the attending physician in charge of the residents, did not play a significant role in the decisions regarding the prisoner's treatment.

Deliberate Indifference and Environmental Hazards

It is common for inmates to smoke. Not only do prisoners smoke, but "squares" (cigarettes) also serve as part of the prison economy. Debts and favors are frequently paid with cigarettes. The United States Supreme Court has taken the opportunity to further apply the deliberate indifference standard to issues of environmental hazards in prisons and jails. The Supreme Court in *Helling v. McKinney* (1993) concurred with a prisoner who brought a § 1983 action claiming that his constitutional rights were violated because he was exposed to secondhand smoke. The prisoner was double-celled with a chain-smoking prisoner and claimed that the smoke endangered his health. Justice White emphasized that when prisoners are exposed to dangerous or unhealthy conditions, they need not wait until they suffer from a serious or life-threatening illness before asserting claims about improper conditions. The Court ruled that Helling did show that the correctional officials' actions under the Eighth Amendment supported a deliberate indifference claim, as he was exposed to high levels of environmental tobacco smoke (ETS) that posed an unreasonable risk of serious danger to his future health (Figure 10.1).

Since the *Helling* decision, numerous correctional officials have enacted a smoking ban within prison living units, and lower courts have frequently rejected prisoner claims of ETS. In three separate cases (*Weaver v. Clarke*, 1997; *Scott v. District of Columbia*, 1998; *Caldwell v. Hammonds*, 1999), prisoners all claimed that correctional officials were "deliberately indifferent" to their medical needs because they were exposed to ETS. In *Caldwell*, the appellate court affirmed a prisoner's claim that he indeed was exposed to ETS. Prison officials had instituted a policy banning smoking within the prison. Cigarettes were still sold in the prisoner canteen and officers permitted smoking in cell blocks. The court found that pervasive unsanitary and unhealthy conditions in the prisoner's cell block were obvious to any observer. The director of corrections was aware of these conditions and was, therefore, deliberately indifferent to them, giving support to the prisoner's claim. In *Weaver* and *Scott*, prison officials were not deliberately indifferent, because they had instituted reasonable measures to ensure that prisoners observed the no-smoking policy and had improved ventilation.

In *Atkinson v. Taylor* (2003), a prisoner filed a lawsuit claiming that his Eighth Amendment rights were violated by being exposed to ETS, which created a serious medical need that posed an unreasonable risk of harm. The prisoner stated that he was constantly exposed, over seven months, to a chain smoker who shared the same cell with him and that correctional officials were aware that tobacco smoke was dangerous. He complained that he suffered numerous symptoms as a result of his exposure to ETS and that no change was made in his housing conditions when he asked to be moved. The appellate court agreed with the prisoner and affirmed the federal district court's decision in denying summary judgment. The court held that there was ample evidence to establish a legitimate claim that the prisoner was exposed to a future of risk harm.

Other claims have been brought against correctional officials in this category beyond issues of secondhand smoke. Several claims have been filed for asbestos exposure. A prisoner brought a pro se action to recover for exposure to asbestos in *Johnson v. DuBois* (1998). The district court ruled that although the prisoner could recover for asbestos exposure without actually suffering from asbestosis, cancer, or other physical injuries, the prisoner failed to establish that he was exposed to asbestos. Based on news articles, the prisoner alleged that almost all buildings erected prior to 1970 used asbestos as fireproofing material, which the court found to be insufficient evidence. The prisoner contended that he was exposed to asbestos while working on several correctional department work crews during his confinement, and that he was not provided with protective clothing or devices. Contrast this with the decision in *LaBounty v. Coughlin* (1998), in which a prisoner brought a § 1983 claim for asbestos exposure in prison. The appellate court overturned summary judgment granted by the lower court, finding that the prisoner stated an Eighth Amendment deliberate indifference claim based on allegations that he was exposed to asbestos while incarcerated, and that prison officials knowingly failed to protect him from such exposure.

Figure 10.1
Helling v. McKinney (1993)

Nevada state prisoner McKinney filed a § 1983 action, claiming that he was exposed to environmental tobacco smoke (ETS) from his cell mate, who smoked five packs of cigarettes a day. He asserted that being subjected to the smoke caused health problems in violation of his Eighth Amendment right to be free from cruel and unusual punishment. The lower court found no medical evidence to support his claim, that he did not have a constitutional right to a smoke-free environment, and that correctional officials were not deliberately indifferent to his rights. The prisoner appealed and the lower court reversed. Correctional officials appealed to the United States Supreme Court.

The Court assessed the issue of whether involuntary exposure to ETS and its potential of a health risk support a § 1983 lawsuit in accordance with the Eighth Amendment. The Court held that a sufficiently high risk of future harm stemming from a prisoner's conditions of confinement could give rise to an Eighth Amendment claim. In such claims, the prisoner must prove that he was exposed to high levels of ETS. The Court further held that a prisoner seeking damages must convince a court that being exposed to such a risk violates contemporary standards of decency. The Court also determined that deliberate indifference was the proper standard with which to evaluate such claims.

This case is significant in that prisoner challenges to such claims need not cause a current health problem in order for the condition to be actionable. The Court agreed that being exposed to secondhand smoke can create a health concern for prisoners and that smoking may be prohibited. This decision grants authority to officials to develop policies that prohibit smoking within prisons and detention facilities. Counterclaims filed by prisoners requesting the right to smoke during confinement are unlikely to prevail.

Deliberate Indifference and Prison and Jail Conditions

Prisoners have initiated numerous lawsuits claiming that the conditions of their confinement are substandard. Allegations emerging from conditions of confinement can include such issues as: poor sanitation, living environment, plumbing, ventilation, heating, hygiene, food, overcrowding, noise, and the "totality" of the conditions themselves. An example of these issues was illustrated in the classic case of *Holt v. Sarver* (1970), depicted in the 1981 film *Brubaker*. In this case, a class action claim was filed by Arkansas prisoners complaining of vermin-infested facilities, rampant sexual assaults by other prisoners, abuse of the trustee system, absence of meaningful rehabilitation programs, conditions of isolation cells, overcrowded living conditions, defective plumbing facilities, excessive use of corporal punishment by correctional officials, and corruption between officers and prisoners. When a lower federal court examined these issues, it ruled that in the "totality of the circumstances"(cumulative impact) the Arkansas prison system, through its deplorable conditions, violated the Eighth and Fourteenth Amendment rights of prisoners.

Prison officials have a responsibility to provide adequate living conditions for prisoners. The Constitution, however, does not mandate "comfortable prisons." "Discomfort in prison is not guaranteed," nor does the Constitution permit "inhumane prisons" (*Rhodes v. Chapman*, 1981; *Farmer v. Brennan*, 1994). The United States Supreme Court expanded the application of the deliberate indifference standard to conditions-of-confinement cases with its decision in *Wilson v. Seiter* (1991). Wilson filed a § 1983 action against Ohio correctional officials, claiming that overcrowding, mixing of healthy and physically and mentally impaired prisoners, excessive noise, inadequate heating and cooling, and a lack of sanitation violated his Eighth and Fourteenth Amendment rights to be free from "cruel and unusual" punishment. The Court noted that "deliberate indifference" is the sole standard for evaluating allegations of inadequate prison conditions. The Court also stated that prisoners filing such claims must show a culpable state of mind on the part of the official. This means that prisoners must show that corrections officials had the "intent" to continue such deplorable prison conditions. The Court's decision is significant because it makes it more difficult for prisoners to prevail in such actions (Figure 10.2).

A prisoner brought a pro se complaint against correctional officials alleging unconstitutional conditions of confinement in *Davis v. Scott* (1998). The appeals court held that the prisoner's three-day confinement in a crisis management cell, which he alleged had blood on the walls and excrement on the floor, did not constitute an extreme deprivation as to violate the prisoner's rights under the Eighth Amendment. The court noted that the prisoner had cleaning supplies available to him. In *Geder v. Godinez* (1995), an Illinois prisoner confined at Statesville Prison filed a claim for cruel and unusual conditions of confinement. He alleged that he was confined in conditions that included defective pipes, sinks and toilets, improperly cleaned showers, a broken intercom system, stained mattresses, accumulated dust and dirt, and infestation by rats and roaches. The district court granted summary judgment for the correctional officials. The court concluded that whether the conditions were viewed separately or cumulatively, they were insufficient to establish a deprivation of human needs sufficient to constitute a violation of the Eighth Amendment. The court further noted that there was nothing to show that prison officials knew of and consciously disregarded an excessive risk to prisoner health or safety. Prison conditions are not unconstitutional under the Eighth Amendment simply because they are restrictive or harsh.

Figure 10.2
Wilson v. Seiter **(1991)**

Wilson sought monetary damages and injunctive relief in a § 1983 action claiming that the conditions of confinement violated his Eighth Amendment right to be free from cruel and unusual punishment. He also brought an action under the Fourteenth Amendment. He asserted that the totality of conditions, including overcrowding, excessive noise, inadequate heating and cooling, improper ventilation, lack of storage space, unsanitary dining facilities, and housing with the mentally impaired violated his rights. The lower courts rejected Wilson's claim and he appealed to the United States Supreme Court.

The Court granted certiorari to assess the issue of whether the deliberate indifference standard applied to conditions of confinement in accordance with the cruel and unusual punishment clause of the Eighth Amendment. In a 5 to 4 decision, the Court held that if conditions of confinement deprive a prisoner of basic human needs, those conditions are not actionable unless the correctional official has acted with a sufficiently culpable state of mind in allowing those conditions to exist. The Court ruled that the appropriate standard to apply to such actions is that of deliberate indifference that satisfies the Eighth Amendment's state of mind requirement. The decision in *Estelle v. Gamble* (1976) dictated this decision.

This case is significant because it grants more authority to correctional officials in operating their facilities. It makes it more difficult for prisoners to prevail in such actions because they must prove that officials had a culpable state of mind—meaning that officials intended, through the conditions, to punish prisoners under the Eighth Amendment. Prisoners must show that correctional officials were deliberately indifferent to the conditions in question and intended harm to the prisoner as a result. It is unlikely that prisoners will prevail on such a claim.

In *Dixon v. Godinez* (1997), a prisoner brought a § 1983 action claiming that the conditions of his protective custody cell violated his Eighth Amendment right to be free from cruel and unusual punishment. The lower court granted summary judgment to correctional officials. On appeal, the court ruled that poor ventilation in the prisoner's cell during the summer did not violate the Eighth Amendment, because the cell had a window that opened, as well as an electric fan. The prisoner's claim that the rank air in the cell exposed him to diseases and caused respiratory problems was not supported by medical or scientific sources. Further, the appellate court affirmed a lower court's holding in *Beverati v. Smith* (1997) that conditions in an administrative segregation cell did not violate his constitutional rights. The court found that conditions within the segregation cell block were not atypical, although the cells allegedly were infested with vermin; smeared with human feces and urine; flooded with water; and unbearably hot. Additionally, there was cold food in small portions; infrequent receipt of clean clothing, bedding, and linen; inability to leave cells more than three or four times per week; denial of outside recreation; and denial of educational or religious services.

Conditions-of-confinement actions frequently contain multiple claims, alleging that the "totality" of prison conditions are cruel and unusual. In *Simpson v. Horn* (1998), a prisoner brought a § 1983 lawsuit against a correctional commissioner and other officials, claiming that the prison was overcrowded in violation of the Eighth Amendment prohibition on cruel and unusual punishment. He also asserted that the classification system for double-cell assignments violated the equal protection clause of the Fourteenth Amendment. The court found that the alleged deficiencies in the prison were not cruel and unusual punishment, and granted summary judgment to the correctional officials. The court noted that prison officials have the right, acting in good faith and in particularized circumstances, to take into account racial tensions in maintaining security, discipline, and good order in prisons and jails. The court found that housing two prisoners in a cell designed for one prisoner does not per se violate the Eighth Amendment proscription against cruel and unusual punishment, but it may if it results in deprivation of essential food, medical care, sanitation, or other conditions intolerable for human confinement. The prisoner had alleged that as a result of overcrowding, prisoners were not provided with adequate furniture, cleaning supplies, laundry service, ventilation, bedding, clothing, recreational equipment, or telephones. He also alleged that food was served cold 85 percent of the time and that the dining hall was not kept clean or free of vermin.

Detention centers holding pretrial detainees and sentenced offenders have been prime targets for litigation regarding inadequate jail conditions. In *Ingalls v. Floyd* (1997), severe jail conditions, including extreme overcrowding, continuous periods of sleeping on the floor, physical fights over toilet paper availability, frequent food contamination, and lengthy periods without outdoor exercise, warranted denial of qualified immunity to the sheriff. Moreover, a pattern of continued assaults by both officers and prisoners, including severe physical injuries during a riot and even a correctional officer poisoning a prisoner, which were known but not remedied, presented triable issues of deliberate indifference. A practice of double-celling pretrial detainees was found to be unconstitutional in *Newkirk v. Sheers* (1993). Despite the availability of cots, pretrial detainees were forced to sleep on mattresses on the floor and to sleep adjacent to small toilets for lengthy periods. Qualified immunity was denied and the court determined that the sheriff was deliberately indifferent to the needs of prisoners. Compare, however, *Hamilton v. Lyons* (1995), in which the court found that temporarily requiring pretrial detainees to sleep on the floor in a cold cell did not violate the Eighth Amendment. Absent the intent to punish, the presence of vermin was not actionable.

Conditions of confinement in which pretrial detainees were forced to endure the following were actionable in *Antonelli v. Sheahan* (1996). The court determined that pretrial detainees stated a claim when they asserted that the jail was serving rancid food, provided no exercise, failed to protect detainees from extreme cold, lacked sufficient lighting, and allowed incessant noise at night over a lengthy period. The court also noted that a pest infestation claim was not defensible by showing two pest control sprayings in 16 months where the problem was persistent and prolonged and resulted in physical harm. The court concluded by stating that the confinement of pretrial detainees must be related to a legitimate and objective goal and that there can be no intent to punish.

The Ninth Circuit Court of Appeals affirmed the lower court's decision not to enjoin correctional officials from placing mentally disturbed or suicidal prisoners in safety cells in *Anderson v. County of Kern* (1995). The court heard testimony that mentally disturbed and suicidal prisoners were violent and dangerous to themselves, requiring temporary placement in a safety cell. In some cases prisoners were so violent that it was necessary to shackle them to a toilet grate for protection against suicide. The court agreed, and also held that the deprivation of sinks, urinals, and beds for short periods during violent episodes was constitutionally justifiable because the prisoners were confined to safety cells only for short periods. Likewise, in *Robeson v. Squadrito* (1999), there was no Eighth Amendment violation for overcrowded jail conditions where the mattress on the dayroom floor was not unsanitarily maintained, minimal exercise did not threaten health, diet was minimally adequate, and there was no deliberate indifference to safety.

Deliberate Indifference and Failure to Protect

Prisons and jails confine a diverse population. Many prisoners are mentally impaired, violent, depressed, chemically addicted, and assaultive. With this population, a variety of confinement behaviors are common, such as violent assaults, including sexual assaults; intimidation; extortion; homosexuality; suicides; and uncontrolled outbursts. Legal actions for failure to protect are often filed against correctional personnel. Correctional personnel must be prepared to respond to a variety of human behaviors. Liability concerns regarding failure to protect arise from three potential situations: prisoner-on-prisoner physical assaults, self-inflicted injuries, and prisoner-on-prisoner sexual attacks.

The United States Supreme Court further expanded the standard of deliberate indifference to claims of failure to protect in *Farmer v. Brennan* (1994). In a unanimous decision, the Court held that prisoners can prevail in suits against correctional officials for prisoner-on-prisoner assaults if they can show that officials knew of a substantial risk of harm and recklessly disregarded that risk. Farmer was serving a lengthy federal prison sentence for multiple crimes. He entered prison as a preoperative transsexual and possessed feminine traits. He was classified as a "biological male" and housed in a male correctional institution. His situation posed problems for a housing assignment by the Federal Bureau of Prisons. Prior to his assault, Farmer was housed in protective custody, away from the general population. After a disciplinary transfer to the U.S. Penitentiary in Terre Haute, Indiana, Farmer was placed in administrative segregation. He was later released to the general population. Approximately one week later he was raped and beaten in his cell after he rejected the sexual advances of another prisoner (Figure 10.3).

Figure 10.3
Farmer v. Brennan (1994)

Farmer brought a *Bivens* action under the Eighth Amendment, claiming that correctional officials were deliberately indifferent to his constitutional right to be safe during his incarceration. Farmer acknowledged that he was a transvestite and suffered from a slight psychotic disorder. Prior to his confinement, Farmer submitted to an unsuccessful "black market" testicle removal surgery. Farmer's appearance resembled a female's, as he had undergone hormonal therapy. Due to his "condition," proper security placement of Farmer was difficult for officials. He was placed in segregation for disciplinary reasons and later released to general population without objection. Within two weeks, Farmer alleged that he was beaten and raped by other prisoners. He filed suit and the lower court and appellate court found in favor of the correctional officials. He appealed to the United States Supreme Court.

The Court examined the issue of whether prison officials may be held liable under the Eighth Amendment for unsafe conditions in prison when they know that prisoners face risks of harm and fail to take measures that would reduce or eliminate such risks. The Court held that the Constitution does not mandate "comfortable prisons," but prison officials do have a duty to protect prisoners from violence at the hands of other prisoners. The Court ruled that a prison official cannot be found liable under the Eighth Amendment unless the official knows of and disregards an excessive risk to the prisoner's health and safety. The Court stated that if the official possessed knowledge that a prisoner faced a substantial risk of serious harm and disregarded that risk by failing to take reasonable measures to alleviate or abate it, a violation under the Eighth Amendment would exist.

This case is significant because the Court applied the deliberate indifference standard to claims of failing to protect prisoners from attacks by other prisoners. This is a high standard for the prisoner to overcome, because he must prove that officials "knowingly disregarded an excessive risk of harm." To win such cases, prisoners must show evidence that a substantial risk of harm existed through long-standing, pervasive, and well-documented assaults that were noted by prison officials, and that they failed to recognize such risks and take steps to alleviate such conduct.

With its decision, the Court expanded the scope of "deliberate indifference" in claims for failure to protect by holding that deliberate indifference can mean "reckless" behavior (on the part of correctional officials) "only when a person disregards a risk of harm of which he was aware." This means that correctional officials are aware of facts from which the inference can be drawn that a substantial risk of serious harm exists and they must draw the inference that the risk exists. To prevail in a lawsuit asserting failure to protect a prisoner, the plaintiff must show that officials consciously and recklessly disregarded a substantial risk of harm to a prisoner.

In order to prove that correctional officials possessed knowledge of a substantial risk of harm, a plaintiff can use circumstantial evidence to show that the risk was obvious. The Court noted three situations in which a plaintiff may prevail: (1) if assaults were pervasive, long-standing, well-documented, and expressly noted by correctional officials; (2) if officials refused to verify underlying facts of such assaults; and (3) if prison officials declined to confirm inferences of risk that they strongly suspected to exist. Prison officials may be held liable if they know of a substantial risk of physical harm to a general class of prisoner but no harm has yet occurred. Prisoners do not have to first be assaulted before protective action is taken by correctional personnel. Moreover, correctional officials will not be held liable when they can show that they responded reasonably to known risks.

There are two levels of deliberate indifference (Silver, 2005). The first level involves a failure to protect from a pervasive risk at an institution. In *Matthews v. Armitage* (1999), the widow of a prisoner who was stabbed by another prisoner brought a civil rights action against prison officials, alleging Eighth Amendment violations. The district court granted summary judgment as a matter of law, holding that the officials did not act with deliberate indifference to the prisoner's health and safety and were entitled to qualified immunity. The court noted that the two prisoners had coexisted in each other's presence in the general population at least 50 times without incident and that there had never been a stabbing in the protective custody unit previously. In *Lopez v. Smith* (1998), a state prisoner filed a § 1983 action against correctional officials alleging violation of his civil rights by placing him in a cell with a dangerous cell mate, providing inadequate medical care, and placing him in a security unit. An appellate court affirmed the lower court's dismissal of the case, finding that the prisoner's 15-day confinement in the security unit while he awaited transfer did not violate his constitutional rights. The court held that officials were not deliberately indifferent for failing to provide the prisoner with a blanket and pillow, absent the prisoner's failure to produce any evidence that he was denied adequate warmth or heating, or that he suffered from the cold. The court further found that the prisoner failed to state a claim regarding his alleged placement in a cell with a dangerous prisoner who subsequently broke his jaw.

The second level of deliberate indifference involves a failure to protect a prisoner after a specific reported threat, irrespective of the dangerous nature of the prison. Correctional officials were denied summary judgment in *Dowling v. Hannigan* (1998) when a state prisoner brought a claim of failure to protect from other prisoners' assaults. The district court found that correctional officials abdicated their responsibility to protect prisoners from attacks by other prisoners. A correctional officer had received a note stating that one prisoner was going to attempt to kill or injure the plaintiff because he had informed authorities about a drug transaction. Prison officials failed to inform the plaintiff about the threat, and he was attacked with an edged weapon (a razor blade melted in a toothbrush). The court found that there were factual issues, precluding summary judgment, regarding the adequacy of the official's response. Likewise, in *Freeman v. Godinez* (1998), the court denied summary judgment for correctional officials, finding that the prisoner stated a claim arising from a physical attack by other prisoners. The court held that the prisoner need not exhaust administrative remedies prior to filing a § 1983 claim. The prisoner claimed that prison officials knew he was on a "hit list" and interrogated him about gang activities that may have put him in danger. He requested and was twice denied protection. He was later attacked by three prisoners and stabbed in the back, chest, and face, and beaten with pipes.

Failure to protect litigation has also emerged from situations in jails. In *Lopez v. Le Master* (1999), a pretrial detainee brought a § 1983 claim against the sheriff, asserting that he was beaten by fellow prisoners. The appellate court reversed the summary judgment granted by the lower court. The detainee was placed in a general population cell and later threatened by another prisoner. The prisoner notified a correctional officer about the threat, and the officer interviewed the prisoner in an office. The prisoner filed a written statement regarding the threat, and the officer placed him back in the cell. The plaintiff was later attacked and beaten by several prisoners. The plaintiff was taken to the hospital for treatment of his injuries, brought back to the jail, and released the next day. Upon his release he again went to the hospital and was diagnosed with postconcussion syndrome and a severe strain to the cervical, thoracic, and lumbosacral spine. The appellate court found that material issues of fact precluded summary judgment in that the sheriff was deliberately indifferent by failing to monitor prisoners, failing to protect prisoners, maintaining a policy of understaffing the jail, and failing to respond to the prisoner's medical needs.

The Eighth Circuit Court of Appeals affirmed a lower court's granting of summary judgment for detention officers and the sheriff in *Perkins v. Grimes* (1998). The plaintiff filed a § 1983 claim, alleging that he was raped by another prisoner. The appellate court ruled that neither the jailers nor the sheriff were deliberately indifferent to the detainee's safety when they housed him with a prisoner who later raped him. The court noted that although officers were on notice that the prisoner was easily provoked, they also knew that the detainee and the prisoner had previously been housed together without incident, and the officers neither knew, nor had reason to know, that the prisoner was a violent sexual aggressor. The plaintiff had been confined in a holding cell for public intoxication. Another prisoner, who was larger and heavier and confined for the same charge, was subsequently raped. The detainee alleged that a detention officer was aware of the assault and failed to intervene.

Special threat groups have emerged as a source of assaults, disturbances, escapes, and a threat to the security of prisons and jails. In *Plamer v. Marion County* (2003), a detainee who was severely beaten by other detainees brought a § 1983 claim against officers for failing to protect him and a claim against the county for deliberate indifference to the adequate training of officers and supervisors. The detainee alleged that jail officials were indifferent to the housing and classification of detainees by race and gang member status, who controlled the jail. The appellate court affirmed that the lower court's decision to grant qualified immunity to jail officials. The court held that the affidavit filed by the detainee, who claimed that he observed the practice of segregating detainees by race, placing gang members with non-gang members, not segregating detainees who felt threatened, and not intervening to stop detainee fights in the cell blocks, was insufficient to show that the county had either a widespread practice of allowing detainees to fight or segregating them by race.

The Prison Litigation Reform Act and the Antiterrorism and Effective Death Penalty Act

As evidenced by the above discussion, prisoners in both jails and prisons have filed numerous lawsuits over the years asserting the deprivation of various constitutional rights. While it is acknowledged that some lawsuits have assisted in bringing reform to corrections, many of them have been categorized as baseless and frivolous. The determining factor of what distinguishes a legitimate lawsuit from a frivolous lawsuit can be problematic. In an effort to constrain the surge in prison litigation and to more carefully define a legitimate lawsuit, Congress enacted the Prison Litigation Reform Act in 1996 (PLRA) and Title I of the Antiterrorism and Effective Death Penalty Act (AEDPA). It was signed into law as part of H.R. 3019, Omnibus Appropriations Bill, and codified at 18 U.S.C. § 3626. The PLRA pinpoints actions addressing conditions of confinement, and the AEDPA focuses on state and federal habeas corpus petitions.

The PLRA did not curtail the right of a prisoner to file a lawsuit. The purpose of the new legislation was to limit the ability of prisoners to complain about prison conditions and to limit the jurisdiction of the federal courts to issue orders relieving conditions of confinement that allegedly violated the constitutional rights of prisoners (Palmer & Palmer, 1999). The Act is also intended to grant more authority to the states to manage their correctional systems and, at the same time, to limit the federal courts' "hands-on" intervention of managing prisons from the bench. The days of the court holding correctional administrators accountable for requirements not mandated by the Constitution and continuing to maintain some level of oversight for many years may be ending. There are numerous sections of the PLRA; only five will be discussed.

Section 802 of the Act addresses appropriate remedies with respect to prison conditions and seeks to resolve these actions in the least intrusive means necessary to correct the violation. This section ostensibly pertains to consent decrees. A consent decree is a binding agreement made outside of court between two conflicting parties and is established with time limits. For example, correctional officials would agree to build more prisons to alleviate prison overcrowding within five years.

For years, many correctional systems have entered into consent decrees (sometimes involuntarily), primarily due to overcrowding problems, as one alternative to resolving a prisoner lawsuit. This provision terminates existing court-ordered consent decrees unless the court finds continuing constitutional violations. This section mandates that courts shall not enter or approve consent decrees unless they comply with correcting a harm found by the court and the court requires preliminary relief to correct such harm. This can be a double-edged sword. On the one hand, terminating a consent decree requiring a population cap on a crowded prison may appease the legislature. On the other hand, it may create a whole new set of problems for correctional personnel. The impact of this provision is viewed as violating the Constitution's separation of powers clause. At least one legal scholar states that consent decrees constitute final judgments that cannot be reopened by Congress (Alexander, 1996). It remains to be seen how this provision will be further implemented.

Section 803 of the Act states that lawsuits brought by prisoners alleging poor conditions of confinement may not be filed until available administrative remedies have been exhausted. This means that the grievance system within the institution must be exhausted first. Prior to enactment of § 803, the federal courts could require prisoners to pursue internal remedies if such a system was certified by the Department of Justice or a federal district court. There appear to be at least two potential problems with this provision. First, the U.S. Supreme Court held in *McCarthy v. Madigan* (1992) that federal prisoners need not exhaust the prison grievance procedures prior to filing a *Bivens* action for damages. The Court did not believe that policy reasons required judicial imposition of an exhaustion requirement. Moreover, the Court also held that a plaintiff bringing suit under § 1983 need not first exhaust available state judicial or administrative remedies (*Patsy v. Florida Board of Regents*, 1982). The Court, however, in *Farmer v. Brennan* (1994) did indicate that prisoners bypassing "adequate" internal prison procedures might be denied relief. The Court emphasized that "an inmate who needlessly bypasses such procedures may properly be compelled to pursue them."

In *Morgan v. Arizona Dept. of Corrections* (1997), the court addressed the issue of exhausting the prison system's grievance system prior to submitting a § 1983 action alleging an assault by other prisoners. The district court dismissed the action, finding that the prisoner failed to file an initial grievance under the corrections department's procedures, depriving the court of jurisdiction because he failed to exhaust his administrative remedies. According to the court, the PLRA has made exhaustion provisions mandatory rather than discretionary, and courts no longer have the discretion in the absence of exhaustion. The prisoner had requested a 30-day continuance to amend his complaint to prove that he had exhausted his administrative remedies.

Requiring exhaustion of administrative remedies presents a second potential problem. Maahs and del Carmen (1995) reported that in 1995 few states had a certified grievance system in place. This is primarily due to the slow and cumbersome certification process. Theoretically, this provision appears to assist in reducing the number of actions that can be filed by a prisoner, because it requires conflicts to first be confronted at the institutional level. Further examination, however, reveals that it may be unconstitutional, because the Supreme Court has traditionally held that such remedies need not first be exhausted. Also, if an institution does not have such a system in place, a lack of internal remedies may create more administrative problems than the Act was intended to resolve. In addition, this section limits the awards for attorney's fees and recovery of damages.

Luong v. Hatt (1997) is illustrative of a federal district court in Texas dismissing a prisoner civil action and denying the recovery of damages in conjunction with the PLRA. A prisoner brought an action against prison officials, alleging that they failed to protect him from an assault by other prisoners. The court dismissed the case, finding that the prisoner failed to demonstrate violations of his rights sufficient to support an order from the court requiring his transfer to another institution. The court also held that the prisoner could not recover damages in the absence of any indication that he suffered a "physical injury" within the meaning of the PLRA. According to the court, cuts, scratches, and minor bruises suffered by the prisoner did not constitute the requisite level of physical injury.

The United States Supreme Court has twice addressed the issue of whether it is constitutional to require prisoners to first exhaust administrative remedies before filing a lawsuit. In *Booth v. Churner* (2001), the Court held that Congress did indeed intend for prisoners to exhaust available remedies prior to filing a civil action. Before submitting his civil action, Booth only exhausted the first step of the institutional grievance system. The Court concluded that completion of every step is required by statute. It is not enough to file a grievance only at the institutional level; if further appeals are available, they must be completed prior to filing the action in federal court. Second, prisoners are not allowed to bypass the grievance system merely because they believe that doing so is an exercise in futility.

In a second case the Court reaffirmed their decision in *Booth*. In a unanimous decision, the Court ruled in *Porter v. Nussle* (2002) that prisoners in jails and prisons may not bring any action into federal court until they have exhausted administrative remedies available to them at the institutional level. Nussle filed a § 1983 lawsuit claiming that correctional officers used excessive force, that officers threw him up against a wall, pulled his hair, "kneed" him in the back, and struck him several times. He further claimed that the officers threatened to kill him if he reported the beating. The federal district court dismissed the case, relying on the exhaustion of administrative remedy requirement. He appealed and the appellate court reversed the lower court's decision, holding that exhausting administrative remedies did not apply to use-of-force allegations. The court made a distinction between conditions of confinement claims and use-of-force claims.

The United States Supreme Court granted certiorari and determined that Congress did not intend to divide prisoner petitions into subcategories for judicial review (i.e., civil actions and habeas corpus petitions). The Court concluded that Congress did not intend to exempt use-of-force cases from prison condition cases under the PLRA and that, therefore, prisoners could not skip the administrative remedy process at the institutional level. The Court held that the exhaustion of administrative remedies requirement was important so that correctional administrators could know of correctional officers' misconduct. Authorizing prisoners to bypass the internal grievance process excluded the possibility that administrators would take corrective actions when they might be warranted. The Court held that the PLRA's exhaustion requirement applied to all prisoner suits about prison life, whether they involved general circumstances or particular episodes, and whether they alleged excessive force or some other wrong.

Section 804 of the PLRA addresses the issue of filing fees. Generally, the filing fee for a civil action is approximately $150, and previously the fee had been waived for prisoners. The law now requires prisoners to pay the full filing fee, and it requires institutional officials to verify the funds that the prisoner may have at his or her disposal. Additionally, this section provides for the appointment of an attorney if any person is unable to afford one. Bona fide indigent prisoners will not be affected by this stipulation. The court will dismiss the action at any time if it determines that the poverty claim is untrue. Lower courts have begun to rule on this provision. In *Hampton v. Hobbs* (1997) and *Roller v. Gunn* (1997), both courts found the PLRA filing fee requirement to be rationally related to curtailing meritless prisoner litigation and that it did not violate the equal protection clause of the Fourteenth Amendment.

Section 809 provides for the revocation of earned good time or early-release credit of a federally incarcerated prisoner should that prisoner file a malicious or false civil action. It is, however, not definitive what characterizes a "malicious" civil action. Some guidance is given in this section because the PLRA has its own version of "three strikes and you're out." States that have legislated the three-strikes law incarcerate for life individuals who have three convictions of the same type of crime or violent crimes. The PLRA version provides that a prisoner who has had three previous lawsuits dismissed for failing to state a claim, or as frivolous or malicious, is banned from filing further lawsuits without paying the full filing fee in advance. The exception to this is if the prisoner is under "imminent danger or serious physical injury." Reaction by the courts to this provision appears to be split. In *Lyon v. Vande Krol* (1996), the court found the provision to be unconstitutional. In *Abdul-Wadood v. Nathan* (1996), however, the court upheld the provision.

Liability and Parole Decisions

The most frequently used prison sentence is the indeterminate sentence, which stipulates a minimum and maximum number of years to be served. For example, an individual may receive a sentence of five to ten years for breaking and entering into a residence. In many states, the prisoner may be eligible for parole (early release) just prior to his five-year minimum or before the maximum term is served. The state parole board has jurisdiction and authority to decide when a prisoner is released on parole. With this decision-making authority, issues of liability often emerge for the parole board and subsequently for the supervising parole officer.

The United States Supreme Court has examined decisionmaking by a parole board. In *Martinez v. California* (1980), the Court held that the Parole Board of California was absolutely immune from liability in its decision to parole a prisoner who committed a homicide five months after release. Martinez sued the state of California after his daughter was murdered by a parolee who was a known sex offender. He brought a state claim and a § 1983 claim, asserting that the parolee deprived his daughter of life without due process. The lower courts found in favor of the defendants, and Martinez appealed the decision to the U.S. Supreme Court. The Court held that under these circumstances of the decision to parole, the death was too remote a consequence of the parole board's action to hold them responsible. The Court further stated that the decision to parole the inmate was an action by the state and that the action of the parolee five months later cannot be fairly characterized as state action. The Court upheld a state statute providing absolute immunity from suit for the parole board as valid.

In *Sellars v. Procunier* (1981), the Court denied review and remanded the case to a lower court. The Ninth Circuit Court of Appeals determined that parole board officials' decision in granting parole was similar to that of a judge, who is absolutely immune from liability. The court stated that parole board members enjoy absolute immunity from lawsuits by individuals denied parole insofar as the suit attacks the decision on their parole. In *Montero v. Travis* (1999), a former parolee brought a pro se § 1983 action against parole board officials, alleging that his parole was revoked in violation of his due process rights. The district court dismissed the case and the appeals court affirmed. The appeals court held that the parole board commissioner who presided over the parole revocation hearing was entitled to absolute immunity, notwithstanding the official's administrative function. The official was serving in a quasi-judicial function when he revoked the parolee's parole. The court further held that the claim against a second parole board official was frivolous given the failure to allege facts describing the official's personal involvement in the alleged constitutional violations.

Likewise, the Tenth Circuit Court of Appeals found that the Utah Parole Board was entitled to absolute immunity in *Malek v. Haun* (1994). A parolee brought a § 1983 action against parole board members, alleging that he was denied the opportunity to appeal the parole board's decision to deny parole. The court determined that the parole board has complete discretion in making parole decisions once an offender is eligible, and is immune from civil liability.

Parole officers, however, have qualified immunity and may be liable for actions that violate a parolee's rights. In *Greer v. Shoop* (1998), the administrator of a decedent's estate brought a § 1983 action against state probation and parole officers based on their failure to warn the decedent that a parolee placed into the decedent's home, who had been the decedent's boyfriend, was infected with HIV. The district court entered summary judgment for the defendants, and the appeals court affirmed. The appeals court held that the defendants were entitled to qualified immunity because the law was not clearly established at the time of the incident. Likewise, in *Olds v. Hogg* (1991), a prisoner brought a § 1983 action against parole officers in Missouri, alleging that they had made false statements in a pre-parole hearing report. The federal district court found that the parole officer was entitled to qualified immunity from § 1983 damages for liability and granted summary judgment.

One of the primary issues that parole officers face is the task of performing searches of parolees and their property to ensure that they are abiding by the conditions of the parole. The court's views on probable cause and conducting a search are different for parolees than free citizens, as the parolee is still serving a sentence but under supervision in the community. The status of the prisoner is slightly altered and therefore application of the Fourth Amendment is slightly altered as well.

In *United States v. Tucker* (2002), a parolee convicted for possession of child pornography appealed his conviction, challenging a warrantless parole search of his residence. The district court held that the parole search was supported by reasonable suspicion and that seizure of the defendant's computer was justified under the plain view doctrine. The court noted that probable cause is not required for a parole search that is conducted under a valid parole agreement and that the defendant had agreed to allow searches of his residence, diminishing his expectation of privacy.

Summary

Prisoners have used § 1983 as the primary vehicle for filing actions against correctional officials that allege constitutional rights deprivations for more than 40 years. From the mid-1970s to the late 1990s, prisoner civil litigation flooded the court system and many subsequent decisions have significantly affected correctional operations. Correctional litigation is comprised of a wide array of topics, but this chapter has dealt with the standard most commonly applied to prisoner allegations.

A common standard applied to correctional issues is that of "deliberate indifference." The standard is applied to correctional issues in prisons in accordance with the Fourteenth, Fifth, and Eighth Amendments, and in jails under the Fourteenth and Fifth Amendments. Deliberate indifference means that officials have consciously chosen to disregard the rights of a prisoner. It is a high standard for the plaintiff to prove and is applied by the courts on a case-by-case basis. Primary issues include medical and mental health care, conditions of confinement, and failure to protect. The United States Supreme Court has also expanded the standard to apply to issues relevant to environmental hazards in confinement facilities and claims filed under the ADA. Because of its common applicability in correctional matters, correctional officials should be aware of their custodial responsibilities in light of this standard a

Liability issues also emerge when confining the mentally impaired. Detention facilities house a significant number of this population. Whether in prison or jail, supervising and medicating the mentally ill raises certain liability concerns that officers and correctional officials should address. Procedures and practices for involuntarily medicating these prisoners should be implemented and officers should receive periodic training in how to respond to this population.

Perhaps the most significant impact on prisoner litigation has been the establishment of the Prison Litigation Reform Act. The PLRA was passed by Congress and has been implemented in an effort to reduce the number of frivolous lawsuits filed by prisoners. The PLRA pinpoints prison condition litigation and since 1996 its restrictions have reduced the number of civil actions filed by prisoners. As a result, habeas corpus petitions have increased sharply. Prisoners who file "frivolous" claims may be subject to losing earned good time, and prisoners in many situations must first submit an institutional grievance in an effort to resolve a complaint prior to filing a civil claim. In most cases, filing fees must be paid by prisoners. The PLRA applies to state correctional institutions and jails alike. The United States Supreme Court has twice addressed Congress's intent to require prisoners to exhaust administrative remedies before filing a civil action. This factor alone has more than likely assisted in reducing the number of lawsuits that prisoners file. The Court does not distinguish between classifications of lawsuits in applying the requirement. Correctional agencies should continue to ensure that their internal remedy mechanisms are functional in an effort to resolve prisoner disputes at the institutional level.

References

Administrative Office of the United States Courts (2000). "Civil and Trial Statistics: Twelve-Month Periods. Table C-2A, Statistics Division." *Annual Report to the Director—1999*. Washington, DC: Author.

Alexander, E. (1996). "Inmate Advocate Raises Questions About PLRA's Constitutionality." *Correctional Law Reporter* 8:19, 26.

Krantz, S. (1997). *The Law of Sentencing, Corrections, and Prisoners' Rights*, Fifth Edition. St. Paul, MN: West Publishing.

Maahs, J.R. & R.V. del Carmen (1995). "Curtailing Frivolous Section 1983 Inmate Litigation: Laws, Practices, and Proposals." *Federal Probation* 59:53-61.

Maruschak, L. (1997). "HIV in Prisons and Jails, 1995." *Bureau of Justice Statistics Bulletin*. Washington, DC: U.S. Department of Justice.

Palmer, J.W. & S.E. Palmer (1999). *Constitutional Rights of Prisoners*, Sixth Edition. Cincinnati, OH: Anderson Publishing Co.

Plitt, E.A (1997). *Police Civil Liability and the Defense of Citizen Misconduct Complaints Manual*. Chicago, IL: Americans for Effective Law Enforcement, Inc.

Ross, D.L. (1997). "Emerging Trends in Correctional Civil Liability Cases: A Content Analysis of Federal Court Decisions of Title 42 United States Code Section 1983: 1970-1994." *Journal of Criminal Justice* 25:501-515.

Silver, I. (2005). *Police Civil Liability*. New York, NY: Matthew Bender & Co.

Cases Cited

Abdul-Wadood v. Nathan, 91 F.3d 1023 (7th Cir. 1996)

Anderson v. County of Kern, 45 F.3d 1310 (9th Cir. 1995)

Antonelli v. Sheahan, 81 F.3d 1422 (7th Cir. 1996)

Arnold v. Lewis, 803 F. Supp. 246 (D. Ariz. 1992)

Atkinson v. Taylor, 316 F.3d 257 (3d Cir. 2003)

Beckford v. Irvin, 49 F. Supp. 2d 170 (W.D.N.Y. 1999)

Beverati v. Smith, 120 F.3d 500 (4th Cir. 1997)

Blackmore v. Kalamzoo County, 390 F. 3d 890 (6th Cir. 2004)

Booth v. Churner, 532 U.S. 731 (2001)

Bragdon v. Abbott, 526 U.S. 1131 (1999)

Caldwell v. Hammonds, 53 F. Supp. 2d 1 (D.D.C. 1999)

City of Canton, Ohio v. Harris, 489 U.S. 378 (1989)

Davis v. Scott, 157 F.3d 1003 (5th Cir. 1998)

DeShaney v. Winnebago County Department of Social Services, 489 U.S. 189 (1989)

Dixon v. Godinez, 114 F.3d 640 (7th Cir. 1997)

Dowling v. Hannigan, 995 F. Supp. 1188 (D. Kan. 1998)

Estelle v. Gamble, 429 U.S. 97 (1976)

Farmer v. Brennan, 511 U.S. 825 (1994)

Freeman v. Godinez, 996 F. Supp. 822 (N.D. Ill. 1998)

Geder v. Godinez, 875 F. Supp. 1334 (N.D. Ill. 1995)

Giron v. Corrections Corp. of America, 14 F. Supp. 2d 1252 (D.N.M. 1998)

Greer v. Shoop, 141 F.3d 824 (8th Cir. 1998)

Gutierrez v. Peters, 111 F.3d 1364 (7th Cir. 1997)

Hamilton v. Lyons, 74 F.3d 99 (5th Cir. 1995)

Hampton v. Hobbs, 106 F.3d 1281 (6th Cir. 1997)

Hanson v. Sangamore Co. Sheriff's Dep't, 991 F. Supp. 1059 (C.D. Ill. 1998)

Harris v. Thigpen, 941 F.2d 1495 (11th Cir. 1991)

Hawley v. Evans, 716 F. Supp. 601 (N.D. Ga. 1989)

Helling v. McKinney, 509 U.S. 25 (1993)

Holt v. Sarver, 309 F. Supp. 362 (E.D. Ark.1970)

Ingalls v. Floyd, 968 F. Supp. 193 (D.N.J. 1997)

Johnson v. DuBois, 20 F. Supp. 2d 138 (D. Mass. 1998)

LaBounty v. Coughlin, 137 F.3d 68 (2d Cir. 1998)

Lancaster v. Monroe County, Alabama, 116 F.3d 1419 (11th Cir. 1997)

Lopez v. Le Master, 172 F.3d 756 (10th Cir. 1999)

Lopez v. Smith, 160 F.3d 567 (9th Cir. 1998)

Luong v. Hatt, 979 F. Supp. 481 (N.D. Tex. 1997)

Lyon v. Vande Krol, 940 F. Supp. 1433 (S.D. Iowa 1996)

Malek v. Haun, 26 F.3d 1013 (10th Cir. 1994)

Martinez v. State of California, 444 U.S. 277 (1980)

Matthews v. Armitage, 36 F. Supp. 2d 121 (N.D.N.Y. 1999)

McCarthy v. Madigan, 503 U.S. 140 (1992)

McNally v. Prison Health Care Services, Inc., 28 F. Supp. 2d 671 (D. Me. 1998)

Meyers v. Maryland Div. of Corrections, 782 F. Supp. 1095 (D. Md. 1992)

Montero v. Travis, 171 F.3d 757 (2d Cir. 1999)

Morgan v. Arizona Dept. of Corrections, 976 F. Supp. 892 (D. Ariz. 1997)

Newkirk v. Sheers, 834 F. Supp. 772 (E.D. Pa. 1993)

Olds v. Hogg, 774 F. Supp. 1202 (E.D. Mo. 1991)

Patsy v. Florida Board of Regents, 457 U.S. 496 (1982)

Perkins v. Grimes, 161 F.3d 1127 (8th Cir. 1998)

Pennsylvania Dept. of Corrections v. Yeskey, 524 U.S. 206 (1998)

Polanco v. Dworzack, 25 F. Supp. 2d 148 (W.D.N.Y. 1998)

Porter v. Nussle, 534 U.S. 516 (2002)

Reed v. McBride, 178 F.3d 849 (7th Cir. 1999)

Rivera v. Alvarado, 240 F. Supp. 2d 136 (D. P.R. 2003)

Rhodes v. Chapman, 452 U.S. 337 (1981)

Robeson v. Squadrito, 57 F. Supp. 2d 642 (N.D. Ind. 1999)

Roe v. County of Com'n of Monongalia County, 926 F. Supp. 74 (N.D. W. Va. 1996)

Roller v. Gunn, 107 F.3d 227 (4th Cir. 1997)

Rouse v. Plantier, 997 F. Supp. 575 (D.N.J. 1998)

Scott v. District of Columbia, 39 F.3d 940 (D.C. Cir. 1998)

Sell v. United States, 123 U.S. 2174 (2003)

Sellars v. Procunier, 641 F.2d 1295 (9th Cir. 1981)

Simpson v. Horn, 25 F. Supp. 563 (E.D. Pa. 1998)

Singleton v. Norris, 319 F.3d 1018 (8th Cir. 2003)

Thompson v. Davis, 295 F.3d 890 (9th Cir. 2002)

Tucker v. Randall, 840 F. Supp. 1237 (N.D. Ill. 1993)

United States v. Tucker, 305 F.3d 1193 (10th Cir. 2002)

Washington v. Harper, 494 U.S. 201 (1990)

Weaver v. Clarke, 120 F.3d 852 (6th Cir. 1997)

United States v. Weston, 134 F. Supp. 115 (D.D.C. 2001)

Williams-El v. McLemore, 213 F. Supp. 2d 783 (E.D. Mich. 2002)

Wilson v. Seiter, 501 U.S. 294 (1991)

Wolff v. McDonnell, 418 U.S. 539 (1974)

Chapter 11

Section 1983 Actions in Law Enforcement

The essence of contemporary law enforcement has made the patrol officer a prime target for litigation. In a democratic society police represent the legitimate force of government to compel citizens, if necessary, to obey laws that the majority of citizens, at least theoretically, have participated in creating. Despite the legitimacy of police authority and power, there are many citizens in society who resist such authority. When the government, through law enforcement, is required to intervene in the lives of the citizenry, a conflict emerges between the protection of individually protected constitutional rights and the exercise of the rule of law. In a democracy, an informal contract exists whereby citizens have a duty to abide by the law. When that contract is breached, other citizens rely on the police to intervene and enforce the law.

Intervening and responding on behalf of society by enforcing the law is the point at which the police become vulnerable to civil liability. When police officers perform their primary functions, they must be accountable to the rule of law. Just as citizens must comply with the law, police must know the law, make prudent decisions when enforcing the law, and exercise their authority within the boundaries of the law. A vast majority of police officers perform their duties in accordance with their sworn oath of office. As in many professions, there are some officers who cross the line, violate their oath, and exercise their authority outside its legal limits. As previously described in this text, § 1983 was enacted so that citizens who believe their protected rights have been violated by police may redress such actions.

Enforcing the First and Fourth Amendments through police intervention can generate civil actions against the police. When a protester exercises his or her freedom of speech at a rally, police may have to intervene if the protester violates the law. The protester may be arrested through the use of force and charged with a crime. The protester may later file a civil lawsuit claiming that his right to freedom of speech was denied, that he was falsely arrested and imprisoned, and that the officers used excessive force when making the arrest. The officers may have acted within their legitimate authority, but must be able to defend their actions. This chapter will examine § 1983 actions that arise out of common functions that the police perform regularly. In reviewing these cases, officers should consider their state's statutes and their agency's policies and practices.

False Arrest

Police officers are authorized to enforce the law and to arrest law violators. Officers frequently are sued for false arrest and false imprisonment. "Arrest" is defined as taking a person into custody against his or her will for the purpose of criminal prosecution or interrogation (*Dunaway v. New York*, 1979). An arrest occurs only when there is a governmental termination of freedom of movement through means intentionally applied (*Brower v. County of Inyo*, 1989). There must be some form of restraint used by the police, because words alone are insufficient. As a Fourth Amendment issue, arrest is a type of seizure, because a person's liberty must be restricted by law enforcement officers, such that the person is not free to leave. Allegations of false arrest or false imprisonment are actionable under both state tort law and § 1983.

Arrest is a legal conclusion that is used to describe a complex series of events that have taken place (Klotter, 1999). Depending upon the circumstances, there are at least three possible components of an arrest. First, an essential component is the intent of the arresting officer to take the person into custody. Without the requisite intent there is no arrest, even though a person may be temporarily detained. Stopping a speeding motorist and citing him or her for violating the posted speed limit is not an arrest. There is no intent on the part of the officer to take the person into custody.

Second, under criminal law, an officer making an arrest must have the authority to restrict the person's liberty. An officer acting within the "scope of his authority," as provided by law, may make a legal arrest, providing that the elements for the arrest exist. An example may be when an officer arrests under an invalid warrant or makes an arrest for a misdemeanor not committed in his or her presence, where such an arrest is not authorized by state law. Arrest authority is granted by state law and agency regulations.

Third, the person must come under the control and custody of the officer. This can be accomplished by two means. First, a person may voluntarily submit to the authority and control of the officer. Second, the officer may use physical force to take the person into custody. In *United States v. Mendenhall* (1980), the U.S. Supreme Court stated that a person is seized only when, by means of physical force or show of authority, his freedom of movement is restrained. Informing a person that he is under arrest shows the intent of the officer, but does not constitute an arrest. The required restraint of the individual accompanied by taking control of the person is necessary.

In order to validate the arrest, the officer must have probable cause. In *Draper v. United States* (1959), the Supreme Court defined probable cause as: "facts and circumstances within the arresting officers' knowledge and of which they had reasonably trustworthy information are sufficient in themselves to warrant a man of reasonable caution in the belief that an offense has been or is being committed." This is applied on a case-by-case basis. The officer may form probable cause through three means: (1) his or her knowledge of the facts and circumstances; (2) acquiring information through a third party or an informant; or (3) gaining information and corroboration. Pursuant to federal constitutional standards, probable cause is required in all arrests, whether the arrest is being made with or without a warrant.

Claims of warrantless arrests without probable cause constitute one of the most frequently litigated issues in § 1983 cases, as the arrest is unquestionably a "seizure" of a person under the Fourth Amendment (Silver, 2005; Klotter et al., 2005). In a false arrest claim, the plaintiff asserts that the arresting officer or officers deprived him of his liberty without proper authority. The plaintiff will generally allege that the officer acted without probable cause. Claims of false arrest may also emerge when an officer executing an arrest warrant arrests the wrong person or an individual not named in the warrant. The officer must demonstrate that the arrest was valid and that he or she was acting in accordance with probable cause. In *Brodnicki v. City of Omaha* (1996), probable cause existed when a nine-year-old girl described a suspect, identified his car license plate, and identified the plaintiff in a showup at his home. A few inconsistencies in matching the plaintiff to the initial description did not alter the determination. The showup was not impermissibly suggestive and probable cause existed prior to it.

Compare, however, *Washington v. Lambert* (1996), in which the court denied qualified immunity to officers. The court held that a forcible stop involving displaying weapons, cuffing, frisking, searching the car, and detention in a patrol car for up to 25 minutes was a functional arrest. This intrusive action was not warranted by any alleged resemblance to armed robbery suspects. The court determined that under ordinary circumstances, when police have only reasonable suspicion to make an investigatory stop, drawing weapons and using handcuffs and other restraints will violate the Fourth Amendment. The court further held that only factors such as uncooperativeness, information that the suspect is currently armed, suspicion of committing a violent crime, and specificity of information about the crime may permit intrusive action. In this case the factors were extremely vague and the suspects did not match the descriptions.

In *Iacobucci v. Boulter* (1999), the court denied qualified immunity for arresting an individual for videotaping a meeting in which the person was not disorderly. The nondisruptive conduct of the plaintiff in videotaping a public meeting was legal, despite the fact that the arresting officer repeatedly told him to cease recording. The court stated that a police officer is not a law unto himself; he cannot give an order that has no colorable basis and then arrest a person who defies it. Further, in *Spiller v. City of Texas City* (1997), arresting a person for uttering a profanity was invalid. An arrest made by a plainclothes officer for disorderly conduct for demanding that the officer move his vehicle away from a gas pump was not based on probable cause. The court determined that the word "damn" was not likely to incite an immediate breach of the peace under Texas law, and it was unreasonable to arrest an individual for merely using one profane word.

The court also denied qualified immunity to officers in *Beier v. City of Lewiston* (2004). Beier and his wife were separated and seeking a divorce. Beier's wife was granted a protective order by the court and the judge ordered him to stay 300 feet away from her residence and place of employment. The order prohibited him from visiting his two sons. Several days later, Beier attended church where he was a member and sat a few rows behind his wife and sons. Beier's wife called the police after he would not leave on the request of one of his sons. Beier's wife informed the responding officer that she had an order and that her husband was violating it, but she did not show it to the officer, nor did he inquire about its stipulations or ask to read it. The officer instructed Beier to leave, but he claimed that he was not violating the order and ask the officer to review it. A second officer responded and they arrested Beier for violating the order. A scuffled ensued as one of Beier's sons attempted to intervene. The officers were trained in how to assess, serve, and enforce protection orders and they admitted that they were supposed to review the contents of an order to determine whether a violation had occurred. Beier was arrested for violating the order, resisting arrest, and malicious injury to property. The charges were later dismissed.

Beier filed a lawsuit for false arrest in violation of the Fourth Amendment. The lower court and the appellate court denied the officer's motion for qualified immunity. The appellate court concluded that the officers did not have probable cause to arrest Beier as they incorrectly relied upon his wife's statement that he was violating the order. Probable cause could not be established by relying on the wife's incorrect understanding of the order. The officers should have relied on the contents of the order, not their unsubstantiated understanding of the order's terms. The court reasoned that there were no exigent circumstances warranting the failure to determine the applicable terms of the order. The court determined that the officers should have asked dispatch for details of the order and failed to review the order themselves. Because the officers made no attempt to review the contents of the order, the arrest of Beier was unjustified.

False Imprisonment

False imprisonment is the unlawful confining of a person, which deprives that person of their liberty. False imprisonment may occur because of false arrest or, more commonly, as the result of an illegal detention after a valid arrest (Silver, 2000). An excessive delay in producing an arrestee before a magistrate may give rise to a valid § 1983 action. For example, a person may be legitimately arrested in accordance with probable cause, but held in a detention facility uncharged for 15 days (false imprisonment). The United States Supreme Court held in *Baker v. McCollan* (1979) that a "mistaken identity" arrest and a short detention under a warrant failed to give rise to a § 1983 action. The warrant was valid and the arrest was reasonable at the time it occurred. The fact that the police failed for several days to even investigate the plaintiff's assertion of innocence did not violate any constitutional right.

Prolonged detention can give rise to a false imprisonment claim under § 1983. The United States Supreme Court determined in *County of Riverside v. McLaughlin* (1991) that delays of up to 48 hours, if not taken for improper purposes, may be actionable. In *Kyle v. Patterson* (1997), the court ruled that a 61-hour delay before presentation before a magistrate due to the prosecutor delaying about what charges to bring against the arrestee was unconstitutional. Compare, however, *Sanchez v. Swyden* (1998) and *Brennan v. Township of Northville* (1996), in which qualified immunity was granted despite delays in bringing the arrestees before a magistrate. In *Sanchez*, officers detained the plaintiff for 26 hours before taking him before the magistrate. In a mistaken identity arrest, officers possessed the actual suspect's photos, fingerprints, and tattoo information within two hours of the arrest. Baker was cited and more than negligence was required. In *Brennan,* the court, citing *McLaughlin*, found that the overnight detention of an arrestee for 22 hours for domestic violence without giving an opportunity to post bail was not actionable under § 1983. The court concluded that there was no constitutional violation, no harassment, nor was a magistrate available that evening.

In *Brady v. Dill* (1999), officers mistakenly arrested an individual on a valid warrant. He was arrested and placed in detention for 36 hours over a weekend. Officers attempted to contact the prosecutor and judge but were unsuccessful. After discovering their mistake, the officers failed to release the arrestee. The plaintiff filed a § 1983 action, claiming false imprisonment. The officers' failure to release was qualifiedly immunized, at least because they had actually attempted to secure the person's release. The court held that in egregious cases where officers failed to inform a prosecutor or judge, liability would most likely attach. Although prolonged detention occurred in this case, the court acknowledged that neither the judge nor the prosecutor was available and that the officers made a bona fide effort to contact them.

In *Sivard v. Pulaski County* (1992), qualified immunity was denied on a false imprisonment claim. A 17-day detention between a warrantless arrest, a hearing, and a continued post-hearing detention, due in part to a probable cause finding and also an out-of-state request to detain a warrant obtained one month after the arrest, was illegal. Even though the defendants were orally informed of the indictment within hours of the arrest, they failed to comply with the ordinary promptness requirements or the state of Indiana's Extradition Act by not bringing the arrestee before a magistrate who could have ordered further detention.

The court granted summary judgment to arresting officers in *Wilder v. Village of Amityville* (2003), when a protester was arrested for attempting to block the removal of tree. When town officials attempted to remove a tree, Wilder and other protestors cited religious and environmental concerns and stood in front of the tree, blocking workers from cutting it down. Police officers responded and a sergeant instructed Wilder to leave numerous times. Wilder claimed that while she was playing the flute she became confused about what the sergeant wanted her to do. The sergeant moved her, handcuffed her, and charged her with obstructing a governmental function in the second degree. Wilder sued, claiming false arrest, excessive force, false imprisonment, malicious prosecution, and interference with her free speech rights.

The federal district court granted summary judgment to the sergeant. The court concluded that the sergeant had probable cause to arrest Wilder for obstructing governmental administration, and her other claims also failed. The law prohibited a person from intentionally preventing public servants from performing their official functions. It was undisputed that Wilder failed to move when ordered several times by the sergeant. Her excessive force claims failed because although her wrists may have been sore, they were uninjured, and this was not enough to be considered to be unlawful conduct in a lawful arrest situation. Her claims of expressing her right to free speech also failed as she could not prove that the village harbored any ill-will against her.

Police Pursuits

A common task of many patrol officers is operating their police vehicle in a high-speed pursuit. Such pursuits may involve citizens attempting to elude police. The chase may involve misdemeanants or felons. It is not uncommon for the driver, passenger, or an innocent third party to be seriously injured or die, because many pursuits end in crashes. As a consequence, it is highly likely that a § 1983 lawsuit will be filed against the officers involved and the police agency.

Research studies on police pursuits are limited (Beckman, 1987; Gallagher, 1989; NIJ, 1998; Falcone et al., 1994). Alpert (1997), however, conducted a national study on the training of police officers and their agency policies on engaging in pursuits. He studied 436 agencies of 737 contacted. Of the respondents, 90 percent indicated that they had written policies on allowing and restricting officers to pursue fleeing motorists. Sixty percent require officers to be trained in pursuit driving in the police academy (14 hours) and provided an average of three hours of in-service training annually.

In an attempt to perform their legally sworn duties when engaged in a pursuit, law enforcement personnel frequently find themselves in a no-win situation. They are criticized for pursuing and for not pursuing an eluder. While police may be open to civil litigation, Kappeler et al. (1997) found that plaintiffs prevail in approximately 31 percent of the § 1983 claims filed against them. The lawsuit generally asserts that the officer, by initiating the pursuit, should be held liable for violating the constitutional rights of the injured party. The lawsuit may also claim that the officer was motivated by the intent to harm, failed to follow agency policy and training, and acted with indifference to the rights of the injured party. Frequently, supervisors will also be named in the civil litigation for failing to train, supervise, and direct officers in regard to engaging in such pursuits.

Several issues have emerged regarding the practice of police officers performing high-speed pursuits. One important issue surrounding police pursuits is that of whether pursuits and roadblocks constitute a "seizure" under the Fourth Amendment. The United States Supreme Court in *Brower v. County of Inyo* (1989) determined that roadblocks designed to stop an individual from fleeing from the police are "seizures" under the Fourth Amendment. The plaintiff asserted a viable claim that placing a large tractor-trailer across the highway as a "roadblock" behind a curve without illumination and the pursued driver being blinded by police car headlights as he approached constituted an "unreasonable seizure." Applying *Brower*, the court in *Frye v. Town of Akron* (1991) reviewed a high-speed police chase involving a motorcycle in which the passenger died. The accident was not a constitutional seizure in the absence of any evidence that the officer intended to seize the person by colliding with them to force them off the road. If there was any evidence that the officer acted so recklessly as to amount to a complete disregard for the safety of the passenger, a substantive due process claim may be stated. The court concluded that proof of the department not providing training to its officers concerning high-speed pursuits may, however, state a policy claim against the government entity. Compare, however, the court's decision in *Adams v. St. Lucie County Sheriff's Department* (1992). Several deputies from the St. Lucie County Sheriff's Department attempted to stop a motorist for committing a misdemeanor. The driver sped off and deputies engaged in a high-speed pursuit. During the chase, the deputies intentionally rammed the eluder's car, which later crashed, killing the passenger. The court denied qualified immunity for the deputies. The court determined that intentional ramming constituted an unreasonable seizure that would have been apparent to a reasonable officer.

A second important issue concerning high-speed police pursuits addresses the appropriate standard of review the courts apply in such cases. Over the years, lower courts have applied different standards, such as deliberate indifference, shocking to the conscience, and objective reasonableness to police pursuits in determining whether liability should attach. These standards have caused confusion among the courts, police, and lawyers. The U.S. Supreme Court, in *County of Sacramento v. Lewis* (1998), agreed with the philosophy of many lower courts concerning pursuits by endorsing the "shocks the conscience" standard. The Court concluded that a high-speed pursuit will violate substantive due process only where a purpose to cause harm unrelated to the legitimate object of the arrest "shocks the conscience."

Figure 11.1
County of Sacramento v. Lewis (1998)

In *Lewis*, a deputy attempted to stop a motorcyclist (with a passenger) who had driven between two deputies' patrol vehicles at a high rate of speed. The pursuit, which exceeded 80 miles an hour, ended when the motorcycle overturned, and the deputy's vehicle skidded into the motorcycle. The driver of the motorcycle survived, but the passenger was killed. The driver of the motorcycle attempted to elude the deputies because he was restricted from operating the motorcycle. In operating their police vehicles at speeds of more than 80 miles per hour, the deputies violated their department's policy regarding proper pursuit speeds.

Lewis's family filed a § 1983 claim under the Fourteenth Amendment asserting the deprivation of Lewis's substantive due process right to life. The lower court granted summary judgment for the deputy, but the Ninth Circuit Court of Appeals reversed, holding that the appropriate standard in a police pursuit is deliberate indifference to a person's right to life. The Supreme Court granted certiorari to examine the issue of determining the appropriate standard in police pursuit cases. The Court rejected the standards of deliberate indifference and reckless disregard. The Court determined that in circumstances of a high-speed chase aimed at apprehending a suspected offender, where unforseen circumstances demand an instant judgment by the officer who feels the pull of competing obligations, only a purpose to cause harm unrelated to the legitimate object of the arrest will satisfy the "shocks the conscience" test. Chases conducted with no intent to physically harm suspects or worsen their legal plight do not give rise to the substantive due process liability.

This is a significant case because the Court for the first time established that the "shocks the conscience" standard was the appropriate standard in police pursuit cases. While the decision involved the death of a passenger, its broad language appears to apply to all injuries, including injuries sustained by bystanders, regardless of whether the police vehicle or the pursued vehicle was involved in the accident. This is a high standard for the plaintiff to overcome, because the intent and motive of the officer to cause harm must be proved.

Since the *Lewis* decision, a few lower courts applied the standard with varying interpretations. In *Trigalet v. City of Tulsa* (2001), officers pursued a motorist who stole a minivan. There was no indication that the fleeing suspect had committed any violent felony or was known for violent behavior. The eluder drove through several stop signs, at speeds of more than 40 miles per hour, and later drove through a red light, where he struck another vehicle, killing the three occupants. The estates of the victims sued the city, claiming that it was liable for civil rights violations for its policies and practices governing high-speed chases. The department's policy stated that all pursuits were to be supervised and that officers were to terminate pursuits "when the hazards outweigh the benefits." The officers allegedly did not inform any supervisor of the pursuit. The city requested summary judgment, but the lower court refused their request and they appealed. The appellate court reversed, concluding that the officers' actions did not violate the plaintiffs' constitutional rights. Testimony revealed that the officers had received 24 hours of hands-on training regarding operating a vehicle and additional training on the philosophy of pursuits. The court stated that the officers would violate a bystander's substantive due process rights only when they acted with reckless indifference to the risk created and directed by their actions toward the bystander. Here, nothing indicated that the officers intended to harm the victims. Thus, the officers did not violate the victims' constitutional rights. The court further stated that because the officers did not violate the victims' constitutional rights, the city could not be held liable.

In *Puglese v. Cobb County, Georgia* (1998), the court found that it was reasonable to shoot a fleeing intoxicated felon to end his flight and because the driver had driven his vehicle at the officer. The court ruled that the shooting was a seizure under the Fourth Amendment in accordance with *Brower*, was reasonable under *Graham v. Connor* (1989), and did not shock the conscience, despite a collision and injury sustained by the driver. Similarly in *Scott v. Clay County* (2000), the court ruled that police shooting the tires of a fleeing vehicle did not rise to the "shocks the conscience" level. The Sixth Circuit Court of Appeals ruled that a chase lasting more than 20 minutes, reaching speeds ranging from 80 to 100 miles per hour, and officers shooting the tires out, with two bullets hitting the passenger in the car, was not shocking to the conscience. The driver of the car attempted to drive over an officer prior to the chase. The court stated that the driver led the officers on a high-speed chase and attempted to harm the officer, and thus the officer was justified in firing at the vehicle in order to seize it. The officer could not violate the passenger's rights because he did not know she was there.

The Third Circuit Court of Appeals affirmed summary judgment for officers involved in the pursuit of a stolen vehicle in *Davis v. Township of Hillside* (1999). Matching the description of a stolen vehicle, two patrol officers in separate patrol cars attempted to investigate the theft as the vehicle was stopped at a stop sign. As the officers approached the driver of the stolen vehicle, he pulled away. A pursuit reaching speeds of more than 70 miles per hour ensued. Officers activated their overhead lights but not their sirens. One patrol car bumped the rear of the eluder's car, causing the driver to hit his head on the steering wheel, rendering him unconscious. The car spun out of control, hitting a parked car, which struck a pedestrian standing on the sidewalk. The pedestrian (Davis) suffered severe injury and filed a civil action against the police. The lower court granted summary judgment and Davis appealed.

Davis argued that the officers' ramming of the eluder's vehicle amounted to deadly force and that such action was foreseeable where harm or injury that "shocks the conscience" was likely. The appellate court concluded that the officers were performing a lawful duty by attempting to investigate the stolen vehicle, and faced lawless behavior when the driver drove off. The officers' actions were taken out of necessity, not to cause injury. The court reasoned there was no evidence that their actions, if reckless or imprudent, were "tainted by an improper or malicious motive." Their actions did not shock the conscience and the court subsequently affirmed summary judgment.

Because of the stringent standard established in the *Lewis* case, many plaintiffs are seeking relief in state courts when a pursuit ends in a fatality. Claims are filed in accordance with wrongful death statutes. In *Nguyen v. City of Westminster* (2002), police observed a stolen van and attempted to stop it but the driver fled from them. The chase traveled through a high school parking lot, and through an adjacent athletic field. The van proceeded into a second parking lot, where numerous students were standing. The officer twice rammed the van but it continued toward the students. The van hit a pool of water, skidded, and crashed into a trash dumpster, striking and seriously injuring several students. The family sued for negligence and after a student died the family added a wrongful death claim. Under California law, the officer was immune from liability for the death and injury resulting from operating an emergency vehicle in a pursuit of a suspected criminal. The lawsuit therefore was directed at the city for adopting a faulty pursuit policy that contributed to the death of the student. The city's policy identified 11 factors for officers and supervisors to consider when engaging, continuing or discontinuing a pursuit. Such factors included the seriousness of the offense, the safety of the public and officers, traffic concerns, location of pursuit, speed, time of day, radio communication, and road conditions, to mention a few. The policy also directed that the officer should use his or her discretion as the policy could not address every conceivable factor involved in a pursuit. Determining that the policy satisfied the law's requirement, the court granted summary judgment to the city and the family appealed.

The appellate court affirmed the lower court's decision. The court noted that the city followed the law when it designed their policy. The law was intended to encouraged public agencies to adopt clear and specific standards that were intended to reduce the frequency of accidents but to leave the agency discretion as to when to conduct vehicle pursuits without threat of liability. The policy alone made the officer immune, regardless of whether he followed it. Because the policy complied with the law, the city was immune from liability.

Conversely, in *Ewing v. City of Detroit* (2002), the plaintiff prevailed in a pursuit case. Police engaged in a high-speed chase and the driver of the vehicle crashed into a third party. As a result of the collision an innocent motorist and her child were severely injured. The family filed suit in state court, claiming that the police were the proximate cause of the injuries. The court agreed and awarded the family $2.2 million.

High-speed pursuits are a high liability area in policing, despite the standard established in the *Lewis* decision. As discussed in Chapter 6, claims attacking administrators revolve around failure to train, failure to supervise, and failure to direct officers through established written policies and procedures. Police pursuits are a highly controversial topic with the public, the news media, and the courts. It is critical that administrators provide a written policy for their officers and that policy training, as well as behind-the-wheel training, be provided. Figures 11.2 and 11.3 illustrate components that should be considered when deciding to engage in a pursuit and identify essential elements of a pursuit policy (Nerbonne, 1998; Michigan Municipal Risk Management Authority, 1997).

Figure 11.2
Factors in Determining Whether to Undertake a Police Pursuit

- Type of crime involved
- Type of location where pursuit occurred
- Time of day or night
- Likelihood of harm from not apprehending the suspect
- Availability of backup
- Weather and road conditions
- Condition of the police vehicle
- Safety of officer and citizens
- Traffic conditions
- Communication with supervisor
- Presence of passengers in fleeing vehicle
- Likelihood of apprehending the suspect
- Officer's knowledge of the area
- Whether suspect can be apprehended later
- Whether suspect has been positively identified

Figure 11.3
Essential Components of a Pursuit Policy

- Department philosophy regarding pursuits
- Definition of high-speed pursuits
- Initiation of a pursuit
- Activation of emergency equipment
- Use of marked versus unmarked vehicles
- Pacing
- Notification of supervisor
- Bumping and ramming
- Safety of officer
- Pursuits in and out of jurisdiction
- Compliance with state and local laws
- Use of roadblocks
- Use of strips
- Number of police vehicles
- Types of crimes
- Speed limits
- Authority to terminate
- Radio communications
- Information on suspect when available
- Shooting from or at a moving vehicle
- Environmental factors (weather, roads, city, highway, residence, business, rural, etc.)
- Safety to citizens
- Defining supervisory role
- Description of alternatives that may be used
- Establishing the speed that police vehicles may travel
- Requiring reports and review process
- Tracking the number and nature of pursuits annually

Administrators should also consider adopting a pursuit management continuum, which provides guidance in decisionmaking for officers (Ashley, 2006). This continuum is similar to that of a use-of-force continuum that has been used in law enforcement and corrections for many years. The pursuit continuum graphically illustrates various types of pursuit circumstances and aligns recommended pursuit tactics (control) for officers to consider based on the situation. The Ashley continuum can be divided into three suspect activities based on the severity of the hazards involved in the flight of the suspect and three levels of pursuit control tactics, including trailing techniques, blocking techniques, and contact techniques. he concept is to teach officers how to assess suspect activities and respond with reasonable and justifiable techniques based on the numerous variables involved in any pursuit. The continuum should be integrated with the pursuit policy, combined with classroom and scenario-based field training, to enhance the decision-making and motor skills of officers.

Failure to Protect

Section 1983 claims emerging from a failure to protect assert that the police officer's action or inaction caused harm to the plaintiff. To state a cause of action, the plaintiff must show that a police officer or municipality was aware of a particular danger or risk to which the plaintiff was exposed, and/or the injury occurred while the plaintiff was in the immediate control of the police. Common claims for failure to protect involve allegations of failure to intervene, failure to arrest a drunk driver, delay or failure in responding to a call, failure to protect a witness, leaving citizens in a place of danger, domestic violence situations, and failure to summon assistance. In a highly publicized case, the city of Milwaukee, Wisconsin, settled out of court for $850,000 for claims of failing to intervene and failing to protect a 14-year-old boy from Jeffrey Dahmer in *Estate of Sinthasomphone v. City of Milwaukee* (1995). Police were summoned to investigate a youth who was drugged, bleeding, and running naked in the neighborhood. After investigating, the officers came to believe that the incident involved a homosexual love matter between the youth and Dahmer (it was unknown to the officers at the time that he was a serial killer). The officers left the youth in Dahmer's custody in his apartment, where he was later murdered by Dahmer. The estate filed suit against the city, alleging that the officers violated the rights of the youth by not intervening.

An important case on liability under § 1983 for claims of failure to protect comes from a case that is unrelated to policing. The U.S. Supreme Court in *DeShaney v. Winnebago County Department of Social Services* (1989) held that there is no constitutional right to protection under the due process clause. This decision holds that, with some exceptions, the state and its officers are not liable under § 1983 for failure to protect persons from injury caused by private persons (Figure 11.4).

Figure 11.4
**DeShaney v. Winnebago County
Department of Social Services (1989)**

After a divorce, four-year-old Joshua DeShaney was placed into the custody of his father. Over a period of time, social workers received several complaints that Joshua was being abused by his father. The department of social services took limited measures to protect the boy, but did not remove him from his father's custody. Joshua was later beaten by his father and sustained permanent brain injuries that caused him to be mentally retarded. His father was prosecuted, found guilty of child abuse, and sentenced to prison. His mother filed a § 1983 action against the department of social services, claiming that they violated the child's Fourteenth Amendment right to due process by failing to protect him from his violent father. The district court held in favor of the county, and the appellate court affirmed.

The United States Supreme Court examined the issue of whether the state has a duty to protect individuals not in their custody from harm by a private person. The Court decided that the Fourteenth Amendment does not require a state to protect a person from harm by a private person who is not in their custody. While the Fourteenth Amendment does protect citizens from the actions and power of the state, it does not impose any requirement on the state to protect their citizens' life, liberty, and property from invasion of a private party. The Court concluded that a state's failure to protect an individual against private violence does not constitute a violation of the due process clause.

This decision is significant because the Court held for the first time that state and public officials are not liable to citizens for failing to protect them from harm incurred through the actions of a private person. While this case does not involve criminal justice personnel, it is important for those who have care and custody of prisoners and detainees. The Court reasoned that when the state takes a person into custody and detains that person against his or her will, the Constitution imposes a duty to provide some level of protection against harm for that person. This would apply to detention centers and correctional facilities. The state has some responsibility to provide for the safety of those in their custody. A breach of such a duty would subject the state and its officers to civil liability.

This decision is important to public officials. Absent any duty to protect, it makes little difference whether inaction was intentional, malicious, reckless, or negligent, so long as the public officials in some substantial way do not actively participate in the infliction of harm (*Bryson v. City of Edmond*, 1990). The Court in *DeShaney* stated that one element under § 1983 was absent—the violation of a constitutional right. A § 1983 action cannot succeed when the harm comes from the hands of a third person. However, governmental entities that detain or incarcerate prisoners could be sued under

§ 1983 for failure to protect. Thus, officials working in detention centers and prisons must provide security to those in their custody.

In *Stemler v. City of Florence* (1997), the court denied qualified immunity to officers who physically forced a woman to accompany her intoxicated boyfriend in his truck and drive away, resulting in an accident and her subsequent death. She had been beaten by her boyfriend earlier. While custody was not required in this case, it was present. The court determined that constitutional arbitrariness was a predicate for liability. The court further ruled that police officers should know that they cannot force an incapacitated woman to drive away with an obviously drunk man who they believed had beaten her. This action of the police, the court stated, "is a chilling and unacceptable vision of the role of the police in our society."

Responding to domestic violence situations can, in many jurisdictions, involve a considerable amount of time for the police. Generally, the police do not owe a constitutional duty to protect people from domestic violence. In light of *DeShaney*, it has been argued that there is a special duty to provide protection from domestic violence, including spouse abuse. Liability, however, will not normally attach against police officers in domestic violence incidents unless the officer or the department increases an individual's danger or interferes with other actions that may have been available (such as informing an abused spouse not to go to court because they would protect her (Plitt, 1997).

While no individual has the right to demand or expect protection from all harm, when the police have knowledge and are "on notice" concerning a domestic violence situation, such as through a protective order, the potential for liability increases. It becomes paramount to respond to such calls for service when there is knowledge or the department has notice of such domestic problems. Gone are the days when these types of incidents could simply be dismissed.

In *Siddle v. City of Cambridge* (1991), a protection order created a protected interest on the part of a woman who was beaten and abused by her husband. The duty to enforce the law is, however, normally only owed to the public at large and not to any specific person. If complaints and enforcement regarding protective orders are treated differently from other types of complaints, an equal protection claim can be upheld. In *Siddle*, a woman had been abused and harassed by her husband and was granted a court-issued protection order. When her husband violated the order, she would summon the police. They responded every time she called. The prosecutor chose not to prosecute some of the violations of the protection order, which was not the fault of the police officers. The court granted qualified immunity to the police, because each time they responded, it was a reasonable response.

In *Sadrud-Din v. City of Chicago* (1995), liability attached against the department for failing to protect a wife from her husband, who had killed her. A female officer was married to a male officer and he had threatened to kill her on several occasions. She secured a protection order and also filed a complaint with the police department. Two officers had seen him point a gun at her. Over a period of time, several officers were summoned to her residence for this type of violent behavior. Two days before the husband shot and killed her, she called for help and two officers responded. She demanded that they arrest him but they failed to intervene and called their supervisor. The supervisor arrived and failed to intervene. Two days later, the husband killed his wife and himself. Her estate filed a § 1983 claim and the department argued that it had no duty to protect her. The court held that there was sufficient evidence to establish a special relationship, because they knew about the danger and played a part in placing her in a position of danger. There were more than six incidents in which no action was taken by supervisors or officers when the department had such knowledge.

Consider, however, *McKee v. City of Rockwell, Texas* (1989), in which the police were granted qualified immunity for not arresting the boyfriend in a domestic violence case. A woman was beaten by her live-in boyfriend and demanded that the police arrest him. While in the officer's presence, the boyfriend threatened to burn her belongings should she follow through on her complaint. The police decided not to arrest the boyfriend, because there was no evidence of an assault and he appeared to be calm and rational. The police decided to drive the woman to an undisclosed place, where later the boyfriend discovered and stabbed her. The court, citing *DeShaney*, found the case to be relevant to an equal protection claim, but ruled in favor of the officers, finding no constitutional requirement to arrest the boyfriend. The court further ruled that probable cause did not exist, given the lack of a noticeable injury and the fact that the woman was not trapped in the apartment. The court declined to consider a statement apparently made by the chief that officers do not like to make arrests for domestic violence, stating that this did not establish a policy of nonarrests. The court further found arrest statistics in domestic violence cases and other assault cases to be inconclusive in supporting the plaintiff's claim.

Citing *DeShaney*, the Sixth Circuit Court of Appeals in *Summar v. Bennett* (1998) affirmed the lower court's decision in favor of officers who the plaintiff claimed had failed to provide protection. Summar was arrested for possession of marijuana and decided to offer his services as a confidential informant in exchange for an undercover officer's promise to inform the prosecutor of his cooperation and to assist in future drug investigations. The officer submitted the necessary paperwork and Summar became an informant for the officer. The officer asked that he assist in buying drugs and testifying against a drug dealer. Summar refused and the officer interpreted the failure as an abandonment of the earlier agreement. Several months later, the officer gave information to the prosecutor to prepare charges against a drug dealer and also gave the name of Summar as the confidential informant. The indictment stated that Summar had purchased drugs from the drug dealer. Several days after the indictment had been issued on the drug dealer, Summar was found shot to death. Summar's father filed a § 1983 action claiming the officer's actions exhibited a deliberate failure to protect the plaintiff's identity and personal safety, because it was foreseeable that harm would result should his identity become known.

The lower court dismissed the case and Summar's father appealed. The appellate court affirmed the lower court's ruling, holding that the officer did not have a special duty to protect Summar. The court concluded that Summar voluntarily chose to act as a confidential informant and was not forced to do so by the officer. The court further added that Summar's voluntary decision to become a confidential informant, with all of the dangers it presented, not to mention his prior decision to fraternize with criminals in the first place, played a much greater role in his demise than did the officer's action in helping the prosecutor prepare the indictment.

The court in *Barber v. Guay* (1995) denied summary judgment to a deputy who arrested a mentally impaired individual for theft. The plaintiff was a veteran who had a psychological disability and was considered a "drunk." He was receiving psychological treatment at a Veterans' Administration hospital. The plaintiff claimed that the deputy illegally arrested him, used excessive force during the arrest, and failed to protect him due to his disability. The state dropped the theft charge. Despite the state's failure to prosecute, the court determined that the deputy did not make a false arrest. The court, however, ruled that the deputy was not justified in using force by improperly applying handcuffs on the plaintiff's wrist and knuckles, wrenching his shoulder, and throwing him headfirst into the patrol car. Such force, the court concluded, was excessive because the plaintiff did not resist arrest, did not attempt to flee, and did not pose a threat to the officers or others. In applying the force in such a manner, coupled with the plaintiff's disability, the court held that the deputy failed to protect him during arrest and custody.

In *Russell v. Steck* (1994), police were denied qualified immunity when they forced an inebriated person to drive home and injury resulted. An officer responded to a call regarding a drunk and disorderly person at a hotel. After being ordered by the officer to drive away, the guest later was injured in a car accident. The court held that *DeShaney* standards regarding a duty to protect applied and the officer created a danger, violating the person's Fourteenth Amendment due process rights. The court further concluded that a reasonable officer should have known that forcing a person to drive while intoxicated amounted to an unjustifiable intrusion on that person's interest in personal security.

A different theory of liability stemming from claims of failure to protect addresses property interests in enforcing restraining orders. Under the due process clause it was argued that a restraining order creates a property interest to the protected party, and failure to enforce the order by law enforcement officers deprives the party of due process of law. The United States Supreme Court addressed this argument in *Town of Castle Rock v. Gonzales* (2005).

Jessica Gonzales, the mother of three daughters, obtained a restraining order against her estranged husband. The order was later modified and the husband was granted visitation rights on alternate weekends and the ability to visit the home to pick up the children. The husband picked up the children one evening and took them to an amusement park in Denver without prior arrangements with his wife. She noticed that they were not in the yard or in the house, but assumed that they were with her husband at about 5:30 P.M. She called the police and sought their assistance in finding her children and enforcing the order. The police informed her that there was nothing that they could do as the children were with their father but to call back later if the girls were not returned by 10:00 P.M. At 8:30 P.M., Mrs. Gonzales received a call from her husband who reported that he had the children and they were at the amusement park. She immediately called the police again, asking that an all-points bulletin be initiated for her husband, gave the police his description and a description of his vehicle, and asked that they make a check at the park. She was told by the police to wait until 10:00 P.M. to see if the girls returned. Mrs. Gonzales waited until 10:10 P.M. and called the police a third time and reported that the girls were still not home and the police told her to wait until midnight. At midnight she drove to her husband's apartment and did not find him home. She called the police and was told to stand by. After 40 minutes she filed a complaint at the police department and the police did not begin a search for her children. At 3:20 A.M. Mr. Gonzales showed up at the police department and began firing a rifle at the building. Officers returned fire and killed Mr. Gonzales. The officers searched the truck and found that Mr. Gonzales had killed his daughters.

Mrs. Gonzales filed a lawsuit alleging that the inaction of police violated her procedural due process rights under the Fourteenth Amendment and that this violation led to the death of her children. The district court granted the town's motion to dismiss, but the Tenth Circuit Court of Appeals reversed, holding that Mrs. Gonzales had alleged a cognizable procedural due process claim because a Colorado statute established the state legislature's clear intent to require police to enforce restraining orders. The court also determined that Mrs. Gonzales had a protected property interest in the enforcement of the restraining order. The town appealed and the United States Supreme Court granted certiorari to examine the issue of property interests in enforcing restraining orders.

The Court overturned the appellate court's decision holding that the due process clause does not protect everything that might be described as a government "benefit." A benefit is not a protected entitlement if officials have the discretion to grant or deny it. The Court reasoned that as Colorado law has not created a personal entitlement to enforcement of restraining orders, it does not appear that state law truly made such enforcement mandatory. Police officers have an established tradition of discretion in mandatory arrest statutes. The Colorado statute, the Court held, does not require an officer to arrest or to enforce a restraining order but provides for allowances in discretion in enforcing a restraining order. The statute did not say anything about the right of a person to demand enforcement and arrest by the police. Even if the Court thought the statute mandated officer response, it is not clear that an individual is entitled to enforcement of the order constituting a "property interest." The Court held that Mrs. Gonzales failed to demonstrate that she was "entitled" to the protection of the police and due process property interests were not violated by the inactions of the police in her regard.

In arriving at their decision the Court reiterated its previous position that the Constitution does not require a duty of the government to protect a third party from harm and the ability of the states to enact legislation that recognizes such protection as a matter of state law if the state so chooses. The Court stated: "in light of today's decision and that in *DeShaney*, the benefit that a third party may receive from having someone else arrested for a crime generally does not trigger protection under the due process clause, neither in its procedural nor in its "substantive" manifestations. This result reflects our continuing reluctance to treat the Fourth Amendment as 'a font of tort law." But it does not mean states are powerless to provide victims with personally enforceable remedies. Although the framers of the Fourteenth Amendment and the Civil Rights Act of 1871, 17 Statute 13 (the original source of § 1983) did not create a system by which police departments are generally held financially accountable for crimes that better policing might have prevented, the people of Colorado are free to craft such a system under state law.

The application of this decision generally means that: (1) officers must be familiar with their state's statutes regarding the enforcement of restraining orders; (2) law enforcement generally has no constitutional duty to protect citizens from third-party harm; (3) a duty may be found if the police have "created" or "enhanced" the danger to an individual; and (4) a duty to protect may be more likely found in situations in which officers have an individual in custody against his or her will and the person is harmed.

Searches

By nature of their law enforcement function, police officers search people, vehicles, residences, businesses, and other enclosed facilities. Police are authorized to conduct searches with a warrant. Warrantless searches incident to a valid arrest are limited to the person and the surrounding area (*Chimel v. California*, 1969). Searches are generally performed to discover contraband, fruits of a crime, instrumentalities of a crime, and evidence of a crime. The Fourth Amendment protects people from any governmental intrusion into a person's reasonable expectation of privacy and therefore police officers must abide by its requirements (*Katz v. United States*, 1967). The U.S. Supreme Court stated in *Johnson v. United States* (1948) that the point of the Fourth Amendment, which often is not grasped by zealous officers, is not that it denies law enforcement the support of the usual inferences that reasonable men draw from evidence. Its protection consists in requiring that those inferences be drawn by a neutral and detached magistrate instead of being judged by the officer engaged in investigating crime.

A search may be reasonable at its inception, but may become unreasonable in its execution (Silver, 2000). A search can be defined as *any governmental intrusion into a person's reasonable and justifiable expectation of privacy*. All searches must be based on probable cause. The key is the legal concept of "reasonableness." Many civil actions have been filed challenging the reasonableness of a search (Kappeler et al., 1997). In their study of more than 1,300 published § 1983 actions from 1978 to 1994, plaintiffs prevailed in 72 percent of the strip-search allegations. This category represented the largest winning percentage by the plaintiff, and the average award was $24,329. The Associated Press (2001) reported that the city of New York agreed to pay up to $50 million to settle a lawsuit on behalf of 50,000 people who were illegally strip-searched. The subjects of the searches, which were conducted by officers in the jail at Queens and Manhattan over the course of 10 months in 1996 and 1997, were often first-time offenders arrested for minor infractions such as loitering and disorderly conduct. The settlement will disburse awards that range from $250 to $22,500.

Police come into contact with many different people in a variety of situations. Stopping and detaining or frisking "suspicious" individuals during a street encounter has been controversial Fourth Amendment subject matter. The basic principle is that, even lacking probable cause, a police officer has the right to stop and detain a person whom he or she reasonably suspects has committed or is about to commit a crime (*Terry v. Ohio*, 1968). In *Terry* a police officer stopped a suspect on a city street after he observed the suspect and two other men "casing" a store. The officer stopped the suspect and conducted a pat-down search of the outside of his clothing for weapons without placing him under arrest. The officer removed a handgun from the suspect's coat pocket. The holding by the U.S. Supreme Court emphasized that police officers may detain a suspect and conduct a frisk only for the protection of the officer and are limited to patting down, rather than a full-scale search of the person. The officer must be able to reasonably articulate that the individual was armed and dangerous and have reasonable suspicion to stop and detain a person.

The Court expanded the stop-and-frisk to seizure of contraband detected through an officer's sense of touch during a protective pat-down search in *Minnesota v. Dickerson* (1993). Performing a *Terry* stop, an officer felt a lump in a suspect's coat. The search did not yield a weapon, but the officer felt a plastic bag that was later revealed to contain cocaine. The Court ruled that officers may seize contraband as long as they stay within the bounds of *Terry*. While the Court expanded the application of *Terry* to contraband, the Court found the seizure of cocaine in *Dickerson* to be unconstitutional, because the officer never thought the lump was a weapon and did not immediately recognize it as cocaine.

In *Painter v. Robertson* (1999), the court denied immunity to officers who ignored *Terry* requirements. Officers responded to a bar after the manager summoned them following a fight. When the manager would not consent to a search of the facility, the officers frisked him and found a handgun in his jacket. The officers knew the manager was a law-abiding person, carried a weapon, and had expelled several intoxicated and dangerous customers earlier in the evening. The court concluded that the officers failed to establish reasonable suspicion that the manager was armed and potentially dangerous. The court further ruled that the officers ignored the *Terry* requirements and denied them qualified immunity.

The court in *Gainor v. Douglas County, Georgia* (1998) found that officers made a *Terry* stop of an individual who was at the scene of a burglary. Officers responded to a burglary, detained an individual, then grabbed him because he became uncooperative. The court found that the officers' seizure of the individual was reasonable because it was initiated to question him. As he became uncooperative and attempted to leave, the officers grabbed him, which was reasonable and proportional under the circumstances, and placed him under arrest. The actions of the suspect, coupled with being at the scene with no visible means of transportation, established reasonable suspicion of criminal behavior. The court granted qualified immunity to the officers.

A warrantless search may be conducted incident to a lawful arrest, and probable cause is not needed. In *Osabutey v. Welch* (1988), the stop and search of a vehicle failed to yield any contraband. The court concluded that the automobile search and "search incident to arrest" exceptions applied and, based on an informant's tip, probable cause was present. In *Commonwealth v. Knoche* (1996), however, an officer's search of a passenger's purse for weapons was not justified as a search incident to arrest. The officer impounded a vehicle and offered the passenger a ride. He searched her purse for weapons prior to allowing her into the patrol car. The search was not an inventory search because the passenger was not arrested, and there was no probable cause or reasonable suspicion to perform the search. The court concluded that the officer should have obtained consent prior to searching the purse.

Searches incident to arrest are not always performed to discover contraband, but to ensure the safety of the officer, the arrestee, and others in the area. Where there is reasonable suspicion to believe that during a legal arrest an armed or dangerous person may be present, such as an accomplice, a "protective sweep" of the area is permissible. The rationale is that there may be other persons at the location who could pose a threat to the arresting officers or destroy evidence.

The United States Supreme Court held in *Maryland v. Buie* (1990) that conducting a limited protective sweep of an apartment was constitutional when based upon reasonable suspicion that other dangerous accomplices might be hiding in the apartment. The Court ruled that, as a precautionary matter, officers may search closets and other rooms immediately adjoining the place of arrest from which an assault may be launched. It is objectively reasonable to suspect without probable cause that an accomplice may be present and to perform a search of the area.

The lower courts have expanded upon this rationale. In *United States v. Biggs* (1995), the court upheld a protective sweep of the premises 20 to 75 feet away from the actual arrest location. The arrest of the suspect occurred inside a motel room and a search was conducted outside the motel. Officers had reasonable suspicion, based upon prior knowledge that others, who were armed, were present and they did not know if they were in the room or outside. Consider, however, *United States v. Blue* (1996). Federal agents had an arrest warrant for a suspect named Elton Ogarro. When drug enforcement agents entered the apartment, Ogarro was pushed through the door of another person's (Blue's) apartment. Officers began searching Blue's apartment and looked between his mattress and box spring. The court held that the search was unconstitutional. Although Blue was a potential danger to the agents, he was handcuffed and controlled by an agent larger than himself. According to the court, the bed, which was two feet away, was not accessible or within a "grab area." The court rejected the idea that the interior of the bed could have hidden a third person. In *United States v. Pixley* (1998), a protective sweep was considered unreasonable by the court. Officers arrested a suspect on the main floor of a home. A sweep of a second-floor bedroom, which involved searching under a mattress on a bed that would not conceal another person, was rejected by the court.

In *United States v. Gwinn* (2000), officers responded to a 911 call regarding a domestic violence situation. An officer was informed that Gwinn was inside a trailer threatening to kill his girlfriend. From behind his patrol car, the officer ordered Gwinn to exit the trailer. He complied, wearing only blue jeans. The officer applied handcuffs, performed a pat-down search, and placed him in the squad car. The officer entered the trailer to speak with the girlfriend, Diane Harrah, and a second officer entered the trailer and performed a protective sweep search. Harrah informed the first officer that Gwinn was drunk, had waved a handgun at her, and threatened to kill her. The officers searched for the handgun but instead found a shotgun under the couch. The officers seized the shotgun and retrieved Gwinn's boots and shirt. As the officer picked up the boots, he noticed they were heavy. Looking inside the boot, the officer observed a handgun, showed it to Harrah, and she confirmed that it was the weapon Gwinn had used to threaten her.

Gwinn filed a civil action for an illegal seizure during a warrantless search. The lower court agreed with respect to the shotgun, but refused with respect with the handgun, finding that the second search and seizure were proper based on the plain view doctrine. He appealed and the appellate court affirmed. The court held that the officer entering the trailer was proper because Gwinn was partially dressed and it was part of the officer's duty to care for an arrestee in his custody. There was no evidence that entering the trailer was pretexual. The intrusion was minor, temporary, and limited to the purpose of obtaining his boots and shirt.

Police are frequently confronted with searching for and seizing contraband or evidence of a crime from a home. The general requirement for performing a search or seizure within a home is to first obtain a warrant. Performing a warrantless search, however, is not always an unreasonable search that would give rise to a civil action, and the plaintiff bears the burden of proof. The United States Supreme Court in *Payton v. New York* (1980) held that, absent exigent circumstances, nonconsensual entry into a person's home is prohibited under the Fourth Amendment. There are a variety of rationales that constitute exigent circumstances. Some of the more common circumstances can involve a belief that a crime is being committed, hot pursuit of a suspect, protective sweeps, and searching for a criminal. Probable cause to believe that a crime is being committed is not per se an exigent circumstance. By these types of circumstances police are justified in entering a residence to effect an arrest, but their actions may be later scrutinized in a civil action. In *United States v. Timberlake* (1990), the court concluded that undercover officers who smelled PCP could not legitimately enter a location when there was no evidence that entry was initiated by fear of an explosion and there was no danger of evidence being destroyed.

In *United States v. Bates* (1996), the court held that an informant's tip regarding a weapon that was concealed in an apartment did not establish exigent circumstances to enter the premises and search for the weapon. Despite the door being barricaded and the potential for drugs being destroyed, the court reasoned that the presence of a weapon alone was insufficient to enter the apartment. There was no indication of violence and officers had not been threatened. Consider, however, the court's ruling regarding an entry into a home to search for an arrestee in *Valdez v. McPheters* (1999). Officers had an arrest warrant and reasonably believed that the suspect lived at his parents' residence. They also believed the suspect was in the home at the time the officers were there. Officers entered the home and arrested the suspect. The court upheld the entry because the officers possessed a valid arrest warrant and they "reasonably believed" the suspect lived at his parents' home, as evidenced by his lifestyle.

Likewise, in *Fletcher v. Town of Clinton* (1999), the court granted qualified immunity to officers who entered a home to enforce a domestic violence restraining order. Officers had previously received numerous calls for help from the female complainant and she would change her mind once the officers responded. Officers entered the home and, despite no evidence of violence, arrested the boyfriend, who had violated the restraining order and bail conditions. The complainant, who objected and interfered with the arrest, was also arrested and later filed a civil action against the police. The court granted qualified immunity to the officers for the warrantless entry due to exigent circumstances because the officers believed her safety was at risk.

Neither valid consent nor exigent circumstances allowed a warrantless entry into a home in *Howe v. State* (1996). The court concluded that a suspect merely stepping away from the doorway, without more information, was not clear and persuasive evidence that the person gave consent. Officers were at the home based on the belief that the suspect was growing marijuana, and had a generalized fear that he may have been destroying evidence by burning the marijuana, so they entered the home. The court held that even if there was probable cause to make the arrest, a warrantless search was not justified as being incident to arrest. Likewise, in *Guie v. Wright* (1998), the court denied qualified immunity in the warrantless entry and arrest of a person identified by a police officer as a suspect in several armed robberies. Exigent circumstances were absent because several officers on the scene could have surrounded the house to prevent an escape.

The Sixth Circuit Court of Appeals affirmed summary judgment to officers when a woman consented to a warrantless search of her residence in *Saltsman v. Campbell* (1998). A department of social services worker was denied admittance into a house to check on the welfare of children inside as well as the alleged condition of the home. The worker returned to her office and her supervisor instructed her to return with a police officer. The next day the worker and an officer returned to the house and were met at the porch by the same woman. She informed them that her attorney had instructed her not to allow them entrance into the house and that they needed a search warrant. The officer informed her that he did not need a warrant, because he was with a social worker. The woman retreated inside and closed the door. After a few minutes she returned and on advice of her attorney consented to the search. During the search the social worker did not find any evidence to support the allegations and closed the case. The woman filed a § 1983 action claiming that her Fourth and Fourteenth Amendment rights had been violated. The lower court granted summary judgment to the officer and the appellate court affirmed.

The plaintiff claimed that the officer coerced her into allowing him into the house. The court concluded that the search was consensual and therefore was within the consent exception to the warrant requirement. She allowed the officer entrance into her residence on the advice of her attorney, and she was in constant contact with the officer the entire 20 minutes he was there. The plaintiff failed to show that the officer violated her constitutional rights.

The Third Circuit Court of Appeals determined that exigent circumstances existed when an officer heard "eerie silence" after loud crying in *United States v. Coleman* (2003). A woman who was noticeably upset, nervous, shaking, and talking fast, approached an officer and informed him that her sister was being beaten by her boyfriend (Coleman) a few blocks away. She also informed the officer that earlier she observed "a lot of blood" in the bedroom. The officer called for backup and two other officers responded. As the officers approached a common area of the apartment building, Coleman noticed them and ran back to the apartment and slammed the door shut. The officers could hear a female crying coming from inside the apartment and heard muffled voices, yelling and some kind of commotion. The officers began banging on the door repeatedly yelling "Police, open the door!" The noise continued for several more minutes, no one came to the door, and another officer arrived. Suddenly, the noise in the apartment ceased, which disturbed the officers, fearing for the woman's safety. The officers did not have a warrant to enter the apartment and after making a warning, an officer kicked in the door and the police entered. Inside the apartment the officers observed a woman sitting on a couch holding her young son. She had bruises on her neck and she was crying, shaking, afraid, talking fast, and hyperventilating. She told the officers that Coleman had held her against her will, had a shotgun, pointed it at her, and threatened to kill her. Coleman emerged from the bedroom. The girlfriend led the officers to the bedroom and showed them the shotgun under the bed. An officer retrieved the gun and also observed a plastic bag containing what appeared to be crack cocaine.

The police arrested Coleman and obtained a warrant to search the rest of the apartment for narcotics. The search yielded more cocaine and a scale. At trial, the court denied Coleman's motion to suppress the shotgun and drugs found in the apartment. The appellate court affirmed the lower court's verdict, stating that there were exigent circumstances justifying the officers' entrance into the apartment. The court ruled that exigent circumstances justify a warrantless entry where officers reasonably believe that someone is in danger, and that they must act to avert the danger. The sister's description of the apartment and the situation, hearing a commotion, crying, and yelling, followed by silence, and Coleman's reaction when the police entered the apartment, reasonably led the police to believe that a woman was in imminent danger.

Officers sometimes perform strip searches. Although an arrest may be valid, a strip search or body cavity search incident to an arrest may not be authorized. Every strip search and body cavity search must be justified by the circumstances of the arrest, or the search will be considered unconstitutional. Civil liability may also attach.

Neither exigent circumstances nor probable cause existed in an arrest and strip search in *Flores v. City of Mount Vernon* (1999). A narcotics unit with a warrant searched a pub based on an informant's tip. The search failed to yield any narcotics within the pub. Three patrons and the bartender were arrested for drug possession even though there was no evidence that the bartender was involved in any criminal behavior. At the station house, the bartender was strip-searched, but not charged with a crime. The bartender filed a civil action and the court held that the officers lacked probable cause to arrest or strip-search the bartender. She was arrested without any evidence that she was harboring drugs, and no exigent circumstances supported the strip search.

While exigent circumstances did not play a part in *Nelson v. McMullen* (2000), the arrestee was strip-searched. An officer stopped a woman for speeding. Checking her license, he found an outstanding warrant for someone matching her name, date of birth, and general description. The warrant indicated that the wanted person had a tattoo on her chest. The officer explained the warrant and instructed the woman to show him the tattoo. The woman refused to cooperate and go to the station house. The officer insisted on seeing the tattoo, and the woman exposed her breasts, revealing no tattoo. The woman filed a civil action, claiming an illegal search. The lower court granted summary judgment and she appealed. The appellate court affirmed the lower court's decision. The court agreed that a strip search is an extreme invasion of personal rights. The government, however, has a significant interest in pursuing lawful warrants and, in this case, confirming the woman's identity. While the officer did not have authority to conduct a roadside strip search, he did have reasonable suspicion to check her physical description. The court concluded that the officer did not ask for consent to search or command her to submit to a search. The plaintiff chose to pull her top down far enough to expose herself.

In *Doe v. Calumet City* (1993), the city decided to settle out of court a lawsuit involving strip searches of female arrestees. The case involved repeated strip searches of female traffic and misdemeanor arrestees by officers without the reasonable belief that they had weapons or contraband. The city had adopted a policy prohibiting such searches, but failed to supply it to the officers responsible for performing the searches. The city settled the suit for $6.1 million.

The United States Supreme Court addressed the issue of whether an officer could search a vehicle incident to arrest after the arrest was made outside the vehicle in *Thorton v. United States* (2004). Thorton was driving his vehicle next to an officer and slowed down so that he would not be directly across from him. The officer did not notice him until he slowed his vehicle. The officer allowed Thorton to pass him and ran a check on his plates and learned that the plates were for another car—*not* the one Thorton was driving. Thorton pulled over into a parking lot, parked his car, and left it. The officer pulled into the lot, confronted Thorton, asked him for his driver's license, and informed him that the plates did not match the car that he was driving. Thorton became nervous, sweating, licking his lips, and began to ramble. Fearing for his safety, the officer asked Thorton if he had any drugs on his person and he said no and allowed the officer to search him. During the pat-down search, the officer discovered several bags of marijuana and crack cocaine. After the search the officer secured Thorton in the patrol car and searched Thorton's vehicle and found a handgun under the front seat. Thorton was charged with possession of drugs and a handgun and asked that the court suppress the evidence based on an illegal search. Thorton argued that the officer could not search his vehicle because he initiated contact with him outside his vehicle. Thorton's motion was denied, he was convicted, and he appealed.

Ultimately the United States Supreme Court reviewed the case and affirmed the lower court's decision. The Court ruled that, after lawfully arresting a person, officers could search the arrestee and the area immediately surrounding him without first obtaining a warrant. The purpose of a search incident to an arrest is to secure any dangerous weapons and to prevent the concealment or destruction of evidence. If the arrestee was the recent occupant of a vehicle, the Court treated the passenger compartment as the area surrounding him, thereby making a search of the area a lawful search incident to an arrest. The Court reasoned that it did not make a difference that Thorton left his vehicle prior to the initiation of the police encounter. In its decision the Court did not distinguish whether the arrestee was outside or inside the vehicle, as the safety concerns for the officer are the same.

Special Response Teams

In response to incidents involving high-risk and extraordinary situations beyond patrol officers' normal duties, numerous police agencies and sheriffs' departments have developed special response teams (SRT). The purpose of these teams is to perform special tactical and weapons responses to situations that may involve hostage taking, barricaded individuals, high-risk drug seizure operations, executing warrants on known violent individuals, and other incidents requiring tactical procedures and weapons. These teams have been in operation since the late 1960s and, depending on the region of the country and the specific use of the team, the frequency of call-outs for the team can be quite high. Because of the high-profile nature of these teams, some of their operations have generated § 1983 claims. Plaintiffs may allege claims of excessive force, illegal arrest, illegal search or seizure, or delay in responding to a call-out. For example, civil litigation has been filed against several police departments based on the Columbine High School (Littleton, Colorado) shooting in 1999, in which two students killed 13 fellow students and later committed suicide. The family of one of the deceased victims sued the Jefferson County Sheriff's department for their alleged delay in the special response team's deployment to the incident (*Denver Post*, 2000).

The plaintiff in *Kirk v. Watkins* (1999) filed a § 1983 claim against a special response team when they executed a warrant for his arrest. An informant informed a drug task force unit that he had observed drugs, guns, and drug paraphernalia in Kirk's residence. The unit obtained a no-knock warrant to search the home, and the department's special response team was sent to execute it. Kirk was known to be violent, known to carry guns, and had a previous conviction for assault and battery with a deadly weapon. It was well known that if the police ever came to arrest him, he would use deadly force against them. The police approached the house and threw a flash-bang distraction device into the bedroom. The device landed on the bed and started a fire, which burned Kirk and his wife.

Kirk filed suit, claiming that the officers violated his constitutional rights. The lower court found in favor of Kirk and the officers appealed. The appellate court reversed and held that the officers were entitled to qualified immunity. The court concluded that the officers had reason to believe Kirk had loaded weapons, had threatened to kill officers if they attempted to arrest him, and had a history of violence. The purpose of the warrant was to arrest him and seize the drugs, which was a volatile combination. An officer could have reasonably believed that using a distraction device would lessen the possibility of injury in executing the warrant.

In *Boyd v. Benton County* (2004), the use of a flash-bang device by a response team to enter a residence was again criticized. A confidential informant informed police that three men that robbed a jewelry store two days earlier could be found at an apartment that he had frequented and where he had purchased drugs. The informant had been in the house and heard the men bragging about the heist. Officers watched the house and observed two of the men and they appeared to fit the description of the men who robbed the store. The two men left in their car and the police followed. A high-speed chase ensued and the officers arrested the two men. The third man was still in the apartment and the police radioed for the county SWAT unit to assist in securing the apartment. A briefing was conducted outlining the nature of entry, the number of people that may be in the apartment, the potential for high-powered weapons, and that the third man was potentially in the residence. As result of the briefing, the team supervisor decided that a "flash-bang device be used against the front wall of the apartment as it was believed that the risk of someone sleeping there was minimal. Without looking, a deputy on the team tossed in the flash-bang a few feet from the door and Boyd was burned on the arm when it ignited. Boyd sued the officers for using excessive force in violation of his Fourth Amendment rights when they threw in the flash-bang device. The lower court granted summary judgment for the officers and Boyd appealed.

The Ninth Circuit Court of Appeals affirmed the lower court's verdict, but commented that the officers used poor judgment. The court noted that the officers did not consider alternatives such as controlled evacuation of the premises. The officers' contention that an armed person might be situated in the loft of the apartment was insufficient to justify throwing the device, without either looking or sounding a warning first. The court noted that it cannot be reasonable to throw a device "blind" into a room with several innocent people nearby. Because there had been no case decided by the United States Supreme Court on what constitutes a Fourth Amendment violation when using a flash-bang, the court concluded that the officers were entitled to qualified immunity.

In *Tapia v. City of Greenwood* (1992), upon receiving information that a fugitive, who had an outstanding arrest warrant for murder, was in town to attend a funeral, the city's special response team was deployed. Information conveyed to the police was that Tapia's nephew was staying at her house. Upon arrival at Tapia's home, officers asked her to open the garage door and she left before the team entered the house. Tapia claimed she was ordered out of her house and forcibly pulled from the garage. The team searched the home but did not find the wanted nephew.

Tapia filed suit, claiming that the team conducted an illegal search and that the city failed to train its officers in regard to warrantless searches and failed to provide officers with policies with which to conduct searches. A jury awarded Tapia $200,000 and the city appealed. The appellate court reversed the judgment, stating that the search was not unconstitutional nor did there exist an unconstitutional policy directing the duties of the team in performing the search. The court further added that there was no evidence that the city failed to train the team about search warrants; therefore, the verdict could not stand.

Due to the volatile nature of the calls to which special response teams are deployed, civil actions have been filed citing that the actions, tactics, and weapons used to respond to such a situation violated the constitutional rights of the arrestee. Other claims have been filed that attack the tactical procedures the team used during a particular entry.

Tactical procedures used by a special response team were challenged in *Baldwin v. Seattle* (1989). Seattle police attempted to evict Baldwin for non-payment of rent. When a police officer attempted to enter the residence to evict Baldwin, Baldwin killed the officer with a sword and barricaded himself in the apartment. The special response team responded, along with a hostage negotiation team. Baldwin refused to communicate for 17 hours, and the commander believed that further negotiating efforts would be pointless.

Commanders of the units decided that a tactical entry would be justified because Baldwin might be injured, officers having shot five rounds at him earlier. The plan called for tear gas to be launched into the apartment, followed by the use of a stun grenade, and then immediate entry. Unfortunately the response team experienced equipment failure and poor communications. When the apartment door was opened, Baldwin charged the officers and stabbed one officer in the knee with the sword. Baldwin was shot by an entry team member and then retreated into the bathroom. A stun grenade was thrown into the bathroom, and Baldwin stuck his sword out the open bathroom door. Baldwin exited the bathroom after the grenade exploded, and the officers (thinking he was going to charge them with the sword) shot him 21 times in the side and back.

Baldwin later died and his estate sued the city. The court ruled in favor of the estate and held that the decision to make a tactical entry was inappropriate and violated established procedure. The court further stated that a tactical response is a final option to be exercised only when the actions of the criminal subject cannot be allowed to continue without danger to any party (officer, hostage, or bystander). Examples of such actions requiring immediate intervention include the execution of hostages, gunshots directed at officers or bystanders, and attempts to escape from the area of containment.

In *Handle v. City of Little Rock* (1991), an entry team was summoned to remove people from trailers. A supervisor was on the scene and coordinated the team's response from outside the trailer. Handle was forcibly removed from the trailer, and as he was brought out by team members, he began screaming and cursing. He complained to the supervisor that the officers used excessive force against him. The supervisor did not see any readily observable injuries. Handle brought a civil action, claiming that the city and supervisors engaged in a custom and practice of using excessive force. The court granted summary judgment to the entry team and its supervisor. In support of his claim, Handle offered numerous citizen complaints that were filed against the team for using excessive force. The court rejected this theory because it was without merit. The court further held that Handle failed to show there was a custom requiring excessive force, police regulations fostering excessive force, or regulations that required officers to act unconstitutionally.

The deployment of a special response team was criticized in *Williams v. Richmond County, Georgia* (1992). Family members of a mentally impaired woman summoned police to assist in an involuntary commitment for treatment of the woman, who had refused transport to a mental health facility. A special response team was deployed after officers had spoken with the woman, and she threatened to shoot the officers and swung a butcher knife at one officer. The team responded, attempted to talk to her, and she again responded in the same manner. When she swung the knife at a team member, an officer shot her. They took custody of her and she was transported to the hospital. The family sued and the court determined that it was not an unreasonable use of force or seizure in light of the facts and circumstances of the situation. In *Salas v. Carpenter* (1992), neither the county nor the sheriff was liable for the death of a hostage taken at the courthouse. During a court proceeding, an individual took a hostage and made several demands. The special response team and hostage negotiation team later responded. After several hours, the sheriff ordered the removal of the teams and they were replaced with county personnel not trained in response team or negotiation procedures. The hostage was later killed and a civil action was filed. The court determined that the sheriff did not violate any of the hostage's constitutional rights, because there was no constitutional duty to have a special response team or trained hostage negotiators.

Allegations that a response team used excessive force measures emerged in *Federman v. County of Kern* (2003). Neighbors complained to the police about a man's odd behaviors at his home. Deputies from Kern County responded and after interaction with Federman, a sergeant determined that he needed to be taken into custody for an involuntary psychiatric evaluation. The sergeant did not advise Federman of this nor did he seek a warrant, but called the department's SWAT team. After four hours of surrounding the house and attempting to coax him out, the team lured him to a window and sprayed him with pepper spray. imultaneously, five members of the team, armed with submachine guns and shotguns, kicked in the door and entered the house. Allegedly, Federman shot a rifle at the officers and they retreated. Team members fired three rounds of tear gas into the house, threw a flashbang into the house, and re-entered. Federman dropped his rifle, pulled a knife, and began walking toward the officers, in a final act of surrender, according to his family. The family stated that one officer fired four rounds of wooden less-lethal shots at Federman, but three other officers opened fire with standard munitions, striking him 18 times and killing him. The family sued the sheriff and the officers on claims of excessive force and a warrantless entry of the home. The district court denied summary judgment and the officers appealed.

The appellate court affirmed the lower court's decision and determined that the officers recklessly entered Federman's home with a SWAT team and violated his constitutional rights. The court held that officers aggressively entered the home without a warrant, to detain Federman for a psychiatric evaluation due to his "odd behavior," provoked him to resist, and turned a relatively minor situation into a fatal shooting. The court held that no reasonable officer could have believed that he was entitled to make such an entry. The family also showed that the officers used excessive force—Federman was not a suspect of any kind, and using lethal force against a person who was allegedly surrendering, was unreasonable.

Racial Profiling

The use of race solely as the bias for law enforcement decisionmaking has been a debatable tactic for many years. The debate has enlarged since the World Trade Center Towers were attacked on September 11, 2001. When it comes to using race as the criterion to screen, stop, question, or treat someone with a degree of suspicion in a proactive matter, it means that many perfectly innocent people will be forced to undergo scrutiny that others would not, based solely on their race. This is at odds with the constitutional principles of due process and equal protection.

Law enforcement officers must balance the interests of the individual against the interests of the government. Hickman (2005), reporting for the Bureau of Justice Statistics, defines "profiling" as racial profiling, or *stopping a person based solely on their perceived race or ethnicity instead of individualized suspicion*. Police agencies have been collecting traffic stop data for several years and Hickman reported that 29 of 49 state police patrol agencies in the United States have required their officers to report race and ethnicity for every traffic stop. Stopping motorists for traffic offenses based only on a demographic characteristic and without individualized suspicion is a violation of the U.S. Constitution and the constitutions of all states (Raterman, 2004). The question becomes "What is the proper response by law enforcement when using race and or other factors to stop, detain and/or arrest someone in protecting citizens from threats to national security and or other types of criminals?"

The United States Supreme Court held in *Wayte v. United States* (1985) that the constitution prohibits selective enforcement of the law based on race under the equal protection standards. The Court, however, ruled in *United States v. Drayton* (1999) that there is a diminished expectation of privacy in public transportation facilities (such as airports) and the conveyances that operate from them, and therefore individuals may be singled out for increased scrutiny. When other factors can be articulated combined with race it appears that surveillance and stopping, detaining, and arresting individuals may be justifiable. The Court's decision in *Whren v. United States* (1996) is instructive. Officers stopped Whren and others for traffic violations, even though departmental policies instructed undercover officers not to conduct traffic stops. The officers observed drugs in plain view, and the occupants of the vehicle were convicted on the basis of drugs discovered during the stop. On appeal, Whren claimed that the stop was a pretext to discover drugs and that such stops violated the Fourth Amendment's prohibition of unreasonable searches. The Court ruled that officer's subjective motivation for making a traffic stop is irrelevant as long as there is probable cause to justify the traffic stop. The Court reasoned that the test is not whether the officer would have made the stop, but whether he "could have" made the traffic stop. In other words, if a person is committing or believed to be committing an offense, and the individual officer has sufficient reason to believe this is the case, a stop or detention will likely be upheld.

Lower courts have had occasion to examine cases alleging unconstitutional detentions based on factors less than probable cause. In *United States v. Moore* (2004), an appellate court upheld a lower court's decision not to suppress evidence acquired during a traffic stop. Detectives secluded themselves in an observation room at an Amtrak station to investigate drug couriers coming through the station who were using trains to distribute narcotics. The detectives spotted Moore, who saw them in the observation room, and expressed a "surprised" look on his face, and began to walk quickly away. The officers decided to stop and question him. By the time they reached the exit area, Moore had boarded a taxi and sped away. The detectives followed the taxi from a patrol car and an unmarked car. The officer in the patrol car stopped the taxi, and approached the driver, while the other detective approached the passenger side and asked Moore to answer a few questions. Unable to provide identification and giving inconsistent information about where he was going, which later proved to be false after a computer check, the officers asked Moore to step out of the taxi for a consent search. He complied and an officer felt a hard object in his jacket pocket. The officer reached in to retrieve the object and Moore fled. The detectives chased Moore into a hotel and found him hiding in a bathroom stall. The officers unwrapped the object and found 11 grams of crack.

The appellate court upheld the lower court's denial of Moore's suppression motion because Moore voluntarily consented to the search and the drugs were discovered pursuant to the search. The court held that as part of traffic stop, officers are permitted to question any passenger without triggering a Fourth Amendment violation. Further, the questioning of Moore and his responses to the questions did not violate his rights because Moore consented to the inquiries. The stop was not unconstitutional, as the taxi driver consented to the stop and questioning may occur as part of a lawful stop. Moreover, the search was not unlawful because Moore consented to the pat-down search of his outer clothing consistent with a *Terry* stop. The crack was admissible because Moore consented to the search.

In *United States v. West* (2004), agents of the Bureau of Alcohol, Tobacco, and Firearms (ATF) were finishing an investigation and from the vehicle in the parking lot of a sporting goods store, they observed a car park in the lot. The occupants stared at the agents and became nervous and hesitant to leave their car. They finally exited their car and began walking toward the store, but continued to look back and forth at the agents several times. The agents became more suspicious and one called an employee inside the store. The two men purchased ammunition and as they approached their car, they nervously walked into each other as though they were unsure of their movements. Agents also noticed a small package in the waistband of the pants of one of the men.

The agents decided to approach the two men, identified themselves, and asked them what they were doing. West stated that they had purchased ammunition for a friend, and gave the agent his identification card when asked. The other man could not produce any identification. While one agent ran a background check, the other noticed that West began fidgeting with his car keys, which were in the ignition. The agent at the car discovered that West had a previous conviction for car theft and the agent conducting the background check learned that he also had prior arrests for drug violations, aggravated assault, and receiving stolen property. Moreover, he had an outstanding arrest warrant for violating probation. The agents arrested West and charged him with the felony probation violation of possession of ammunition. West asked the court to suppress the ammunition, claiming the agents' actions violated his Fourth Amendment rights. The court denied West's request and he appealed.

The appellate court affirmed, holding that momentarily detaining the two men was supported by reasonable suspicion that they were in engaged in criminal activity and therefore the evidence was admissible. The court determined that under the Fourth Amendment, law enforcement officers are authorized to conduct a brief investigative stop if they could point to specific and articulable facts which, when taken collectively, a reasonable inference from the facts establishes reasonable suspicion to believe the suspects are engaged in criminal activity. The court stated that prior case decisions allow officers to investigate even legal behavior that supports reasonable suspicion, if based on the totality of circumstances, when actions lead to an inference of criminal activity. While nervousness in and of itself can not support reasonable suspicion, the collective nature of the nervousness, the men tripping over each other, the clerk informing the agents that one man purchased ammunition, and noticing that West had a package in his waistband, all supported reasonable suspicion that the men were engaging in criminal activity. The court held that the agents did not violate West's constitutional rights.

Summary

This chapter has examined seven areas in policing that can increase the liability potential for officers: false arrest, false imprisonment, pursuits, failure to protect, searches, racial profiling, and special response teams. These seven categories represent critical dimensions of police work and the potential for liability exposure. With the exceptions of failure to protect and police pursuits, each category is based on incidents controlled by court decisions emerging from the Fourth Amendment to the U.S. Constitution. Since 1950, the United States Supreme Court has decided more than 300 cases involving Fourth Amendment issues. When officers conduct searches and seizures, allegations of unreasonable conduct will emerge, providing an avenue of civil litigation.

Officers also engage in vehicle pursuits. Because pursuits are high-profile events, when a serious injury or death of a citizen results, they have spawned civil lawsuits under the Fourteenth Amendment. The United States Supreme Court has established the standard for reviewing such claims under the *Lewis* decision as "shocks the conscience." This standard is difficult to overcome. In order to prevail, the plaintiff must prove that the officer intended to cause harm as a result of the pursuit. Because the standard is difficult to prove in federal court, many plaintiffs file a claim in state court and if a fatality occurred, the claim is filed under the state wrongful death statute.

Failure-to-protect allegations can also stem from violations of the Fourteenth Amendment. Failure-to-protect claims can cover a wide range of possible circumstances. The Supreme Court, in the *DeShaney* decision, however, made it more difficult for the plaintiff to prevail in failure-to-protect claims. The Court's decision in *Town of Castle Rock v. Gonzales* further restricts exposure to liability regarding protective orders. Collectively these two decisions will make it much more difficult for a plaintiff to prevail when alleging that the police failed to protect. Administrators, trainers, and officers should ensure that their policy reflects these two decisions and their state's statute regarding protective orders and their enforcement. Periodic training should be conducted to address this issue. In addition, allegations of racial profiling and bias have emerged as a concern in civil litigation. In light of national and local security concerns, policies, practices, and training that address this issue should direct officers in performing such duties within the framework of legal precedents.

The categories of litigation in this chapter represent areas of the law that are the most likely to change regularly. In light of the cases reviewed in this chapter, police administrators should keep abreast of the changes in the law and the potential for civil litigation. Administrators should keep their polices and procedures current with respect to each category and ensure that officers and supervisors in their department regularly review these policies and receive ongoing training. Training and direction provided for officers enforcing constitutional requirements of the Fourth Amendment may include:

making arrests, conducting searches with or without a warrant, obtaining warrants, the scope of searches during short detentions, the scope of searches incident to a lawful arrest, proper methods for seizing items, proper intervention in domestic disputes, and engaging in pursuits of fleeing individuals.

Police officers also should be aware of their potential liability when performing these duties. Officers should be aware of the current status of the law and be familiar with their agency's policies and procedures. When practical, and as circumstances dictate, officers should obtain a warrant for arrests, searches, and seizures. Properly executing warrants is also important. Officers should be aware of circumstances that do not require a warrant. They should also adhere to the law, department policies, and training when performing these duties. Compliance with the law, acting reasonably and in accordance with probable cause, and properly using their authority will not totally protect officers from civil lawsuits. It will, however, be useful in defending a civil lawsuit from claims that the officer violated a citizen's constitutional rights and help to support the qualified immunity defense.

References

Alpert, G.P. (1997). *Police Pursuits: Policies and Training*. Washington, DC: National Institute of Justice.

Ashley, S. (2006). "Reducing Pursuit Liability." *The Law Enforcement Trainer* (Jan./Feb.):26-29

Associated Press (2001). "NY Settles Strip Search." (January 10).

Beckman, E. (1987). "Identifying Issues in Police Pursuits: The First Research Findings." *The Police Chief* (July):57-63.

Denver Post (2000). "U.S. Courts to Hear All Suits." (September 10):A3.

Falcone, D.N., M.T. Charles & E. Wells (1994). "A Study of Pursuits in Illinois." *The Police Chief* (July):59-64.

Gallagher, G.P. (1989). "Managing the Risk of Police Pursuits." *Government Risk Management Reports* (December):1-6.

Hickman, M.J. (2005). *Traffic Stop Data Collection: Policies of State Police in 2004*. Washington, DC: Bureau of Justice Statistics.

Kappeler, V.E., S.F. Kappeler & R.V. del Carmen (1997). "A Content Analysis of Police Civil Liability Cases: Decisions of the Federal District Courts: 1978-1990." In V.E. Kappeler (ed.), *Critical Issues in Police Civil Liability*, Second Edition. Prospect Heights, IL: Waveland Press, Inc.

Klotter, J.C., J. Walker & C. Hemmens (2006). *Legal Guide for Police: Constitutional Issues*, Seventh Edition. Newark, NJ: LexisNexis/Matthew Bender.

Michigan Municipal Risk Management Authority (1997). *Pursuit Driving*. Livonia, MI: Author.

National Institute of Justice (1998). *Pursuit Management Task Force*. Washington, DC: U.S. Department of Justice.

Nerbonne, T. (1998). *Policy Development for Emergency and Pursuit Driving: Training Manual*. Big Rapids, MI: Criminal Justice Institute, Ferris State University.

Plitt, E. (1997). *Police Civil Liability and the Defense of Citizen Misconduct*. Chicago, IL: Americans for Effective Law Enforcement.

Raterman, M.T. (2004). *Putting Race in Its Proper Place: Profiling, Law Enforcement and Post-9/11 America*. A Special Report. Boston, MA: Quinlan Publishing.

Silver, I. (2005). *Police Civil Liability*. New York, NY: Matthew Bender & Co.

Cases Cited

Adams v. St. Lucie County Sheriff's Department, 962 F.2d 1563 (11th Cir. 1992)

Baker v. McClollan, 443 U.S. 137 (1979)

Baldwin v. City of Seattle, 776 P.2d 1377 (Wash. Ct. App. 1989)

Barber v. Guay, 910 F. Supp. 790 (D. Md. 1995)

Beier v. City of Lewiston, 354 F.3d 1058 (9th Cir. 2004)

Brady v. Dill, 187 F.3d 104 (1st Cir. 1999)

Brennan v. Township of Northville, 78 F.3d 1152 (6th Cir. 1996)

Boyd v. Benton County, 374 F.3d 773 (9th Cir. 2004)

Brodnicki v. City of Omaha, 75 F.3d 1261 (8th Cir. 1996)

Brower v. County of Inyo, 489 U.S. 593 (1989)

Bryson v. City of Edmond, 905 F.2d 1386 (10th Cir. 1990)

Chimel v. California, 395 U.S. 752 (1969)

Commonwealth v. Knoche, 678 A.2d 395 (Pa. 1996)

County of Riverside v. McLaughlin, 500 U.S. 44 (1991)

County of Sacramento v. Lewis, 523 U.S. 833 (1998)

Davis v. Township of Hillsdale, 190 F.3d 167 (3d Cir. 1999)

DeShaney v. Winnebago County Department of Social Services, 489 U.S. 189 (1989)

Doe v. Calumet City, 754 F. Supp. 1211 (N.D. Ill. 1993)

Draper v. United States, 358 U.S. 307 (1959)

Dunaway v. New York, 442 U.S. 200 (1979)

Estate of Sinthasomphone v. City of Milwaukee, 785 F. Supp. 1343 (E.D. Wis. 1995)

Ewing v. City of Detroit, 651 N.W. 2d 780 (Mich. Ct. App. 2002)

Federman v. County of Kern, 61 Fed. Appx. 438 (9th Cir. 2003)

Fletcher v. Town of Clinton, 196 F.3d 41 (1st Cir. 1999)

Flores v. City of Mount Vernon, 41 F. Supp. 2d 439 (S.D.N.Y. 1999)

Frye v. Town of Akron, 759 F. Supp. 1320 (N.D. Ind. 1991)

Gainor v. Douglas County, Ga., 59 F. Supp. 2d 1259 (N.D. Ga. 1998)

Graham v. Connor, 490 U.S. 386 (1989)

Guie v. Wright, 147 F.3d 747 (8th Cir. 1998)

Handle v. City of Little Rock, 772 F. Supp. 434 (E.D. Ark.1991)

Howe v. State, 916 P.2d 153 (Nev. 1996)

Iacobucci v. Boulter, 193 F.3d 14 (1st Cir. 1999)

Johnson v. United States, 333 U.S. 10 (1948)

Katz v. United States, 389 U.S. 347 (1967)

Kirk v. Watkins, 182 F.3d 932 (10th Cir. 1999)

Kyle v. Patterson, 957 F. Supp. 1031 (N.D. Ill. 1997)

Maryland v. Buie, 494 U.S. 325 (1990)

McKee v. City of Rockwell, Texas, 877 F.2d 409 (5th Cir. 1989)

Minnesota v. Dickerson, 508 U.S. 366 (1993)

Nelson v. McMullen, 207 F.3d 1202 (10th Cir. 2000)

Nguyen v. City of Westminster, 103 Cal. App. 4th 1161 (Cal. App. 2002)

Osabutey v. Welch, 857 F.2d 220 (4th Cir. 1988)

Painter v. Robertson, 185 F.3d 557 (6th Cir. 1999)

Payton v. New York, 445 U.S. 573 (1980)

Puglese v. Cobb County, Georgia, 4 F. Supp. 2d 1172 (N.D. Ga. 1998)

Russell v. Steck, 851 F. Supp. 859 (N.D. Ohio 1994)

Sadrud-Din v. City of Chicago, 883 F. Supp. 270 (N.D. Ill. 1995)

Salas v. Carpenter, 980 F.2d 299 (5th Cir. 1992)

Sanchez v. Swyden, 139 F.3d 464 (5th Cir. 1998)

Saltsman v. Campbell, 145 F.3d 1333 (6th Cir.1998)

Scott v. Clay County, No. 98-6157 (6th Cir. 2000)

Siddle v. City of Cambridge, 761 F. Supp. 503 (S.D. Ohio 1991)

Sivard v. Pulaski County, 809 F. Supp. 631 (N.D. Ind. 1992)

Spiller v. City of Texas City, 130 F.3d 162 (5th Cir. 1997)

Stemler v. City of Florence, 126 F.3d 856 (6th Cir. 1997)

Summar v. Bennett, 157 F.3d 1054 (6th Cir. 1998)

Tapia v. City of Greenwood, 965 F.2d 336 (7th Cir. 1992)

Terry v. Ohio, 392 U.S. 1 (1968)

Thorton v. United States, 541 U.S. 615 (2004)

Town of Castle Rock v. Gonzales, 543 U.S. 1047 (2005)

Trigalet v. City of Tulsa, 239 F.3d 1150 (10th Cir. 2001)

United States v. Bates, 84 F.3d 790 (6th Cir. 1996)

United States v. Biggs, 70 F.3d 913 (6th Cir. 1995)

United States v. Blue, 78 F.3d 56 (2d Cir. 1996)

United States v. Coleman, 68 Fed. Appx. 300 (3d Cir. 2003)

United States v. Drayton, 536 U.S. 194 (2002)

United States v. Gwinn, 219 F.3d 326 (4th Cir. 2000)

United States v. Mendenhall, 466 U.S. 544 (1980)

United States v. Moore, 375 F.3d 580 (7th Cir. 2004)

United States v. Pixley, 7 F. Supp. 2d 52 (D.D.C. 1998)

United States v. Timberlake, 896 F.2d 592 (D.C. Cir. 1990)

Valdez v. McPheters, 172 F.3d 1220 (9th Cir. 1999)

Wayte v. United States, 470 U.S. 598 (1985)

United States v. West, 103 Fed. Appx. 460 (3d Cir. 2004)

Washington v. Lambert, 98 F.3d 1181 (9th Cir. 1996)

Whren v. United States, 517 U.S. 806 (1996)

Wilder v. Village of Amityville, 288 F. Supp. 2d 341 (E.D.N.Y. 2003)

Williams v. Richmond County, Ga., 804 F. Supp. 1561 (S.D. Ga. 1992)

Chapter 12

Liability and Wrongful Custodial Death

Police are increasingly taking custody of citizens who are intoxicated by alcohol or drugs, exhibit symptoms of a mental illness, and violently resist arrest, forcing officers to use higher levels of force, and nonlethal force equipment. A vexing problem has emerged from these confrontations, because annually a small number of arrestees die suddenly in police custody. The individual may be violent toward himself, others, or officers, requiring several officers to restrain him or her. In a majority of arrests, the person is physically controlled and restrained without being injured. In some cases, however, the arrestee was maximally restrained in a restrictive position, commonly referred to as being "hogtied" (hands and legs restrained, connected together, legs bent back toward the hips, and placed on his stomach). In a majority of cases the person has been controlled and restrained, and within minutes officers may notice that the once-combative person is unresponsive. Emergency procedures may be initiated and medical assistance summoned, and it is determined that the individual is dead, all within a few minutes or hours of the arrest.

Additionally, detention facility personnel confine a diverse population, who are often mentally impaired, intoxicated, depressed, hostile, or addicted. Members of this population periodically attempt or commit suicide while confined in a jail or police lockup. The estate of the deceased prisoner will generally file a civil action claiming that jail personnel were deliberately indifferent in protecting the prisoner from him or herself, indifferent to his mental or medical health needs, or were in some way negligent in performing their duties, which led to the prisoner's death. It is common for the estate to file a wrongful death claim against the agency administrators, the municipality or county, and the officers involved.

This chapter describes the civil liability issues commonly associated with wrongful custodial deaths, including deaths following restraint incidents and deaths due to prisoner suicides. Liability issues involving standards of care in state courts are examined, as well as the standards for use of force, restraints, medical care in accordance with actions based on claims of negligence, and § 1983. Sudden deaths in police custody after a use-of-force confrontation are emerging as a critical area in police civil litigation. While many of these lawsuits are settled out of court, cases that are decided by trial yield a number of important legal issues that are of concern to police officers and administrators. A custodial death normally results in a civil lawsuit by the estate. The plaintiffs attempt to demonstrate that the officers and the government entity should be held responsible for the wrongful death.

Wrongful Custodial Deaths

A lawsuit filed in a wrongful custodial death will allege that the agency as a whole was intentionally negligent, grossly negligent, or deliberately indifferent to the needs of the deceased. The lawsuit generally will assert that the department's custom, policy, and procedures (or lack thereof) were the "proximate cause" of the death. The plaintiff will attempt to show that the department ignores industry standards, historically ignores problems in the agency, and typically fails to correct constitutional deficiencies.

The claim may also assert that the department fails to keep abreast of changes in the profession, and that it takes a death or a lawsuit before the agency makes necessary changes. Allegations made against public officials in a sudden wrongful death suit generally include the following factors: that arresting officers used excessive force; that officers assaulted and battered the deceased; that the officers' use of restraints contributed to the decedent's death; that the officers were grossly negligent or deliberately indifferent to the medical and/or psychological needs of the deceased; that officers failed to assess or monitor the medical condition or provide medical assistance for the deceased; that officers failed to transport the deceased to the nearest hospital or summon medical assistance at the arrest scene; that the officers failed to follow department policy; that the decedent in a maximum restrained position was transported in a police vehicle that contributed to his death; that officers violated the decedent's constitutional rights; that officers acted outside the scope of their authority; and that officers conspired to injure or cause the death of the deceased.

The claim may also assert that administrative personnel failed to provide officers with policies that would direct them in responding to "special needs" arrestees (intoxicated or mentally impaired), failed to provide officers with training in how to properly respond and use control techniques with "special needs" arrestees, failed to provide officers with appropriate equipment to perform their duties, failed to supervise their officers, failed to train supervisors, negligently entrusted equipment to their officers without training or competency evaluation, condoned excessive force measures with arrestees, failed to articulate directives in how to transport "special needs" arrestees, failed to develop a protocol for responding to violent arrestees' medical/psychological needs, failed to conduct an internal investigation, or failed to conduct an independent investigation of the death, conspired to cause the death of the deceased, or covered up the death with an inadequate internal investigation. Each case will have numerous variables for the plaintiff to attack, although in any lawsuit not all initial allegations will withstand judicial scrutiny. The agency should, however, be prepared to defend each claim.

Negligence Components

The common law and statutes generally provide that police officers may take custody of the apparently mentally ill or those who appear to be dangerous (Silver, 2000). Negligence claims against police officers for wrongful deaths of arrestees are based on state tort law. Negligence tort definitions differ from state to state and are generally differentiated from other torts, as they include inadvertent behavior that results in injury or damage (Barrineau, 1994). In some states, slight negligence will suffice, while other states require gross negligence, which involves a reckless disregard of the consequences. When an arrestee dies in police custody, a presumption of negligence may arise if the arresting officers failed to follow department policies regarding force measures, use of restraints, medical concerns, and transporting procedures.

Wrongful death torts, usually established by law and found in all states, arise whenever a death occurs as a result of an officer's unjustified action (del Carmen, 1991). These lawsuits are based in state statutes and are brought by the estate of the deceased (Kappeler, 1997). Frequently, wrongful death claims emerge from a deadly force incident; however, deaths in custody after a physical force altercation and custodial suicides have become the subject of more wrongful death litigation. The possibility of a wrongful death lawsuit arises any time a death is caused by criminal justice personnel. However, no liability attaches unless the death was unjustified. Further, the claim must be based on a recognized tort theory. Compensatory and punitive damages can be awarded.

The standard applied in negligence torts is whether the officer's act or failure to act created an unreasonable risk to another. When police officers exercise custodial control over a person they have a duty to provide reasonable care (*Thomas v. Williams*, 1962; *Wagar v. Hasenkrug*, 1980; *Abraham v. Maes*, 1983). Custody applies to police arresting or transporting, and to detention officers confining prisoners and the mentally impaired. This means that the police have a legal duty to take reasonable precautions to ensure the health and safety of persons in their custody, render medical assistance as warranted, and treat arrestees humanely. Establishing negligence is difficult. To prove a negligence claim, four components must be established: legal duty, breach of duty, proximate causation, and actual injury.

A legal duty requires an officer either to act or refrain from acting in particular situations. The duty may arise from laws, customs, judicial decisions, or agency regulations (Kappeler et al., 1991). Second, once a duty has been proven by the plaintiff, it must be demonstrated that the officer breached the duty by failing to act in accordance with the legal responsibility. Courts recognize that the police are only liable to specific individuals and not the general public (*Harris v. District of Columbia*, 1991). Some special knowledge or circumstances must exist that sets the individual citizen apart from the general public and shows a relationship between that citizen and the police (Kappeler, 1997). Next, if the plaintiff can show that the officer owed a duty and breached that duty, it must be established that the officer was the proximate cause of the harm or the damage (Barrineau, 1994). A close causal link between the officer's negligent conduct and the consequent harm to the arrestee must be proven. This may be determined by asking, "But for the officer's conduct, would the plaintiff have sustained the injury, damage, or death?"

These components provide the structure in which a state tort claim for negligence in a wrongful custodial death will be examined. Proximate cause is defined differently by many courts. It may be enough to show that the officer's act or omission rose to a level that caused injury to or death of the arrestee. Other courts, however, may rely on a higher standard of recklessness, wanton conduct, or gross negligence before negligence will be attached. For example, in *Tindall v. Multnomah County* (1977), there was no negligence when an officer took an intoxicated individual to jail rather than a treatment facility after being notified by hospital personnel that they would not take drunks. The officer did not inform detention personnel that the arrestee had fallen and had a bump on his head. There was no violation of a state statute, because the statute applied only when the arrestee was incapacitated or in immediate danger, and if a treatment facility was available. A cause for liability was upheld in *Brinkman v. City of Indianapolis* (1967), however, when an officer took a severely sick man to jail rather than a hospital, provided no medical assistance, and notified his relatives that they could not post bond until the morning.

Special Duty of Care

Courts have also established that an officer may owe a special duty when he or she has reason to believe that the arrestee presents a danger to himself. When it is evident that a particular arrestee has a diminished ability or cannot exercise the same level of care as an ordinary person due to mental illness or intoxication, police must ensure that reasonable measures are taken in order to care for the person in their custody (*Thomas v. Williams*, 1962; *Shuff v. Zurich*, 1965).

The concept of special duty is based on two factors: (1) the officer's knowledge of the arrestee's mental state, and (2) the extent to which the condition renders the arrestee unable to exercise ordinary care. If it is foreseeable (i.e., a reasonable anticipation that the injury or damage is likely a result of an act or omission) that a circumstance shows that an arrestee's condition creates a hazard, a general duty of care is required of police that becomes a special duty of care that may lead to liability if the duty is breached. If an officer possesses sufficient knowledge of an arrestee's mental state or intoxicated condition and the arrestee is rendered helpless, a special duty may exist.

A special duty of care creates increased responsibilities and may include cases of unexpected custodial deaths. In *Fruge v. City of New Orleans* (1993), the estate brought a wrongful death claim for a diabetic arrestee who gave the appearance of intoxication. The arrestee was placed in an isolation cell, where he later was observed to be foaming at the mouth. He was transported to the hospital and died two hours later. The attending doctor stated that he had a moderately enlarged liver, which can cause sudden death. The court found that officers were negligent in their decision to incarcerate, because they owed a duty to a prisoner to protect him from harm and preserve his safety. The court concluded that the city failed in its responsibility by not ascertaining his medical condition and transporting him to a hospital. The arrestee's apparent intoxication triggered the need for a higher degree of care by the police.

In *Del Tufo v. Township of Old Bridge* (1996), the estate of an arrestee who died from a cocaine overdose while in police custody brought a wrongful death action for negligence. The estate claimed that officers failed to provide the arrestee with emergency medical assistance upon arrest. Officers responded to a traffic accident and found the driver sitting at the wheel with the motor running. Officers attempted to subdue and restrain him, but he struggled violently with them. Other officers responded and the driver was restrained with his hands behind his back and placed in the back seat of the patrol car. In the patrol car he began kicking the windows, and during transport the officer observed him to be shaking violently. At police headquarters the arrestee collapsed outside the car. The officer removed the handcuffs, began CPR, and radioed for medical assistance. The individual died an hour later at the hospital from cardiac failure due to ingesting 1.5 to 3.5 grams of cocaine.

The court acknowledged that the police have a duty to provide emergency medical assistance to those in their custody. The court rejected, however, the idea that drug abusers fall into the same category as the elderly and the mentally ill, because they have the responsibility to advise the police that they have consumed drugs—self-inflicted harm equates to self-care responsibility. The plaintiff failed to prove that the officers were the proximate cause of the death of the arrestee by a delay of medical care, and comparative fault was used as the defense for the officers: "a policy of individual responsibility for voluntary behavior."

The estate in *Brown v. Lee* (1994) brought a wrongful death claim when a prisoner died in the police lockup from an overdose of methylene-dioxy-methamphetamine (also called Ecstasy). The plaintiff asserted that the sheriff had a duty to obtain medical treatment for him. The lawsuit alleged negligent failure to provide medical care and negligence in monitoring arrestees in the lockup. The prisoner was arrested on charges of disturbing the peace, because he was walking in the middle of traffic, sweating, and grimacing. The arresting officer detected the odor of alcohol and during transport asked him if he had used the drug Ecstasy. He denied any drug use, although he acted "hyper" and was sweating. During booking, the arrestee said he was fine. Medical attention was offered, but he refused and was placed in a cell.

During the night, a trustee noticed that the prisoner was experiencing breathing difficulties and shaking, and called for the officers. Responding officers found the arrestee dead. An autopsy revealed that he died from a drug overdose. The court acknowledged that officers owe a duty to provide care for arrestees and that a higher degree of care is owed to an intoxicated person who cannot care for himself. Because the arrestee denied being under the influence and rejected medical care when it was offered, and because the drug condition is often not fatal, the court dismissed the claim, stating that it is "unreasonable to impose a duty on the sheriff to provide medical treatment to every intoxicated arrestee."

These cases illustrate that courts determine whether a special duty exists on a case-by-case-basis. The courts expect the police to provide a level of care and caution when taking custody of arrestees who exhibit signs of intoxication and mental illness. Legal duties are obligations recognized by the courts that require police officers to act or refrain from acting in a given situation (Kappeler, 1997). While a plaintiff may be able to prove that the officer owed a duty and breached that duty, he or she must next prove that the officer was the proximate cause of the injury or death. This is not a simple endeavor, because there are considerable differences among the courts' interpretations of "proximate cause." In these unexpected death cases, one method of determining this is to ask: "But for the officer's action, would the arrestee have died?" Careful consideration must be given to the decedent's medical and psychological history and his or her condition during the hours prior to arrest and during the arrest to determine the actual cause of death. In some incidents, the officer's action or inaction may be a significant factor and rise to a level of culpability that results in liability. The courts will determine the degree of knowledge the police had at the time or obtained relative to the arrestee's condition.

While a definitive test for foreseeability does not exist, the courts will rely on the facts of the particular case and on precedent when analyzing the case. Figure 12.1, as adapted from Kappeler, Vaughn, and del Carmen (1991), illustrates how the courts determine liability based on negligence factors, special duty, and knowledge or foreseeable factors concerning sudden/wrongful deaths in custody. Many courts will evaluate the case based on the totality of circumstances. Other courts, however, will consider the knowledge the officers had about the arrestee who exhibited symptoms associated with other sudden deaths and whether the death was foreseeable. The interaction between judicial decisionmaking and factual circumstances that indicate a breach of duty ultimately determines liability for negligent failure to prevent a wrongful death (del Carmen & Kappeler, 1991).

Figure 12.1
Liability Decision-Making Model in Police Custodial Deaths

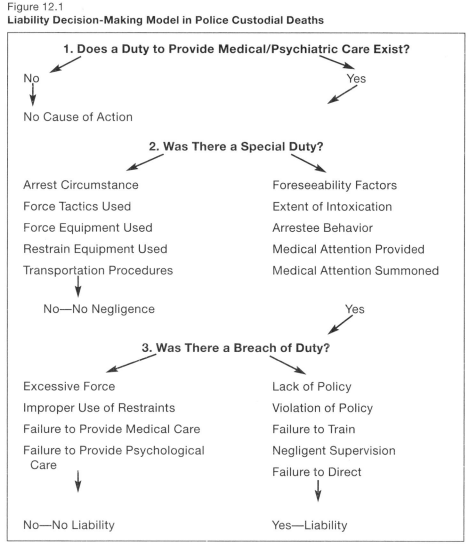

Source: Adapted from Kappeler, V., M. Vaughn & R.V. del Carmen (1991). "Death in Detention: An Analysis of Police Liability for Negligent Failure to Prevent Suicide." *Journal of Criminal Justice* 19:381-393.

Wrongful Custodial Death Claims Under § 1983

Wrongful death actions are recognized in all states, therefore, such laws may be used in a § 1983 action. Section 1983 authorizes the application of any state remedial law that is consistent with the purposes of § 1983 to any situation for which federal civil rights laws do not provide an appropriate remedy (Silver, 2000). Wrongful death claims may be filed under § 1983 when the death has resulted from excessive force, failure to attend to medical needs, or any other constitutional violation, and the conduct of the defendants was the proximate cause of the death under intentional tort principles (*Wright v. Collins*, 1985).

Figure 12.2
Sudden Deaths in Police Custody Liability Issues Matrix

Arrestee			
Issue	**Applicable Amendment**	**Precedent**	**Standard of Review**
Use of Force and Restraints	Fourth	Graham v. Connor (1989) Tennessee v. Garner (1985)	Objective Reasonableness
Medical/Psychological (§ 1983)	Fourteenth	Revere v. Mass. General Hospital	Deliberate Indifference
Policy/Custom	Fourteenth	Monell v. Dept. of Social Services (1978)	Deliberate Indifference Proximate Cause
Training	Fourteenth	City of Canton v. Harris (1989)	Deliberate Indifference
Pretrial Detainees			
Use of Force and Restraints	Fifth and Fourteenth	Johnson v. Glick (1973) Bell v. Wolfish (1979) Rochin v. California (1952)	Shocks the Conscience Due Process Clause
Medical/Psychological	Eighth and Fourteenth	Estelle v. Gamble (1976) Revere v. Mass. General Hospital (1983)	Deliberate Indifference
Failure to Protect	Eighth and Fourteenth	DeShaney v. Winnebago (1989) Farmer v. Brennan (1994)	Deliberate Indifference Special Relationship
Policy/Custom	Fourteenth	Monell v. Dept. of Social Services (1978)	Deliberate Indifference Proximate Cause
Training	Fourteenth	City of Canton v. Harris (1989)	Deliberate Indifference

Unexpected custodial death cases filed under § 1983 are evaluated within the purview of the Fourth and Fourteenth Amendments, based on the standards of "deliberate indifference," "objective reasonableness," and "conduct shocking to the conscience." Figure 12.2 presents a matrix that summarizes various liability issues, court decisions, and applicable standards of review when analyzing the factors involved in sudden deaths in police custody. Liability concerns regarding citizens who are arrested, restrained, and suddenly die shortly after arrest are analyzed according to the Fourth Amendment standard of objectively reasonable force, and primarily involve issues of excessive force/restraints, failure to train, failure to render medical/psychological care, and policy and customs issues that are alleged to have violated the decedents' constitutional rights. As an arrestee's status changes to that of a pretrial detainee, the standard of reviewing claims of excessive force relies on the "conduct shocking to the conscience" standard under the Fourteenth Amendment. Medical, psychological, and failure to protect concerns are generally examined under the Eighth Amendment deliberate indifference standard. Arrestee behaviors that are consistent with the inability to care for themselves, such as the intoxicated or mentally ill, pose a particular dilemma for responding officers. The following § 1983 case analysis of wrongful deaths in police custody reveals how the courts determine liability.

Excessive Force Claims

A significant number of sudden death restraint incidents involve the violent behavior of an arrestee, requiring police to use higher levels of physical control measures and nonlethal force equipment or implements. As a result, the primary claims filed against the responding officers are allegations of excessive force that occurred during arrest, at the station, or in a detention cell.

In *Estate of Phillips v. City of Milwaukee* (1996), officers used force to subdue a large schizophrenic man with ballpoint pens in each hand. After a lengthy struggle, he was subdued, handcuffed behind his back, and placed in leg restraints. He was on his stomach for one minute and suddenly stopped breathing. Cardiopulmonary resuscitation was initiated and emergency medical personnel responded, but they were unable to revive him. The arrestee died a day later, and the medical examiner determined that the restraint contributed to his death. The estate filed a § 1983 lawsuit for use of excessive force, denial of medical care, and failure to train. The court held that the officers did not use excessive force in controlling the arrestee. Police actions were analyzed based on the totality of circumstances and the resistive behaviors they encountered. Deliberate indifference to the medical needs of the deceased was not established and officers were shielded from liability under qualified immunity. Moreover, the court noted that "police officers facing unpredictable and oftentimes dangerous situations must be free to perform their duties utilizing their training, experience, and judgment with confidence that courts will not scrutinize their discretionary decisions with microscopic detail."

In *East v. City of Chicago* (1989), however, the court held that officers used excessive force when East died of a drug overdose in their custody. During a drug raid, East swallowed a packet of cocaine. Approximately four hours later, in the interrogation room at the station, he experienced hallucinations, began yelling, and attempted to hide under a table. Several officers removed him from under the table, kicked him in the head and between his legs, and hit him with a nightstick in an attempt to handcuff him. East told the officers that he had ingested cocaine, but they ignored him and responded "You're just afraid to go to jail." He was placed in a cell with another prisoner, who later informed police that East needed medical attention. At an unknown time, paramedics were summoned, responded, and transported East to the hospital, where he later died.

The court cited the *Graham v. Connor* (1989) decision, but acknowledged that the arrestee was in custody at the station when force was applied. They ruled that in post-arrest situations, when dealing with a pretrial detainee, the Fourteenth Amendment "shocks the conscience" standard applies. The officers were found liable for beating the arrestee, deliberate indifference to his medical needs under *Estelle v. Gamble* (1976), and the city was also liable for failing to train officers in the appropriate use of force.

In cases of sudden death after force is used, two questions are commonly asked: "Was the officer's force excessive?" and "Did the amount of force used contribute to the detainee's death?" Answering these questions is not easy. Excessive force claims stemming from arrests must be examined under the Fourth Amendment's "reasonableness" standard based on the Supreme Court's decision in *Graham*. The "reasonableness" inquiry in an excessive force claim is an objective inquiry. While there is no precise definition for the test of reasonableness, applying the standard requires careful attention to the facts and circumstances confronting the police, without regard to their underlying intent or motivation. Each case must be evaluated from the perspective of a reasonable officer on the scene, based on the severity of the crime, the resistance level of the arrestee, the threat posed by the arrestee, and whether the circumstances were rapidly evolving.

The courts recognize that use-of-force incidents can be tense and officers often must respond quickly, with the understanding that there are numerous variables to consider. Using the objective reasonableness standard, the court will determine whether excessive force was used by officers by evaluating the totality of the circumstances, including the unpredictability, danger, and violent behavior manifested by the arrestee, and whether the force or control tactics used were reasonable or proportional in light of the behavior encountered. Objectively reasonable and lawful force is force used at the moment it is needed and in response to the arrestee's behavior, regardless of the outcome. The *East* case, however, provides an example of excessive force, because officers kicked the arrestee in the head and between the legs, and then continued to beat him with an impact weapon. After establishing control, officers failed to provide timely medical assistance. In light of the circumstances, these tactics were considered excessive and disproportional. Failure to follow up with necessary medical care amounted to deliberate indifference.

Use of Restraint Claims

Associated with excessive force allegations is a second level of claims that often asserts that the police maximally restrained the deceased, which purportedly contributed to his death. The assertion is frequently made that the deceased died as a result of "positional, postural, restraint, compressional, or mechanical asphyxia," because he was placed in the hogtied position. The claim may also assert that the individual died from asphyxia due to the weight of the officers on his body for an extended period during control and restraint. These allegations may be further supported by results of an autopsy or independent autopsy conducted by the estate claiming that the method of restraint contributed to asphyxia, which caused death. Moreover, this assertion will attempt to prove excessive force by using restraints without considering the obvious medical needs of the arrestee.

A federal court found the city of Chicago liable for contributing to the death of an arrestee who was under the influence of cocaine and phencyclidine in *Animashaun v. O'Donnell* (1994). While restrained and lying face-down on the ground, the arrestee began experiencing breathing difficulties. He was transported to the hospital in a maximally restrained position, where he was pronounced dead. His estate filed a § 1983 action, claiming that he had died from positional asphyxia due to the nature of restraint methods used by the police. The city contended that it was unaware of the relationship between restraining an arrestee in this manner and the occurrence of positional asphyxia. The plaintiff attached a memorandum of a similar death in 1988 regarding this problem, and the city deliberately ignored it. The court held that the city was on notice that its officers were responding to recurring situations yet chose to ignore it and this omission rose to a level of deliberate indifference in training their officers. Likewise, in *Johnson v. City of Cincinnati* (1999), policy and training issues that arose from *Monell v. Department of Social Services of New York* (1978) were not dismissed. The court denied summary judgment because the city knew that taking custody of highly agitated people was a recurring problem, and it was aware of the potential risks of placing a person showing signs of delirium in a prone restraint that could result in sudden death.

Similarly, in *Cruz v. City of Laramie, Wyoming* (2001), the Tenth Circuit found that hogtying individuals with diminished capacity was excessive force and denied summary judgment for the city of Laramie. Cruz was found by officers to be naked and running wildly. Believing he was on some type of drug, officers summoned an ambulance; verbal calming attempts were unsuccessful. He fought with the officers, who restrained him with handcuffs, and due to his kicking, a nylon strap was placed on his ankles and connected to the handcuffs. Cruz calmed down, but officers noticed his face had blanched and removed the restraints. Although emergency medical personnel initiated CPR, Cruz died at the hospital. An autopsy revealed a large amount of cocaine in his system. His family filed a civil action claiming he died of restraint asphyxia, which was supported by one medical expert, while another medical expert claimed his death was solely from cocaine abuse.

A dispute emerged over whether Cruz was hogtied or hobbled. The lower court determined that had the officers separated Cruz's ankles further from his restrained hands, by two feet or more, Cruz would have been hobbled. The court reasoned that the hogtied restraint technique does not per se constitute a constitutional right violation; rather, officers may not apply the technique when an individual's diminished capacity is apparent. Such diminished capacity may result from intoxication, the influence of controlled substances, a discernible mental condition, or any other condition apparent to officers. The appellate court ruled that the officers knew Cruz was under the influence and using the hogtie restraint amounted to excessive force. Liability attached against the city for failing to train officers in the use of hobble restraints.

In *Price v. County of San Diego* (1998), an arrestee who had a history of methamphetamine use fought violently with police, was restrained in a hogtied position, stopped breathing, and died two days later in the hospital. A § 1983 claim for violation of constitutional rights, wrongful death, and excessive force was filed, along with state negligence claims. One medical examiner argued in court that restraint asphyxia contributed to the decedent's death, while another medical examiner testified that the hogtied position did not dangerously affect oxygen levels, nor contributed to the arrestee's death based on new medical research concerning restraint asphyxia (Chan et al., 1997). Based on the medical research, the judge ruled that hogtying in and of itself did not cause the arrestee's death, that the deputies did not use excessive force, and acknowledged that the consequences of abusing drugs led to a heart attack that, more than anything else, killed him. The case was dismissed. In a companion case, *Guseman v. Martinez* (1998), a federal district court in Kansas found that the police officers' method of restraint did not rise to the level of deliberate indifference, despite the arrestee dying in custody, and granted the city's motion for summary judgment.

Likewise, in *Young v. Mt. Ranier* (2001), the court awarded summary judgment to the defendant officers despite Young's dying in restraints. Police officers responded to a call that Young was exhibiting bizarre behaviors and was extremely agitated, and upon initial response found him lying on the ground. The officers attempted to take him into custody, but he struggled with them. The officers used pepper spray and restrained him with handcuffs and leg restraints. He was transported to the hospital, where he died. An autopsy revealed that Young had PCP in his system and the cause of death was listed as sudden cardiac arrhythmia. Young's parents claimed the officers were deliberately indifferent to his medical needs. The Fourth Circuit determined that the officers did not violate Young's rights, as he struggled and the officers were unaware that he had consumed PCP.

The *Graham* standard of using force is also applied to the reasonable use of restraints in controlling a combative arrestee. Liability attaches only if excessive force is used on an individual that proximately causes injury, in this case death. The use of restraints must be reasonably related to the behavior and safety of the individual, the need to control him or her, and the safety concerns of the responding officers. It is standard practice to handcuff an arrestee after a use-of-force altercation. In combative arrest scenarios (as illustrated by these cases), officers generally need to further restrain the person, as he or she frequently will kick and continue the violent behavior. In response to the citizen's behavior, police officers are authorized to graduate their response to the demands of any particular situation. It is reasonable to handcuff and restrain an individual's legs (*Maynard v. Hopwood*, 1997).

A federal district court found, however, that a restraint procedure known as the "total appendage restraint procedure (TARP) amounted to excessive force and contributed to the death of an arrestee. In *Nelson v. County of Los Angeles* (2003), Nelson stood in the middle of street and began firing a loaded gun in the air and at passing motorists. Police were summoned and deputies from the Los Angeles County Sheriff's Department responded. Nelson was handcuffed and placed in the back seat of the patrol car and began thrashing around. The deputies removed him and placed him the "total appendage restraint procedure" (TARP). When the deputies secured him they noticed that he was unconscious. They rolled him over and observed that he was not breathing. Rescue personnel were summoned but could not revive him. The arrest and restraint process was videotaped from a deputy's car camera. An autopsy was performed and the pathologist reported that he died of positional asphyxia. The family filed a lawsuit alleging that the officers used excessive force and restraints that contributed to the wrongful death of their son. At trial the pathologist testified that the officers used the TARP procedure, which "hogtied" Nelson, compromising his breathing, and thus killing him. Nelson had an underlying heart condition and had cocaine in his system, but the pathologist did not believe these factors contributed to his death. Finding for the estate of Nelson, the jury awarded $2 million in compensatory damages. The court reduced the amount to $1.3 million as Nelson was 35 percent at fault.

The county appealed and the court affirmed the lower court's decision but found the award was excessive and ordered the amount reduced. The court determined that there was enough evidence to show that Nelson died due to the TARP procedure and positional asphyxia. The court found that Nelson's heart condition and cocaine use did not contribute to his death.

The use of restraints may be considered unreasonable force if they were used inappropriately to the need, officers were not trained in their proper use, or officers failed to follow the department's restraint policy. There must be proof that a particular violation of a federal right was a "highly predictable" consequence of the failure to equip police officers with specific tools to handle recurring situations. The question that emerges from these restraint deaths is whether asphyxia deaths are highly foreseeable or a predictable consequence of restraining persons prone in the hogtied position? The *Graham* standard of objectively reasonable force will be applied in restraint cases. The *Price* case is illustrative of this, as the court, relying on scientific evidence regarding "hogtying," found the restraint procedure in and of itself not to be excessive force and that it did not cause asphyxia. The court found that drugs caused the individual's death and not the restraint procedure. In analyzing these cases, courts will review the totality of circumstances, cause of death, extent of the person's medical or psychiatric condition, restraints authorized and methods used, other alternatives available, officer's perception of safety, and the resistive behaviors requiring further immobilization of the person. As evidenced in these cases, the courts are split in their opinions as to whether the hogtied procedure should be considered excessive force. This type of restraint litigation is still emerging and changes in court interpretations may be forthcoming.

Deliberate Indifference to Obvious Medical or Psychological Needs

Beyond the claims of excessive force and improper use of restraints, allegations for failure to recognize behaviors and medical symptoms commonly associated with sudden custodial deaths will be filed. The duty to protect a detainee from harm and to provide reasonable medical care is based partially on the notion that the government is responsible for these individuals because it has deprived them of the ability to look after themselves (Silver, 2005). The duty begins at arrest and continues through the process of detention. The police, however, are not considered absolute insurers of the health and safety of those in their custody. The assertion may be made that officers were deliberately indifferent to the medical or psychological needs of the arrestee. This legal claim may be framed within the context of the Fourteenth Amendment in accordance with the U.S. Supreme Court's decision in *City of Revere v. Massachusetts General Hospital* (1983). This case concluded that municipalities have a constitutional duty to obtain necessary medical care for detainees in their custody. Failing to obtain such care may rise to the level of deliberate indifference.

In *Harris v. District of Columbia* (1991), the estate brought a wrongful death claim under the Fourteenth Amendment, alleging that officers were deliberately indifferent to the decedent's medical needs and misused restraints. Harris was "freaking out" on PCP. He was handcuffed, with legs restrained, locked in a police van, and later transported to a hospital. Medical care was delayed at first due to filling out forms (per hospital policy), and then it was delayed because the forms were incorrectly completed, according to the attending emergency room physician. Harris was pronounced dead two hours and 20 minutes after the arrest, due to a drug overdose. The court held that the police had not entered into a special relationship when they restrained him and locked him in the van, in that he had not been formally committed, either by conviction, involuntary commitment, or arrest. Thus there was no duty to obtain medical assistance. Officers were entitled to qualified immunity because they acted reasonably in light of the circumstances. The court also noted that the officers had not entered into a special relationship requiring a duty to provide medical care, because Harris demonstrated a lack of care for himself when he ingested the PCP. The court's reasoning compared the police officers' duty of custody with that of ambulance drivers, stating that "they are not subject to a constitutional obligation every time they pick up a patient."

In *Cottrell v. Caldwell* (1996), police officers responded to a 911 call and arrested a man with a history of mental illness who had stopped taking his medication. The family wanted the officers to transport him to the hospital. After a 20-minute struggle to control the individual, he was subdued, restrained with handcuffs and leg restraints, and placed face-down on the floor of the car. He was transported to the station and during transport died of "positional asphyxiation." Using the deliberate indifference standard, the court ruled that in "custody mistreatment claims," gross negligence is not part of the standard of review. The standard is deliberate indifference to a "substantial risk of serious harm." The plaintiff must show a deprivation that is "objectively, sufficiently serious," meaning that the officers' actions resulted in the denial of the minimal civilized measure of "life's necessities." The court found no evidence that the officers knew of, and consciously disregarded, the risk that the arrestee would suffocate, and the plaintiff failed to show a violation of due process. The police did not act with deliberate indifference to the medical and due process rights of the arrestee, nor did they use excessive force in restraining him.

In *Simpson v. Hines* (1990), the estate brought a § 1983 action against 10 officers for alleged excessive force and lack of medical care under the Fourth and Fourteenth Amendments, as well as state claims. The chief of police was sued on grounds of failure to supervise. After an arrest and confrontation, officers were attempting to search an individual at the station. The arrestee was in a drug-induced state, became violent, and refused to be searched. A struggle ensued, and one officer placed him in a "neck hold," while other officers grabbed his arms and legs and forced him to the floor in order to handcuff him. A large officer sat on his chest. After control was established, the arrestee was rolled on his side, handcuffed with his hands behind his back, and his legs were restrained. Once restrained, the arrestee became silent, and was left in his cell to recover. During the night he was checked twice, and the officers noted that he did not move from that position. Approximately five hours later, an officer noticed a pool of blood near his head. Rigor mortis had apparently occurred. The medical examiner reported that the arrestee died as a result of asphyxia due to trauma to the neck during the struggle to subdue him. On the medical claim the court held that the officers were deliberately indifferent to the medical needs of the deceased by leaving him unconscious in the cell. The court stated that the officers owe a duty of reasonable care to pretrial detainees under the Fourteenth Amendment.

The applicable standard with regard to medical care issues is deliberate indifference pursuant to *Estelle v. Gamble* (1976). The plaintiff must establish actual omissions that are sufficiently harmful to evidence deliberate indifference to serious medical needs. To hold officers liable, it must be shown that they intentionally denied or delayed access to treatment or interfered with treatment. The Court in *Estelle* held that an inadvertent failure to provide adequate medical care does not rise to the level of a constitutional violation.

In *Hoyer v. City of Southfield and County of Oakland* (2003), five officers responded to contain a mentally impaired man, partially clothed, who was running in traffic. Officers attempted to make verbal contact with him, but he ignored them. An officer attempted to control him and he violently fought with responding officers. One officer struck him with a baton three times, while another officer sprayed him with pepper spray, another officer applied a brachial stun to the side of his neck and several knee strikes to the outside of this thigh in an effort to control him. All of these attempts were unsuccessful, but the officers eventually were able to place him on the ground, control, and handcuff him. Hoyer was transported to the jail and three officers received treatment at the hospital for injuries sustained. Within 20 minutes, Hoyer became violent in his jail cell and began banging his head on the wall, shouting, and attempting to destroy the toilet. Paramedics were summoned and an extraction team forcibly removed him from the cell. During transport in the ambulance he became unresponsive and later died at the hospital. The family filed a lawsuit claiming excessive force and deliberate indifference to Hoyer's medical condition The family claimed that the officers should have transported him directly to the hospital rather than the jail. The pathologist who performed the autopsy reported that Hoyer died due to acute cocaine intoxication, with about 4 grams of cocaine in his system, and agitated delirium. The court granted summary judgment to both of the defendants. The defendants were not found to be deliberately indifferent to Hoyer's medical condition nor used excessive force in subduing him.

The courts do not hold police officers to the same level of care as a physician, although officers have a responsibility to determine the medical or psychological well-being of a person in their custody. The plaintiff may attempt, however, to prove that officers failed to provide medical needs under the ruling in *DeShaney v. Winnebago County Department of Social Services* (1989). In this case, the United States Supreme Court recognized that a special relationship can exist between the state and a person, giving rise to a constitutional duty on the state to assume some responsibility for the person's medical needs, only "when the State takes a person into its custody and holds him against his will." Police officers are under no constitutional obligation to protect or provide medical services to the general public, even if they know of a particular person's need and regardless of whether that obligation is imposed by state tort law, unless the government has entered into a "certain special relationship" with the person. There are three primary components that must be considered in determining whether a "special relationship" may exist for medical purposes, which include that the police: (1) created the danger to which the plaintiffs were exposed; (2) had knowledge of the impending danger; and (3) had custody of the plaintiff. Thus, liability for police officers may attach when the need for medical care of an arrestee in their custody was created after a use-of-force situation (e.g., baton strikes, physical control techniques, during restraint, etc.) and the person sustained an injury, and officers knew that the person needed medical assistance through verbal inquiry or assessment or requests made by the individual. As illustrated in the *Harris* case, medical care liability in sudden custodial deaths may not attach, because in a significant number of incidents the police take custody and restrain an individual after they have already consumed drugs or alcohol. With this in mind, police officers should take reasonable precautions to assess and monitor the condition of the arrestee, and summon medical care as warranted after a violent use-of-force restraint confrontation.

Failure to Train

A frequent claim in unexpected death actions are allegations that police supervisors failed to train officers. The assertion is that officers have not been properly instructed or trained by the supervisor or agency and thus lack the skills, knowledge, or competency required in a range of items, such as: use of appropriate force measures, including the use of restraints and other equipment; recognizing the hazards of drug-induced violent behavior; deficiency in training to obvious medical or psychiatric behaviors; recognizing the risks of hogtying; and a lack of training in policies and procedures for responding to "special needs" prisoners (those intoxicated or mentally impaired).

In *Elmes v. Hart* (1994), a § 1983 claim and state tort claims were filed by an estate when an arrestee who was high on LSD and marijuana died in police custody. Officers responded to a disturbance at a party where they observed an individual choking a female guest. Due to an intense struggle, several officers were needed to subdue the violent male. Handcuffs and leg restraints were secured on the kicking arrestee, and he was hogtied with flex-cuffs and leg restraints. The medical examiner was summoned to the scene and found the arrestee hogtied and learned that he had stopped breathing after several minutes of being hogtied. An ambulance was summoned, but there was no attempt to resuscitate, because there was no CPR mask available, and officers were fearful of contracting AIDS. They had felt for a pulse and, finding none, thought CPR would be futile. Death was caused by "mechanical asphyxiation." The court ruled that the officers did not "intentionally kill the arrestee." An excessive force claim was made against the officers in which the court found that the officers used excessive force in arresting the deceased. The city, however, was not found to be deliberately indifferent for failing to train its officers.

In *Swans v. City of Lansing* (1998), the jury found in favor of the estate of an arrestee who died in a detention cell. Upon being admitted into the detention center, Swans kicked the booking sergeant in the head and fought with officers. He was restrained with handcuffs but the officers were unable to secure him in a restraint chair. He was forcibly moved to a cell where he continued to violently fight with the officers. In the cell, five officers and a lieutenant attempted to further restrain him with a Kick-Stop restraint strap, like they had used in numerous other situations with violent detainees. The strap broke and the officers restrained Swans with additional handcuffs and leg irons connected to his ankles. The officers left Swans on his side/stomach, monitored him by closed circuit television, and returned to the cell within 10 minutes. The officers found Swans lying in urine and unresponsive. They moved him to the hallway, removed the restraints, initiated CPR, and summoned medical personnel. Medical personnel found him pulseless, continued life-saving efforts, and transported him to the hospital where he was pronounced dead. An autopsy revealed that he died from cardiac dysrhythmia caused by postural asphyxia during custodial restraint. The jury determined that officers used excessive force, misused the restraints, and that administrative personnel had failed to train, supervise, and direct officers in how to properly respond to and restraint mentally impaired detainees. The jury awarded $10 million to Swans' estate.

The court in *Pliakos v. City of Manchester, New Hampshire* (2003) held that physically controlling a combative subject who twice kicked and beat off a police dog, fought with several officers, fought through a two-second burst of pepper spray, was not unreasonable nor excessive force. After Pliakos was restrained he remained on his stomach for approximately three minutes, became unresponsive, and later died. Pliakos suffered from bipolar affective disorder, an enlarged heart, and was under the influence of cocaine during the confrontation. Pliakos' estate claimed that the chief failed to train officers in properly restraining agitated persons and monitoring them while in restraints. The court reasoned that in light of the circumstances the officers did not violate their training and it was not unreasonable to keep Pliakos restrained on his stomach for his and the officers' safety.

Conversely, the court found in *Watkins v. New Castle County* (2005) that the department was deliberately indifferent to the training needs of their officers regarding factors pertinent to positional asphyxia. Officers responded to a domestic call to remove a man from the residence. A person at the scene informed the officers that he had a long history of cocaine abuse. The officers met the man and noticed that he had a dazed look on his face, spoke incoherently, and complained of feeling sick. The man engaged in a struggle with him and then he tensed up. The officers struck him in the face several times, struck him on the wrist with a collapsible baton, sprayed pepper spray in his eyes. He fell to the floor and an officer dropped his weight on his back to handcuff him. The officers held him down on his chest and secured his wrists and ankles together. Within several minutes he became unresponsive and died. The court denied summary judgment and found that the evidence revealed that the department failed to adequately train their officers in the risks of cocaine-induced delirium and the potential serious health consequences of restraining persons with their hands and ankles bound together.

Claims of excessive force and failing to train officers in the proper use of the restraint chair have been filed due to the deaths of several detainees in detention facilities. In *Jones v. Devaney* (2004) and *Bishop v. Corsentino* (2004), prisoners became combative, requiring officers to further restrain them in the restraint chair due to their continued self-injurious behaviors. The prisoners were placed in the chair, monitored, and later became unresponsive. Life-saving efforts were initiated and both prisoners died due to unspecified medical conditions. In both cases the courts granted summary judgment, as it was shown that the officers were guided in the proper use of the chair by agency policy. Training in the policy and the mechanics of using the chair was provided by the agency and the policy also provided for officer monitoring and intervals of medical personnel assessment. In both cases the procedures and officer training was followed, and the courts determined that the use of the chair failed to amount to excessive force in restraining the violent prisoners.

Section 1983 claims of this nature will focus on the U.S. Supreme Court case of *City of Canton v. Harris* (1989). The Court established that the inadequacy of police training may serve as a basis for § 1983 liability only when the failure to train amounts to deliberate indifference to the rights of persons with whom the police come into contact. The plaintiff must show that the custom or policy of the department was to ignore officer training and that this was the moving force behind a constitutional violation. In custodial death cases, the plaintiff must show that the alleged lack of training with regard to the use of force and restraints and the alleged lack of medical or psychiatric care for "special needs" prisoners is closely related and actually caused the officers' deliberate indifference to the serious medical needs of the arrestee.

The courts appear to be split on the issues of failure to train officers regarding restraint and use-of-force procedures, and recognizing symptomologies of medical and psychological care for these arrestees. For example, *in Swans v. City of Lansing* (1998), *Johnson v. Cincinnati* (1999), *Cruz v. City of Laramie, Wyoming* (2001), and *Watkins v. New Castle County* (2005), the courts denied summary judgment on claims of failure to train. The courts noted that administrators were deliberately indifferent to the training needs of their officers when they contact and intervene with the mentally ill and/or those who are experiencing a drug-induced psychosis. In the *Cruz* case, the court specifically held that there must be more than 14 inches separating the restraints between the ankles and wrists when retraining a violent arrestee who appears to be under the influence of drugs. Moreover, the *Swans* case is illustrative of how a jury may view restraining a mentally impaired person who suddenly dies in police custody.

Conversely, in the decisions *of Sims v. Greenville* (2000), *Bozeman v. Orum* (2002), *Hoyer v. City of Southfield* (2003), *Pliakos v. City of Manchester, New Hampshire* (2003*), Bishop v. Corsentino* (2004), *and Jones v. Devaney* (2004), the courts held that officers used proper force and followed their policies and training, granting summary judgment. These cases are instructive as the officers had received training in responding to the mentally impaired, training on substance abuse, and training in use-of-force techniques, multiple officer response, and restraint training. As evidenced in these case examples, the courts are more likely to grant summary judgment to the responding officers and agencies when they can justify the appropriate level of force, based on the circumstances facing them, and when the officers have been provided with proper training, and were guided by policy.

Claims Against Detention Personnel

The claims most frequently filed against detention officers are allegations of excessive force, positional asphyxia, and failure to provide medical care, like their police counterparts. The jury returned a "no cause" for action verdict in *Love v. Bolinger* (1998). During a hearing to determine the competency to stand trial of a bipolar individual, the detainee became agitated and rushed the judge's bench. Five officers struggled with the detainee and sprayed him twice with pepper spray. Once he was finally subdued, his hands were secured in front with two sets of handcuffs. He was escorted from the courtroom, down one floor, to a padded cell in the detention center. The detainee continued to struggle during the escort and fought with officers, kicking them once they placed him in the cell. While officers were removing the handcuffs, one officer noticed he had stopped breathing, and began CPR, while another officer summoned medical personnel. Within several minutes paramedics responded and continued life-saving efforts. A pulse was restored but it stopped during transport to the hospital, where he was pronounced dead. The estate filed a § 1983 action, claiming that he died of asphyxiation from a choke hold and the officers placing their weight on him in the cell. Two other pathologists reviewed the autopsy and each determined that he died of an enlarged heart. Over five days the jury listened to the officers' and expert witness testimony. They found in favor of the officers, finding they did not use excessive force, nor did they cause the death of the detainee.

Detention facilities have experienced sudden custodial deaths of detainees who have consumed a quantity of drugs prior to admission. In *Smith v. Wilson County* (2000), Smith died of acute cocaine intoxication in the detention center and his family filed a § 1983 action against the facility for failing to provide medical care at time of arrest and while confined. Smith resisted arrest for failing to stop at a stop sign. Officers noticed he was chewing something and he attempted to remove it. Smith stated he swallowed a marijuana cigarette, and then said it was rock cocaine, and then said it was marijuana. The arresting officer asked if he wanted medical attention, Smith refused, and he was transported to the police department for processing. At the station, Smith informed the lieutenant that he had not swallowed cocaine. The lieutenant instructed the officer to take Smith to the magistrate. The magistrate set Smith's bond and Smith did not complain about needing medical care nor did he appear to be under the influence of drugs. He was booked into the detention center, being unable to post bond. Smith was placed in a holding cell and shortly became agitated and began yelling. Officers moved him to an isolation cell and Smith stated that the "rock of cocaine he swallowed is killing me." Smith then stated he only swallowed a marijuana cigarette. Officers did not summon medical personnel, as Smith did not appear to need medical treatment.

During a standard security check three hours later, Smith was found unconscious in his cell. Medical personnel were summoned and life-saving efforts were initiated but proved unsuccessful and Smith was pronounced dead at the hospital, approximately five hours after he was arrested. The autopsy revealed that Smith had not suffered any "acute external injuries." The pathologist determined the cause of death to be from cocaine intoxication, which caused an idiosyncratic reaction of the heart due to Smith's heart being enlarged from extensive cocaine abuse.

The family filed a legal action claiming the arresting officers used excessive force in taking Smith to the ground and were deliberately indifferent in failing to provide medical care in violation of his Fourth and Fourteenth Amendment rights. The court awarded summary judgment to the arresting officers. The family also filed claims against the detention facility officers and the sheriff for wrongful death, officers failing to recognize and respond to a medical emergency, and failing to train, supervise, and direct officers in the care of intoxicated prisoners, under the Fourteenth Amendment. The court also granted summary judgment to the detention personnel, finding no evidence that the officers or the sheriff were deliberately indifferent to Smith's medical needs.

In *Sims v. Greenville County* (2000), a detainee was being moved from a holding area to a holding cell in order to serve a meal. The detainee resisted the detention officers, and four officers took him the floor. One officer applied a choke hold on the fighting detainee. The detainee was maximally restrained with handcuffs and leg restraints and placed in the holding cell. The detainee became unresponsive and attempts at medical intervention were unsuccessful. He later died and the pathologist determined that the cause of death was positional asphyxia. The detainee filed a legal action claiming that the officers used excessive force and inappropriately used a "multiple officer takedown" technique. Claims against the sheriff alleged that he failed to train officers and instituted an unconstitutional policy of using a multi-officer takedown maneuver. The appellate court affirmed summary judgment by the lower court, determining that Sims failed to present evidence that the defendants used excessive force. Simms failed to show that the sheriff maintained unconstitutional policies that would subject detainees to excessive force measures.

In *Bozeman v. Orum* (2002), the estate of a deceased detainee brought a § 1983 claim against the sheriff and several officers, alleging the force used caused his death, thereby violating his Fourteenth Amendment right against the use of excessive force. The detainee had become violent in the jail and the officers had threatened to "kick his ass" if he did not cease. He continued and the officers apparently punched or slapped the detainee and he subsequently died as a result of the officers' actions. The court granted summary judgment to the officers and sheriff, noting that some level of force was necessary to restore order where the detainee was going through a mental breakdown in his cell. The court noted that the sheriff had provided adequate training in the proper use of force, including training on positional asphyxia, and was not liable for failing to train or supervise the officers.

Suicides in Detention

A suicide by a prisoner or pretrial detainee poses a serious problem for detention and prison personnel. Civil litigation in this topic area has increased since the 1970s, and millions of dollars have been awarded as a result of attempted or actual suicides. The prevailing trend for plaintiffs, however, declined during the 1990s and through 2005. These civil actions normally assert that the confining agency and its officers failed to take the proper measures to prevent such an incident.

A wrongful death claim resulting from a prisoner suicide may be brought under § 1983 or as described earlier under state tort law. In accordance with § 1983, the plaintiff's claim will invariably allege that the defendant was deliberately indifferent to the deceased by failing to properly screen the prisoner upon reception into a detention facility; failing to recognize signs of symptoms of suicide; failing to train detention personnel; failing to protect the prisoner from himself by providing a safe environment; failing to properly search the prisoner and seize items that might be used to commit suicide; a deficiency in the design and structure of the confining facility; failing to "watch" the suicidal prisoner on a continuous basis; and failing to provide mental health services (Cohen, 1992).

A typical complaint will allege multiple theories of liability. In *Frey v. City of Herculaneum* (1995), for example, an intoxicated arrestee hanged himself in his cell with bed sheets. The estate claimed that the defendants were deliberately indifferent to the medical needs of Frey insofar as they knew or should have known that he was a suicide risk; knew or should have known he was in immediate need of medical attention; inadequately monitored the jail cells; failed to take precautions to remove dangerous items from the arrestee's cell; and knew or should have known that the jail was defective and dangerous.

Suicide and Deliberate Indifference

In Chapter 9, the deliberate indifference standard was described and applied to correctional issues. Recall that deliberate indifference originated in *Estelle v. Gamble* (1976), which involved prisoner medical care issues. In *Bell v. Wolfish* (1989), the U.S. Supreme Court held that pretrial detainees at the very least possess the same rights as convicted prisoners. While the Court has never specifically recognized a prisoner's right to protection from self-harm, the principles and analysis of *Bell* and *Estelle* have been applied to prisoner suicide cases.

Consider, however, the *Farmer v. Brennan* (1994) decision, in which the Court held that in order for liability to attach in a civil rights action against correctional personnel, deliberate indifference to a prisoner's safety and health must be based on a showing that they were subjectively aware of the risk. Correctional officials are not absolute guarantors of the safety of prisoners, but cannot ignore obvious risks or dangers to prisoners in their custody. The official must be aware of the facts from which the inference could be drawn that a serious risk of harm exists. Although Farmer is not a suicide case per se, it is instructive in that it is a deliberate indifference case involving issues of "knew or should have known" and should strengthen the ability to defend suicide cases involving issues of knowledge. *Deliberate indifference* describes a state of mind that is more blameworthy than negligence and requires more than an ordinary lack of due care, but can be satisfied with less than acts or omissions with knowledge that harm will result. In *Hare v. City of Corinth* (1996), the Fifth Circuit applied *Farmer* standards to a pretrial detainee suicide claim. The court ruled that the duty not to be deliberately indifferent was minimally established. A check on the prisoner who had threatened suicide while in withdrawal from drugs consumed prior to arrest was made by an officer, although he failed to remove a blanket from the cell. The officer's belief that the detainee was too weak to tear it was objectively reasonable.

To prevail in a § 1983 suit for violation of rights under the Fourteenth or Eighth Amendments, the plaintiff must establish that the defendant displayed deliberate indifference to a "strong likelihood" of suicide rather than a mere possibility. The plaintiff must prove that officials were deliberately indifferent to the prisoner's serious needs. Deliberate indifference is more than making a mistake. In suicide cases, deliberate indifference means: (1) officials knew or should have known that the prisoner was a suicide risk and steps were not taken to prevent it; and/or (2) the officers and agency were deliberately indifferent to the prisoner's serious medical or mental health needs (Plitt, 1997). Accordingly, when an official fails to act in the face of an obvious risk of which he or she *should have been* aware, the official has not inflicted punishment in violation of the Eight Amendment.

In *Popham v. City of Talladega* (1990), the court applied the "strong like-lihood" test of deliberate indifference in the suicide of an intoxicated pre-trial detainee. The estate brought a § 1983 action against city and jail officials, claiming that their son had the right to be protected from committing suicide while confined, that officials failed to properly monitor him, and that officers were not properly trained to recognize indicators of suicide. Popham was placed in a holding cell, and his belt, shoes, socks, and the contents of his pockets were removed. His cell was monitored by closed-circuit televi-sion, and he was periodically monitored physically. The last physical check was at 11:00 P.M. At 5:00 A.M., he was discovered hanging from his cell bars by his jeans.

The appeals court affirmed the lower court decisions that jail personnel were not deliberately indifferent because they were unaware of any suicidal tendencies. The court held that suicides in custody are analogous to the fail-ure to provide medical care, and deliberate indifference is the proper standard of review in such cases, regardless of the status of the prisoner. The deliberate indifference standard as applied to suicide cases requires a strong likelihood, rather than a mere possibility, that self-inflicted harm will occur. Personnel followed standard procedures and a failure to train officers in screening for suicidal tendencies did not provide a basis for imposing liability. Further, in *Bell v. Stinger* (1991), the court ruled that although an intoxicated detainee threatened to kill himself and officers failed to respond or to remove his belt during a search, this did not rise to the level of deliberate indifference, because there was no "strong likelihood" of a suicide attempt.

In *Sanders v. Howze* (1999), the Eleventh Circuit Court of Appeals fol-lowed the same line of reasoning as *Popham*. After the lower court denied summary judgment, the appellate court reversed the decision and held that the jail officials were entitled to qualified immunity in the suicide of the detainee. Several weeks after his confinement, the detainee removed the razor from a disposable razor and cut his wrists. He was transported to the local hospital, per jail policy, and was later transferred to a state hospital, where he remained for several months. He returned to the jail and was placed in the general population, where within two days he used a pencil to reopen his ear-lier wound. He was again transported to the hospital and treated. He was transferred to the state hospital a second time and later released back to the jail and placed in an observation cell. The county petitioned the court for a psychiatric evaluation, but before the request was granted the detainee hanged himself with a bed sheet. The court ruled that jail officials were not deliberately indifferent to the needs of the detainee and followed established policy in responding to him.

Suicide Risk Factors

The question of whether a detainee's past or current behaviors are indicative of a suicidal "profile" often arises. This question posed is asserted by the plaintiff in many legal actions regarding custodial suicide. The claim is that the decedent "fit" the profile and officers failed to recognize it, and therefore should be held liable. In an attempt to establish a foundation for such an argument, the plaintiff will cite studies suggesting that the decedent characterized the "typical" in-custody suicide.

The use of a profile is highly controversial, and the research on suicide points toward patterns and risk factors that correctional personnel should observe. It is important to recognize that a definitive profile of potential custodial suicide on which all researchers agree does not exist (Plitt, 1997). With any research there are methodological problems that can skew the data. A significant problem in suicide research is that studies all examine the suicide without fully comparing the victim to other confined prisoners (Kennedy & Homant, 1988). In other words, why did other detainees in the same facility not commit suicide? Does one "profile" fit all prisoners and all locations? These types of questions are ignored in many studies. Rather than claiming that a prisoner fit a profile and committed a jail suicide, it would be more precise to state that a suicide happened to occur while a detainee was confined in a jail. Thus, a "typical suicide" does not exist in the confinement setting. What should be addressed are factors that may alert correctional personnel to potential risks of a detainee suicide and what constitutes awareness of suicide (see Figure 12.3). While such factors are not inclusive of every possible factor and may not apply to every detainee, they may be useful in training correctional personnel about the behavior of all detainees in housing assignments, and in potential medical care of the detainee. Understanding the behavior of all detainees in a detention or correctional setting can assist officers in being more proactive in reception procedures, removing items from a cell or from the detainee that could be used to commit suicide, utilization of cells and housing assignments, monitoring procedures, and services provided to prisoners. The mere fact that a detainee fits a "suicide profile," independent of other factors, does not support liability against correctional personnel that the prisoner was likely to commit suicide.

In *Zwalesky v. Manistee County* (1990), a detainee hanged himself 90 minutes after being placed in a detoxification cell at the jail. He had been arrested for spouse abuse, was intoxicated, and threatened to kill his relatives, the transporting officer, and himself. The court granted summary judgment to jail officials, because there was no showing that the jail officials violated any clearly established right possessed by the detainee.

Figure 12.3
Prisoner Suicide Awareness Factors

- Nature of arrest/transporting from transporting officer
- Prisoner's mental state/mental health history
- Prisoner expresses feelings of hopelessness
- Prisoner expresses he is thinking about killing himself
- Prisoner's history of suicide attempts
- Prisoner's intoxicated state
- Prisoner shows signs of depression
- Prisoner shows concern about a loss: a job, family, position in community, etc.
- Prisoner's behavior is anxious, afraid, angry, strange
- Prior arrests and convictions
- Prisoner's medical/medication history
- Prisoner charged with a "shocking" crime

Further, the court concluded that the right actually being asserted is the right of a detainee to be screened for suicidal tendencies and to have appropriate preventive measures taken. The general right to medical care, the court ruled, is not sufficient to establish a clear constitutional right to be screened for psychological problems.

In *Estate of Frank v. City of Beaver Dam* (1996), the estate of a detainee who committed suicide while confined in jail brought a § 1983 action against a detention officer. The court dismissed the case, holding that the officer was entitled to qualified immunity because he was not deliberately indifferent to the rights of the detainee. The court noted that although one officer was informed that the detainee had exhibited severe mood swings during transport to the jail, the detainee did not make any threats, cause any disturbances, stagger, slur his speech, or do anything bizarre that would have caused the officer to believe he was suicidal. The court determined that the detainee's quiet behavior as he walked to the cell and unresponsiveness to questions asked by the officer did not suggest that he was an imminent danger to himself. The court also noted that once the detainee was placed in his cell he later ate breakfast and engaged in a telephone conversation.

The district court in *Vinson v. Clarke County, Alabama* (1998) granted summary judgment to the defendant sheriff and detention officers in a detainee suicide. The estate brought a § 1983 claim against the sheriff and officers, asserting that the intoxicated detainee, with a blood-alcohol content of .205, clearly fit a suicidal profile in that he committed suicide within 30 minutes of confinement. The court determined that the county was not deliberately indifferent to the risks of suicide. The court further held that the risk of suicide among intoxicated detainees was not so obvious that the county's failure to remedy conditions of confinement that gave detainees the opportunity to commit suicide could be seen as showing deliberate indifference.

The Eighth Circuit Court of Appeals affirmed a lower court's decision to grant summary judgment for jail officials after a detainee committed suicide in *Liebe v. Norton* (1998). The court found that detention officers were not deliberately indifferent to the detainee's health and safety, because they classified him as a suicide risk, took precautionary measures by placing him in a holding cell, removed his shoes and belt, and periodically checked on him. The intake officer classified the detainee as a "suicide risk" because he admitted to previously attempting suicide and was taking clonazepam and Valium. Officers checked on the detainee at intervals ranging from 7 to 21 minutes, but did not turn on the audio system in the holding cell. The detainee used his long-sleeved shirt to hang himself from an electrical conduit in the cell. The family asserted that the officers failed to supervise their son, and that the county failed to test officers on their policy manual regarding custodial suicides. The court found that the county was not deliberately indifferent to the training of officers, because the policy manual outlined their duties step-by-step.

The issue of suicide risk was examined in *Payne for Hicks v. Churchill* (1998) by the Seventh Circuit Court of Appeals. The family brought a wrongful death action against city jail officials following the suicide of their son. The appellate court affirmed the lower court's dismissal on the suicide issue, but remanded the case on the excessive force claim. According to the court, the detainee's intoxication, his tattoo that questioned life, and his angry cursing did not indicate an obvious, substantial risk of suicide. The court found that failing to monitor the arrestee or recognize the risk of suicide was, at most, negligence. The man was admitted to a holding cell at 1:00 A.M. and died of suffocation after hanging himself with a blanket prior to 4:00 A.M.

Some courts, examining custodial suicides, have focused on the decedent's own responsibility in committing suicide rather on the alleged omissions of the officers. For example, in *Soles v. Ingham County* (2004), the court determined that the detainee was the direct cause of his death and not the actions or omissions of the detention officers or social worker. Frayer, the decedent, was placed in an observation cell for making comments about taking his life. After several days he promised a social worker that he would not kill himself and the social worker instructed officers to return him to the general population. During the afternoon prior to Frayer's suicide, a correctional officer noticed that he was acting strangely but did not transfer him back to the observation cell. Later that night Frayer committed suicide. His estate filed a legal action claiming that the social worker and the detention officer's actions amounted to deliberate indifference to Frayer's mental health needs. The court granted summary judgment to the defendants. The court concluded that Frayer's suicide was not the result of the defendants' actions or nonfeasance, but was a direct cause of his own actions. The court ruled that Frayer committed suicide while he was alone in his cell by hanging himself with a bed sheet, which was a result of his own volitional self-destructive action.

The Sixth Circuit Court of Appeals applied the deliberate indifference standard from the *Farmer* decision in *Bradley v. City of Ferndale* (2005) and also focused on the actions of the decedent. Bradley was admitted to the City of Ferndale's lock-up facility and placed in a cell pending transport to the Oakland County jail on an outstanding warrant. Admitting officers could smell alcohol on Bradley and heard him state that an officer should give him a gun so that he could kill himself. Booking officers followed the standard booking process, and removed his belt, shoes wallet, and jacket, but he was allowed to retain his shirt and pants. He was also given a blanket. Bradley was the only detainee in the lockup. At the time Bradley was admitted, Ferndale officers were handling a barricaded gunman situation, which left one officer, one supervisor, and a dispatcher at the stationhouse. At some point after placing Bradley in his cell, an officer observed him sleeping on his bunk with the blanket. The officers returned to monitoring the barricaded gunman situation. About 36 minutes after Bradley was placed in his cell, an officer made another cell check, and discovered Bradley unconscious, with the blanket tied around his neck. Officers immediately initiated CPR and summoned emergency medical personnel, but revival efforts were unsuccessful. Bradley's estate filed a § 1983 lawsuit claiming that the officers and city were deliberately indifferent to Bradley's known suicidal tendencies in violation of the Fourteenth Amendment.

The district court granted the defendant's motion for summary judgment and the plaintiff appealed. The appellate court affirmed the lower court's verdict. The court found that there was no evidence that the officers acted with deliberate indifference to the needs of Bradley. The court noted that the officers followed the proper booking procedures and departmental monitoring practices of making cell checks every 15 minutes. In fact, the court noted that the officers set a timer to remind themselves to make the checks. The court reasoned that removing the blanket from Bradley may have prevented his suicide but that did not equate to deliberate indifference and the policy of the department allowed numerous alternatives for officers to consider, but did not prohibit the removal of blankets. The court concluded that Bradley's own actions were the direct cause of his death and that the officers' actions did not manifest a conscious disregard for his welfare. Moreover, the court found no evidence that the city failed to train their officers in the risks and hazards of suicide prevention.

Failure to Train

As described earlier, claims of failure to train will frequently emerge in a wrongful death lawsuit. The same claim is commonly asserted in litigation arising from a suicide. The plaintiff will cite *Canton v. Harris* (1989), alleging that the agency was deliberately indifferent by failing to train officers in recognition of suicide indicators, policy issues, monitoring procedures, how to obtain medical or mental health care, and resuscitation procedures. As discussed below, the training standard of deliberate indifference is a high hurdle for the plaintiff to overcome.

In *Vine v. County of Ingham* (1995), a § 1983 claim was filed alleging deliberate indifference in training officers to recognize signs of drug or alcohol intoxication. In response to a disorderly conduct complaint, a deputy took into custody a male who complained of pain from ingesting methyl alcohol. Transport to a hospital was refused when the arrestee complained of stomach pain. The deputy transported the arrestee to the city lockup and transfer of custody was established. Vine was placed in the city lockup without medical examination, although he appeared intoxicated. During booking, he became belligerent and, due to prior suicide attempts, was placed in handcuffs in a maximum-security observation cell. During a security check later in the day, Vine was observed to have mucus or vomit coming from his mouth or nose. He had been in the cell for approximately two hours without medical attention, because officers thought he was sleeping. He was later transported to the hospital in a comatose condition and died shortly thereafter. The court ruled in favor of the officers, stating that there was no evidence of deliberate indifference to the medical needs of the arrestee, nor to the training of officers, because they had been trained in accordance with state minimum standards.

In *Pyka v. Village of Orland Park* (1995), the court granted summary judgment to city jail personnel in a case regarding the suicide of an 18-year-old detainee. The estate brought a § 1983 action claiming, among other things, that officials failed to properly train officers about the risks of prisoner suicides. The court held that officials were not liable for the suicide on the theory of failure to train officers on suicide awareness, absent any evidence that the municipality had a large suicide problem that it was ignoring or that statutes or regulations required officers to perform CPR on the detainee after he was discovered hanging in his cell.

In *Mathis v. Fairman* (1997), the Seventh Circuit Court of Appeals affirmed summary judgment granted by the lower court in a suicide that occurred in the Cook County Jail. The court found that jail personnel did not exhibit deliberate indifference toward the detainee. The court noted that after hearing that the detainee was fearful that someone might kill him, an officer placed the detainee in a holding cell and requested that a mental health professional speak with him. A psychologist concluded that the detainee did not pose a threat to himself, and officers placed him in the general population. The mother of the detainee alleged that jail officials failed to train officers about prisoner suicides and that they failed to adequately staff the facility. The court held that while it was the officer's first day on the job, he reported the strange behaviors of the detainee to a supervisor. These actions failed to rise to a level of deliberate indifference, despite only having completed a five-day orientation course. The court ruled that although officers may not have been trained in suicide prevention, the jail maintained a psychiatric unit for that purpose.

Compare, however, *Owens v. City of Philadelphia* (1998), in which the federal district court denied summary judgment to the defendants, ruling that the training program was deliberately indifferent to detainees' needs. According to the court, the detainee's statement to an officer that he felt "schizy" and that he was "going to hurt myself" raised questions of fact on issues of knowledge and deliberate indifference. The court held that it was not necessary to show that an officer believed harm would actually befall the detainee; rather, the plaintiff need only show that the official acted or failed to act despite his knowledge of substantial risk of serious harm. The officer summoned a psychiatrist knowing that she intended to issue a pass for the detainee to go to the mental health unit, but failed to note in the logbook the detainee's statement about harming himself. There was nothing in the record that indicated the pass was ever issued. The court further found that the officials' alleged conduct as policymakers with respect to inadequate training to prevent suicide by pretrial detainees was actionable under § 1983.

In examining claims for failure to train officers regarding issues of suicide awareness, a majority of courts are rejecting plaintiffs' claims if the defendants can show evidence of training or policies that direct officers in responding to detainees who exhibit a strong likelihood of suicide. For example, in *Harvey v. County of Ward* (2005), *Howard v. City of Atmore* (2004), and *Gray v. Tunica, Mississippi* (2003) the courts granted summary judgment, finding that the administrators had addressed issues surrounding suicides, including booking procedures, contacting health care personnel, initiating and monitoring detainees, and suicidal symptomologies, through training sessions and policies and procedures. In *Wever v. Lincoln County* (2004), however, the sheriff was denied qualified immunity on claims that he was deliberately indifferent to the training needs of detention officers and the risk of suicides in the jail. The jail incurred two suicides in a short period when officers gave blankets to detainees who were confined in isolation cells.

Summary

Two emerging areas of liability that have increased allegations of wrongful deaths have been described. Sudden deaths in police custody are a rare occurrence after a use-of-force confrontation, but the liability potential for a wrongful death can be critical. Law enforcement officers and administrators have many responsibilities for individuals in their custody. The police are not absolute guarantors of health, but they do owe a duty of care to arrestees in their custody who otherwise cannot care for themselves.

Based on case analysis, police agencies can insulate their officers and themselves from liability by taking a proactive stance in considering the following policy and training recommendations. Because these arrest situations allege excessive force, administrators are encouraged to first review and revise their use-of-force policy to ensure that officers are directed in using "objectively reasonable" force in accordance with the *Graham* holding. It should direct officers in the proper escalation and de-escalation in a variety of physical force techniques and equipment based on the arrestee's behavior. Included in the force policy should be a section devoted to the use of authorized restraints. This section should direct officers in using department-issued restraint devices that specify how to further restrain combative and "special needs" detainees. Because in a significant number of these incidents more than three officers respond, officers should receive training in "multiple officer response" or "team-takedown response." Such training can assist officers in using physical control techniques and force equipment more efficiently when faced with a violent encounter (Ross & Chan, 2005).

A second area of concern is transportation. Preliminary questions that need to be addressed are: Under what circumstances will police transport a maximally restrained person? How many officers should be involved? What type of vehicle will be used? If police do not transport, who will? These issues need to be examined and addressed pursuant to policy prior to the need arising. Procedures that direct officers in responding to the mentally or chemically impaired (special needs detainees) should be revised or developed. This policy should be structured within state standards for dealing with detainees who require medical or psychiatric treatment or hospitalization. The policy should direct officers in how to respond to this population, when to summon backup or a supervisor, when to summon medical or psychological assistance, and to what facility they should be transported. Taking proper precautions with at-risk detainees begins with policies that direct officers in justifiable decisions when encountering such individuals.

In compliance with the *Canton* decision, administrators are also encouraged to provide officers with regular training relevant to the policies identified. In many jurisdictions, police frequently encounter "special needs" individuals. As shown in the case examples, regular training should be provided in assisting officers in responding to "special needs" individuals, in recognizing behaviors and symptoms associated with in-custody deaths, such as the mentally ill and intoxicated. Officers should routinely receive realistic training that addresses skill competency and use-of-force decision-making in all authorized physical control tactics and restraint equipment (Ross & Jones, 1996). Further training should be regularly provided to officers in how to assess the medical/psychiatric condition of detainees, monitoring needs of detainees in restraints, and when to summon medical assistance for detainees involved in a violent force confrontation. Administrators are encouraged to require officers to maintain certification in first aid and CPR in order to help them recognize and respond to medical emergencies. Finally, periodic training that addresses the critical issues to be contained in an incident report should be provided.

If an agency experiences an in-custody death or suicide, the administrator should immediately contact his or her risk manager and legal counsel, and ensure that a thorough internal investigation is conducted. Using an independent agency to conduct the investigation should be considered. Moreover, the administrator is encouraged to immediately initiate an ongoing file by compiling all relevant policies, officer incident reports, training files of personnel involved, autopsy report, attending physician reports, emergency medical personnel reports, investigation reports, statements of all witnesses, photos and video of the incident scene, retrieving/saving all taped radio communications throughout the incident, in order to develop a timeline of the incident.

Liability concerns regarding custodial suicides were also discussed. The standard of review in these cases is whether there was a strong likelihood that the detainee or prisoner would commit suicide and whether officials were deliberately indifferent to a substantially known risk of harm. It is common for the plaintiff to allege that the decedent fit a suicide profile and that officers failed to recognize such symptoms.

While a "typical" suicide profile is nonexistent, the review of cases illustrates that detention agencies are likely to prevail in this type of litigation when proactive measures have been instituted and followed by agency personnel. It is important to underscore that maintaining a detention or correctional facility requires an understanding of prisoner behavior. Guidelines that direct officers in the performance of their duties in order to provide an orderly and safe operation should be developed. Not all custodial suicides can be prevented, but many can be averted through proper planning and careful adherence to a system of fundamental correctional strategies. This system should include a twofold approach: policy development and training. When developing a suicide awareness policy, administrators are encouraged to consider the following components: intake screening/assessment procedures for all prisoners, proper classification/housing of prisoners, levels of supervision and monitoring protocols, documentation of security checks, communication between detention officers and health care workers, when to summon health care professionals, detailed reporting, investigation of a suicide, and debriefing of facility personnel. Administrators should ensure that all directives comply with state minimum standards and court decisions for confining prisoners.

Moreover, all personnel having contact with prisoners should be trained in policies that direct decisions in responding to and supervising prisoners. Training should involve recognizing and understanding human behavior and common prisoner behavior, particularly toward understanding behavior of the mentally impaired and the chemically addicted.

References

Barrineau, H.E. III (1994). *Civil Liability in Criminal Justice*, Second Edition. Cincinnati, OH: Anderson Publishing Co.

Chan, T., G. Vilke, T. Neuman & J. Clausen (1997). "Restraint Position Asphyxia." *Annals of Emergency Medicine* 30:578-586.

Cohen, F. (1992). "Liability for Custodial Suicide: The Information Base Requirements." *Jail Suicide Update* 4:1-9.

del Carmen, R.V. (1991). *Civil Liabilities in American Policing: A Text for Law Enforcement Personnel*. Englewood Cliffs, NJ: Brady.

del Carmen, R.V. & V. Kappeler (1991). "Municipal and Police Agencies as Defendants: Liability for Official Policy and Custom." *American Journal of Police* 10:1-17.

Kappeler, V. (1997). *Critical Issues in Police Civil Liability*, Second Edition. Prospect Heights, IL: Waveland Press, Inc.

————, M. Vaughn & R.V. del Carmen (1991). "Death in Detention: An Analysis of Police Liability For Negligent Failure to Prevent Suicide." *Journal of Criminal Justice* 19:381-393.

Kennedy, D.B. & R.J. Homant (1988)." Predicting Custodial Suicides: Problems with the Use of Profiles." *Justice Quarterly* 5:441-456.

Plitt, E.A. (1997). *Police Civil Liability and the Defense of Citizen Misconduct*. Chicago, IL: Americans for Effective Law Enforcement.

Ross, D.L. & T.C. Chan (2006). *Sudden Deaths in Custody*. Totowa, NJ: Humana Press.

Ross, D.L. & M. Jones. (1996). "Frequency of Training in Less-Than-Lethal Force Tactics and Weapons: Results of a Two-State Study." *Journal of Contemporary Criminal Justice* 12:250-263.

Silver, I. (2000). *Police Civil Liability*. New York, NY: Matthew Bender & Co.

Cases Cited

Abraham v. Maes, 436 So. 2d 1099 (La. Dist. Ct. App. 1983)

Animashaun v. O'Donnell, 1994 U.S. Dist. Lexis 17339 (N.D. Ill.)

Bell v. Wolfish, 441 U.S. 520 (1979)

Bell v. Stinger, 937 F.2d 1340 (8th Cir. 1991)

Bozeman v. Orum, 199 F. Supp. 2d 1216 (M.D. Ala. 2002)

Bishop v. Corsentino, 371 F. 3d 1203 (10th Cir. 2004)

Bradley v. City of Ferndale, 148 Fed. Appx. 499 (6th Cir. 2005)

Brinkman v. City of Indianapolis, 231 N.E.2d 169 (Ind. Ct. App. 1967)

Brown v. Lee, 639 So. 2d 897 (La. Dist. Ct. App. 1994)

City of Canton v. Harris, 489 U.S. 378 (1989)

City of Revere v. Massachusetts General Hospital, 463 U.S. 239 (1983)

Cottrell v. Caldwell, 85 F.3d 1480 (11th Cir. 1996)

Cruz v. City of Laramie, Wyoming, 239 F.3d 1183 (10th Cir. 2001)

DeShaney v. Winnebago County Department of Social Services, 489 U.S. 189 (1989)

Del Tufo v. Township of Old Bridge, 685 A.2d 1267 (N.J. 1996)

East v. City of Chicago, 719 F. Supp. 683 (N.D. Ill. 1989)

Elmes v. Hart, 1994 Tenn. App. Lexis 278 (Tenn. Ct. App. 1994)

Estate of Fank v. City of Beaver Dam, 921 F. Supp. 590 (E.D. Wis. 1996)

Estelle v. Gamble, 429 U.S. 97 (1976)

Estate of Phillips v. City of Milwaukee, 928 F. Supp. 817 (E.D. Wis. 1996)

Farmer v. Brennan, 511 U.S. 285 (1994)

Frey v. City of Herculaneum, 44 F.3d 667 (8th Cir. 1995)

Fruge v. City of New Orleans, 613 So. 2d 811 (La. Dist. Ct. App. 1993)

Graham v. Connor, 490 U.S. 386 (1989)

Gray v. Tunica County, Mississippi, 279 F. Supp. 2d 789 (N.D. 2003)

Guseman v. Martinez, 1 F. Supp. 2d 1240 (D. Kan. 1998).

Hare v. City of Corinth, 74 F.3d 633 (5th Cir. 1996)

Harris v. District of Columbia, 932 F.2d 10 (D.C. Cir. 1991)

Harvey v. County of Ward, 352 F. Supp. 1003 (D.N.D. 2005)

Hoyer v. City of Southfield, 2003 U.S. Dist. Lexis 5835 (E.D. Mich.)

Howard v. City of Atmore, 887 So. 2d 201 (N.D. Ala. 2003)

Johnson v. City of Cincinnati, 39 F. Supp. 2d 1013 (S.D. Ohio 1999)

Johnson v. Glick, 481 F.2d 1028 (2d Cir. 1973)

Jones v. Devaney, Lexis 13700 107 Fed. Appx. 709 (9th Cir. 2004)

Liebe v. Norton, 157 F.3d 574 (8th Cir. 1998)

Love v. Bolinger, 927 F. Supp. 1131 (E.D. Ind. 1998)

Mathis v. Fairman, 120 F.3d 88 (7th Cir. 1997)

Maynard v. Hopwood, 105 F.3d 1226 (8th Cir. 1997)

Monell v. Department of Social Services, 436 U.S. 658 (1978)

Nelson v. Los Angeles County, 113 Cal. App. 4th (Cal. App. 2003)

Owens v. City of Philadelphia, 6 F. Supp. 2d 373 (E.D. Pa. 1998)

Payne for Hicks v. Churchill, 161 F.3d 1030 (7th Cir. 1998)

Pliakos v. City of Manchester, New Hampshire, 2003 U.S. Dist. Lexis 12589 (D.N.H.)

Popham v. City of Talladega, 908 F.2d 1561 (11th Cir. 1990)

Price v. County of San Diego, 990 F. Supp. 1230 (S.D. Cal. 1998)

Pyka v. Village of Orland Park, 906 F. Supp. 1196 (N.D. Ill. 1995)

Rochin v. California, 342 U.S. 165 (1952)

Sanders v. Howze, 177 F.3d 1245 (11th Cir. 1999)

Shuff v. Zurich, 173 So. 2d 393 (La. Dist. Ct. App. 1965)

Simpson v. Hines, 903 F.2d 400 (5th Cir. 1990)

Sims v. Greenville County, 221 F.3d 1265 (4th Cir. 2000)

Smith v. Wilson County, 10 Fed. Appx. 118 (E.D.N.C. 2000)

Soles v. Ingham County, 316 F. Supp. 2d 536 (W.D. Mich. 2004)

Swans v. City of Lansing, 65 F. Supp. 2d 625 (W.D. Mich. 1998)

Tennessee v. Garner, 471 U.S. 1 (1985)

Thomas v. Williams, 124 S.E.2d 409 (Ga. Ct. App. 1962)

Tindall v. Multnomah County, 570 P.2d 979 (Or. Ct. App. 1977)

Vine v. County of Ingham, 884 F. Supp. 1153 (W.D. Mich. 1995)

Vinson v. Clarke County, Alabama, 10 F. Supp. 2d 1282 (S.D. Ala. 1998)

Wagar v. Hasenkrug, 486, F. Supp. 47 (D. Mont. 1980)

Watkins v. New Castle County, 374 F. Supp. 2d 379 (D. Del. 2005)

Wever v. Lincoln County, 388 F.3d 601 (8th Cir. 2004)

Wright v. Collins, 766 F.2d 841 (5th Cir. 1985)

Young v. City of Mount Ranier, 238 F.3d 567 (4th Cir. 2001)

Zwalesky v. Manistee County, 749 F. Supp. 815 (W.D. Mich. 1990)

Chapter 13

Personnel Issues and Liability

In Chapters 6 and 7, theories of administrative and supervisory liability under § 1983 were discussed. A citizen or prisoner plaintiff may bring a § 1983 action for deficient hiring and retention practices, failure to properly assign or supervise, failure to direct, negligent entrustment, and failure to train subordinate personnel. An additional emerging area of liability for administrators is personnel litigation. Line-level personnel have brought legal actions against superiors for civil rights violations, sexual harassment, wrongful termination, Americans with Disabilities Act violations, fair labor law violations, and general discrimination in the workplace. This chapter will address the liability issues associated with employment and personnel issues.

Liability and Sexual Harassment

Sexual harassment has become one of the most potentially critical management problems faced by the administrator. More than 15,500 lawsuits alleging sexual harassment in the workplace are initiated annually. Sexual harassment claims filed with the Equal Employment Opportunity Commission have more than doubled since 1991 (Toplitt, 1999).

Claims of sexual harassment fall within the purview of Title VII of the Civil Rights Act of 1964 under the general prohibition of sexual discrimination in the "terms, conditions, or privileges of employment." Title VII prohibits employment discrimination based on gender, race, national origin, or religion. Failure to act appropriately not only has adverse effects for the agency, but also may result in supervisory liability and disciplinary action.

The courts are increasingly reviewing sexual harassment cases, and several have emerged in corrections. *In Speed v. Ohio Dep't of Rehabilitation and Correction* (1994), the court awarded a female correctional officer

$7,500 in damages for invasion of privacy based on a male supervisor's obser-vation of her from the ceiling of a prison restroom. In *Holland v. New Jer-sey Department of Corrections* (2001), the court awarded $3.74 million to correctional employees who alleged racial and sexual harassment and dis-crimination in the workplace. Conversely, in *Spicer v. Commonwealth of Vir-ginia Department of Corrections* (1995), the Court of Appeals found correctional officials not liable for employees who made sexual remarks about a female employee's breasts when the department made a prompt and effec-tive response to remedy the situation after she complained. In addition, the Missouri Department of Corrections settled four sexual harassment cases over 18 months totaling $177,500 (Associated Press, 2004). The cases involved four female correctional officers who had been harassed by male officers and supervisors. Collectively, the cases showed a departmental culture of poli-cies and practices that condoned harassment and tolerated a "code of silence." The DOC reported that it disciplined 22 employees for sexual harassment over three years: three were fired, one was reprimanded, and the rest were suspended for varying amounts of time.

Claims of sexual harassment have also emerged in policing. Ross (2000) reported in a review of more than 1,500 § 1983 published decisions from 1989 to 1999 that "police as plaintiff" is an emerging liability area that cites admin-istrators for failure to train officers. Throughout the 1990s, a significant num-ber of claims alleging sexual harassment were filed primarily by female officers against their supervisors and fellow male officers. Vaughn, Cooper, and del Carmen (2001) found, in a survey of 849 Texas police chiefs, that 12 percent of the respondents had incurred a lawsuit from an officer within the preceding three years. These chiefs reported that they lost 41 percent of the cases. They also reported that they are commonly sued for allegations of: sexual harassment (25%), disciplinary actions (24%), employment dis-crimination (13%), overtime/compensation/pay issues (10%), race dis-crimination/reverse discrimination (7%), and disability discrimination (4%).

The city of Los Angeles, California, was ordered to pay $1.7 million for Los Angeles police employees claiming sexual discrimination and racial harassment (Associated Press, 2000a). A total of 24 women and four men alleged acts of discrimination, sexual harassment, or retaliation while serv-ing on the force in cases filed from 1994 to 2000. The lead plaintiff claimed that she was subjected to racist remarks, sexist comments, and on one occa-sion was grabbed by a fellow officer while other officers watched and laughed. It was alleged that female officers who complained about sexual harassment were subjected to death threats and left stranded without backup in emergencies. One female officer settled out of court for $175,000. Other cases involved male employees who said their supervisors harassed them. Two officers claimed that they faced retaliation after their wives sued the LAPD.

Other examples include two separate sexual harassment claims that were settled by the FBI in 1993 and in 2000. The Associated Press (1993) reported that a former female agent was awarded $300,000 because she claimed that her superior harassed her for 10 years. This was the first sexual harassment case brought against the FBI. In the 2000 case, the Associated Press reported that another former female FBI agent had settled a sex discrimination claim for $150,000. She claimed that she had been harassed by co-workers and her supervisor over a period of many years, denied equal job treatment, and was punished when she complained.

Sexual Harassment Defined

The Equal Employment Opportunity Commission (EEOC) guidelines on sexual harassment (29 C.F.R. § 1604.11, 1995), define sexual harassment as "unwelcome sexual advances, requests for sexual favors, and other verbal or physical conduct of a sexual nature." These factors constitute sexual harassment when: (1) such conduct is made a term or condition of employment; (2) such conduct is used as a basis for employment decisions affecting the person; and (3) such conduct has the purpose or effect of interfering with an employee's performance, or creates an intimidating, hostile, or offensive work environment. In *Anthony v. County of Sacramento Sheriff's Department* (1994), a female deputy stated a cause of action for sexual harassment claiming a hostile work environment and inadequate training in department policy. In *Farmers Insurance Group v. County of Santa Clara* (1995), the county settled out of court in a sexual harassment claim for $1,283,000 for failing to train and develop policy on sexual harassment. A male deputy's sexual harassment of three female deputies, including one for whom he had training responsibility, was not within the scope of his employment.

Types of Sexual Harassment

Sexual harassment claims have been separated into two categories. The first, *quid pro quo* sexual harassment, occurs when a supervisor conditions an employment benefit or continued employment on the employee's acquiescence in sexual behavior. The liability associated with this term is limited to circumstances in which a "tangible economic action" has been taken with respect to the employee.

The second type is known as "hostile or offensive work environment" sexual harassment. No employment benefits need be gained or lost, and this type of harassment may be engaged in not only by managers or supervisors, but also by co-workers or persons who are not even employed by the employer. This type of sexual harassment occurs when sexual jokes, graffiti, suggestive remarks, cartoons, physical interference with movement such as blocking or following, or sexually derogatory comments create a hostile work environment. Thus, if a supervisor said to an employee, "Go out with me and you will do well in the organization," this would be considered *quid pro quo* sexual harassment, even if nothing detrimental (or positive) actually occurred. If no "tangible economic action" resulted, such a comment would be considered part of a hostile work environment.

Evans v. Leelanau County Sheriff's Department (1994) is illustrative of both types of sexual harassment. Evans, a female correctional officer, was the victim of sexual harassment from the sheriff, her sergeant, and several correctional officers over a period of 18 months. The sheriff told her that she should lose weight, wear her uniform so that it would outline her "figure" better, and that she had a nice set of "jugs." The sheriff would summon Evans to his office, where he would have open in plain view a lingerie catalog and state that he would "enjoy seeing her in one of those outfits." The sheriff would occasionally brush up against her in the hallway, and pat and stroke her hair. The department primarily employed males and there was only one restroom. Male employees left pornographic magazines opened in the restroom and would also leave them opened on the booking counter, dispatch area, officers' control room, and virtually any area to which officers had access. Pictures of nude women were pinned on several of the walls in the control room. Evans complained to her sergeant and later to the sheriff, but nothing changed. There was no policy against sexual harassment within the department. She filed a lawsuit asserting hostile work environment sexual harassment. The county settled out of court for an undisclosed amount.

Plaintiffs have also filed legal actions alleging retaliation because they reported or filed a sexual harassment complaint. In *Barth v. The Village of Mokena* (2004), a female police officer prevailed when she sued on a claim of retaliation. Barth claimed that the chief customarily condoned a work climate of harassment. She alleged that she was subject to ongoing incidents of harassment and because she reported the incidents to supervisors, she was treated differently. She claimed that she was denied assignments, subjected to unwarranted and disproportionate disciplinary action, denied backup, and denied compensation for training time. Further, she claimed that the chief discriminated against women because of gender and that the chief, as the policymaker, created and perpetuated a hostile work environment. The chief denied the claims and filed a motion with the court for a dismissal.

The court rejected the chief's motion and held that he violated Barth's constitutional rights as he was the official policymaker. In that capacity, the court concluded that his actions expressed a widespread practice and official policy that was well settled, amounting to a custom of official conduct, creating a hostile work environment. Barth did not have to be any more specific with her claims to demonstrate examples of retaliation for reporting sexual harassment.

United States Supreme Court Decisions

In three landmark decisions, the United States Supreme Court set the standard for administrative liability in cases alleging sexual harassment. The cases of *Faragher v. City of Boca Raton* (1998) and *Burlington Industries, Inc. v. Ellerth* (1998) established the rule that an administrator is responsible for the misdeeds of an employee when that employee uses the agency relationship to accomplish the misbehavior. The Court in *Ellerth* declared that a tangible employment action was a "significant change in employment status, such as hiring, firing, failing to promote, reassignment with significantly different responsibilities, or a decision causing a significant change in benefits." The supervisor's action must inflict some direct economic harm. If the harassment does not result in a tangible job detriment, an employer still may be liable for hostile work environment sexual harassment engaged in by managers or supervisors. The Court stated that in such instances, the employer may affirmatively avoid liability if it can show that: (1) it used reasonable care to prevent and correct harassment (such as having a policy on the subject), and (2) the employee unreasonably failed to make a complaint under the policy or to avoid harm otherwise.

Justice Souter noted that the primary purpose of Title VII "is not to provide redress but avoid harm." In keeping with Congress's intent to prevent sexual harassment, the Court decided to model its rule on the premise that an administrator should be rewarded for making an effort to stop harassment. Along with the administrator's responsibility to thwart sexual harassment, the Court also recognized the victim's responsibility to avoid harm by using the agency's antiharassment policy.

In a third case, the Court further expanded employer liability under Title VII. In *Oncale v. Sundowner Offshore Services, Inc.* (1998), the Court held that sexual harassment includes same-sex harassment. Oncale worked for Sundowner on an oil rig as a "roustabout" with an eight-man crew. He alleged that he was subjected to sex-related, humiliating actions against him by members of the crew, including his supervisor. On more than one occasion, he alleged he was physically assaulted in a sexual manner and threatened with rape. He finally filed suit against the company after repeated complaints to management were ignored. The district court and the Fifth Circuit Court of Appeals found in favor of the company. Oncale appealed to the United States Supreme Court and they granted certiorari.

The Court examined the issue of whether same-sex harassment is actionable under Title VII. The Court held that same-sex sexual harassment is clearly actionable. The Court ruled that "when members of one sex are exposed to disadvantageous terms or conditions of employment to which members of the opposite sex are not exposed," such conduct is actionable. Moreover, the Court explained that Title VII is not a "civility" code designed to remedy all interpersonal problems in the workplace. It forbids only objectively offensive conduct that alters the conditions of the victim's employment. The Court cautioned courts and juries to distinguish this type of conduct from ordinary socializing in the workplace, such as "intersexual flirtation" or "male-on-male horseplay," which are not within the scope of the antidiscrimination law.

The decisions in *Burlington* and *Faragher* emphasize that if an employer shows that it acted reasonably to prevent and correct sexual harassment, and that the employee unreasonably failed to avoid harm, it can successfully avoid liability. If, however, the employer fails to satisfy the Court's requirements, liability will attach (Collins & Vaughn, 2004). In some cases in which the employer is unable to avoid liability completely, the affirmative defense may be used to mitigate damages if the employee could have avoided some but not all of the harm that occurred.

Gonzales v. New York State Department of Corrections (2002) provides an instructive example of an employer failing to take action when there was knowledge. A female correctional officer brought suit under Title VII on allegations of sexual harassment and a hostile work environment. The court ruled in favor of the officer, finding that she been subjected to a hostile work environment for more than a year and that the department failed to take any action after she had repeatedly reported it to supervisory personnel. The court found that she had incurred a pattern of offensive behaviors almost daily, which included male officers using derogatory terms such as "nigger" and "spic" in her presence, and calling her and other female officers "bitches." The court concluded that such unchecked behavior amounted to a hostile work environment in accordance with Title VII and awarded her $100,000.

In *Pennsylvania State Police v. Suders* (2004), the United States Supreme Court examined the issue of sexual harassment and constructive discharge in a police department for the first time. Suders was a communications operator for the Pennsylvania State Police and claimed that from the beginning of her employment male supervisors harassed her. Suders claimed that the harassment continued throughout her employment, which eventually led to her quitting the job. She alleged that supervisors would talk about having sex with animals, would talk about how to "satisfy" a man orally, and would make obscene gestures in her presence. She complained to the EEOC in Pennsylvania but did not receive any relief. In retaliation, she was arrested by PSP on false charges and before they could officially file the charges, she resigned.

She filed a Title VII claim, alleging sexually harassment and claimed that she was constructively discharged from her job. The lower court granted judgment for the department, stating that Suders never gave the department a chance to respond to her complaints. The court did not address her claim that she was forced to resign because of the hostile work environment. She appealed and the appellate court reversed the lower court's decision. The court determined that the lower court should have addressed her constructive discharge claim and that constructive discharge was a tangible employment action, thereby making the department automatically (and strictly) liable for the supervisors' actions in the event Suders proved her sexual harassment claim. The Supreme Court reviewed the case to determine whether the employer could be held liable. The appellate court's decision that a constructive discharge was always a tangible employment action was too limiting.

In an 8 to 1 decision, the Court reversed the decision and remanded the case to the lower court for further proceedings. The Court reasoned that an employee's decision to quit could be construed as a constructive discharge where the abuse endured was so "intolerable" that resignation was deemed a "firing response." The employer, however, would have a defense to such a claim when it could prove: (1) it had a "readily accessible and effective policy" in place for reporting and resolving sexual harassment complaints and (2) the employee failed to take advantage of the employer's policy. The Court also held that the employer would not have a defense, however, if the employee could demonstrate the decision to quit resulted from "an employer-sanctioned adverse action," which resulted in an official change in employment status or situation, e.g., humiliating demotion, severe pay cut, or transfer to a position where the employee would be faced with unbearable working conditions.

Sexual Misconduct by Correctional Employees

A related and emerging area for correctional supervisors are claims of sexual misconduct by correctional staff with female prisoners. Correctional employee-on-prisoner misconduct involves a range of behaviors, ranging from lewd comments to voyeurism to assault and rape. Since 1999, the federal government, 41 states, and the District of Columbia have passed laws criminalizing some types of staff sexual misconduct (GAO, 1999). Supervisors must be diligent in investigating prisoner complaints about correctional officer sexual misconduct.

To investigate this emerging problem, researchers from the General Accounting Office (GAO, 1999) conducted a study of female prisoners and sexual misconduct by correctional staff. The study examined 506 allegations of sexual misconduct between 1995 and 1998 in four jurisdictions: California Department of Corrections, the Federal Bureau of Prisons, the Texas Department of Corrections, and the District of Columbia. Only adult female institutions were studied and not detention facilities. Of the 506 claims filed, 18 percent were sustained in which a high percentage of staff resigned or were terminated. All four jurisdictions were involved in at least two civil lawsuits. Allegations ranged from verbal harassment, improper surveillance, improper touching, and/or consensual sex. Allegations of rape or other types of forced sexual assault were relatively rare. None of the jurisdictions had a tracking system in place that readily made available comprehensive data on the topic.

The GAO also reported that at least 23 departments of corrections had faced class action or individual damage suits related to sexual misconduct. During the 1990s, the Justice Department filed civil lawsuits alleging systemic sexual misconduct by male correctional staff in womens' prisons in two states (Arizona and Michigan). Both suits were filed in 1997 under the Civil Rights of Institutionalized Persons Act of 1980, which is designed to protect the rights of people housed in state and local government institutions. In 1999 the state of Arizona and the Justice Department entered into a settlement agreement, which requires Arizona to revise employee and prisoner training, strengthen investigative techniques, and requires male officers to announce their presence prior to entering female housing units, when feasible. Moreover, the state of Michigan also entered into a similar settlement with the Justice Department regarding male officers working in female housing units.

The court in *Women Prisoners v. District of Columbia* (1994) found a pattern of sexual harassment by employees, including assaults, a lack of response and, at times, an inadequate response. Part of the harassment involved unjustified invasions of privacy by male officers. Medical examination policies were not followed and illnesses were not responded to. Prenatal care of pregnant prisoners was grossly inadequate, as were general prison conditions. The evidence revealed a level of sexual harassment that was so malicious that it violated the Eighth Amendment.

Although the GAO study focused on adult prison systems, county detention facilities have incurred civil liability for officer sexual misconduct. In *Ware v. Jackson County* (1998), widespread and condoned misconduct of jail employees created county liability when "rampant sexual misconduct" toward female prisoners was proven. Refusal to terminate an assaultive employee, to monitor him after a termination recommendation had been made, or to investigate several incidents demonstrated deliberate indifference. Compare, however, *Thomas v. Galveston County* (1997), in which liability did not attach against the county. A female prisoner alleged that a male detention officer sexually assaulted and harassed her during the three months she was confined in the jail. She did not complain to the officer's superiors, because he threatened her until after the final assault. She notified a supervisor and an investigation began immediately. The investigation revealed that several officers had assaulted the plaintiff and other female prisoners. Based on the investigation, the officers were disciplined and one officer was terminated and criminally prosecuted. The county was granted summary judgment because there was no evidence that the county knew about the officers' conduct and disregarded it. Female prisoners did not inform officials until after the last assault, and the investigation revealed the officers' misconduct. The county had policies in place, and once they were informed of the misconduct they promptly investigated, disciplined the officers, and terminated one officer.

Likewise, consistent discipline with officers by supervisors rebuffed claims of sexual assault in *Hegenmiller v. Enda Mahan Correctional Institution for Women* (2005). Two female prisoners alleged that a correctional officer sexually assaulted them over a two-year period of their confinement.

When a captain learned of the allegations, he reported the allegations to his superiors and an investigation led to the termination and prosecution of the officer. Further investigation revealed that another officer was involved and the first officer had covered for his participation in the repeated assaults. The second officer was also fired.

Prior to the assaults, the prison had instituted policies and training for the officers that prohibited sexual contact with prisoners. Further, administrators verbally informed officers that they would be investigated, fired, and prosecuted if they had sexual contact with prisoners. Prior to the firing of the two officers, there were six incidents involving six officers for such assaults on female prisoners. Five were fired and prosecuted. The prisoners claimed that the administration knew of other incidents of sexual assault but failed to investigate them and filed a lawsuit, claiming deliberate indifference to the risk of assaults. They also claimed that the administration failed to provide training to officers and failed to implement adequate policies on prisoner and officer contacts. The lower court granted summary judgment to the prison administration and the prisoners appealed. The appellate court affirmed the lower court's decision, concluding that the administration was not deliberately indifferent to sexual assaults in the prison. Moreover, the court ruled that the administrators did not fail to train the officers. The prisoners failed to show that the administration's actions were linked to the conduct of the officers who were fired. They also failed to show that they faced a substantial risk of harm to which the administration acted with deliberate indifference. The court underscored the fact that the administration vigorously enforced their own policy; had investigated, fired, and prosecuted officers in the past, as well as in this incident. The court failed to find any evidence that the administration looked the other way or tried to intervene on behalf of any officer who violated the no-contact rule.

Supervisory Liability

While some claims of sexual harassment against co-workers have been cited, a significant number have been filed against the employee's supervisor or administrator. An administrator is generally liable for sexual harassment of his or her employees when the harassment results in a "tangible employment action," such as termination, demotion, or unwarranted transfer; and the harassment results in a severe or pervasive hostile work environment created by the supervisor. Regarding conduct between co-workers, an employer is responsible for acts of sexual harassment in the workplace when the employer knows, or should have known, of the harassment. Supervisory liability will not attach when the supervisor can show evidence of acting reasonably to prevent harassment by acting promptly to correct the behavior. In *Williamson v. City of Houston, Texas* (1998), a police officer repeatedly complained to her sergeant that a male officer was sexually harassing her by commenting on her body, pulling her hair, sticking his tongue in her ear, and trying to look up her skirt and down her neckline. The female officer then asserted that after she complained, the sergeant retaliated against her by criticizing and taunting her, giving her a written reprimand, and transferring her to a less desirable position. Rejecting the city's claim that it should not be held liable because it did not have proper notice of the harassment, the Fifth Circuit Court of Appeals held that when the officer first complained to the sergeant, a supervisor, the city was placed on notice.

In *Wright v. Rolette County* (2005), an appellate court reversed a lower court's decision on a sexual harassment and constructive discharge claim. Wright complained that she was subjected to sexist and offensive language daily and was embarrassed that men in the department called her a "big-breasted Canadian secretary," a dizzy [expletive]," and "Canadian bacon." The sheriff admitted that he participated in the name-calling in front of others, including at a peace officer's meeting. The sheriff also implied that there was a camera in the female restroom, so she began using the restroom designated for female prisoners. The sheriff allegedly made vulgar comments about Wright's anatomy and requested a sexual favor. Wright claimed that she objected to these comments but they were ignored. While she attended correctional officer training, she completed sexual harassment training but did not make a formal complaint, fearing she would lose her job. She did complain to a county commissioner but he stated that there was nothing that he could do. She also complained to the county attorney, but the county did nothing to remedy the situation.

A week later, Wright was diagnosed by her physician with high blood pressure, anxiety, depression, and he prescribed her medication. Wright gave notice a few days later, alleging that the sheriff's behavior caused a hostile work environment. Wright was placed on paid leave pending an investigation, after which an attorney concluded the comments were inappropriate but not unwelcome. Wright returned to work and quit three months later, claiming she was constructively discharged. She sued, alleging sexual harassment and the sheriff requested qualified immunity; the lower court refused, and he appealed.

The sheriff was not immune on Wright's harassment charges, but the court did grant immunity on the claims of constructive discharge. According to the court, the sheriff's conduct could be considered sexual harassment even if he did not touch Wright or make sexual advances toward her. Wright's allegations showed a violation of her constitutional rights, requiring her to seek medical treatment. Because the sheriff received complaints from Wright and did nothing to address the allegations, liable attached. The court, however found that Wright failed to show that she was constructively discharged because of the harassment, and the sheriff was granted qualified immunity. Wright failed to demonstrate that the working conditions were intolerable for a reasonable person as it appeared that the harassment stopped after she returned to work.

Responding with an investigation to a claim of sexual harassment and following through with appropriate discipline was useful in defending such a claim. In *Rudd v. Shelby County* (2006), Rudd, a deputy sheriff, filed a complaint of sexual harassment with her superior and an investigation was conducted by internal affairs. Rudd reported that a sergeant handcuffed her in a bent-over position, to a file cabinet. She also reported that the sergeant rubbed himself against her, draped a chain around her neck, and asked her over the intercom, if it was "too hot in the kitchen for her." During the investigation Rudd was allowed to work in a separate facility to avoid contact with the sergeant. Within a month, the department reprimanded two of Rudd's supervisors. The sergeant was demoted to patrol officer, suspended for 30 days, and placed on probation for six months. The sergeant ultimately retired under a settlement agreement. Rudd left her job within two weeks of the harassment and sued, claiming that the sergeant's actions constituted sexual harassment, gender discrimination, and a hostile work environment under federal and state law. The court denied the county's motion for summary judgment and a jury awarded her $1 million in compensatory damages, back pay, and lost future wages.

The county appealed the award and the appellate court reversed the judgment. Because the sergeant was Rudd's co-worker and not her supervisor, Rudd had to show that her employer knew or should have known of the harassment and failed to take prompt action. The court agreed that the sergeant's conduct was shocking, but because the county responded with good faith to safeguard Rudd, liability did not attach. The court determined that Rudd did not prove that the county failed to take prompt action. Within several weeks the sergeant was disciplined and the county followed through with the discipline.

In *McCurdy v. Arkansas State Police* (2004), the court examined whether a single incident of supervisor harassment was enough to hold the employer strictly liable. McCurdy was a dispatcher for the Arkansas State Police (ASP) and within a short time of her employment her supervisor began harassing her. The one-time incident occurred in the dispatch room and McCurdy quickly left the room following the action, where there was offensive touching. McCurdy informed another dispatcher but would not report the episode until a higher-ranking supervisor responded. A subsequent investigation found that McCurdy's supervisor had violated departmental policy against sexual harassment and was subsequently disciplined. McCurdy filed a lawsuit claiming a hostile work environment and sexual harassment. The court rejected the claim and granted judgment for the department. The court concluded that there was no tangible employment action that occurred and because the department followed the principles in the *Suders* case by promptly investigating and disciplining the harasser, liability could not attach.

The Supreme Court has sent a clear message that Title VII requires employers to try to prevent sexual harassment in the workplace and to provide appropriate discipline as warranted. These cases require administrators not only to have a sexual harassment policy, but the agency must also aggressively enforce that policy by promptly correcting any sexually harassing behavior (Rossi, 1998; Figure 13.1) Supervisors must be familiar with the agency's sexual harassment policy and provide periodic training to all employees.

Figure 13.1
Procedures to Follow When Investigating Harassment Claims

- Fully investigate all complaints

- Ensure that investigators are well trained

- Upon receiving the complaint, do not delay the investigation

- When practical, reassign employees involved in the complaint

- Use an impartial investigator

- Remain neutral with the individual you are interviewing

- Keep the investigation confidential

- Interview all potential witnesses

- Stay in touch with the complainant, accused, and witnesses

- Take action, regardless of the investigation outcome

- Take advantage of the opportunity to e-educate the department about harassment

When the supervisor is on notice of sexual harassment, Title VII requires the administrator to take some action to stop the harassment. This still is not sufficient to avoid liability. The administrator must prove that the complainant unreasonably failed to prevent or correct the problem by taking advantage of the sexual harassment policy or by correcting the problem in some other way. To meet this component of the defense, administrators must encourage their employees to take advantage of the policy by promptly investigating and documenting all complaints and by preventing retaliation against those who do complain. Further, in accordance with the Supreme Court's decision in *Suders*, if an employee can prove that she or he resigned as a result of prohibited conduct by a supervisor, while the supervisor acted under his or her official capacity, the employer will be automatically liable for that supervisor's conduct, i.e., the employer will not have a defense to a constructive discharge claim. Administrators are encouraged to critically assess their current sexual harassment policy and assess how sexual harassment claims are handled.

Americans with Disabilities Act

The Americans with Disabilities Act (ADA) was signed into law on July 26, 1990, and applies to agencies with at least 15 employees. The Act is codified at 42 U.S.C. §§ 12101-12213 and provides that employers may not discriminate in employment against qualified individuals with disabilities. The ADA protects individuals with disabilities from discrimination in public services and accommodations. The Act does not repeal Title VII of the Rehabilitation Act of 1973, nor does it preempt any statute or federal law that establishes a higher standard of protection. The courts have the final opinion on ADA disputes. In its relatively short existence, the courts have increasingly examined cases to interpret the meaning of the statute.

Practices and Activities Covered by the ADA

The ADA prohibits discrimination in all employment practices, including job application procedures, hiring, firing, promotion, compensation, training, as well as other terms, conditions, and privileges of employment. It applies to recruitment, advertising, tenure, layoff, leave, fringe benefits, and all other employment-related activities.

Persons Protected by the ADA

Employment discrimination is prohibited against "qualified persons with a disability." This includes applicants for employment and employees. An individual is considered to have a "disability" if he has a physical or mental impairment that substantially limits one or more major "life activities," has a record of such an impairment, or is regarded as having such an impairment.

Commonly recognized physical impairments that may interfere with the performance of life activities include blindness, deafness, muscular dystrophy, cerebral palsy, and cardiac problems. Any mental or psychological disorder generally recognized by medical authorities, such as schizophrenia or bipolar disorder, that interferes with an individual's performance or major life activities is a disability (*Sutton v. United Airlines, Inc., 1999*). Individuals discriminated against because they have a known association or relationship with an individual with a disability are protected.

A "qualified person with a disability" is one who meets legitimate skill, experience, education, or other requirements of an employment position that she or he holds or seeks, and who can perform the essential functions of the job with or without reasonable accommodation. Requiring the ability to perform "essential" functions assures that an individual with a disability will not be considered unqualified simply because of inability to perform marginal or incidental job functions. If the individual is qualified to perform essential job functions except for limitations caused by disability, the employer must consider whether the person could perform those functions with a reasonable accommodation. If written job descriptions have been prepared in advance of advertising or interviewing applicants for a job, this would be considered as evidence, although not conclusive evidence, of the essential functions of the job.

The term "major life activity" means activities like walking, sitting, standing, seeing, hearing, breathing, performing manual tasks, caring for oneself, learning, and working. The inability to work at one job may not count, because it is not substantial enough a limitation on the ability to work. A person with a disability must also be "qualified." This means someone who "satisfies the requisite skill, experience, education, and other job-related requirements of the job and who, with or without reasonable accommodation, can perform the essential functions of the job."

"Essential functions" means job tasks that are fundamental and not marginal. Thus, if a person with a disability can do the essence of the job despite having a disability, the employer cannot discriminate against that person because of the disability. The employer must also reasonably provide accommodations for the disabled person that do not create an undue hardship for the employee. This means doing things like making facilities accessible to persons with disabilities, restructuring nonessential parts of the job, altering work schedules, modifying equipment or machinery, and providing someone to aid the disabled worker. An accommodation is not reasonable if it imposes an "undue hardship" on the agency's work by requiring "significant difficulty or expense."

The ADA does not protect individuals because of homosexuality, bisexuality, transvestitism, transsexualism, pedophilia, exhibitionism, voyeurism, gender identity disorder not resulting from physical impairments, compulsive gambling, kleptomania, pyromania, or psychotic substance use disorders resulting from current illegal drug use. An alcoholic is protected, but not if his or her current use of alcohol interferes with performance of the job or poses a direct threat to property or the safety of others.

Enforcement of the ADA

The Equal Employment Opportunities Commission (EEOC) is charged with enforcing the provisions of the ADA. An individual with a disability who believes he or she has been discriminated against may file a complaint with the EEOC, after which an investigation will be conducted. The EEOC has broad investigatory authority, including subpoenaing witnesses and evidence. After the investigation, the commission will state its findings and can compel an agency to comply with the provision by hiring the person. The commission and/or the complainant may submit civil actions against the agency. In cases of a political subdivision, the statute reserves the decision to pursue remedies to the Attorney General (Colebridge, 2000). Compensatory and punitive damages may be available in cases of intentional discrimination or when an employer fails to make a good faith effort to provide a reasonable accommodation.

The ADA and Job Descriptions

Although it is a prudent management strategy to have current job descriptions and to revise them periodically, the ADA does not require employers to do so. Written job descriptions that are prepared prior to advertising a position or interviewing applicants for a job will be considered as evidence along with other relevant factors. Job descriptions should be reviewed to make sure they accurately reflect the actual functions of a job. Job descriptions should focus on outcomes or results of a job function, not solely on the way it is customarily performed.

It is important that management specify essential job functions. The courts have been instrumental in identifying the essential functions of police officers. Case law has established that firing a weapon and making forcible arrests are essential job functions of a police officer (*Davoll v. Webb*, 1999). Driving a police vehicle is also essential (*Gonzalez v. City of New Braunfels, Texas*, 1999), as is collecting evidence (*Holbrook v. City of Alpharetta*, 1997). This does not totally quantify or exhaust other essential functions of the job, but specifying core tasks can avert claims of discrimination under the ADA (see Figure 13.2).

The EEOC suggests that when considering essential job functions, an employer should consider written job descriptions, the amount of time spent performing the function, the consequences of not requiring performance of the job, collective bargaining agreements, and the experience of the job incumbent or incumbents in similar positions.

Must Employers Give Preference to a Qualified Applicant with a Disability?

An employer is free to select the most qualified applicant available and to make decisions based on reasons unrelated to a disability. For example, an essential function in corrections is to be able to walk for extended periods and climb stairs in a housing unit. Two people apply for a correctional officer position and the employer administers a mandatory physical step test for five minutes and provides a reasonable accommodation for the person with a disability. The person without the disability obtains a better score on the performance test. The employer can hire the applicant with the better score.

Figure 13.2
Essential Job Functions of Law Enforcement Officers

- Effect an arrest, using force if necessary, and restraints
- Physical aspects—running, climbing, jumping, swimming, rescuing, standing for prolonged periods, searching, and investigating in various environments. Subdue resisting subjects with control tactics. Pursue suspects on foot in different types of terrain. Lift, carry, and drag objects and people.
- Communicate effectively, give directions/commands, give information, listen to people, and testify in court
- Conduct visual and audio surveillance for extended periods
- Enter and exit vehicles quickly. Operate motor vehicles under normal and emergency conditions, during day or night
- Exercise independent judgment within legal requirements
- Gather information in criminal investigations by conducting interviews
- Load/unload and fire different types of weapons from varying positions
- Use other equipment such as batons, aerosol sprays, flashlights, cones, etc.
- Direct traffic for extended periods
- Prepare written reports and other documents and perform mathematical computations
- Read and comprehend laws, rules, regulations, and policies
- Manage interpersonal conflicts to maintain order and restore peace

Limitations on Medical Examinations Prior to Employment

An employer may not ask or require a job applicant to take a medical examination before making a job offer. The employer cannot make any preemployment inquiry about a disability or the nature or severity of a disability. An employer may ask if an applicant has a driver's license or can drive but may not ask questions regarding a visual impairment. An employer may, however, ask questions about the ability to perform specific job functions and may, with certain limitations, ask a person with a disability to describe or demonstrate how he or she would perform these functions.

An employer may condition a job on the satisfactory result of a post-offer medical examination or medical inquiry if this is required of all entering employees in the same job category. A post-offer examination or inquiry does not have to be job-related and consistent with business necessity. If the person is not hired after the medical examination, the reason or reasons for not hiring must be job-related and consistent with business necessity. The employer must show that no reasonable accommodation was available that would enable the person to perform the essential job functions, or that accommodations would impose an undue hardship. An "undue hardship" refers to an accommodation that would be unduly costly, extensive, substantial, or disruptive, or that would alter the operation of the business. A post-offer medical examination may not disqualify an individual with a disability who is currently able to perform essential job functions because of speculation that the disability may cause a risk of future injury.

Tests for illegal use of drugs are not medical examinations under the ADA and are not subject to the restrictions of such examinations. Information from all medical examinations and inquiries must be kept apart from general personnel files as a separate, confidential medical record, available only under limited conditions.

Alcoholics and the ADA

While a current illegal user of drugs is not protected by the ADA if an employer acts on the basis of such use, a person who currently uses alcohol is not automatically denied protection. An alcoholic is a person with a disability and is protected by the ADA if he or she is qualified to perform the essential functions of the job. An employee may be required to provide an accommodation to an alcoholic. An employer, however, may discipline, discharge, or deny employment to an alcoholic whose use of alcohol adversely affects job performance or conduct. Moreover, an employer may prohibit the use of alcohol in the workplace and can require that employees not be under the influence of alcohol.

Requirements to Make Reasonable Accommodation

An employer is only required to accommodate a "known" disability of a qualified applicant or employee. The requirement generally will be triggered by a request from an individual with a disability, who frequently will be able to suggest an appropriate accommodation. Accommodations must be made on an individual basis, because the nature and extent of a disabling condition and the requirements of a job will vary in each case.

The ADA and Performance Standards

An employer can hold employees with disabilities to the same standards of performance as other similarly situated employees without disabilities for performing essential job functions, with or without reasonable accommodation. An employer also can hold employees with disabilities to the same standards of performance as other employees regarding marginal functions unless the disability affects the person's ability to perform those marginal functions. If the ability to perform marginal functions is affected by the disability, the employer must provide some type of reasonable accommodation, such as job restructuring, but may not exclude an individual with a disability who is satisfactorily performing a job's essential functions.

Criminal Justice Cases Involving the ADA

The Ninth Circuit Court of Appeals rejected an ADA challenge to a correctional officer who challenged a policy of assignment rotation in *Kees v. Wallenstein* (1998). The union sued on behalf of four Seattle correctional officers to block officer rotation policies. One officer had a neck and back injury and could suffer paralysis if reinjured. Another officer had residual injuries from a prisoner assault. A third officer had a toe amputated and a fourth officer had a displaced vertebra. The district court found that the plaintiffs were not "qualified" for their employment because of their "no prisoner contact" medical restrictions. The court of appeals agreed. The court held that the "ability to restrain prisoners during an emergency is critical to jail security," and jail safety is jeopardized by the plaintiff's inability to respond to emergencies. The court also noted that the bargaining agreement provided that correctional officers were expected to rotate among several positions, most of which require prisoner contact.

In *Miller v. City of Springfield, Missouri* (1998), the Eighth Circuit Court of Appeals upheld the use of the Minnesota Multiphasic Personality Inventory (MMPI) for testing of police applicants. A woman who had served as a police officer for 10 years moved to Springfield, Missouri, where she was hired as a dispatcher. After twice failing the police officer agility test, she passed that portion, but scored a 66 on the MMPI-2, indicating above-normal depression. She sued under the ADA, claiming that management perceived her as disabled, and challenging the MMPI as not job-related. The appellate court held she presented no evidence that she was disabled, and the fact she was hired as a dispatcher meant the city did not perceive her as disabled. Regarding the MMPI, the court held that it was appropriate as a psychological screening mechanism, is job-related, and consistent with business necessity where the selection of individuals to train for the position of police officer is concerned.

Two police officers and the union in New Jersey challenged a 12-year-old policy requiring officers of all ranks to be psychologically tested every three years in *PBAL-319 v. Township of Plainsboro* (1998). One of the officers was later directed to participate in counseling for anger management. The officers filed suit, claiming they were forced to reveal personal and private information that was unrelated to work performance and their fitness for duty as police officers; the process violated their right to due process; and the screening caused humiliation, embarrassment, emotional distress, anguish, and harm to their personal reputations. The court dismissed the case, concluding that periodic psychological screening is constitutional, provided that management provides for the privacy of officers' files and records and respects their rights to due process. No appeal was filed.

In *Williams v. Philadelphia Housing Authority* (2004), a 24-year veteran challenged his termination by the department based on his mental instability. Near the end of his employment, Williams' behavior became erratic—yelling at co-workers and threatening them. PHA suspended him without pay and two days later they ordered him back to work and he called in sick daily for several days. The PHA ordered Williams to undergo a psychological exam with the departmental psychologist and he went on medical leave for two months. The chief informed Williams that he would be exhausting his sick leave and annual benefits within a month and that if needed additional leave, he needed to request a medical leave of absence or it would be deemed a voluntary resignation. Prior to the end of the sick leave, the psychologist cleared Williams to return to work on restricted duty, provided he would be prohibited from carrying a weapon. The chief contended that he could not accommodate him because there were no non-firing bearing positions open at the time, although there was one position open in the radio room. The chief again asked Williams to seek a medical leave of absence to in order to keep his job. Williams did not respond and the department fired him. Williams filed several claims against the PHA, including an ADA claim for failing to accommodate his disability. The federal court granted judgment to PHA, finding that Williams was not disabled within the meaning of the ADA.

Williams appealed and the court reversed the decision. The court reasoned that Williams met the definition under the ADA. Although Williams agreed that he should not carry a weapon, he argued that he could do other jobs at the police department, like working in the radio room. The court looked to the EEOC regulations for guidance. EEOC regulations stated that working was substantially limited where one was significantly restricted in the ability to perform either a class of jobs or a broad range of jobs in various classes as compared to the average person having comparable training, skills, and abilities. Testimony at court revealed that Williams' disability did not preclude him from working in a "broad range of jobs." Williams requested the accommodation and the court agreed that he should be allowed to work in the radio room in accordance with the provisions of the ADA.

Measures that Managers Should Take in Light of the ADA

An agency should review its Equal Employment Opportunity and discrimination and harassment policy statements to ensure that they include statements to the effect that discrimination on the basis of disability will not be tolerated. Moreover, these statements should be amended to include an explanation about a disabled individual's right to request accommodations. Managers should review all mandatory fitness standards applied to applicants to ensure compliance with the ADA. Further, managers should ensure that medical information is retained in a separate file from other nonconfidential information.

While the ADA does not require maintenance of job descriptions, identifying essential job functions is critical in determining whether an applicant or employee is a qualified individual with a disability entitled to the protections of the ADA. It is a prudent management practice to develop and revise job descriptions regularly. From job descriptions, all employees learn what the job requirements are and performance evaluations should be based on these requirements. Managers should identify the core job functions of each employee and categorize them as "major," "essential," or "critical" duties and "other" duties or responsibilities. Employers should review their recruiting programs and particularly the notices and advertisements placed for individual jobs to ensure that they accurately reflect essential job functions.

Employers should revise their application forms, and hiring and interview processes. Employers cannot ask direct questions on an application about whether the applicant is disabled or has a disabling condition. During an interview the applicant cannot be asked such questions about a disability. A review of all interview forms and revisions should be made as warranted. Interviewers should be trained to ask questions related to the essential functions of the job.

An employer may be held liable under ADA for discrimination as a result of the use of a standardized test, whether of physical or mental aptitude capabilities. In order to avoid liability for what appear to be neutral testing programs, an employer must make sure that the testing used is: (1) job-related, and (2) consistent with business necessity. In other words, employers should review any testing programs to determine that the testing is designed and administered to measure actual ability to do the essential functions of the job in question.

Wrongful Termination

Employment-at-Will

The law generally examines employment as a matter of contract and the legal status of the employee will dictate the legal requirements of supervisors' interactions with employees. When issues of employment law emerge, the first question to be analyzed is whether the relationship involves employment or another kind of contractual relationship. In most, if not all, criminal justice agencies, the employer has the right to control what the employee does, when the employee does it, and how it is accomplished. This type of situation is considered an employment relationship.

In the public sector, when an employer hires a person, the legal presumption that governs their working relationship is that the employment is "at will." This means that the employee works at the pleasure of the employer and the employer may dismiss the employee at any time without explanation or legal penalty. This is known as the "American rule." In seventeenth-century England, there was a presumption that employment was for one year unless otherwise stated. The United States courts adopted the one-year rule after the American Revolution. The courts reexamined this philosophy at the end of the nineteenth century as individual freedom to contract expanded. The courts adopted the rule that an employee without a definite term of employment was an employee at-will and may be discharged without reason (Avery, 1997).

Employment-at-will has, over the years, meant that the employer could terminate an employee for no cause, good cause, or even for "causes morally wrong" (*Hutten v. Waters*, 1915). An example of this is illustrated in many sheriff's departments after an election. A newly elected sheriff enters office and fires employees for no cause other than he wants to hire employees whom he believes will work best with his goals. The terminated employees basically had no recourse or protections.

The example above is not completely accurate today, because there are no true employment-at-will situations. The concept has been eroded by Congress and state legislatures, which have passed laws restricting employers from terminating at-will employees. Federal statutes that modify employment-at-will include the Civil Rights Act of 1964, which prohibits discharge for discriminatory reasons; the Age Discrimination in Employment Act, which prohibits discharge solely on the basis of age; and the Rehabilitation Act of 1973, which bars dismissal of an otherwise qualified handicapped employee when reasonable accommodation of the handicap can be made (Allred, 1995). State legislatures have also passed similar antidiscrimination laws that protect employees as well as civil service commissions. Antidiscrimination laws, both state and federal, also generally prohibit retaliation. Thus, workers cannot be fired for filing discrimination charges against their employers. Nor can they be discriminated against for other reasonable actions taken in opposition to discrimination by their employers.

Employment today is protected in many ways. In many states, employees are represented by unions and collective bargaining agreements with employers. Employees who have bargained for individual contracts of employment or who are covered by employer policy manuals or other manifestations of promises that the workers have job security are generally protected. Many employees are covered by their state personnel act, which stipulates that an employee may not be fired for reporting improper government activities. Whistle-blowing statutes protect employees from retaliation if they report improper activity. Most states provide that a career employee cannot be fired for failing to meet job performance requirements without first showing prior written warnings documenting poor job performance. The system provides for hearings to ensure that due process rights are guaranteed. Other exceptions to the employment-at-will rule include formal written contracts, personnel handbooks, and implied good faith. Violations of these standards can subject employers to civil litigation.

It is improper to say today that a public employer can simply discharge an employee for any reason. It is most accurate to hold that employment-at-will has been significantly modified.

Due Process and Discharge

Many courts recognize an exception to employment-at-will rule based on the tort of wrongful discharge. This holds that an employer may not discharge an employee in violation of a public policy contained in a statute (*Brockmeyer v. Dun & Bradstreet*, 1983). In its broadest sense, an employer may not discharge an employee for reasons of malice, bad faith, or retaliation, because to do so contravenes public policy. Public policy has generally been defined as no citizen can lawfully do that which has a tendency to be injurious to the public or against the public good. Some have held that this principle implies a contract, including at-will employees, and good faith. A bad faith discharge would breach the stipulations of the contract and conceivably result in a civil lawsuit (Allred, 1995).

Wrongful termination lawsuits emerge when an employee believes the employer has terminated her or him for no legitimate reason in violation of their constitutionally protected rights secured under the Fourteenth Amendment. The Fourteenth Amendment protects individuals from being deprived of property or liberty without due process of law. This language has been linked to a property interest in employment matters (*Cleveland Board of Education v. Loudermill*, 1985). Property interests arise when a public employer demonstrates a reasonable expectation of ongoing employment, because the employer has created a binding policy that discharge will occur only for stated reasons, such as for just cause.

Property interests or rights in employment are created by acts of the employer. Property rights are established by state laws, local ordinances, or statutes, not by the Constitution (*Board of Regents v. Roth*, 1974). If one of these items protects the public employee against discharge except for just cause, the employee will automatically have a property interest in employment. Employee handbooks, policy manuals, and contracts normally create property interests for employment purposes. If a claim of wrongful discharge emerges, the court will examine state laws to decide whether the employee has a valid claim to employment. The United States Supreme Court stated in the *Roth* decision that "for the proposition that to demonstrate a property right in employment, the employee clearly must have more than an abstract need or desire for it. He must have more than a unilateral expectation of it. He must, instead, have a legitimate claim of entitlement."

It is important to recognize that a property interest only applies to continued employment. A right to a particular position or duties is nonexistent. Management may reassign employees to new responsibilities or duties without infringing on property rights of their employees (Avery, 1997).

Employers may not infringe on property rights of vested employees without first ensuring due process of law. Vested employees are those who have successfully completed the probationary status of the department. Probationary employees do not have a property interest.

Employers may not discharge employees with property interests without first providing due process. The central feature of due process is a hearing. In *Cleveland Board of Education v. Loudermill* (1985), the United States Supreme Court held that the "root requirement of the due process clause is that an individual be given an opportunity for a hearing before he is deprived of any significant property interest." Loss of property interests can involve disciplinary actions such as suspensions, severe disciplinary actions, and dismissal. This means that a hearing must be conducted prior to the termination of employment. This protection is to ensure that employees with property interests are granted the essence of fundamental fairness. This provides a balance to the interest of the employee in retaining their job and the employer's interest in simultaneously reducing the risk of error.

A hearing is required, but it need not be formal. The Court in *Loudermill* stated "that a pre-termination hearing, though necessary, need not be elaborate. The formality and procedural requisites for the hearing can vary, depending upon the importance of the interests involved and the nature of the subsequent proceedings." Due process also requires that advance notice be given to the employee before the hearing and the notice should be given in writing at least 24 hours prior to the actual hearing. The charges should be conveyed to the employee prior to the hearing. There is no requirement that an attorney be allowed during the hearing or that the employee be given the right to consult with one during the hearing. Any investigatory reports that have been submitted should be given to the employee. Documentation of the hearing and transcripts should be recorded. Other proactive strategies for administrators to consider are identified in Figure 13.3.

After a discharge, the employee must be granted a full hearing before an impartial decisionmaker. This can be someone inside or outside the department. Legal representation and cross-examination of witnesses should be allowed. The final decision should be placed in writing and the employee informed that he or she may file an appeal. These procedures will be useful in ensuring that the employee is provided with the requirements of due process and will place the employer in a more defensible position should the employee file a civil lawsuit for wrongful discharge.

Figure 13.3
Proactive Strategies for Avoiding Wrongful Discharge Claims

- Develop employee handbooks that describe at-will employment
- Develop written guides and statements regarding discipline and termination policies
- Develop and maintain a progressive disciplinary system and consistently enforce it
- Distribute discipline statements to all employees
- Train all supervisors and investigators in the disciplinary process
- Performance appraisals should be candid and should reflect the employee's actual job performance
- Progressive discipline that is properly documented provides evidence that a good faith effort was made to give an employee an opportunity to correct performance
- Provide a reasonable opportunity for an employee to meet agency expectations
- When practical, suspend employees pending an investigation by an impartial supervisor—thoroughly investigate any dispute prior to taking action
- Discharge decisions should have a second review by another person
- Document all complaints, investigations, and supervisory actions with an employee
- If possible, allow an employee to resign instead of being fired
- When feasible, resolve disputes through arbitration or mediation

In *Garner v. Gwinnet County* (1999), the court upheld the discharge of a mentally unstable police officer. A police officer's performance began to deteriorate and he developed suicidal thoughts and a vivid fantasy of killing the chief. The chief had him examined by three different doctors, who determined that he was unsuited for police work. One doctor stated that he was burned out and should not be on the street carrying a weapon. The chief demoted him to animal control officer. The officer demanded reinstatement and filed an EEOC complaint. The officer's behavior deteriorated further and the chief fired him after giving him a hearing. The officer filed a legal action demanding reinstatement and sought damages for emotional injuries from observing animals being euthanized.

The court found in favor of the chief, holding that he had competent medical evidence that the officer posed a threat to himself and others. The chief's actions were proper, the court ruled, because it would have been reckless to reinstate an employee whom defendants perceived posed a threat to the community.

In *Spades v. City of Walnut Ridge* (1999), a police officer attempted suicide by shooting himself in the head. Because of his "violent use of a firearm" and the city's exposure to liability, he was terminated. After receiving counseling, medication, and treatment for his physical and psychological injuries, he sought reinstatement. When rejected, he filed a civil action claiming that he was wrongfully discharged, and filed a claim under the ADA. He alleged that he was illegally terminated because of his disabling depression and that management failed to grant him federally mandated medical leave.

The court found that the city had a legitimate reason for terminating the officer. The court reasoned that increased potential liability associated with an employee's past behavior is a legitimate concern of the city, particularly when there is known violent history. Claims of improper hiring, supervision, and retention loom large in the minds of employers and their lawyers. Liability did not attach because the court held that the city articulated a nondiscriminatory reason for his termination.

The question of providing a presuspension hearing was examined by the U.S. Supreme Court in *Gilbert v. Homar* (1997). A campus police officer was charged with felony drug possession and suspended without pay pending an investigation. The officer filed a civil action claiming that his property interest rights and his Fourteenth Amendment due process rights were violated because the university failed to give him a presuspension hearing. The Court held that the due process clause of the Fourteenth Amendment does not require a formal or informal hearing prior to a temporary deprivation of an officer's property interest. The Court did hold that a post-suspension hearing was required within a reasonable period.

In *Pittman v. Wilson County* (1988), the county had adopted a personnel resolution to govern employment decisions. The resolutions regarding employment were placed in an employee handbook and distributed to all employees. A central feature of the resolution dealt with disciplinary procedures for errant employees, and it stated that an employee may be dismissed by a department head or the county manager. The clause also stipulated that employees could be dismissed only for causes related to poor job performance after three prior warnings. The policy did allow for a predismissal conference between the supervisor and the employee.

Dispatcher Pittman of the Wilson County Sheriff's Office was accused of misconduct by her supervisor. Instead of being fired, she agreed to resign. Three days later she contacted her former employer and complained that she was coerced into resigning and demanded a discharge hearing. The county refused and she filed a civil action claiming that her Fourteenth Amendment rights were violated in that she was denied a predismissal hearing before an impartial official.

The District Court found in favor of the county, holding that Pittman had no property interest in her job and that she had not been wrongfully discharged from her job as a dispatcher. She appealed and the Fourth Circuit Court of Appeals affirmed, holding that she was an at-will employee with no property interests in continued employment, citing *Roth*. Central to the court's holding was the county's resolution on disciplinary actions. The court concluded that resolutions under North Carolina law were not binding, because they were not in an ordinance or a state statute.

CIVIL LIABILITY IN CRIMINAL JUSTICE

The United States Supreme Court affirmed a city's termination of a police officer in *City of San Diego v. Roe* (2004). Roe was a police officer with the San Diego police department. He made a video showing himself taking off a police uniform and engaging in a sexual act. He sold the video on eBay, which was discovered by his supervisor. Internal affairs conducted an investigation and found that Roe's conduct violated the department's policies. The chief ordered him to cease displaying, manufacturing, distributing, or selling any sexually explicit material or engaging in any similar behaviors. Roe ignored the orders and he was fired for disobedience of lawful orders. Roe sued, claiming the firing violated his First Amendment right to free speech. The district court granted summary judgment to the city but the appeals court reversed, finding Roe's conduct was protected as citizen commentary on matters of public concern because his conduct took place off duty and was unrelated to his job.

The city appealed to the United States Supreme Court and they reversed the appellate court's decision. The Court concluded that Roe's conduct was not a matter of public concern. Public employees had a First Amendment right to speak on matters of public concern, which were typically matters concerning government policies of interest to the public. However, Roe's expression did not qualify as a matter of public concern because his actions did nothing to inform the public about any aspect of the department's operation, workings, or functions. Moreover, even though Roe's actions occurred off-duty, his expression was linked to his official status as a police officer and was designed to exploit his image as an employee. Therefore, there was no basis for finding that Roe's expression was of concern to the community, so his speech was not protected by the First Amendment.

The levels of punishment and the termination of detention officers who abused a juvenile detainee were examined in *Stroud v. Shelby County Civil Service Commission* (2006). Thomas and Stroud were investigated for using excessive force against two juvenile detainees in the jail and were fired. It was also determined that they were untruthful during the investigation. Both officers appealed to the civil service board. After the hearings, the board concluded that both officers used excessive force and had been untruthful during the investigation, warranting their dismissal. The officers appealed the termination and filed a lawsuit for wrongful discharge. The court found that there was evidence to support the claim that the officers were untruthful during the investigation, but found no evidence to support the excessive force claim against Stroud. The court found that the board treated the officers differently from other employees who had received lesser sanctions for similar conduct. The lower court sent the matter back to the civil service board. After a hearing, the board reinstated their earlier decision and the officers appealed again. The lower court overturned the board's decision and found that the officers were treated differently from officers in the past and should receive a 30-day suspension without pay.

The civil service board appealed and the appellate court reversed the lower court's decision, upholding the board's decision to terminate Stroud. The court found that there was sufficient evidence to support the charge that Stroud used excessive force and his termination was warranted under the county's rules. There was a video showing Stroud using excessive force, as well as statements from fellow officers. The investigation report verified the claims, and the officer was found to be untruthful.

Fair Labor Standards Act

Background

During the Great Depression, the Fair Labor Standards Act (FLSA) was enacted to ensure that employers complied with federally mandated minimum wage, equal pay, and overtime standards. Child labor restrictions are also addressed in the Act (Allred, 1995). The provisions of the Act are stipulated in 29 U.S.C. §§ 201-219 and it is enforced by the U.S. Department of Labor. Over the years, the Act has undergone many amendments, and since 1974 it has applied to both private and public employment.

The FLSA and its requirements have been examined by the United States Supreme Court on two occasions. In *National League of Cities v. Usery* (1974), the Court held that the federal government did not have the power under the Tenth Amendment to interfere with "traditional" functions of state and local governments, including the power to decide wage rates to be paid to their employees. The Court reversed its prior decision in *Garcia v. San Antonio Metro Transit Authority* (1985). It ruled that the FLSA could be entirely applied to state and local governments and did not violate the Tenth Amendment. The *Garcia* decision prompted Congress to help the states by enacting Public Law 99-150 in 1986, which gave the states relief from having to pay overtime and provided compensatory time off instead of monetary payments.

Work Time/Overtime

The FLSA provides that salaried executive, administrative, and professional employees are exempt from its minimum-wage and overtime provisions (§ 213). Work time is defined by the Act to mean all hours an employee is engaged in work, including waiting to be engaged in work, or actually at work, authorized or not. Beyond actual hours worked, provisions of the Act define "work time activities" to include actual job-related duties, requiring an employee to wear a pager and refrain from consuming alcoholic beverages, maintaining vehicles when required by the agency, testifying in court, attending mandatory training sessions, and preparing for an employee grievance. Work time does not include attending training that is not mandated, maintenance of physical fitness and preparing for work, outside employment, or uninterrupted mealtime lasting for at least 30 minutes.

The normal work week is established at 40 hours per week during a seven-day period. Work time above this standard is to be compensated at a rate of time and one-half. Section 207k of the FLSA provides an overtime provision. Police officers are paid straight time on an hourly basis. Should they exceed 171 hours in a 28-day period, they would qualify for overtime pay for all hours beyond this period. Sleep time may be excluded from this provision.

Compensatory Time

The FLSA allows compensatory time to be accrued by public officials. In lieu of overtime pay, the FLSA accrual provisions permit up to 480 hours of compensatory time at a rate of one and one-half hours for each hour of overtime. As long as the time off does not conflict with work duties, compensatory time must be granted when an employee requests it. Policy statements should address such a provision. When an employee retires or resigns, cash must be paid.

The use of compensatory time creates a potential financial liability for an agency (Brooks, 2004). Pursuant to Title 29 U.S.C. § 207, when an employee leaves the department, he or she must be paid for accumulated compensatory time based upon their salary when they leave or their average salary over the previous three years, whichever is greater. Accordingly, an agency may want to "force" employees to take compensatory time when it is advantageous to the department. In *Christensen v. Harris County* (2000), the United States Supreme Court ruled that the FLSA permits a public employer to order an employee to take compensatory time off whenever the employer chooses to do so.

This, however, raises another question: Can an employee demand to be allowed to take compensatory time off whenever the employee wants to take the time off? The law on this issue is not as clear. The FLSA (Title 29 U.S.C. § 207) provides that an employee who has earned compensatory time by working overtime must be allowed to take such time off within a reasonable time of the request unless doing so would cause an "undue disruption" to operations. In *Houston Police Officers' Union v. City of Houston* (2003), the Fifth Circuit Court of Appeals addressed the Houston Police Department's policy that placed an inflexible cap prohibiting more than 10 percent of the force being scheduled off on a particular day for such things as annual leave and compensatory leave. Thus, an officer who requested to use compensatory time on a day when 10 percent already had scheduled time off would have that request denied. The court found the policy in compliance with the FLSA, stating that the statute only requires that an agency permit an employee to take compensatory time within a "reasonable" period after the request.

Violation Claims

An employee claiming a violation of the FLSA minimum-wage and overtime requirements may file a civil suit in federal or state court. Moreover, the Department of Labor may file lawsuits on behalf of employees. Employers found to have violated the act are liable for unpaid minimum wages or unpaid overtime compensation.

Police officers and other employees of the Greenville, North Carolina, Police Department won a settlement of $660,000, including $255,000 in attorney's fees and costs, in a lawsuit regarding overtime issues (*Daily Reflector*, 2000). The federal suit, initiated in 1999, alleged that officers were not paid for time spent responding to off-duty pages and phone calls; arriving early for their scheduled shift or staying late; cleaning their department-authorized weapons and assigned vehicles; preparing for court; and reviewing files and completing paperwork. The settlement did not reflect payment for time employees said that they spent "on-call" and "on-standby," but it did release the city from further claims on these issues.

In *Stachowski v. Town of Cicero* (2005), a police officer's termination was upheld for falsifying overtime claims. Stachowski was a 21-year veteran police officer who was accused of making false overtime claims of nearly $53,000.00. He was suspended without pay and the town board initiated termination proceedings. The board denied Stachowski's request for a hearing, noting that the severity of the charges justified his termination, and they fired him. He applied for and received retirement benefits and sued the town for denial of due process and equal protection rights. The lower court dismissed his claims, finding that the board's termination was justified and that he could have appealed the decision. His equal protection claim was also dismissed because he failed to allege that similarly situated officers were treated differently.

Stachowski appealed and the appellate court affirmed the lower court's decision. His claims were dismissed as state law provided that a town's board had the final authority to terminate an employee's employment. The court stated that Stachowski did have the right to appeal the board's decision under state law and because he did not, such failure did not give rise to a due process violation. Further, the court stated that his equal protection claim was meritless because Stachowski was not similarly situated to other officers who retired with untarnished records.

Employee Drug Testing

United States Supreme Court Decisions

The prevalence of substance abuse in our society has caused concern about public officials' fitness for duty. Screening or testing employees for drug use is an evolving area of the law. Because public employees operate equipment and machinery, and make decisions about the liberty of citizens, employers must have the public's as well as the employees' interests in mind and be familiar with the legalities of conducting drug searches with employees.

The Fourth Amendment protects persons from unreasonable searches and seizures. The United States Supreme Court has held that searches without consent or a valid search warrant are unreasonable except in certain specific circumstances (*O'Connor v. Ortega*, 1987). When special needs exceed the normal need in law enforcement, a search may be reasonable even though performed without probable cause. When a special need exists, the court must evaluate and balance the need for the search and the person's Fourth Amendment protected right against an unreasonable intrusion.

Balancing the need to conduct a search against employee privacy was the essential issue before the United States Supreme Court in *Skinner v. Railway Labor Executives Association* (1989). Following a major train accident, a federal regulation authorizing blood and urine testing of employees who violate safety rules by the Federal Railroad Administration (FRA) was implemented. The regulation was prompted by evidence that the accident was a result of widespread drug use by employees working for the railroad. Employees of the union challenged the searches, claiming that they violated their Fourth Amendment right to be free from unreasonable searches.

In a 7-to-2 decision, the Court upheld the regulation as constitutional. The Court determined that drug testing through blood and urine was a search, and the necessity of conducting such searches required neither probable cause or individualized suspicion. The Court found that a compelling government interest to perform such searches outweighed any employee right or privacy interest. The FRA drug testing program withstood constitutional scrutiny based on special needs of the government.

Using the balancing test between the interests of the government and the privacy rights of the individual, the Court again upheld a regulation requiring mandatory drug testing of United States Customs employees in *National Treasury Employees Union v. Von Raab* (1989). The Customs Service implemented a drug-screening program requiring urinalysis of Service employees seeking transfer or promotion to positions having direct involvement in drug interdiction, requiring the incumbent to carry firearms, or handling "classified" material. Customs employees challenged the drug testing requirement, claiming it was a violation of their Fourth Amendment rights.

The District Court agreed and enjoined the program. The Court of Appeals vacated the injunction, holding that the requirement did not violate the Fourth Amendment.

Using the same analysis as in the *Skinner* decision, the United States Supreme Court upheld the requirement that workers seeking such positions within the Customs Service must undergo urinalysis. The Court stated that in view of the fact that the drug problem in society is pervasive, caused primarily by drug smuggling, the government has a compelling interest to ensure agents are physically fit to perform their job functions, particularly agents who carry firearms. The Court ruled that these interests outweigh the privacy interests of those seeking promotion to such positions, and a warrant is not required. The Court further stated that government employees do not have the same privacy expectations as private citizens.

From these two cases, the Court recognized employment issues and drug testing as "special needs" that provide for an exception to the warrant requirement under the Fourth Amendment and individualized suspicion of a particular employee is not required by the Constitution. Moreover, it is not necessary that a documented drug problem exist within the particular workplace to justify such testing. The Court specified three governmental interests that could justify mandatory testing in the absence of individualized suspicion. First, the government has an interest in maintaining the integrity of the workforce. Second, the government has a legitimate interest in maintaining and enhancing public safety. Finally, the government has an interest in protecting sensitive information, and in some situations suspicionless testing of individuals whose jobs involve access to these classified documents. The public safety rationale adopted by the Court in *Von Raab* and *Skinner* outweighs any privacy expectation of the individual governmental employee. Administrators should keep abreast of changes in the law and develop and maintain testing policies that underscore this principle.

Lower Court Decisions

Testing job applicants for drug use may be required after a conditional offer of employment has been made. The ADA neither supports nor abolishes such testing, because they are not medical examinations. An applicant cannot be required to provide medical information prior to a conditional offer of employment. The California Supreme Court upheld the screening of police applicants, but struck down such tests as a condition for promotion with veteran officers in *Loder v. City of Glendale* (1997). Likewise, in *Feliciano v. City of Cleveland* (1993), the Sixth Circuit Court of Appeals upheld a surprise test of police academy cadets and the dismissal of two who tested positive.

A controversial drug testing issue is that of mandatory and random drug testing of public officials, such as police and correctional officers. Conducting random searches has generally been upheld when there is individualized suspicion. Random testing of police officers with notice was upheld in New York in *Clark v. New York City Housing Unit Authority* (1990). A federal district court upheld random testing of prison employees who are issued or given access to firearms in AFGE Council 33 v. Barr (1992). The New Jersey Supreme Court upheld mandatory urinalysis of officers on an articulated, individualized suspicion of drug use in *Rawlings v. Police Department of Jersey City* (1993). Officers who are under custodial arrest are still subject to testing requirements for administrative purposes.

In *Brown v. City of Detroit* (1989), police officers challenged the city's random drug testing program. A Michigan state court issued a temporary restraining order on the strip-search portion of the program. In court, the plaintiff officers argued that *Von Raab* was intensely fact-specific to Customs agents and not applicable to police officers. The court rejected this argument and observed that both positions have the power of arrest and the right to use deadly force. The city's drug testing program was upheld by the court, but the city could not search body cavities for hidden urine absent a reasonable suspicion. Compare, however, *Guiney v. Police Commissioner of Boston* (1991). The Massachusetts Supreme Court struck down random testing of Boston police on state constitutional grounds.

A California appellate court examined a policy on police officers reporting to work with the odor of alcohol on their breath in *Hinrichs v. County of Orange* (2004). Hinrichs reported to work and a supervisor smelled alcohol on her breath and called her to his office. She reported to the office and another supervisor was also in attendance. Sergeant Schmutz informed her that he smelled alcohol on her breath and she responded that she had two beers at lunch several hours earlier and that she was taking Nyquil. The sergeant asked her to take a Breathalyzer test and she agreed, but no test was administered. Henrichs was reassigned for the day and her weapon was taken from her. Sergeant Schmutz submitted a report documenting the incident and the department obtained a statement from a witness who reported that she smelled medicine on Hinrichs' breath. Internal affairs notified her that they were conducting an investigation for the use of alcohol. Her attorney demanded a copy of the report that the sergeant filed and the department stated that if discipline higher than a reprimand was issued they would grant the request. A month later, the department issued a reprimand to Hinrichs for violation of the rules which stipulated that "the odor of an alcoholic beverage on the breath will be considered presumptive evidence of a violation." She appealed the reprimand to the captain and he denied her appeal. She filed an administrative appeal with the human relations department. She also filed a lawsuit claiming that she was denied her right to be informed of the nature of her initial interrogation and her right to obtain copies of the non-confidential reports and witness statements. She also claimed a violation of due process and that the rule was non-specific and overly broad. The lower court denied her lawsuit, stating that her administrative appeal had not been resolved.

Hinrichs appealed and the appellate court reversed the lower court's decision. The court disagreed with her that Sergeant Schmutz did not follow proper procedure in confronting her regarding the smell of alcohol, as this did indeed placed her on "notice." The court agreed, however, that she was denied the sergeant's report and witness statement, and that the department had a duty to provide the documents. The court also determined that the rule was not unconstitutional, but that it was inapplicable in this situation. The letter of reprimand made no reference that Hinrichs' ability to perform the job was compromised, but stated that she could not perform her duties due to the smell of alcohol on her breath. According to the court, the department could not justify how the smell of alcohol impaired her performance and the department admitted that she was not impaired or under the influence, and there was no certain connection between the regulation and the purported violation.

In *Diaz v. City of El Centro* (2005), Officer Diaz was terminated for possessing marijuana, other drugs, and drug pipes against departmental rules and policies. Officer Diaz had been recognized in numerous performance evaluations as one of the department's best training officers. His live-in girlfriend reported to Diaz's supervisors that he had physically abused her by striking her in the head. Two officers went to his home and Diaz denied the accusation, stating that she was jealous because he was dating another woman. Later that day, Diaz's girlfriend called the department and reported that she found drugs in the home. An officer responded to the house and the girlfriend gave him a box that contained marijuana, marijuana pipes, a knife, bullets from a .38 special, and other drugs. She reported that the box was found in Diaz's bedroom closet. The department conducted an investigation and Diaz admitted the box and the contents were his, but denied using drugs while working on duty. He stated that the box was "found property" that he discovered in an abandoned house, and used the items for training. Departmental rules required him to report the items, and he admitted that possessing marijuana was illegal and was against departmental rules.

The chief fired him and Diaz appealed to the personnel appeals board. The board found that there was no illegal search of his home producing the drug and other items. Diaz argued that he did not use drugs and his exemplary performance at the department should be considered in determining a less severe punishment for violating departmental rules. The board upheld the termination. Diaz filed legal action in the state court and the lower court reversed the board's ruling, finding that the city had to show convincing evidence that the officer's warrantless search of the boxes was justified. The court also found that the termination hearing lacked fairness and that the termination was too harsh. The city appealed.

The appellate court upheld the hearing board's decision to terminate Diaz as there was substantial evidence to support its decision. The court concluded that administrative agencies had broad discretion to determine discipline, and the courts should not interfere unless there is a clear abuse of discretion. Further, the court held that the exclusionary rule did not apply to civil and administrative proceedings involving public employee discipline. The department did not conduct the search; rather, Diaz's girlfriend discovered the boxes, opened them, and turned them over. Finally, the court found that the punishment was reasonably justified as Diaz knew that possessing drugs was illegal and the termination was appropriate, due to the loss of trust in such an exemplary officer.

Administrative Considerations

Administrators must balance the need to initiate and carefully maintain a drug screening policy with the privacy rights of employees. This area of the law is unsettled and can be fraught with complex liability issues. State and federal laws must be examined for embarking on such an endeavor. This topic is an obvious area for policy development and enforcement. Numerous issues concerning such a program include whether to mandate testing, proper protocols, what if employees refuse, what system is in place to handle such concerns, what laboratory should be used, how should false positives be handled, how should retesting be processed, what information do supervisors need before a program begins, and will such testing invade employee privacy? These and other questions must be researched and considered prior to establishing a program.

If a program is already in place, administrators must keep abreast of changing state and federal laws to ensure that agency rules are consistent with the law. Review and revision of regulations already in place should be conducted regularly and as laws change. Consistent enforcement of the agency's drug-screening regulations is essential. Instituting or failing to institute a drug-screening program can increase the liability of administrators from employees or an innocent third party injured by an employee. Therefore, criminal justice managers are encouraged to seek assistance through legal counsel and risk management services as they implement and maintain their programs.

Summary

This chapter has highlighted several key areas that may further expose administrators of criminal justice agencies to civil liability. During the past several years, it has become more common for police and correctional officers to become plaintiffs. Supervisors must be familiar with many aspects of personnel legal issues. Contemporary managers can be sued under Title VII of the Civil Rights Act of 1964 for claims of sexual harassment and discrimination based on race, gender, color, religion, and national origin. Claims of sexual harassment against supervisors and co-workers have been emerging with more frequency than other areas, and the United States

Supreme Court has issued three decisions regarding this topic since 1998. The Americans with Disabilities Act provides another avenue of potential supervisor liability that affects hiring and firing aspects of the job. The Fair Labor Standards Act has been examined by the United States Supreme Court on two occasions and stipulates the requirements for proper wages, overtime, and compensatory time. Employee drug testing also emerged as a significant legal area in the early 1980s and requires employers to adhere to essential provisions of the FLSA when performing such searches.

These issues and others are continuing to evolve. Criminal justice managers should keep abreast of these changes in the law and implement the necessary policy and administrative systems that follow the mandatory requirements. Training for mid-level and first-line supervisors, as well as line-level employees, is essential to producing a healthy work environment. Further, adhering to the laws and agency policy on these subjects assists in communicating to all employees and the community that management will not tolerate infringement of protected employee rights in the workplace.

In light of the developments surrounding the issues of sexual harassment, administrators must ensure that their policies on the subject matter are consistent with the *Suders* decision. Sexual harassment and constructive discharge can be linked together if the plaintiff can show that such a climate caused him or her to resign. Training for all personnel should be provided and claims of sexual harassment claims must be investigated promptly and appropriate sanctions implemented as warranted. Case law examples indicate that supervisors should be trained and all investigations and sanctions should be thoroughly recorded. The same consistency and thoroughness should be followed in claims of sexual assaults and decisions to discharge an employee. Supervisors should ensure that they are familiar with their own disciplinary procedures and practices. Such proactive measures can assist in defending claims of unconstitutional supervisory practices. Administrators are also encouraged to research and be familiar with their own state's laws on personnel practices.

Moreover, due to the complexity of the rules regarding the FLSA, administrators should study the issues carefully and comply with contractual terms and state statutes that deal with the same issues. The costs to an agency for failure to adhere to the rules can be minimized when administrators take proactive measures to ensure that employees are treated fairly. As administrators have questions in this area, they are encouraged to contact the Department of Labor.

References

Allred, S. (1995). *Employment Law: A Guide for North Carolina Public Employers*, Second Edition. Chapel Hill, NC: Institute of Government, University of North Carolina.

Associated Press (2004). "State Prison System Settles Four Sex-Harassment Cases in 18 Months." *USA Today* (December, 19):4.

Associated Press (1993). "FBI Agrees to Pay Out $300,000 to Settle Sexual Harassment Suit." *Daily Reflector* (June 5):3.

_____ (2000a). "City to Pay 1.7 Million to Attorneys in L.A. Police Employee Harassment Cases." (October 4).

_____ (2000b). "Ex-FBI Agent Settles California Suit." (October 24).

Avery, I.T. (1997). *Legal Aspects of Police Supervision*. Incline Village, NV: Copperhouse Publishing Company.

Batchelor, T.S. (2000). "Greenville Settles Overtime Suit with Police Employees." *Daily Reflector* (December 30):A1, A7.

Brooke, M.E. (2004). "The Fair Labor Standards Act and Police Competence." *FBI Law Enforcement Bulletin* (June):24-32.

Colebridge, T.D. (2000). "The Americans with Disabilities Act." *FBI Law Enforcement Bulletin* (September):26-31.

Collins, S.C. & M.S. Vaughn (2004). "Liability for Sexual Harassment in Criminal Justice Agencies." *Journal of Criminal Justice* 32:531-545.

Government Accounting Office (1999). "Women in Prison: Sexual Misconduct by Correctional Staff." Report Number: GGD-99-104.

Ross, D.L. (2000). "Emerging Trends in Police Failure to Train Liability." *Policing: An International Journal of Police Strategies and Management* (23):169-193.

Rossi, A.M. (1998). "Twelve Considerations When Investigating Discrimination or Harassment Complaints." Police Department Disciplinary Bulletin (May):2-5.

Toplitt, S.C. (1999). "Establishing and Enforcing Your Sexual Harassment Policy." *Police Department Discipline Bulletin* (July):23.

Vaughn, M.S., T.B. Cooper & R.V. del Carmen (2001). "Assessing Legal Liabilities in Law Enforcement: Police Chief's Views." *Crime and Delinquency* 47:3-27.

Cases Cited

AFGE Council 33 v. Barr, 794 F. Supp. 1466 (N.D. Cal. 1992)

Anthony v. County of Sacramento Sheriff's Department, 845 F. Supp. 1396 (E.D. Cal. 1994)

Barth v. The Village of Mokena, 2004 U.S. Dist. Lexis 8316 (E.D. Ill.)

Board of Regents v. Roth, 408 U.S. 564 (1974)

Brockmeyer v. Dun & Bradstreet, 335 N.W.2d 834 (Wis. 1983)

Brown v. City of Detroit, 715 F. Supp. 832 (E.D. Mich.1989)

Burlington Industries, Inc. v. Ellerth, 524 U.S. 742 (1998)

City of San Diego v. Roe, 543 U.S. 77 (2004)

Christensen v. Harris, 529 U.S. 576 (2000)

Clark v. New York City Housing Unit Authority, 562 N.Y.S. 2d 637 (A.D. 1990)

Cleveland Board of Education v. Loudermill, 470 U.S. 532 (1985)

Davoll v. Webb, 194 F.3d 1116 (10th Cir. 1999)

Diaz v. City of El Central, DO43517 (4th Div. 3 Cal. App. 2005) [unpublished opinion]

Evans v. Leelanau County Sheriff's Department, No. CL 94-78765- NM (1994)

Faragher v. City of Boca Raton, 524 U.S. 775 (1998)

Farmers Insurance Group v. County of Santa Clara, 906 F.2d 440 (9th Cir. 1995)

Feliciano v. City of Cleveland, 988 F.2d 649 (6th Cir. 1993)

Garcia v. San Antonio Metro Transit Authority, 469 U.S. 528 (1985)

Garner v. Gwinnett County, 170 F.3d 189 (11th Cir. 1999)

Gilbert v. Homar, 520 U.S. 924 (1997)

Gonzalez v. City of New Braunfels, Texas, 176 F.3d 834 (5th Cir. 1999)

Gonzalez v. New York Department of Corrections, 122 F. Supp. 2d 335 (N.D.N.Y. 2000)

Guiney v. Police Commissioner of Boston, 582 N.E.2d 523 (Mass. 1991)

Heggenmiller v. Edna Mahan Correctional Institution for Women, 128 Fed. Appx. 240 (3d Cir. 2005)

Hinrichs v. County of Orange, 125 Cal. App. 4th 921 (4th Div. App. 2004)

Holbrook v. City of Alpharetta, 112 F.3d 1522 (11th Cir. 1997)

Holland v. New Jersey Department of Corrections, 246 F.3d 267 (3d Cir. 2001)

Houston Police Officer's Union v. City of Houston, 330 F.3d 298 (5th Cir. 2003)

Hutten v. Waters, 179 S.W. 134 (Tenn. Ct. App. 1915)

Kees v. Wallenstein, 161 F.3d 1196 (9th Cir. 1998)

Loder v. City of Glendale, 59 Cal. Rptr. 2d 696 (A.D. 1997)

Miller v. City of Springfield, MO, 146 F.3d 612 (8th Cir. 1998)

McCurdy v. Arkansas State Police, 375 F.3d 762 (8th Cir. 2004)

National League of Cities v. Usery, 426 U.S. 833 (1976)

National Treasury Employees Union v. Von Raab, 489 U.S. 656 (1989)

Oncale v. Sundowner Offshore Services, Inc., 523 U.S. 75 (1998)

O'Connor v. Ortega, 480 U.S. 709 (1987)

PBAL-319 v. Township of Plainsboro, #C-173-98 (N.J. 1998)

Pennsylvania State Police v. Suders, 542 U.S. 129 (2004)

Pittman v. Wilson County, 839 F.2d 225 (4th Cir. 1988)

Rawlings v. Police Department of Jersey City, 627 A.2d 602 (N.J. S. Ct.1993)

Rudd v. Shelby County, 166 Fed. Appx. 777 (6th Cir. 2006)

Skinner v. National Railway Labor Executives' Association, 489 U.S. 602 (1989)

Spades v. City of Walnut Ridge, 186 F.3d 897 (8th Cir. 1999)

Speed v. Ohio Dept. of Rehabilitation and Correction, 646 N.E.2d 273 (S.D. Ohio 1994)

Spicer v. Commonwealth of Virginia Department of Corrections, 66 F.3d 705 (4th Cir. 1995)

Stachowski v. Town of Cicero, 425 F.3d 1075 (7th Cir. 2005)

Stroud v. Shelby County Civil Service Commission, 2006 Tenn. App. Lexis 89

Sutton v. United Airlines Inc., 974 U.S. 1943 (1999)

Thomas v. Galveston County, 953 F. Supp. 504 (S.D. Tex. 1997)

Ware v. Jackson County, Missouri, 150 F.3d 873 (8th Cir. 1998)

Williams v. Philadelphia Housing Authority, 380 F.3d 751 (3d Cir. 2004)

Williamson v. City of Houston, Texas, 148 F.3d 462 (5th Cir. 1998)

Women Prisoners v. D.C., 877 F. Supp. 634 (D.D.C. 1994)

Wright v. Rolette County, 417 F.3d 879 (8th Cir. 2005)

Chapter 14

Conclusions: Shifting Directions in Civil Litigation

With the decisions by the United States Supreme Court in *Monroe v. Pape* (1961) and *Monell v. Department of Social Services* (1978), § 1983 was resuscitated and expanded. These two decisions have had a profound impact on liability in criminal justice. Since these decisions, numerous cases have been filed alleging that police and correctional personnel misused their authority, which has underscored varying types of liability claims over 40 years. Regardless of position or rank, criminal justice practitioners remain vulnerable to civil litigation and, based on past trends of § 1983 lawsuits, nothing indicates that its use will decline in the future. What appears to be occurring in the civil litigation landscape are shifts in the use of § 1983 and civil lawsuits against public officials.

The law, civil liability, and American jurisprudence are dynamic. As societal conditions change, so do our laws. These changes manifest shifts in legal thinking, establishment of legal standards, and application of these standards to activities of personnel in the criminal justice system. This text has illustrated emerging areas that place criminal justice personnel today in a more vulnerable position of civil liability than in the 1960s. In this chapter, several apparent shifts in civil litigation in criminal justice agencies are addressed in order for practitioners to consider the best possible ways to avert future legal claims.

Cases

The United States Supreme Court's decisions in *Monroe* and *Monell* have assisted in paving the way for line officers and administrators to be held liable under § 1983. Although § 1983 was enacted in 1871, it lay dormant for many years until a shift in the judicial scrutiny of official misconduct changed the interpretation and application of the statute. Civil liability in criminal justice is still evolving, particularly in areas of supervisory and administrative issues. If the past can predict the future, more shifts and expansions in areas already litigated should be expected, as well as new decisions in emerging areas.

Court decisions have established new or significantly expanded legal standards of review in civil liability. Three examples are worth noting. First, in less than 20 years, a shift in case precedents has been noted in the type of immunity granted to public officials. Today, criminal justice personnel possess qualified immunity. Qualified immunity is considered an affirmative defense when allegations are made (*Harlow v. Fitzgerald*, 1982).

Second, a common standard the U.S. Supreme Court has established to review numerous criminal justice topics is that of "deliberate indifference." This standard is applied to police and correctional activities. Since it was first applied in *Estelle v. Gamble* (1976), the Court has expanded its use to include such correctional issues as: conditions of confinement (*Wilson v. Seiter*, 1991), failure to protect (*Farmer v. Brennan*, 1994), and environmental tobacco smoke (*Helling v. McKinney*, 1993). It has also incorporated the standard to the Americans with Disabilities Act with application to prisoners (*Pennsylvania Dep't of Corrections v. Yeskey*, 1998).

In policing and corrections, the Court has shifted the standard by further expanding it to include administrative liability. The Court in *City of Canton v. Harris* (1989) held that a government entity may be held liable for failing to train its employees. This shift has spawned numerous lawsuits and is the foremost claim asserted against administrators today. The standard has also been applied to hiring practices of administrators (*Board of County Commissioners of Bryan County v. Brown*, 1997). Clearly, the standard of deliberate indifference, through the Court's expansion to correctional and police activities, provides a major example of the shift in judicial thinking of applying case precedents. The standard has been applied to Eighth, Fourth, and Fourteenth Amendment issues, making it one of the most common standards in which the courts review actions of criminal justice personnel.

Third, from 1985 to 1992, the Court shifted in its legal thinking in excessive force litigation. From 1973 to 1985, *Johnson v. Glick* (1973) was the precedent-setting case regarding the use of force, although not a Supreme Court decision. The standard of review was applied to issues pertaining to police and correctional officer use of force. The standard used by the courts to examine use-of-force issues at that time was the "shocks the conscience" test. In 1985 the U.S. Supreme Court significantly shifted the use-of-force analysis by separating lethal force decisions by police officers in *Tennessee v. Garner* (1985) and lethal force used in corrections during riots in *Whitley v. Albers* (1986). These two cases marked the first time the Court addressed use-of-force issues and also made a distinction between using lethal force in police situations and using lethal force in corrections.

In *Graham v. Connor* (1989), the Supreme Court made a further shift in assessing force issues by holding that all police use of force is to be considered a Fourth Amendment seizure. The Court established specific standards by which use-of-force cases are examined. The Court further established the "objective reasonableness" standard for analyzing all police use of force. Three years later, another shift in use-of-force cases in corrections took place in the Court's decision in *Hudson v. McMillian* (1992). The Court ruled that serious injury to a prisoner is not to be considered when correctional officers use force. The case established a new standard of review when considering claims of excessive force that may violate the cruel and unusual punishment clause of the Eight Amendment when the force is used maliciously and sadistically for the purpose of causing harm.

These four cases again illustrate a shift in the Court's thinking about civil liability in criminal justice in the use-of-force area. In a short period (1985 to 1992), the Court shifted its former rationale about use-of-force issues and established two decisions with guidelines that specify the legal requirements of using force in corrections and in policing. Two of the cases deal with force used under the Fourth Amendment and two deal with force used under the Eighth Amendment. The Court has clearly bifurcated the use of force by criminal justice personnel. As a result, numerous claims have been filed by citizens or prisoners asserting that their constitutional rights have been violated through the use of excessive force by officers.

Seeking qualified immunity in civil actions is an important component for defendants when asking a court to consider granting summary judgment. The United States Supreme Court's decision in *Brosseau v. Haugen* (2004) further clarified the application of qualified immunity. The Court underscored the two-part test established in their decision in *Saucier v. Katz* (2001) by noting that qualified immunity operates "to protect officers from liability." If an officer had fair notice that his or her conduct is unlawful and is clearly established through case law decisions, that conduct must be viewed within the context of the law and the facts and circumstances that faced the officer at the time of the conduct. If the law is not clearly established at the time of the officer's conduct, the officer should not be subject to liability. Thus, qualified immunity would be granted to the defendant officer or agency. The Court noted that while *Garner* and *Graham* provide standards of review when assessing claims of excessive force, the standard is general and may apply to varying circumstances. According to the Court, the shooting in the *Brosseau* case did not "clearly" underscore the established law of shooting a "fleeing suspect in a vehicle" that would preclude granting qualified immunity. The Court held that the shooting is far from the obvious one where *Graham* and *Garner* alone offer a basis for such a decision. Because the plaintiff could only show a "handful" of cases relevant to the shooting, the Court held that the cases by no means "clearly established" that Brosseau's conduct violated the Fourth Amendment rights of Haugen. Qualified immunity applies to the discretionary functions of the officers and is available on an individual basis. It is an affirmative defense made by an officer through his or her counsel. As these cases show, the courts will make their decisions on a case-by-case basis. The key to qualified immunity includes being proactive prior to performing the duties of a police or correctional officer.

While the Supreme Court provided more clarification regarding granting qualified immunity, they also made clear that an officer will be held liable when he or she knowingly violates the law. The Court's decision in *Groh v. Ramirez* (2004) firmly reminds officers to follow the law while performing their sworn duties. When asserting a claim of qualified immunity, the officer must show that he or she was following the established law at the time of the incident. This suggests that officers actually must be knowledgeable of state law and constitutional law. Officers must show that their actions were reasonable under the circumstances and that a reasonably trained officer would know that the conduct was constitutional or unconstitutional, depending on the situation. These factors should be addressed in agency policy and procedures, as demonstrated in the *Groh* decision. Officers need to train on a regular basis and be evaluated on their performance to ensure that they are complying with policy and that their conduct conforms to constitutional mandates. When performing their sworn duties, officers should clearly and completely document their actions and rationale for actions taken. Adhering to these elements will assist in being granted qualified immunity with more success.

Finally, the Court's decision in *Town of Castle Rock v. Gonzales* (2005) underscores their previous position that the constitution does not require a duty of the government to protect a third party from harm and the ability of the states to enact legislation that recognizes such protection as a matter of state law. The Court stated: "in light of today's decision and that in *DeShaney*, the benefit that a third party may receive from having someone else arrested for a crime generally does not trigger protection under the Due Process Clause, neither in its procedural nor in its 'substantive' manifestations. This result reflects our continuing reluctance to treat the Fourth Amendment as 'a font of tort law'." Because this decision provides further deference to law enforcement responses regarding protective orders, it may be overlooked by the police and administrators. Rather, the decision should serve as a reminder to law enforcement to ensure that a system is in place that directs officers in the proper response in enforcing protection orders. Thus, the application of this decision generally means that: (1) officers must be familiar with their state's statutes regarding the enforcement of restraining orders; (2) law enforcement generally has no constitutional duty to protect citizens from third-party harm; (3) a duty may be found if the police have "created" or "enhanced" the danger to an individual, and (4) a duty to protect may be more likely found in situations in which officers have an individual in custody against his will and the person is harmed. Review of the law, procedural practices, and revisions of policies is recommended in light of this decision.

These shifts in Supreme Court decisions underscore the fact that the law is constantly changing and legal standards are continually expanded and revised. The shifts also illustrate the need for practitioners to keep abreast of changes in the law in order to perform their responsibilities in compliance with legal standards.

Administrative Issues

Officers as Plaintiffs

One of the most notable shifts in civil liability during the 1990s was the increase in the number of officers who filed civil actions against their own departments (MacMannus, 1997). Administrators have perhaps become accustomed to citizens and prisoners filing legal actions against the department, but now must be aware of the emerging area of officers bringing suit against the department for a variety of reasons. The most common area of litigation involves employee-initiated lawsuits alleging sexual harassment (Vaughn et al., 2001; Ross, 2000; Worrall & Gutierrez, 1999). Vaughn, Cooper and del Carmen (2001) reported that Texas chiefs revealed that 12 percent of the civil litigation in 1998 through 2000 was filed by their own employees and that employees prevailed in 41 percent of the cases. Actions were filed for sexual harassment/sex discrimination, disciplinary actions, employment discrimination (hiring, promotion, and discharge), over-time/compensation/pay issues, First Amendment issues (speech/political rights/religion), race discrimination/reverse discrimination, disability discrimination, and employee search/privacy/Fourth Amendment issues. The Texas chiefs study revealed that many of the employee-initiated lawsuits were settled out of court, and average awards were higher than citizens' awards settled out of court. Ross reported that not only do employee-initiated lawsuits emerge from sexual harassment claims, as well as other areas cited, but officers commonly file civil lawsuits against administrators for failing to train in various dimensions of the job and failure to train to competency levels in using job-related equipment.

An increase in officers as plaintiffs should direct administrators in seeking better practices and methods for managing personnel. Previous research (Scogin & Brodsky, 1991) reveals, and Texas chiefs agree in their survey, that treating people fairly is a significant approach to reducing lawsuits. Other methods include better screening of applicants, better supervision, more and better training, early identification of problem officers, following agency policies, and holding officers accountable (Vaughn et al., 2001).

Department of Justice Investigations

With the passage of the Crime Bill in 1994, §§ 14141-14142 of Title 42, United States Code, the Department of Justice (DOJ) was authorized to investigate patterns or practices of misconduct in local police departments and requires the collection of statistics on "police abuse." The statute grants authority to the DOJ to file a civil action on behalf of citizens to obtain declaratory or equitable relief.

Arguably, Section 14141 is one of most significant measures that affects police reform, management practices, and accountability. The DOJ has conducted 22 investigations since 1996, resulting in seven consent decrees and six memorandums of agreement. One case was dropped by the DOJ. Investigations are ongoing in eight agencies (2006). This marks a significant shift in federal oversight of local, state, and county police agencies.

Passage of this legislation has ushered policing into a new era in which the federal government can dictate sweeping changes in the policies and practices of a law enforcement agency. This provision has significantly affected law enforcement operations. In many cases, a revamping of the entire system of police practices has occurred. Mandated changes in reporting, recording, and tracking all aspects of officer and citizen interactions are required in the consent decrees. Revisions in officer performance evaluations and the department's disciplinary system have in most cases been overhauled as well. Start-up and maintenance costs required of a department in order to comply with the stipulations of the consent decree are enormous.

While police accountability is a legitimate concern, it remains debatable whether § 14141 has been successful in achieving police reform or will bring reform to law enforcement. Rather than speculate about the utility of the statute, based on the past trends of its implementation, police administrators should focus on instilling proactive measures that can minimize the likelihood that the federal government will initiate such an investigation in their department. This provision has opened an additional door of liability concern for administrators and officers alike. Police administrators are encouraged to read the stipulations contained within these consent decrees to learn valuable lessons of how to avoid such investigations (see the Justice Department's Web site: www.doj.gov.). Further, administrators are encouraged to regularly assess the policies and practices in the department with respect to hiring practices, training practices, citizen complaint policies, use-of-force training, tracking of use-of-force incidents and traffic stops, practices involving searches and seizures, responding to calls for service, remediation of problem officers, supervising officers, internal affairs investigations, and disciplinary procedures. This will show the community that the department is seeking to increase the organizational effectiveness of the department and is taking proactive measures to avert claims of tolerating a culture of abusing the constitutional rights of citizens. To that end, administrators are encouraged to consider the risk management suggestions identified below and incorporate them into their management system as warranted.

Adopting Risk Management Strategies

Despite the upward trends in civil liability against criminal justice personnel since the 1960s and recognizing that filing of lawsuits will not be declining anytime soon, studies reveal that public officials win more frequently, and that trend is continuing to shift to higher percentages over time (Ross, 1997, 2000; Vaughn et al., 2001). In response to the ongoing potential of civil litigation, many police agencies have adopted proactive measures to reduce the number of lawsuits and place themselves in a better position to defend a civil action. This is directly related to an administrator's management philosophy. This does not entirely imply that liability is solely and directly linked to the management or leadership style of an administrator, but there are facets that link the administrator to liability by his or her practices and policies.

For example, a noteworthy shift by many police agencies since the 1980s is the adoption of some version of "Community-Oriented Policing" (COP). Adopting COP has forced a change in management approaches and policies, and has expanded officer participation in organizational goal setting and decisionmaking at the street level. Tremendous strides have been made in reducing crime rates in many jurisdictions in the United States. As a result, COP has been touted as a major innovation in policing and highly recommended by many criminal justice scholars.

Implementing COP strategies should result in the decline of civil liability over time. Studies that specifically examine the relationship of COP and civil liability are limited. Worrall and Marien (1998), however, hypothesize that due to COP's philosophy of expanding the officer's street-level decisionmaking and advocating more creative risk-taking in solving problems, the risk of civil liability is likely to increase. They theorize that the more risk-taking officers engage in, the greater the chances of civil liability exposure. In theory, COP embraces internal and external changes in managing the police organization and providing police services to the community. Many COP programs are implemented to modernize the agency, change departmental behavior and operations, and change policies and practices, while delegating to officers more input and decision-making authority. Community-oriented policing fully recommends developing partnerships in the community intended to improve police-citizen relationships. If these ideals are incorporated with proper guidelines such as effective supervisory practices; training officers in COP; and implementing, monitoring, and evaluating such practices, liability should be reduced. This should be a fertile ground for future scholarly research and practitioner assessment.

Community-oriented policing is not necessarily a panacea for civil liability in the departments that implement it. A shift in management approaches through COP may create one net outcome in the reduction of civil lawsuits. While studies in this area are limited, the literature recommends that administrators apply risk management strategies to varying management styles that can assist in reducing the number of civil lawsuits (Gallagher, 1990; Collins, 1993; Alpert & Smith, 1994; Katz, 1995; Parsons, 1997).

Regardless of whether the criminal justice agency is police or correctional in nature, adopting a system of risk management within a management philosophy can reduce exposure to civil liability. Risk management identifies problem areas within an organization and addresses the situation through risk control strategies. In light of the ongoing nature of civil litigation and varying shifts in liability, administrators should consider developing risk management approaches as a method for reducing their exposure to liability. A job assessment that reviews the frequency of critical job tasks by examining calls for service, citizen complaints, incident reports, and past litigation and case decisions is an important step in initiating a risk management program. Once a job assessment is performed, job descriptions, as well as policies and procedures, can be revised.

A critical component of implementing a risk management program is to ensure that all policies are current. Policy formulation and effective supervisory implementation can provide a viable strategy in controlling police civil liability (McCormick, 1996). Policies can serve as guides for officer actions in the field, and when properly enforced by supervisors, assist in keeping officers accountable for proper conduct. While policies cannot be written for every conceivable encounter an officer might face, they should provide a range of options for officers to consider when responding to a variety of situations.

Risk Management and Officer Training

Since the *City of Canton v. Harris* (1989) decision, police and correctional administrators have frequently been cited for failing to train their employees. This is the most frequently cited area when a citizen or prisoner files a claim against administrators, followed by failure to supervise and failure to direct officers (Ross, 2000). Kappeler, Kappeler, and del Carmen (1996) reported that from 1978 to 1994, claims of failure to train were won by administrators in only 45 percent of the cases. Ross revealed that from 1989 to 1999, a marked shift took place in favor of administrators in 10 commonly litigated areas in policing. During the 10-year review, administrators prevailed in 64 percent of the claims. While this indicates a significant shift in the winning margin, employees began to file more lawsuits against their departments.

As the trend to prevail in claims increases, criminal justice administrators must remain committed to providing ongoing training for their officers and supervisors. Chapter 7 indicated the 10 most litigated areas in policing and areas in which correctional training should be addressed. These 10 areas identify key topics for training and represent a practical starting point in which regular training should be addressed. Other training topics should include legal issues of arrests, searches, and civil liability of employees, and the constitutional limits of using force. Topics for correctional training should also include prisoner management in housing units, use of force and the use of restraints, verbal skills, report writing, legal and liability aspects of the job, searches and security measures, medical care issues, suicide awareness, classification, critical incident response, supervising special needs populations, and sexual harassment.

An ongoing commitment should also be made to training supervisors. A primary shift in much of the § 1983 litigation since the *Monell* decision is to name the supervisor along with the officer in the lawsuit. There are eight theories of potential supervisory liability, and commonly a plaintiff will assert that supervisory personnel should be held liable for a combination of these theories, such as failure to train, failure to supervise, and failure to discipline. Administrative and supervisory training is therefore critical to organizational operations and reducing civil liability.

Supervisory training is very important for limiting liability. Supervisors should be trained in proper policy implementation and enforcement, expectations of the job and job descriptions, personnel evaluations, sexual harassment/sex discrimination, hiring and firing practices, officer coaching and counseling, and the agency's progressive disciplinary process.

Training is an administrative function that can enhance employee skills, proficiencies, and decisionmaking. Training is a fundamental component of risk management. It can improve overall organizational effectiveness and is a viable approach to reducing the risk of civil liability.

Liability Shifts in Corrections

Prison Litigation Reform Act

Most notable in correctional § 1983 litigation is the passage of the Prison Litigation Reform Act of 1996 (PLRA) and its impact on prisoner litigation. This act was passed by Congress to reduce the number of frivolous lawsuits filed by prisoners. Since its implementation, a shift in § 1983 prisoner filings has occurred. The number of annual prisoner filings has been reduced by approximately 50 percent since 1996, which indicates that the goal of Congress in passing the legislation has been accomplished. The United States Supreme Court has also determined that it is constitutional to require prisoners to exhaust remedial measures at the institutional level prior to filing a civil lawsuit in their decisions in *Booth v. Churner* (2001) and *Porter v. Nussle* (2002). Both decisions underscore the requirement and trends show that prisoner litigation has been considerably reduced as a result.

A by-product of the PLRA is the increase in prisoners filing habeas corpus petitions regarding sentencing issues and conditions of confinement. For approximately 20 years (1976 to 1997), habeas corpus petitions were rarely used by prisoners due to the increased use of § 1983. Since the PLRA was enacted, the use of writs of habeas corpus has been growing steadily. This shift shows that since 1996 habeas corpus petitions have increased by about 60 percent.

Another trend in corrections is the use of consent decrees as a result of prisoner civil litigation. For more than 30 years, many prisons and local jails have consented out of court to stop or start certain practices. Overcrowding has been a prominent issue that has prompted numerous consent decrees. Most state prison systems and numerous detention facilities have been forced to expand their bed space by building new facilities. This has come at a huge price to taxpayers. The consent decree does not result in a loss when compensatory damages are awarded; rather, the cost is from building new facilities and staffing them with the proper number of personnel. Operating the contemporary correctional facility is a large-budget item despite the fact that monetary damages may be awarded in prisoner litigation.

The PLRA assists in not only reducing the filing of frivolous prisoner lawsuits, but also terminates existing court-ordered consent decrees, unless there are continuing constitutional violations. The PLRA only provides for consent decrees when a court finds "harm" occurring within a facility and may order such a decree to correct such harm. While the PLRA has affected the use of consent decrees, the Civil Rights of Institutionalized Persons Act (CRIPA) allows the DOJ to investigate constitutional deprivations of those confined in varying types of institutions. This should be of concern to correctional officials as prisons, jails, and youthful offender facilities make up about 60 percent of the institutions that have been investigated and/or placed under a consent decree. Enforcement trends of CRIPA show that the DOJ has only moderately used the Act and generally when there has been a number of repeated blatant constitutional violations. Even so, CRIPA provides another methodology for plaintiff prisoners to bring allegations of constitutional violations against the agency and administrators must be prepared to defend against such claims.

Sexual Harassment and Sexual Misconduct

An emerging trend in civil litigation in state prisons and detention facilities are claims of sexual harassment. Male supervisors and correctional officers alike are vulnerable to allegations of sexual harassment by female officers, and during the 1990s more allegations were filed and successfully litigated than in previous years. The shift in this litigation brought before lower federal courts prompted the United States Supreme Court to decide three cases that address this issue. While these cases are not criminal justice-related, they apply to all employees and administrative personnel. A system that does not tolerate such behavior, that includes policies and procedures, training, proper investigation, and appropriate discipline must be in place. Criminal justice administrators should work to ensure that such violations do not occur and respond appropriately should allegations surface.

The Supreme Court has specifically addressed sexual harassment and constructive discharge issues in their decision in *Pennsylvania State Police v. Suders* (2005). This is the first time the Court has addressed an allegation of constructive discharge as it relates to claims of sexual harassment in a criminal justice agency. This reveals that the subject matter of sexual harassment continues to be of prime importance in the workforce, despite the advances in case law, policy changes, and implementation of the law and policy. Further, claims of sexual harassment show the primary area where an officer becomes plaintiff and files legal actions against his or her own department. This case also shows a shift in the theory of sexual harassment claims. With this ruling, it is highly predictable that more claims of constructive discharge will be integrated into allegations of sexual harassment, particularly when the plaintiff has terminated his or her employment due to an alleged hostile environment. Administrators are encouraged to review their current policies and practices as they relate to this important decision.

Sexual misconduct, mostly by male correctional officers with female prisoners, has emerged as a civil liability issue during the past 10 years. A study prompted by Congress and conducted by the General Accounting Office (GAO, 1999) in three state prison systems identified numerous reports and claims of sexual misconduct with female prisoners. Further, two additional state prison systems settled out of court regarding allegations against male officers by female prisoners. More lawsuits can be expected, and administrators and officers should work toward eliminating such behavior.

Officer Performance

Despite the growing trend in filing lawsuits and shifts in civil litigation in criminal justice, officers generally win more often than they lose when named in a civil lawsuit. Lawsuits commonly filed against officers include false arrest and imprisonment, excessive use of force, improper searches and seizures, failure to protect, delay or denial of medical care, and vehicle pursuits. When an officer loses in a civil lawsuit, compensatory and punitive damages may be assessed. This shift in awarding punitive damages by the courts remains intact since the United States Court decision in *Smith v. Wade* (1983). This is important as punitive damages are assessed in particularly egregious situations and for blameworthy conduct outside the scope of the officer's authority. As such, strict compliance with the law is required.

Criminal justice practitioners should regularly review agency policies and procedures and seek out supervisors when questions arise. Officers should keep abreast of changes in the law. Frequent changes are noted with Fourth Amendment issues and routinely include making arrests with or without a warrant, searches and seizures, and false arrest or imprisonment. Changes and shifts in the law frequently occur in corrections with Eighth Amendment issues. Keeping current with legal requirements, performing duties within their mandates, and making sound decisions in compliance with agency policy can reduce the occurrence of civil lawsuits. To assert a successful defense of qualified immunity, officers must demonstrate that they acted within the constraints of the law, their experience, and training.

Officers should also maintain competency in job duties that require physical skills (Siddle, 1997) and operating equipment. A common theme in civil liability involves lawsuits claiming that an officer used excessive force and improperly used his or her baton or handcuffs or sprays. Officers should strive to maintain proficiency and competence in all authorized equipment and control techniques. Whether the officer used reasonable force will be determined on the facts of the case, the officer's perception in using force, and the resistive behaviors of the individual. In use-of-force encounters, officers may have to use varying types of equipment and physical skills. Maintaining proficiency in empty-hand control techniques and other equipment can help to prevent civil lawsuits.

Final Thoughts

Shifts in civil litigation require all employees in criminal justice agencies to continually seek methods for complying with court mandates and strategies for reducing the risk of lawsuits. Innovations in management philosophies, technology, risk management approaches, and decisionmaking are all necessary to ensure that civil liability issues are addressed within each agency. The days of adopting a "head in the sand" approach toward civil litigation are outdated, lead to stagnant organizations, and heighten the risk of civil litigation. Administrators and officers must work together to accomplish the mission of the organization while remaining cognizant of legal changes that affect agency operations. In this way, according to Kappeler (1997), "criminal justice executives and officers must begin to monitor shifting judicial philosophies of law enforcement and the responsibility to society while being mindful that today's actions directly affect the future of liability law and their colleagues within the system."

References

Alpert, G.P. & W.C. Smith (1994). "Beyond City Limits and Into the Woods: A Brief Look at the Policy Impact of *City of Canton v. Harris* and *Woods v. Ostander*." *American Journal of Police* 10:19-40.

Collins, S.C. (1993). "Managing Liability for Municipal Law Enforcement Agencies." *Practicing Law Institute: Litigation and Administrative Practice Course Handbook Series* 490:497-508.

Gallagher, C.P. (1990). "Risk Management for Police Administrators." *The Police Chief* 57:18-29.

General Accounting Office (1999). "Women in Prison: Sexual Misconduct by Correctional Staff." *Report Number GGD-99-104*. Washington, DC: General Accounting Office.

Kappeler, V.E. (1997). *Critical Issues in Police Civil Liability*, Second Edition. Prospect Heights, IL: Waveland Press, Inc.

_____, S.F. Kappeler & R.V. del Carmen (1993). "A Content Analysis of Police Civil Liability Cases: Decisions of the Federal District Courts, 1978-1990." *Journal of Criminal Justice* 21:325-337.

Katz, D.M. (1995). "County Pools Seek to Form $20M Captive." *National Underwriter* 102:11-12.

McCormick, R.J. (1996). "Police Perceptions and the Norming of Institutional Corruption." *Police and Society* 6:239-256.

MacMannus, S.A. (1997). "Litigation Cost, Budget Impacts, and Cost Containment Strategies: Evidence from California Cities." *Police Budgeting and Finance* 17:28-47.

Parsons, R.L. (1997). "Risk Management Strategies in Policing." *Police Administrator's Training Manual*. Big Rapids, MI: Criminal Justice Institute, Ferris State University.

Ross, D.L. (2000). "Emerging Trends in Police Failure to Train Liability." *Policing: An International Journal of Police Strategies and Management* 169-193.

Scogin, F. & S.L. Brodsky (1991). "Fear of Litigation Among Law Enforcement Officers." *American Journal of Police* 10:41-45.

Siddle, B.K. (1997). *Sharpening the Warriors' Edge*. Millstadt, IL: PPCT Publications.

Vaughn, M.S., T.W. Cooper & R.V. del Carmen (2001). "Assessing Legal Liabilities in Law Enforcement: Police Chiefs' Views." *Crime & Delinquency* 47:3-27.

Worrall, J.L. & R.S. Gutierrez (1999). "Professional Notes—Potential Consequences of Community-Oriented Policing for Civil Liability: Is There a Dark Side to Employee Empowerment?" *Review of Public Personnel Administration* 19:61-70.

Worrall, J.L. & O. Marien (1998). "Emerging Liability Issues in the Implementation and Adoption of Community Oriented Policing." *Policing: An International Journal of Police Strategies and Management* 21:121-136.

Cases Cited

Board of County Commissioners of Bryan County v. Brown, 520 U.S. 397 (1997)

Booth v. Churner, 532 U.S. 731 (2001)

Brosseau v. Haugen, 534 U.S. 194 (2004)

City of Canton v. Harris, 489 U.S. 378 (1989)

Estelle v. Gamble, 429 U.S. 97 (1976)

Farmer v. Brennan, 511 U.S. 825 (1994)

Graham v. Connor, 490 U.S. 386 (1989)

Groh v. Ramirez, 540 U.S. 551 (2004)

Harlow v. Fitzgerald, 457 U.S. 800 (1982)

Helling v. McKinney, 509 U.S. 25 (1993)

Hudson v. McMillian, 503 U.S. 1 (1992)

Johnson v. Glick, 481 F.2d 1028 (2d Cir. 1973)

Monell v. Department of Social Services, 436 U.S. 658 (1978)

Monroe v. Pape, 365 U.S. 167 (1961)

Pennsylvania State Police v. Suders, 542 U.S. 129 (2004)

Porter v. Nussle, 534 U.S. 516 (2002)

Pennsylvania Department of Corrections v. Yeskey, 524 U.S. 206 (1998)

Saucier v. Katz, 533 U.S. 194 (2001)

Smith v. Wade, 461 U.S. 30 (1983)

Tennessee v. Garner, 471 U.S. 1 (1985)

Town of Castle Rock v. Gonzales, 543 U.S. 1047 (2005)

Whitley v. Albers, 475 U.S. 312 (1986)

Wilson v. Seiter, 501 U.S. 294 (1991)

Index

Fair Labor Standards Act (FLSA), 369-371

sexual harassment, 343-354

wrongful termination, 362-369

"Persons at liberty," use of force, objective reasonableness standard, and, 208-209

Philadelphia, Pennsylvania, payouts by, for damages, 3

Physical impairments. *See* Americans with Disabilities Act (ADA)

Pittsburgh, Pennsylvania, Police Department, consent decree against, 4, 28, 173, 174

Plaintiffs. *See also* Awards; Damages

in civil action, 23

in good faith defense, 90

monetary awards for, 6-7

officers as, 144, 153-156, 385

probable cause and search and seizure and, 91

in § 1983 lawsuits, 71-75

supervisory liability and, 109-111

Plain view doctrine, 290

PLRA. *See* Prison Litigation Reform Act (PLRA)

Police abuse, Violent Crime Control and Law Enforcement Act and, 28

Police civil liability, 4. *See also* Civil liability; Police officers

under color of law, examples of, 5

increase in lawsuits, 5

lack of statistics on, 5

longitudinal analysis of claims, 8-9

monetary awards against, 6-9

out-of-court settlements, 6-7

police success in lawsuits, 8

topics of frequent litigation, 8

Police dogs. *See* Canines

Police equipment, in use-of-force incidents, 216-221

Police misconduct. *See* § 1983 litigation

Police officers. *See also* Criminal justice practitioners; Law enforcement; Negligence; Personnel issues; § 1983 litigation; Training

absolute immunity, 82, 83

under color of law actions, 26-27, 61-62, 64-65

consent decrees and, 184

controversial cases involving, 3

fear of being sued, as occupational hazard, 7-8, 9

foreseeability by, 97, 312-313

job assessment of, 96-97

perceptions of civil liability, 10-11

performance issues, 391-392

as plaintiff, 144, 153-156, 344, 385

probable cause of, 91-94

qualified immunity of, 82, 83-86, 93-94

reasonableness of, 32-33, 86-87, 91

§ 1983 litigation, 12-13

sexual harassment claims of, 344

training of, 100-101

use of force by, 192-195

Police pursuits

canines as use of force in, 220-221

as common liability claim, 8-9

components of (figure), 280

County of Sacramento v. Lewis and, 148-149, 276, 277, 278, 279

emergency vehicles

failure to train and, 148-149

negligent operation of, 37-38

ending in a fatality, 278

factors determining (figure), 279

high-speed, 37-38

pursuit management continuum, 280-281

reckless disregard and, 38, 41

§ 1983 actions, 274-281

as seizure, 275

"shocks the conscience" test, 148-149, 276

shootings during, 277

standards applied to, 148-149

torts and, 37-38

wrongful death from, 40-41

Police shootings

during pursuit, 277

as seizure, 277

wrongful death claims and, 40

Police training litigation. *See* Failure to train

Police vehicles. *See* Emergency vehicles; Police pursuits

Policy

inadequate, 8

risk management and, 94-104

supervisors and, 109-113

Policy and procedure development, risk management and, 97-98

Policymaking, supervisory liability and, 109-113

Political bodies, "person" applied to, 63

Table of Cases